Study Guide

to Accompany

McConnell and Brue

Macroeconomics

Study Guide
to Accompany
McConnell and Brue
Macroeconomics

Robert C. Bingham

Late Professor of Economics
Kent State University

William B. Walstad

Professor of Economics
University of Nebraska—Lincoln

McGraw-Hill Publishing Company

New York   St. Louis   San Francisco   Auckland   Bogotá   Caracas   Hamburg
Lisbon   London   Madrid   Mexico   Milan   Montreal   New Delhi   Oklahoma City
Paris   San Juan   São Paulo   Singapore   Sydney   Tokyo   Toronto

This book was set in Helvetica by Better Graphics, Inc.
The editors were Michael R. Elia, Scott D. Stratford, and Edwin Hanson;
the production supervisor was Salvador Gonzales.
The cover was designed by Binns & Lubin.
Von Hoffmann Press, Inc., was printer and binder.

About the authors

Robert C. Bingham was an undergraduate student at DePauw University and obtained M.A. and Ph.D. degrees from Northwestern University. He taught at the University of Nebraska—Lincoln where he was a colleague of Professor McConnell before coming to Kent State University from which he retired in 1985. He was the author of several other study guides and supplements for the principles of economics courses.

William B. Walstad is a professor of economics at the University of Nebraska—Lincoln where he directs the Center for Economic Education and the National Center for Research in Economic Education. He received his Ph.D. degree from the University of Minnesota and then served on the economics faculty at the University of Missouri—St. Louis before moving to Nebraska. Professor Walstad has been honored by the College of Business Administration at Nebraska with a Distinguished Teaching Award. He also received the Henry H. Villard Research Award for his published research in economic education. He recently co-edited *The Principles of Economics Course: A Handbook for Instructors* (McGraw-Hill) and has developed several national tests on economics for the Joint Council on Economic Education. He enjoys being with his family and likes to travel on occasion.

To
Karen, Laura, and Kristin

Contents

How to use the Study Guide to learn economics

This **Study Guide** is designed to help you read and understand Campbell R. McConnell and Stanley L. Brue's textbook, **Macroeconomics.** If used properly, a guide can be a great aid to you in what is probably your first course in economics.

No one pretends that the study of economics is easy, but it can be made easier. Of course a study guide will not do your work for you, and its use is no substitute for reading the text. You must be willing to read the text, spend time on the subject, and work at learning if you wish to understand economics.

Many students do read their text and work hard on their economics course and still fail to learn the subject. This is because principles of economics is a new subject for them, and they have had no previous experience in learning economics. They want to learn but do not know just how to go about it. Here is where the **Study Guide** can come to their assistance. Let us first see what the **Study Guide** contains and then how to use it.

■ WHAT THE STUDY GUIDE IS

The **Study Guide** contains twenty-five chapters—one for each chapter in the text and a **glossary.** Each of the chapters has ten parts.

1. An **introduction** explains what is in the chapter of the text and how its subject matter is related to material in earlier and later chapters. It points out topics to which you should give special attention, and reemphasizes difficult or important principles and facts.

2. A **checklist** tells you the things you should be able to do when you have finished the chapter.

3. A **chapter outline** shows how the chapter is organized and summarizes briefly the essential points made in the chapter.

4. A list of the **important terms** found in the chapter points out what you must be able to define in order to understand the material in the chapter. A definition of each of these terms will be found in the glossary at the end of the **Study Guide.**

5. **Fill-in questions** (short-answer and list questions) help you to learn and remember the crucial and important generalizations and facts in the chapter.

6. **Problems and projects** assist you in learning and understanding economic relationships and get you to think about certain economic problems.

7. **True-false questions** can be used to test your understanding of the material in the chapter.

8. **Multiple-choice questions** also give you a chance to check your knowledge of the chapter content and to prepare for this type of course examination.

9. **Discussion questions** can be used to test yourself, to identify important questions in the chapter, and to prepare for examinations.

10. **Answers** to fill-in questions, to the problems and projects, to true-false questions, and to the multiple-choice questions are found at the end of each chapter.

■ HOW TO STUDY AND LEARN WITH THE HELP OF THE STUDY GUIDE

For best results, quickly read the introduction, outline, list of terms, and checklist in the **Study Guide** before you read the chapter in the text. Then read the chapter in the text slowly and keep one eye on the outline and the list of terms. Always read with pencil in hand and use your textbook as if you expected to sell it for wastepaper at the end of the year. The outline in the **Study Guide** contains only the major points in the chapter. Outline the chapter as you read it by identifying the major **and the minor** points and by placing appropriate numbers or letters (such as I or A or 1 or a) in the margins. It is also wise to underline the major and minor points in the chapter and to circle the important terms. When you have completed the chapter, you will have the chapter outlined and your underlining will give you a set of notes on the chapter. It is not necessary to keep a separate notebook for textbook notes or outlines. Be careful to underline only the really important or summary statements.

After you have read the chapter in the text through once, turn again to the introduction, outline, and list of terms in the **Study Guide.** Reread the introduction and outline. Does everything there make sense? If not, return to the text and reread the topics that you do not remember well or that still confuse you. Look at the outline. Try to recall each of the minor topics or points that were contained in the text under each of the major points in the outline. When you come to the list of terms go over them one by one. Define or explain each to yourself and then look for the definition of the term either in the text chapter or in the glossary. Compare your own definition or explanation with that in the text or glossary. The quick way to find the definition of a term in the text is to look in the index of the text for the page or pages on which that term or concept is mentioned. Make any correction or change in your own definition or explanation that is necessary.

When you have done all this, you will have a pretty fair general idea of what is in the text chapter. Now take a look at the fill-in questions, the problems and projects, and the self-test questions. Tackle each of these three sections one at a time, using the following procedure. (1) Answer as many questions as you can without looking in the text or in the answer section. (2) Check the text for whatever help you need. It is a good idea to do more than merely look for answers in the text. Reread any section for which you were not able to answer questions. (3) Then consult the answer section at the end of the chapter for the correct answers and reread any section of the text for which you missed questions.

The questions in these three sections are not all of equal difficulty. Do not expect to get them all right the frst time. Some are designed to pinpoint things of importance which you will probably miss the first time you read the text and to get you to read about them again. None of the questions is unimportant. Even those that have no definite answers will bring you to grips with many important economic questions and increase your understanding of economic principles and problems.

In answering the discussion questions—for which no answers are given—it is not necessary to write out answers. All you need to do is mentally outline your answer. For the more difficult discussion questions you may want to write out a brief outline of the answer or a full answer. Do not avoid the difficult questions just because they are more work. Answering these questions is often the most valuable work a student can do toward acquiring an understanding of economic relationships and principles.

Before you turn to the next chapter in the text and **Study Guide,** return to the checklist. If you cannot honestly check off each of the items in the list, you have not learned what the author of the text and of this **Study Guide** hoped you would learn.

■ SOME FINAL WORDS

Perhaps the method of using the **Study Guide** outlined above seems like a lot of work. It is. Study and learning necessarily entail work on your part. This is a fact you must accept if you are to learn economics.

After you have used the **Study Guide** to study three or four chapters, you will find that some sections are of more value to you than others. Let your own experience determine how you will use it. But do not discontinue use of the **Study Guide** after three or four chapters merely because you are not sure whether it is helping you. Stick with it.

In addition to the material in the **Study Guide,** there are questions at the end of each chapter in the text. Some of these questions are similar to questions in the **Study Guide,** but none is identical. It will be worthwhile for you to examine all the questions at the end of each chapter and to work out or outline answers for them. Students who have trouble with the problems in the **Study Guide** will find the end-of-chapter problems useful in determining whether they have actually mastered their difficulties. All students will find many of the end-of-chapter questions more thought-provoking than the discussion questions in the **Study Guide.**

For those of you who either have trouble with or wish to learn more rapidly the sections of the text containing explanations of economic theory (or principles), let me recommend **Economic Concepts: A Programmed Approach,** by Professor Robert Bingham as revised by Professor Harry Pope. A programmed book is a learning device which speeds and increases comprehension. Its use will greatly expand your understanding of economics.

■ ACKNOWLEDGMENTS

This first edition of the **Study Guide to Accompany Macroeconomics** is based on the late Professor Robert

Bingham's study guides for the previous editions of Professor McConnell's **Economics.** He worked with great care and wanted the **Study Guide** to be a valuable aid for students. Many past users of the **Study Guide** will attest to his success. Although Professor Bingham did not participate directly, his work remains the main contribution to this edition.

I must also acknowledge Campbell R. McConnell, who provided helpful comments and support throughout this revision. The team at McGraw-Hill, especially Scott Stratford, Michael Elia, and Edwin Hanson, gave me great assistance with editorial and production work. Despite the many contributions, all responsibility for errors and omissions are mine.

William B. Walstad

Study Guide

to Accompany

McConnell and Brue

Macroeconomics

CHAPTER 1

The nature and method of economics

Chapter 1 introduces you to economics—the study of how people decide how to use scarce productive resources to satisfy material wants. Knowledge of economics is important because it is essential for well-informed citizenship and it has many practical applications to personal decisions. The purpose of this chapter is to explain the nature of the subject and to describe the methods that economists use to study economic questions.

Economists use three different approaches to examine economic topics. The gathering of relevant facts about an economic problem is called **descriptive economics.** **Economic theory** or economic analysis involves the derivation of principles using inductive or deductive methods. **Policy economics** entails the formulation of policies or recommended solutions to economic problems.

The heart of the chapter is the discussion of economic principles in the economic theory section. Economic principles are generalizations. Because the economist cannot employ laboratory experiments to test the generalizations, these principles are always imprecise and subject to exceptions. Economics is a science but it is not an exact science. Economic principles are also simplifications—approximations of a complex world—and both the formulation and application of these principles present many opportunities for making serious mistakes. Economic principles are not the answers to economic questions but are tools—intellectual tools—for analyzing economic problems and for finding policies to solve these problems.

The selection of economic policies to follow depends not only on economic principles but also on the value judgments and the weight given to particular economic goals. Here we move from economic theory and positive economics, which investigates **what is**, to normative economics, which incorporates subjective or value-laden views of **what ought to be**. Many of the apparent disagreements among economists are over normative policy issues and involve deciding which economic goals for our economy are most important in making the case for a policy solution.

Clear thinking about economic questions requires that the beginning student avoid many pitfalls. Errors of commission and omission can occur from bias, loaded terminology, imprecise definitions, fallacies of composition, and confusing correlation with causation. If you can guard against these potential hazards, you can use the economic perspective to improve your understanding of the people's actions and events in the economy at the macroeconomic or the microeconomic level.

■ CHECKLIST

When you have studied this chapter you should be able to:
□ Write the formal definition of economics.
□ Give two (allegedly) good reasons for studying economics.
□ Define descriptive economics, economic theory, and policy economics.
□ Distinguish between induction and deduction in economic reasoning.
□ Explain what an economic principle is and how economic principles are obtained.
□ List the two important characteristics of every economic principle and explain each of these characteristics.
□ Explain what the "other things equal" (**ceteris paribus**) assumption is and why this assumption is employed in economics.
□ Discuss the distinction between macroeconomics and microeconomics.
□ Give examples of positive and normative economics.
□ Identify the eight economic goals.
□ State four significant points about economic goals.
□ Recognize the "pitfalls to straight thinking" when confronted with examples of them.
□ Describe the economic perspective.

■ CHAPTER OUTLINE

1. Economics is concerned with efficiently utilizing limited productive resources to achieve the maximum satisfaction of human material wants.

2. Citizens in a democracy must understand elementary economics in order to understand the present-day problems of their society and to make intelligent decisions when they vote. Economics is an academic rather than a vocational subject, but a knowledge of it is valuable to business executives, consumers, and workers.

3. Economists gather relevant facts to obtain economic principles that may be used to formulate policies which will solve economic problems.

a. Descriptive economics is the gathering of relevant facts about the production, exchange, and consumption of goods and services.

b. Economic theory is the analysis of the facts and the derivation of economic principles.

(1) To obtain and test their principles economists use both the inductive and the deductive methods.

(2) Economic principles are also called laws, theories, and models.

(3) Each of these principles is a generalization.

(4) Economists employ the *ceteris paribus* (or "other things equal") assumption to obtain these generalizations.

(5) These principles are also abstractions from reality.

(6) Economists can derive principles about economic behavior at the macroeconomic or the microeconomic level of analysis.

c. Policy economics is the combination of economic principles and economic values (or goals) to control economic events.

(1) Values are the judgments people make about what is desirable (good, just) and what is undesirable (bad, unjust).

(2) Positive economics concerns **what is**, or the scientific analysis of economic behavior; normative economics suggests **what ought to be** in offering answers to policy questions.

(3) The American society appears to have at least eight major economic goals; these economic goals can be complementary or conflicting or mutually exclusive.

(4) There are three steps in creating a policy designed to achieve an economic goal.

4. Straight thinking in the study and use of economic principles requires strict application of the rules of logic in which personal emotions are irrelevant, if not detrimental. The pitfalls encountered by beginning students in studying and applying economic principles include:

a. bias or preconceived beliefs not warranted by facts;

b. loaded terminology or the use of terms in a way which appeals to emotion and leads to a nonobjective analysis of the issues;

c. the definition by economists of terms in ways which may not be the same as the ways in which these terms are more commonly used;

d. the fallacy of composition or the assumption that what is true of the part is necessarily true of the whole;

e. and the **post hoc fallacy** or the mistaken belief that when one event precedes another the first event is the cause of the second.

5. The economic perspective is a cost-benefit perspective. People, either as individuals or in groups, make economic choices by evaluating the costs and benefits of decisions.

■ **IMPORTANT TERMS**

Economics	**Macroeconomics**
Descriptive economics	**Microeconomics**
Economic theory (analysis)	**Positive and normative statements**
Policy economics	**Economic goals**
Economic principles (law)	**Value judgment**
Induction	**Conflicting or complementary goals**
Deduction	**Loaded terminology**
Generalization	**Fallacy of composition**
Economic model	***Post hoc, ergo propter hoc* fallacy**
Abstraction	**Correlation**
"Other things equal" (*ceteris paribus*) assumption	**Causation**
	Economic perspective

■ **FILL-IN QUESTIONS**

1. Economics as a subject:
a. Is, first of all, the study of the

_____,

_____,

and _____
of the material goods and services that satisfy human wants.

b. But, more formally, it is concerned with the efficient

utilization of _____ productive resources to

achieve the _____ satisfaction of these wants.

2. An understanding of economics is essential if we are to

be well-informed _____ and it has many personal applications even though it is an academic and not a _____ subject.

3. Economics, like other sciences, begins with the facts found in the world around us.

   a. The gathering of relevant facts is the part of the economics called _____ economics.

   b. Economic _____ involves deriving general principles about the economic behavior of people and institutions. When economists develop economic principles from studying facts, they are using the _____ method; whereas the _____ method uses facts to test the validity of hypotheses or economic theories.

   c. The formulation of recommended solutions or remedies for economic problems is referred to as _____ economics.

4. Economic principles are also called _____. These principles are _____ about people's economic behavior and as such necessarily involve _____ from reality.

5. Economists know that the amount consumers spend for goods and services in any year depends upon their after-tax income in that year and several factors other than their income. To look at the relationship between the spending and income of consumers, economists often assume that these other factors are constant and do not change; and when economists do this they make the _____ assumption.

6. Macroeconomics is concerned with the _____ output of the economy and the _____ level of prices, while microeconomics is concerned with output in a(n) _____

_____

and the price of a(n) _____

_____

7. There are two different types of statements that can be made about economic topics. A (positive, normative) _____ statement explains *what is* by offering a scientific proposition about economic behavior that is based on economic theory and facts. A _____ statement includes a value judgment about an economic policy or the economy that suggests *what ought to be*.

Many of the reported disagreements among economists usually involve _____ statements.

8. Eight widely accepted economic goals in the United States are the following:

   a. _____

   b. _____

   c. _____

   d. _____

   e. _____

   f. _____

   g. _____

   h. _____

9. Increases in economic growth that promote full employment would be an example of a set of (conflicting, complementary, mutually exclusive) _____ economic goals. Efforts to achieve an equitable distribution of income that reduce economic efficiency and growth would be an example of a set of _____ economic goals. Actions to expand economic freedom that have no effect on the balance of trade would be an example of a set of _____ economic goals.

10. The three steps involved in the formulation of economic policy are:

   a. _____

   b. _____

   c. _____

11. The economic perspective is a _____ perspective. People and institutions are assumed to make (rational, irrational) _____ decisions by weighing the _____ and _____ of economic actions.

■ **PROBLEMS AND PROJECTS**

1. "In 1982 the Russian demand for wheat in the United States increased and caused the price of wheat throughout the United States to rise." This is a *specific* instance of a more *general* economic principle. Of which economic *generalization* is this a particular example? _____

_____

_____

2. Below are four statements. Each of them is an example of one of the pitfalls frequently encountered in the study of economics. Indicate in the space following each statement the type of pitfall involved.

a. "Investment in stocks and bonds is the only way to build real capital assets." _____

b. "An unemployed worker can find a job if he looks diligently and conscientiously for employment; therefore, all unemployed workers can find employment if they are diligent and conscientious in looking for a job."

_____

c. **Walstad:** "Regulation of public utilities in the United States is an immoral and unconscionable interference with the God-given right of private property and, as you know, old chum, there is no private property in the communist states." **McConnell:** "It is far from that, my boy. You know perfectly well that it is an attempt to limit the unmitigated avarice of mammoth corporations in order, as the Constitution commands, to promote the general welfare of a democratic America." _____

_____

d. "The stock market crash of 1929 was followed by and resulted in 10 years of Depression." _____

3. Below is a list of economic statements. Indicate in the space to the right of each whether they are positive (P) or normative (N). Then in the last four lines below, write two of your own examples of positive statements and two examples of normative economic statements.

a. New York City should control the rental price of apartments. _____

b. Consumer prices rose at an annual rate of 5% last year. _____

c. Most people who are unemployed are just too lazy to work. _____

d. Generally speaking, if you lower the price of a product, people will buy more of that product. _____

e. The profits of drug companies are too large and ought to be used to conduct research on new medicines. _____

f. The Federal government should do more to help the poor in this nation. _____

g. _____ ___P___

h. _____ ___P___

i. _____ ___N___

j. _____ ___N___

■ **SELF-TEST**

Circle the T if the statement is true; and F if it is false.

1. Economics deals with the activities by which humans can earn a living and improve their standard of living. **T F**

2. Economics is academic and of little value because it does not teach the student how to earn a living. **T F**

3. Gathering the relevant economic facts from which economic principles are derived is the part of economics called economic analysis. **T F**

4. In economics the terms "law," "principle," "theory," and "model" mean essentially the same thing. **T F**

5. The "other things equal" or *ceteris paribus* assumption is made in order to simplify the reasoning process. **T F**

6. The deductive method is the scientific method and the method used to derive economic principles from economic facts. **T F**

7. Economic principles enable us to predict the economic consequences of many human actions. **T F**

8. One of the widely (though not universally) accepted economic goals of Americans is an equal distribution of income. **T F**

9. The first step in the formulation of an economic policy, the statement of the goal or desired result, may be an occasion for disagreement because different people may have different and conflicting goals. **T F**

10. Once a single goal or end has been determined as the sole objective of economic policy, there is seldom any question of which policy to adopt to achieve that goal. **T F**

11. If you speak of "capital" to most people, they understand you to be referring to money. The economist, therefore, is obligated to use the term "capital" to mean money. **T F**

12. When value judgments are made about the economy or economic policy this is referred to as positive economics. **T F**

13. Microeconomic analysis is concerned with the performance of the economy as a whole or its major aggregates. **T F**

14. The economic perspective views individuals or institutions as making rational choices based on the analysis of the costs and benefits of decisions.　　**T　F**

15. The statement that "the legal minimum wage should be raised to give working people a decent income" is an example of a normative statement.　　**T　F**

Circle the letter that corresponds to the best answer.

1. Which of the following terms is *not* found in a sophisticated definition of economics?
(a) efficient utilization
(b) unlimited productive resources
(c) maximum satisfaction
(d) human and material wants

2. Economics is a practical field of study in several ways. Which one of the following is *not* an element of its practicality?
(a) every person affects and is affected by the operation of the economy
(b) every person has to earn a living in some manner, and economics develops skills and trains the student in the art of making a living
(c) every person in a democracy is confronted with its political problems and many of them are economic in nature
(d) every person who understands the overall operation of the economy is in a better position to solve personal economic problems

3. One economic principle states that the lower the price of a commodity, the greater will be the quantity of the commodity which consumers will wish to purchase. On the basis of this principle *alone*, it can be concluded that:
(a) if the price of mink coats falls, more mink coats will be purchased by consumers
(b) if the price of mink coats falls, Mrs. James will purchase two instead of one
(c) if the price of mink coats falls and there are no important changes in the other factors affecting their demand, the public will probably purchase a greater quantity of mink coats than it did at the higher price
(d) if more mink coats are purchased this month than last month, it is because the price of mink coats has fallen

4. An economic model is *not*:
(a) an ideal type of economy or an economic policy for which we ought to work
(b) a tool which the economist employs in order to predict
(c) one or a collection of economic principles
(d) an explanation of how the economy or a part of the economy functions in its essential details

5. When economic principles or theories are developed from factual evidence, this method of economic reasoning is called:
(a) descriptive economics
(b) hypothesis testing
(c) deduction
(d) induction

6. Knowing that as the price of a commodity rises the quantity of the commodity sold decreases and that the imposition of a higher tax on a commodity increases its price, the economist concludes that if a government increases the tax on gasoline, less gasoline will be sold. This is an example of:
(a) prediction
(b) control
(c) policy
(d) the fallacy of composition

7. Which of the following economic goals is subject to reasonably accurate measurement?
(a) economic security
(b) full employment
(c) economic freedom
(d) an equitable distribution of income

8. To say that two economic goals are mutually exclusive means that:
(a) it is not possible to achieve both goals
(b) these goals are not accepted as goals in the U.S.S.R.
(c) the achievement of one of the goals results in the achievement of the other
(d) it is possible to quantify both goals

9. Which of the following would be studied in *microeconomics*?
(a) the output of the entire economy
(b) the total number of workers employed in the United States
(c) the general level of prices in the American economy
(d) the output and price of wheat in the United States

10. During World War II the United States employed price control to prevent inflation; this was referred to as "a fascist and arbitrary restriction of economic freedom" by some and as "a necessary and democratic means of preventing ruinous inflation" by others. Both labels are examples of:
(a) economic bias
(b) the fallacy of composition
(c) the misuse of commonsense definitions
(d) loaded terminology

11. If an individual determines to save a larger percentage of his/her income he/she will no doubt be able to save more. To reason, therefore, that if all individuals determine to save a larger percentage of their incomes they will be able to save more is an example of:

(a) the ***post hoc, ergo propter hoc*** fallacy
(b) the fallacy of composition
(c) economic bias
(d) using loaded terminology

12. The government increases its expenditures for road-construction equipment and later the average price of this equipment falls. To reason that the lower price was due to the increase in government expenditures may be an example of:

(a) the ***post hoc, ergo propter hoc*** fallacy
(b) the fallacy of composition
(c) imprecise definition
(d) using loaded terminology

13. Which economic goal is associated with the idea that we want to get the maximum benefits at the minimum cost from the limited productive resources which are available?

(a) full employment
(b) economic growth
(c) economic security
(d) economic efficiency

14. If economic growth tends to produce a more equitable distribution of income among people in a nation, then this relationship between the two economic goals appears to be:

(a) deductive
(b) conflicting
(c) complementary
(d) mutually exclusive

15. When we look at the whole economy or its major aggregates, our analysis would be at the level of:

(a) microeconomics
(b) macroeconomics
(c) positive economics
(d) normative economics

■ **DISCUSSION QUESTIONS**

1. Define economics in both a less and a more sophisticated way. In your latter definition explain the meaning of "resources" and "wants."

2. What are the principal reasons for studying economics?

3. What is the relationship between facts and theory?

4. Define and explain the relationships between descriptive economics, economic theory, and applied economics.

5. What is a "laboratory experiment under controlled conditions"? Does the science of economics have any kind of laboratory? Why do economists employ the "other things equal" assumption?

6. Why are economic principles and models necessarily generalizations and abstract?

7. Why do economists disagree?

8. What does it mean to say that economic principles can be used for prediction?

9. Of the eight economic goals listed in the text, which one would you ***rank*** first, second, third, etc.? Would you add any other goals to this list? If economic goals 2 and 4 were conflicting, which goal would you prefer? Why? If goals 1 and 5 were conflicting, which would you prefer? Why?

10. What procedure should be followed in formulating sound economic policies?

11. Explain each of the following:
(a) fallacy of composition;
(b) loaded terminology;
(c) the ***post hoc, ergo propter hoc*** fallacy.

12. Explain briefly the difference between
(a) macroeconomics and microeconomics;
(b) deduction and induction; and
(c) correlation and causation.

13. What are some current examples of positive economic statements and normative economic statements?

■ **ANSWERS**

CHAPTER 1 THE NATURE AND METHOD OF ECONOMICS

Fill-in questions

1. *a.* production, distribution, consumption; *b.* limited (scarce), maximum

2. citizens, vocational

3. *a.* descriptive; *b.* theory, inductive, deductive; *c.* policy

4. laws (or theories or models), generalizations, abstractions

5. "other things equal" (***ceteris paribus***)

6. total, general, individual industry, particular product

7. positive, normative, normative

8. *a.* economic growth; *b.* full employment; *c.* economic efficiency; *d.* price stability; *e.* economic freedom; *f.* equitable distribution of income; *g.* economic security; *h.* balance of trade

9. complementary, conflicting, mutually exclusive

10. *a.* a clear statement of the objectives and goals; *b.* an analysis of all possible solutions; *c.* an evaluation of the results

11. cost-benefit, rational, costs, benefits (either order for last two)

Problems and projects

1. An increase in the demand for an economic good will cause the price of that good to rise.

2. *a.* definitions; *b.* the fallacy of composition; *c.* loaded terminology; *d.* the **post hoc, ergo propter hoc** fallacy.

3. *a.* N; *b.* P; *c.* N; *d.* P; *e.* N; *f.* N

Self-test

1. T; **2.** F; **3.** F; **4.** T; **5.** T; **6.** F; **7.** T; **8.** F; **9.** T; **10.** F; **11.** F; **12.** F **13.** F; **14.** T; **15.** T

1. *b*; **2.** *b*; **3.** *c*; **4.** *a*; **5.** *d*; **6.** *a*; **7.** *b*; **8.** *a*; **9.** *d*; **10.** *d*; **11.** *b*; **12.** *a*; **13.** *d*; **14.** *c*; **15.** *b*

APPENDIX TO CHAPTER 1 GRAPHS AND THEIR MEANING

This appendix provides an introduction to graphing in economics. Graphs help illustrate and simplify the economic theories and models that will be presented throughout this book. The old saying that "a picture is worth a thousand words" applies to economics; graphs are the way that economists "picture" relationships between economic variables.

You will need to master the basics of graphing if these "pictures" are to be of any help to you. The appendix explains how to achieve that mastery. It begins by showing you how to construct a graph from a table of data on two variables, such as income and consumption. Economists usually, but not always, place the independent variable (income) on the horizontal axis and the dependent variable (consumption) on the vertical axis of the graph. Once the data points are plotted and a line drawn to connect the plotted points, you can determine whether there is a direct or inverse relationship between the variables. Identifying a direct and inverse relationship between variables is an essential skill that will be used repeatedly in this book.

Information from data in graphs and tables can be written in an equation. This work involves determining the slope and intercept from a straight line in a graph or data in a table. Using values for the slope and intercept, you can write a linear equation that will enable you to calculate what the dependent variable would be for a given level of the independent variable.

Some graphs used in the book are nonlinear. With nonlinear curves, the slope of the line is no longer constant throughout but varies as one moves along the curve. This slope can be estimated at a point by determining the slope of a straight line that is drawn tangent to the curve at that point. Similar calculations can be made for other points to see how the slope changes along the curve.

■ APPENDIX CHECKLIST

When you have studied this appendix you should be able to:

☐ Explain why economists use graphs.

☐ Construct a graph of two variables using the numerical data from a table.

☐ Make a table with two variables from data on a graph.

☐ Distinguish between a direct and an inverse relationship when given data on two variables.

☐ Identify dependent and independent variables in economic examples and graphs.

☐ Calculate the slope of a straight line between two points and determine the vertical intercept for the line.

☐ Write a linear equation using the slope of a line and the vertical intercept, and when given values for the independent variable, determine values for the independent variable.

☐ Estimate the slope of a nonlinear curve at a point using a line that is tangent to the curve at that point.

■ APPENDIX OUTLINE

1. Graphs illustrate the relationship between variables to give economists and students another means, in addition to verbal explanation, of understanding economic phenomena. Graphs serve as an aid in describing economic theories and models.

2. The construction of a simple graph involves the plotting of numerical data about two variables from a table.

a. Each graph has a horizontal and a vertical axis that can be labeled for each variable and then scaled for the range of the data points that will be measured on the axis.

b. Data points are plotted on the graph by drawing perpendiculars from the scaled points on the two axes to the place on the graph where the perpendiculars intersect.

c. A line or curve can then be drawn to connect the points plotted on the graph.

3. A graph provides information about relationships between variables.

a. A line that is upward sloping to the right on a graph indicates that there is a positive or **direct** relationship between two variables: an increase in one is associated with an increase in the other; a decrease in one is associated with a decrease in the other.

b. A line that is downward sloping to the right means that there is a negative or **inverse** relationship between the two variables because the variables are changing in opposite directions: an increase in one is associated with a decrease in the other; a decrease in one is associated with an increase in the other.

4. Economists are often concerned with determining cause and effect in economic events.

a. A dependent variable changes (increases or decreases) because of a change in another variable.

b. An independent variable produces or "causes" the change in the dependent variable.

c. In a graph, mathematicians place an independent variable on the horizontal axis and a dependent variable on the vertical axis; economists are more arbitrary about which variable is placed on an axis.

5. Economic graphs are simplifications of economic relationships. When graphs are plotted, there is usually an implicit assumption made that all other factors are being held constant. This "other things equal" or ***ceteris paribus*** assumption is used to simplify the analysis so the study can focus on the two variables of interest.

6. A slope and intercept can be calculated for a straight line and written in the form of a linear equation.

a. The slope of a straight line is the ratio of the vertical change to the horizontal change between two points. A positive slope indicates that the relationship between two variables is direct; a negative slope means there is an inverse relationship between the variables.

b. Where the line intersects the vertical axis of the graph is the vertical intercept.

c. A linear equation is written as ***y = a + bx.*** Once the values for the intercept (*a*) and the slope (*b*) are calculated, then given any value of the independent variable (***x***), the value of the dependent variable (***y***) can be determined.

7. The slope of a straight line is constant, but the slope of a nonlinear curve changes throughout. To estimate the slope of a nonlinear curve at a point, the slope of a line tangent to the curve at that point is calculated.

■ **IMPORTANT TERMS**

Vertical and horizontal axes	**Slope of a line**
Direct (positive) and inverse (negative) relationships	**Vertical intercept**
	Linear equation
Dependent and independent variables	**Nonlinear curve**
	Tangent

■ **FILL-IN QUESTIONS**

1. The relationship between two economic variables can be visualized with the aid of a two-dimensional graph.

a. Customarily, the (dependent, independent) _____ _____ variable is placed on the horizontal axis and the _____ variable is placed on the vertical axis. The _____ variable is said

to change because of a change in the _____ variable.

b. The vertical and horizontal (scales, ranges) _____ on the graph are calibrated to reflect the _____ of values in a table of data points on which the graph is based.

c. Other variables, beyond the two in the graph, that might affect the economic relationship are assumed to be (changing, held constant) _____ . ***Ceteris paribus*** also means that other variables are

_____

2. The graph of a straight line that slopes downward to the right indicates that there is (a direct, an inverse) _____ relationship between the two variables. A graph of a straight line that slopes upward to the right tells us that the relationship is (direct, inverse) _____ . When the value of one variable increases and the value of the other variable increases, then the relationship is _____ ; when the value of one increases, while the other decreases, the relationship is _____

3. The slope of a straight line between two points is defined as the ratio of the (vertical, horizontal) _____ change to the _____ change. When two variables move in the same direction, the slope will be (negative, positive) _____ ; when the variables move in opposite directions the slope will be _____ . The point at which the line meets the vertical axis is called the _____

4. We can express the graph of a straight line with a linear equation that can be written as ***y = a + bx.***

a. ***a*** is the (slope, intercept) _____ and ***b*** is the

_____

b. ***y*** is the (dependent, independent) _____ variable and ***x*** is the _____ variable.

c. If ***a*** was 2, ***b*** was 4, and ***x*** was 5, then ***y*** would be _____ . If the value of ***x*** changed to 7, then ***y*** would be _____ . If the value of ***x*** changed to 3, then ***y*** would be _____

5. The slope of a (straight line, nonlinear curve) _____ is constant throughout; the slope of a

_____ varies from point to point. An estimate of the slope of a nonlinear curve at a point can be made by calculating the slope of a straight line that is

_____ to the point on the curve.

■ PROBLEMS AND PROJECTS

1. Below are three exercises in making graphs. On the graphs plot the economic relationships contained in each exercise. Be sure to label each axis of the graph and to indicate the unit of measurement and scale used on each axis.

_a._ Graph national income on the horizontal axis and consumption expenditures on the vertical axis; connect the seven points and label the curve "Consumption Schedule." The relationship between national income and consumption expenditures is a(n) (direct, inverse)

_____ one and the Consumption Schedule

a(n) (up-, down-) _____ sloping curve.

National income, billions of dollars	Consumption expenditures billions of dollars
$ 600	$ 600
700	640
800	780
900	870
1000	960
1100	1050
1200	1140

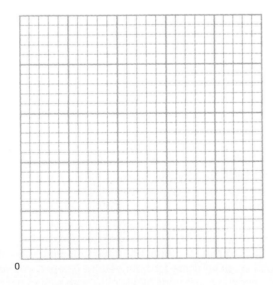

0

_b._ Graph investment expenditures on the horizontal axis and the rate of interest on the vertical axis; connect the

seven points and label the curve "Investment Schedule." The relationship between the rate of interest and investment expenditures is a(n) _____ one and the

Investment Schedule is a(n) _____ sloping curve.

Rate of interest, %	Investment expenditures, billions of dollars
8	$220
7	280
6	330
5	370
4	400
3	420
2	430

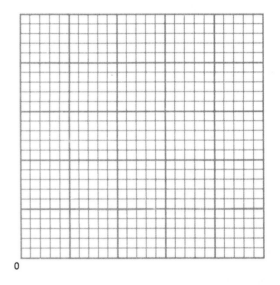

0

_c._ Graph average salary on the horizontal axis and whisky consumption on the vertical axis; connect the seven points.

Average salary, American college professors	Annual per capita whisky consumption in the U.S., gal.
$32,000	1.5
33,000	1.6
34,000	1.7
35,000	1.8
36,000	1.9
37,000	2.0
38,000	2.1

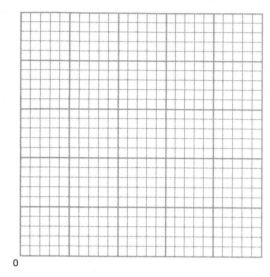

0

(1) The average salary of a college professor and whisky consumption (are, are not) _____

correlated. The higher average salary (is, is not) _____ the *cause* of the greater consumption of whisky.

(2) The relationship between the two variables may be purely _____; or, as is more likely, both the higher salaries and the greater consumption of whisky may be the result of the higher _____ in the American economy.

2. This question is based on the graph below.

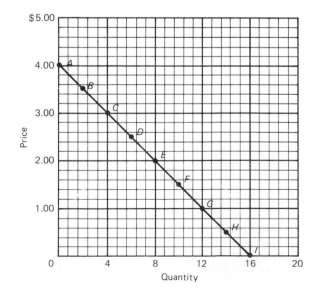

a. Construct a table for points *A–I* from the data shown in the graph.

b. According to economists, price is the (independent, dependent) _____ variable and quantity is the _____ variable.

c. Write a linear equation that summarizes the data.

3. The following three sets of data each show the relationship between an independent variable and a dependent variable. For each set, the independent variable is in the left column and the dependent variable is in the right column.

(1)		(2)		(3)	
A	B	C	D	E	F
0	10	0	100	0	20
10	30	10	75	50	40
20	50	20	50	100	60
30	70	30	25	150	80
40	90	40	0	200	100

a. Write an equation that summarizes the data for each set.

b. State whether each data set shows a positive or inverse relationship between the two variables.

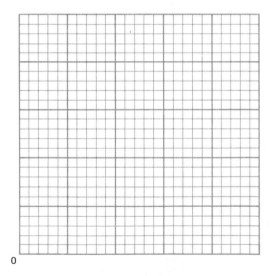

0

c. Graph data sets 1 and 2 on the graph above. Use the same horizontal scale for both sets of independent variables and the same vertical scale for both sets of dependent variables.

4. This problem is based on the following graph.

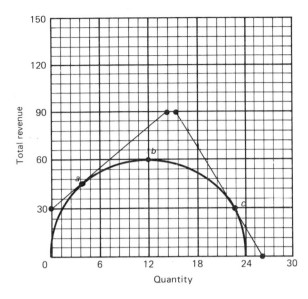

a. The slope of the straight line through point **a** is?
b. The slope of the straight line through point **b** is?
c. The slope of the straight line through point **c** is?

■ SELF-TEST

Circle the T if the statement is true; the F if it is false.

1. Graphs are designed by economists to confuse students and the public.   **T   F**

2. If the straight line on a two-variable graph is downward sloping to the right, then there is a positive relationship between the two variables.   **T   F**

3. A variable that changes as a consequence of a change in another variable is considered to be a dependent variable.   **T   F**

4. Economists always put the independent variable on the horizontal axis and the dependent variable on the variable axis of a two-variable graph.   **T   F**

5. *Ceteris paribus* means that other variables are changing at the same time.   **T   F**

6. In the ratio for the calculation of the slope of a straight line, the vertical change is in the numerator and the horizontal change is in the denominator.   **T   F**

7. If the slope of the linear relationship between consumption and income was .90, then it tells us that for every $1 increase in income there will be a $.90 increase in consumption.   **T   F**

8. If a linear equation was **y** = 10 + 5**x**, the vertical intercept is 5.   **T   F**

9. When a line is tangent to a nonlinear curve, then it intersects the curve at a particular point.   **T   F**

10. If the slope of a straight line on a two-variable (**x**, **y**) graph was .5 and the vertical intercept was 5, then a value of 10 for **x** means **y** is also 10.   **T   F**

11. A slope of −4 for a straight line in a two-variable graph indicates that there is an inverse relationship between the two variables.   **T   F**

12. If **x** is an independent variable and **y** is a dependent variable, then a change in **y** results in a change in **x**.   **T   F**

13. An upward slope for a straight line that is tangent to a nonlinear curve would indicate that the slope of the line is positive.   **T   F**

14. If one pair of **x**, **y** points was (13, 10) and the other was (8, 20), then the slope of the straight line between the two sets of points in the two-variable graph, with **x** on the horizontal axis and **y** on the vertical axis, would be 2.   **T   F**

15. When the value of **x** is 2, a value of 10 for **y** would be calculated from a linear equation of **y** = −2 + 6**x**.   **T   F**

Circle the letter that corresponds to the best answer.

1. If an increase in one variable is associated with a decrease in another variable, then we can conclude that the variables are:
  (a) nonlinear
  (b) directly related
  (c) inversely related
  (d) positively related

2. The ratio of the absolute vertical change to the absolute horizontal change between two points of a straight line is the:
  (a) slope
  (b) vertical intercept
  (c) horizontal intercept
  (d) point of tangency

3. There are two sets of **x**, **y** points on a straight line in a two-variable graph with **y** on the vertical axis and **x** on the horizontal axis. If one set of points was (0, 5) and the other set (5, 20), the linear equation for the line would be:
  (a) **y** = 5**x**
  (b) **y** = 5 + 3**x**
  (c) **y** = 5 + 15**x**
  (d) **y** = 5 + .33**x**

4. In a two-variable graph of data on the price and quantity of a product, economists place:
  (a) price on the horizontal axis because it is the independent variable and quantity on the vertical axis because it is the dependent variable
  (b) price on the vertical axis because it is the dependent

variable and quantity on the horizontal because it is the independent variable

(c) price on the vertical axis even though it is the independent variable and quantity on the horizontal axis even though it is the dependent variable

(d) price on the horizontal axis even though it is the dependent variable and quantity on the vertical axis even though it is the independent variable

5. In a two-dimensional graph of the relationship between two economic variables, an assumption is usually made that:
(a) both variables are linear
(b) both variables are nonlinear
(c) other variables are held constant
(d) other variables are permitted to change

6. When the slope of a straight line to a point tangent to a nonlinear curve is zero, then the straight line is:
(a) vertical
(b) horizontal
(c) upward sloping
(d) downward sloping

The next four questions (7, 8, 9, and 10) are based on the following four data sets. In each set, the independent variable is in the left column and the dependent variable is in the right column.

| (1) | | (2) | | (3) | | (4) | |
A	B	C	D	E	F	G	H
0	1	0	12	4	5	0	4
3	2	5	8	6	10	1	3
6	3	10	4	8	15	2	2
9	4	15	0	10	20	3	1

7. There is an inverse relationship between the independent and dependent variable in data sets:
(a) 1 and 4
(b) 2 and 3
(c) 1 and 3
(d) 2 and 4

8. The vertical intercept is 4 in data set:
(a) 1
(b) 2
(c) 3
(d) 4

9. The linear equation for data set 1 is:
(a) $B = 3A$
(b) $B = 1 + 3A$
(c) $B = 1 + .33A$
(d) $A = 1 + .33B$

10. The linear equation for data set 2 is:
(a) $C = 12 - 1.25D$
(b) $D = 12 + 1.25C$
(c) $D = 12 - .80C$
(d) $C = 12 - .80D$

Answer the next four questions (11, 12, 13, and 14) on the basis of the following diagram.

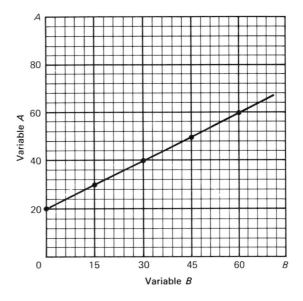

11. The variables **A** and **B** are:
(a) positively related
(b) negatively related
(c) indirectly related
(d) nonlinear

12. The slope of the line is:
(a) .33
(b) .67
(c) 1.50
(d) 3.00

13. The vertical intercept is:
(a) 80
(b) 60
(c) 40
(d) 20

14. The linear equation for the slope of the line is:
(a) $A = 20 + .33B$
(b) $B = 20 + .33A$
(c) $A = 20 + .67B$
(d) $B = 20 + .67A$

Answer the next two questions on the basis of the following diagram:

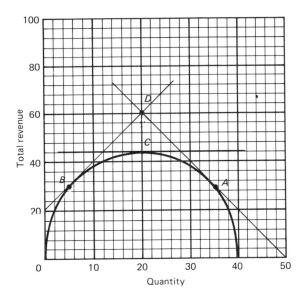

15. The slope of the line tangent to the curve at point **A** is:
(a) 2
(b) −2
(c) −1.5
(d) −0.5

16. The slope of the line tangent to the curve at point **B** is:
(a) −2
(b) 2
(c) 3
(d) 0.5

17. The slope of the line tangent to the curve at point **C** is:
(a) −1
(b) 1
(c) 0
(d) undefined

■ **DISCUSSION QUESTIONS**

1. Why do economists use graphs in their work? Give two examples of a graph that illustrates the relationship between two economic variables.

2. What does the slope tell you about a straight line? How would you interpret a slope ot 4? A slope of −2? A slope of .5? A slope of −.25?

3. If the vertical intercept increases in value but the slope of a straight line stays the same, what happens to the graph of the line? If the vertical intercept decreases in value, what will happen to the line?

4. How do you interpret a vertical ilne on a two-variable graph? How do you interpret a horizontal line?

5. When you know that the price and quantity of a product are inversely related, what does this tell you about the slope of a line? What do you know about the slope when the two variables are positively related?

6. Which variable is the dependent and which is the independent in the following economic statement: "A decrease in business taxes had a positive effect on investment spending." How do you tell the difference between a dependent and independent variable when examining economic relationships?

7. Why is an assumption made that all other variables are held constant when we construct a two-variable graph of the price and quantity of a product?

8. How do mathematicians and economists differ at times in the way that they construct two-dimensional graphs? Give an example.

9. If you know that the equation relating consumption (**C**) to income (**Y**) is **C** = 10,000 + 5**Y**, then what would consumption be when income is $5,000? Construct an income-consumption table for five different levels of income.

10. How do the slopes of a straight line and a nonlinear curve differ? How do you estimate the slope of a nonlinear curve?

■ **ANSWERS**

APPENDIX TO CHAPTER 1 GRAPHS AND THEIR MEANING

Fill-in questions

1. *a.* independent, dependent, dependent, independent; *b.* scales, ranges; *c.* held constant, held constant

2. an inverse, direct, direct, inverse

3. vertical, horizontal, positive, negative, vertical intercept

4. *a.* intercept, slope; *b.* dependent, independent; *c.* 22, 30, 14

5. straight line, nonlinear curve, tangent

Problems and projects

1. *a.* direct, up-; *b.* inverse, down-; *c.* (1) are, is not; (2) coincidental, incomes (standard of living, or some other such answer)

2. *a.*

Point	Price	Quantity
A	$4.00	0
B	3.50	2
C	3.00	4
D	2.50	6
E	2.00	8
F	1.50	10
G	1.00	12
H	.50	14
I	.00	16

b. independent, dependent; *c.* $P = 4.00 - .25Q$

3. *a.* (1) $B = 10 + 2A$; (2) $D = 100 - 2.5C$; (3) $F = 20 + .4E$; *b.* (1) positive; (2) inverse; (3) positive

4. *a.* 5; *b.* 0; *c.* -10

Self-test

1. F; **2.** F; **3.** T; **4.** F; **5.** F; **6.** T; **7.** T; **8.** F; **9.** F; **10.** T; **11.** T; **12.** F; **13.** T; **14.** F; **15.** T

1. *c;* **2.** *a;* **3.** *b;* **4.** *c;* **5.** *c;* **6.** *b;* **7.** *d;* **8.** *d;* **9.** *c;* **10.** *c;* **11.** *a;* **12.** *b;* **13.** *d;* **14.** *c;* **15.** *b;* **16.** *b;* **17.** *c*

An introduction to the economizing problem

The aim of Chapter 2 is to explain the central problem of economics. The problem is that resources—the ultimate means of satisfying material wants—are scarce *relative* to the insatiable wants of society. Economics as a science is the study of the various aspects of the behavior of society in its effort to allocate the scarce resources—land, labor, capital, and entrepreneurial ability—in order to satisfy as best it can its unlimited desire for consumption.

The production possibilities table and curve are used in this chapter to illustrate the meaning of the scarcity of resources and increasing opportunity costs. It is both an illustrative device that will help you to understand several economic concepts and problems and a tool that has many applications in the real world.

Every economy is faced with the problem of scarce resources and has to find ways to respond to the economic problem. No economy answers the problem in the same way that another economy does. Between the extremes of pure (or laissez faire) capitalism and the command economy (communism) are various economic systems; all these systems are different devices—different methods of organization—for finding an answer to the economic problem of relative scarcity. Chapters 3 through 8 will explain in greater detail how the United States economy is organized and operates to address the economizing problem.

In Chapter 2 of the textbook are a number of economic definitions and classifications. It would be worthwhile for you to learn these definitions *now.* They will be used later on and it will be necessary for you to know them if you are to understand what follows.

■ CHECKLIST

When you have studied this chapter you should be able to:
- ☐ Write a definition of economics that incorporates the relationship between resources and wants.
- ☐ Identify the four economic resources and the type of income associated with each.
- ☐ State the four assumptions made when a production possibilities table or curve is constructed.
- ☐ Construct a production possibilities curve when you are given the appropriate data.
- ☐ Define opportunity cost and utilize a production possibilities curve to explain the concept.
- ☐ State the law of increasing opportunity costs and, in as few words as possible, present the economic rationale for this law.
- ☐ Use a production possibilities curve to illustrate economic growth, underemployment of resources, and increasing opportunity costs.
- ☐ Give real-world applications of the production possibilities curve.
- ☐ List the two major characteristics of pure capitalism and the command economy.

■ CHAPTER OUTLINE

1. The bases upon which the study of economics rests are two facts.
   a. Society's material wants are unlimited.
   b. The economic resources which are the ultimate means of satisfying these wants are scarce in relation to the wants.
   (1) Economic resources are classified as land, capital, labor, and entrepreneurial ability.
   (2) The payments received by those who provide the economy with these four resources are rental income, interest income, wages, and profits, respectively.
   (3) Because these resources are scarce (or limited) the output the economy is able to produce is also limited.

2. Economics, then, is the study of how society's scarce resources are used (administered) to obtain the greatest satisfaction of its material wants.
   a. To be efficient in the use of its resources an economy must achieve both full employment and full production.
   b. The production possibilities table indicates the alternative combinations of goods and services an economy is

capable of producing when it has achieved full employment and full production.

(1) Four assumptions are made when a production possibilities table is constructed.

(2) The table illustrates the fundamental choice every society must make: what quantity of each product it wants produced.

c. The data contained in the production possibilities table can be plotted on a graph to obtain a production possibilities curve.

d. Which of these alternative combinations society chooses—which product-mix it selects—depends upon the preferences of that society; and preferences are subjective and nonscientific.

e. The opportunity cost of producing an additional unit of one product is the amounts of other products that are sacrificed; and the law of increasing opportunity costs is that the opportunity cost of producing additional units of a product increases as more of that product is produced.

(1) The law of increasing opportunity cost results in a production possibilities curve that is concave (from the origin).

(2) The opportunity cost of producing additional units of a product increases as more of the product is produced because resources are not completely adaptable to alternative uses.

(3) The production possibilities curve illustrates the concepts of scarcity, choice, opportunity cost, and increasing opportunity costs.

3. The following modifications make the production possibilities concept more realistic.

a. The failure to achieve full employment or full production reduces the output of the economy.

b. Improvements in technology and increased amounts of resources expand the output the economy is capable of producing.

c. The combination of goods and services an economy chooses to produce today helps to determine its production possibilities in the future.

d. There are many real-world applications of the production possibilities curve and table.

4. Different economic systems differ in the way they respond to the economizing problem

a. At one extreme is pure capitalism which relies upon the private ownership of its economic resources and the market system.

b. At the other extreme, the command economy uses the public ownership of its resources and central planning.

c. Economies in the real world lie between these two extremes and are hybrid systems.

d. Some underdeveloped nations have traditional (or customary) economies which are shaped by the customs and traditions of the society.

■ IMPORTANT TERMS

The economizing problem

Unlimited wants

Scarce resources

Land, capital, labor, and entrepreneurial ability

Investment

Consumer goods

Capital goods

Real capital

Money (financial) capital

Rental income, interest income, wages, and profit

Underemployment

Economic growth

Utility

Pure (laissez-faire) capitalism

Factors of production

Economics

Economic efficiency

Full employment

Full production

Production possibilities table

Production possibilities curve

Optimal product mix

Opportunity cost

Law of increasing opportunity costs

Unemployment

Command economy (communism)

Authoritarian capitalism

Market socialism

Traditional (customary) economies

■ FILL-IN QUESTIONS

1. The two fundamental facts that provide the foundation of economics are:

a. _____

b. _____

2. Complete the following classification of resources:

a. _____

(1) _____

(2) _____

b. _____

(1) _____

(2) _____

3. Both consumer goods and capital goods satisfy human wants. The consumer goods satisfy these wants (directly, indirectly) _____ and the capital goods satisfy them _____

4. The incomes of individuals are received from supplying resources. Four types of incomes are _____ ,

_____ , _____ ,

and _____

5. Economics can be defined as _____

_____

_____

6. Economic efficiency requires that there be both full

_____ of resources and full _____

7. When a production possibilities table or curve is constructed, four assumptions are made. These assumptions are:

a. _____

b. _____

c. _____

d. _____

8. Below is a production possibilities curve for tractors and suits of clothing.

a. If the economy moves from point **A** to point **B** it will

produce (more, fewer) _____ tractors and

(more, fewer) _____ suits of clothing.

b. If the economy is producing at point **X,** some of the

resources of the economy are either _____

or _____

c. If the economy moves from point **X** to point **B** (more,

fewer) _____ tractors and (more, fewer)

_____ suits will be produced.

d. If the economy is to produce at point **Y,** it must either

_____ or _____

9. All the combinations of products shown in the production possibilities table (or on the curve) can be achieved only if there are full employment and full production in the economy; the best combination of products depends upon

the (values, resources, technology) _____
of that society and is a (scientific, nonscientific)

_____ matter.

10. The quantity of other goods and services an economy must go without in order to produce more low-cost hous-

ing is the _____

_____

of producing the additional low-cost housing.

11. The cost of producing a commodity tends to increase

as more of the commodity is produced because _____

_____

12. The more an economy consumes of its current pro-

duction, the (more, less) _____ it will be capable of producing in future years if other things are equal.

13. In:

a. pure capitalism property resources are (publicly, pri-

vately) _____ owned and the means employed to direct and coordinate economic activity is the

_____ system.

b. a command economy the property resources are

_____ owned and the coordinating device

is central _____

■ **PROBLEMS AND PROJECTS**

1. Below is a list of resources. Indicate in the space to the right of each whether the resource is land, capital (C), labor, entrepreneurial ability (EA), or some combinations of these.

a. Fishing grounds in the North Atlantic _____

b. A cash register in a retail store _____

c. Uranium deposits in Canada _____

d. An irrigation ditch in Nebraska _____

e. The work performed by the late Henry Ford _____

f. The oxygen breathed by human beings _____

g. An IBM plant in Rochester, Minnesota _____

h. The food on the shelf of a grocery store _____

i. The work done by a welder at an auto plant _____

j. The tasks accomplished in perfecting a new computer for commercial sales _____

2. A production possibilities table for two commodities, wheat and automobiles, is found below. The table is constructed employing the usual assumptions. Wheat is measured in units of 100,000 bushels and automobiles in units of 100,000.

Combination	Wheat	Automobiles
A	0	7
B	7	6
C	13	5
D	18	4
E	22	3
F	25	2
G	27	1
H	28	0

a. Follow the general rules for making graphs (see Chapter 1); plot the data from the table on the graph below to obtain a production possibilities curve. Place wheat on the vertical axis and automobiles on the horizontal axis.

b. Fill in the table below showing the opportunity cost per unit of producing the 1st through the 7th automobile.

Automobiles	Cost of production
1st	_____
2d	_____
3d	_____
4th	_____
5th	_____
6th	_____
7th	_____

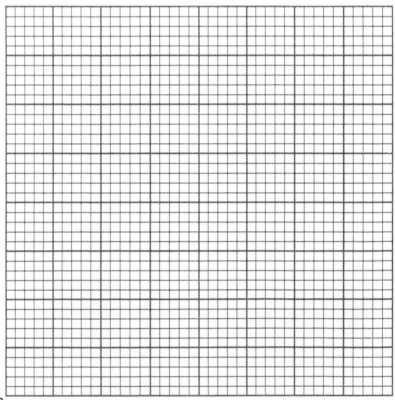

0

3. Below is a production possibilities curve.

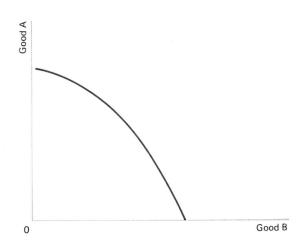

Draw on this graph:

a. A production possibilities curve which indicates greater efficiency in the production of good *A*.

b. A production possibilities curve which indicates greater efficiency in the production of good *B*.

c. A production possibilities curve which indicates an increase in the resources available to the economy.

4. Below is a list of economic goods. Indicate in the space to the right of each whether the good is a consumer good (CON), a capital good (CAP), or that it depends (DEP) upon who is using it and for what purpose.

a. An automobile _____

b. A tractor _____

c. A taxicab _____

d. A house _____

e. A factory building _____

f. An office building _____

g. An ironing board _____

h. A refrigerator _____

i. A telephone _____

j. A quart of Scotch whisky _____

k. A cash register _____

l. A screwdriver _____

■ **SELF-TEST**

Circle the T if the statement is true; the F if it is false.

1. The wants with which economics is concerned include only those wants which can be satisfied by goods and services. **T F**

2. Money is a resource and is classified as "capital." **T F**

3. Profit is the reward paid to those who provide the economy with capital. **T F**

4. Resources are scarce because society's material wants are unlimited. **T F**

5. The opportunity cost of producing antipollution devices is the other goods and services the economy is unable to produce because it has decided to produce these devices. **T F**

6. The opportunity cost of producing a good tends to increase as more of it is produced because resources less suitable to its production must be employed. **T F**

7. Drawing a production possibilities curve concave to the origin is the geometric way of stating the law of increasing opportunity costs. **T F**

8. It is not possible for an economy capable of producing just two goods to increase its production of both. **T F**

9. Economic growth means an increase in the ability of an economy to produce goods and services; and it is shown by a movement of the production possibilities to the right. **T F**

10. The more capital goods an economy produces today, the greater will be the total output of all goods it can produce in the future, other things being equal. **T F**

11. It is economically desirable for a nation to have unemployed resources at the outset of a war because it can increase its production of military goods without having to decrease its production of civilian goods. **T F**

12. In the economic system called authoritarian capitalism most property is publicly owned but the market system is used to coordinate economic activity. **T F**

Circle the letter that corresponds to the best answer.

1. An "innovator" is defined as an entrepreneur who:
(*a*) makes basic policy decisions in a business firm
(*b*) combines factors of production to produce a good or service
(*c*) invents a new product or process for producing a product

(*d*) introduces new products on the market or employs a new method to produce a product

2. An economy is efficient when it has achieved:
(*a*) full employment
(*b*) full production
(*c*) either full employment or full production
(*d*) both full employment and full production

3. When a production possibilities schedule is written (or a production possibilities curve is drawn) four assumptions are made. Which of the following is *not* one of those assumptions?
(*a*) Only two products are produced
(*b*) the nation is not at war
(*c*) the economy has both full employment and full production
(*d*) the quantities of all resources available to the economy are fixed

4. At point **A** on the production possibilities curve in the following illustration:

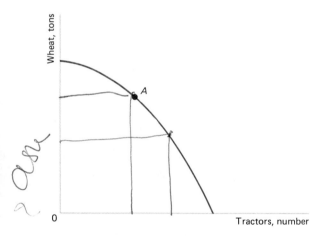

(*a*) more wheat than tractors is being produced
(*b*) more tractors than wheat are being produced
(*c*) the economy is employing all its resources
(*d*) the economy is not employing all its resources

5. The combinations of products in a society's production possibilities table which is its optimal product-mix depends upon that society's:
(*a*) resources
(*b*) technology
(*c*) level of employment
(*d*) values

6. The production possibilities curve is:
(*a*) concave
(*b*) convex

(*c*) linear
(*d*) positive

7. A farmer who produces his crops by inefficient methods is:
(*a*) an unemployed worker
(*b*) an underemployed worker
(*c*) a fully employed worker
(*d*) an apparently unemployed worker

8. If there is an increase in the resources available within the economy:
(*a*) more goods and services will be produced in the economy
(*b*) the economy will be capable of producing more goods and services
(*c*) the standard of living in the economy will rise
(*d*) the technological efficiency of the economy will improve

9. If the production possibilities curve on the graph below moves from position **A** to position **B,** then:
(*a*) the economy has increased the efficiency with which it produces wheat
(*b*) the economy has increased the efficiency with which it produces tractors
(*c*) the economy has put previously idle resources to work
(*d*) the economy has gone from full employment to less-than-full employment

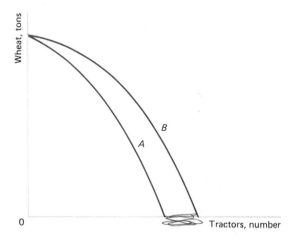

10. The private ownership of property resources and use of the market system to direct and coordinate economic activity is characteristic of:
(*a*) pure capitalism
(*b*) the command economy
(*c*) market socialism
(*d*) the traditional economy

11. The public ownership of property resources and the use of a market system to direct and coordinate economic activity is characteristic of:
(a) pure capitalism
(b) the command economy
(c) market socialism
(d) authoritarian capitalism

12. The opportunity cost of a new public stadium is the:
(a) money cost of hiring guards and staff for the new stadium
(b) cost of constructing the new stadium in a future year
(c) change in the real estate tax rate to pay off the new stadium
(d) other goods and services that must be sacrificed to construct the new stadium

Answer the next three questions (13, 14, and 15) on the basis of the data given in the following production possibilities table.

	Production possibilities (alternatives)					
	A	B	C	D	E	F
Capital goods	100	95	85	70	50	0
Consumer goods	0	100	180	240	280	300

13. The choice of alternative B compared with alternative D would tend to promote:
(a) a slower rate of economic growth
(b) a faster rate of economic growth
(c) increased consumption in the present
(d) central economic planning

14. If the economy is producing at production alternative D, the opportunity cost of 20 more units of consumer goods is:
(a)   5 units of capital goods
(b) 10 units of capital goods
(c) 15 units of capital goods
(d) 20 units of capital goods

15. In the table, the law of increasing opportunity costs is suggested by the fact that:
(a) greater and greater quantities of consumer goods must be given up to get more capital goods
(b) smaller and smaller quantities of consumer goods must be given up to get more capital goods
(c) capital goods are relatively more scarce than consumer goods
(d) the production possibilities curve will eventually shift outward as the economy expands

■ DISCUSSION QUESTIONS

1. Explain what is meant by the "economizing problem." Why are resources scarce?

2. In what sense are wants satiable and in what sense are they insatiable?

3. What are the four economic resources? How is each of these resources defined? What is the income earned by each of them called?

4. When is a society economically efficient? What is meant by "full production" and how does it differ from "full employment"?

5. What four assumptions are made in drawing a production possibilities curve or schedule? How do technological advance and an increased supply of resources in the economy affect the curve or schedule?

6. Why cannot an economist determine which of the combinations in the production possibilities table is "best"? What determines the optimal product-mix?

7. What is opportunity cost? What is the law of increasing opportunity cost? Why do costs increase?

8. What is the important relationship between the **composition** of the economy's current output and the **location** of future production possibilities curves?

9. Describe some real-world applications of the production possibilities curve.

10. Pure capitalism and the command economy differ in two important ways. Compare these two economic systems with each other and with authoritarian capitalism and market socialism.

■ ANSWERS

CHAPTER 2 AN INTRODUCTION TO THE ECONOMIZING PROBLEM

Fill-in questions

1. a. society's material wants are unlimited; b. economic resources, which are the ultimate means of satisfying these wants, are scarce in relation to these wants

2. a. property resources; (1) land or raw materials, (2) capital; b. human resources; (1) labor, (2) entrepreneurial ability

3. directly, indirectly

4. rental income, interest income, wages, profits

5. the social science concerned with the problem of using or administering scarce resources to attain maximum fulfillment of unlimited wants

6. employment, production

7. *a.* the economy is operating at full employment and full production; *b.* the available supplies of the factors of production are fixed; *c.* technology does not change during the course of the analysis; *d.* the economy produces only two products

8. *a.* fewer, more; *b.* unemployed, underemployed; *c.* more, more; *d.* increase resource supplies, improve its technology

9. values, nonscientific

10. opportunity cost

11. economic resources are not completely adaptable among alternate uses

12. less

13. *a.* privately, market; *b.* publicly, planning

Problems and projects

1. *a.* land; *b.* C; *c.* land; *d.* C; *e.* EA; *f.* land; *g.* C; *h.* C; *i.* labor; *j.* EA

2. *b.* 1, 2, 3, 4, 5, 6, 7 wheat

4. *a.* DEP; *b.* CAP; *c.* CAP; *d.* CAP; *e.* CAP; *f.* CAP; *g.* DEP; *h.* DEP; *i.* DEP; *j.* DEP; *k.* CAP; *l.* DEP

Self-test

1. T; **2.** F; **3.** F; **4.** T; **5.** T; **6.** T; **7.** T; **8.** F; **9.** T; **10.** T; **11.** F; **12.** F

1. *d.* **2.** *d;* **3.** *b;* **4.** *c;* **5.** *d;* **6.** *a;* **7.** *b;* **8.** *b;* **9.** *b;* **10.** *a;* **11.** *c;* **12.** *d;* **13.** *b;* **14.** *b;* **15.** *a*

Pure capitalism and the circular flow

Chapter 3 has three principal aims: to outline six ideological and institutional characteristics of pure capitalism, to explain three practices found in all modern economies, and to sketch in extremely simple terms the fundamental operation of a capitalistic economy. A more detailed explanation of the institutions, practices, and behavior of the United States economy—which is not *purely* capitalistic—is found in the chapters that follow. If the aims of this chapter are accomplished, you can begin to understand the system and methods employed by our economy to find answers to the economizing problem discussed in Chapter 2.

The resources of the American economy are owned by its citizens, who are free to use them as they wish in their own self-interest; prices and markets serve to express the self-interests of resource owners, consumers, and business firms; and competition serves to regulate self-interest—to prevent the self-interest of any person or any group from working to the disadvantage of the economy as a whole and to make self-interest work for the benefit of the entire economy.

The three practices of all modern economies are the employment of large amounts of capital, extensive specialization, and the use of money. Economies use capital and engage in specialization because it is a more efficient use of their resources; it results in larger total output and the greater satisfaction of wants. But when workers, business firms, and regions within an economy specialize they become dependent on each other for the goods and services they do not produce for themselves. To obtain these goods and services they must engage in trade. Trade is made more convenient by using money as a medium of exchange.

The circular-flow-of-income model (or diagram) is a device which illustrates for a capitalistic economy the relation between households and businesses, the flow of money and economic goods and services between households and businesses, their dual role as buyers and sellers, and the two basic types of markets essential to the capitalistic process.

Understand these essentials of the economic skeleton first; then a little flesh—a little more reality, a little more detail—can be added to the bones. Understanding the skeleton makes it much easier to understand the whole body and its functioning.

■ CHECKLIST

When you have studied this chapter you should be able to:

☐ Identify and explain the six important institutional characteristics of capitalism.

☐ Name and explain the three characteristics of all modern economies.

☐ Draw the circular flow diagram; and correctly label the real and money flows and the two major types of markets.

■ CHAPTER OUTLINE

1. The United States economy is not pure capitalism, but it is a close approximation of pure capitalism. Pure capitalism has the following six peculiarities that distinguish it from other economic systems.

a. Private individuals and organizations own and control its property resources by means of the institution of private property.

b. These individuals and organizations possess both the freedom of enterprise and the freedom of choice.

c. Each of them is motivated largely by self-interest.

d. Competition prevents them as buyers and sellers from exploiting others.

e. Markets and prices (the market system) are used to communicate and coordinate the decisions of buyers and sellers.

f. And the role of government is limited in a competitive and capitalistic economy.

2. In common with other advanced economies of the world, the American economy has three major characteristics.

   a. It employs complicated and advanced methods of production and large amounts of capital equipment to produce goods and services efficiently.

   b. It is a highly specialized economy; and this specialization increases the productive efficiency of the economy.

   c. It also uses money extensively to facilitate trade and specialization.

3. The circular flow model is a device used to clarify the relationships between households and business firms in a purely capitalistic economy.

   a. In resource markets households supply and firms demand resources and in product markets the firms supply and households demand products. Households use the incomes they obtain from supplying resources to purchase the goods and services produced by the firms; and in the economy there is a real flow of resources and products and a money flow of incomes and expenditures.

   b. The circular flow model has at least six limitations.

■ **IMPORTANT TERMS**

Private property	**Money**
Self-interest	**Medium of exchange**
Competition	**Barter**
Market	**Coincidence of wants**
Freedom of choice	**Circular flow model**
Freedom of enterprise	**Households**
Roundabout production	**Resource market**
Specialization	**Product market**
Division of labor	

■ **FILL-IN QUESTIONS**

1. The ownership of property resources by private individuals and organizations is the institution of _____ _____

2. Two basic freedoms encountered in a capitalistic economy are the freedoms of _____ _____ and _____

3. Self-interest means that each economic unit attempts to _____ ; this self-interest might work

to the disadvantage of the economy as a whole if it were not regulated and constrained by _____

4. According to the economist, competition is present if two conditions prevail; these two conditions are:

   a. _____

   b. _____

5. If the number of buyers and sellers in a market is large, no single buyer or seller is able to _____ the price of the commodity bought and sold in that market.

6. In a capitalistic economy individual buyers communicate their demands and individual sellers communicate their supplies in the _____ of the economy; and their decisions are coordinated by the _____ determined there by demand and supply.

7. In the ideology of pure capitalism government is assigned (no, a limited, an extensive) _____ role.

8. The three practices or institutions common to all modern economies are _____ _____, _____, and _____

9. Modern economies make extensive use of capital goods and engage in roundabout production because it is more _____ than direct production.

10. If an economy engages in extensive specialization the individuals living in the economy are extremely _____ ; and if these individuals are to enjoy the benefits of specialization there must be _____ among them.

11. Modern economies practice specialization and the division of labor because the self-sufficient producer or worker tends to be a(n) _____ one.

12. In modern economies money functions chiefly as a(n) _____

13. Barter between two individuals will take place only if there is a(n) _____

14. For an item to be "money," it must be _____ _____

15. In the circular flow model:
 a. Households are demanders and businesses are suppliers in the _____ markets; and businesses are demanders and households are suppliers of the _____ markets of the economy.
 b. The two flows are called the _____ flow and the _____ flow.
 c. The expenditures made by businesses are a _____ to them and become the _____ of households.

■ **PROBLEMS AND PROJECTS**

1. In the circular flow diagram below, the upper pair of flows (*a* and *b*) represent the product market and the lower pair (*c* and *d*) the resource market.

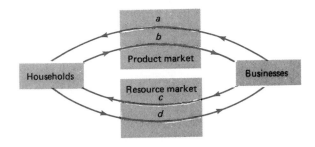

Supply labels or explanations for each of the four flows:

a. _____ Good & Services _____

b. _____ Consumption Expenditures

c. _____ Cost _____

d. _____ Peso   Resource Market _____
   4 factors of prod.

■ **SELF-TEST**

Circle the T if the statement is true; the F if it is false.

1. The United States economy can correctly be called "pure capitalism." **T F**

2. There are in the United States legal limits to the right of private property. **T F**

3. The freedom of business firms to produce a particular consumer good is always limited by the desires of consumers for that good. **T F**

4. When a market is competitive the individual sellers of the commodity are unable to reduce the supply of the commodity enough to drive its price upward. **T F**

5. In a purely capitalistic economy it is consumers who ultimately decide what goods and services the economy will produce. **T F**

6. The market system is not employed in communistic and socialistic economies. **T F**

7. The employment of capital to produce goods and services requires that there be "roundabout production" but it is more efficient than "direct" production. **T F**

8. Increasing the amount of specialization in an economy generally leads to the more efficient use of its resources. **T F**

9. Money is a device for facilitating the exchange of goods and services. **T F**

10. "Coincidence of wants" means that two persons desire to acquire the same good or service. **T F**

11. Cigarettes may serve as money if sellers are generally willing to accept them as money. **T F**

12. In the circular flow model, the household functions on the demand side of the resource and product markets. **T F**

13. The pursuit of economic self-interest is the same thing as selfishness. **T F**

14. A gas station is an example of a market. **T F**

15. Human and geographic specialization are both essential in achieving efficiency in the use of resources. **T F**

Circle the letter that corresponds to the best answer.

1. Which of the following is **not** one of the six characteristics of capitalism?
 (*a*) Competition
 (*b*) central economic planning
 (*c*) private property
 (*d*) freedom of enterprise and choice

2. Maximization of profits appears to be in the self-interest of:
 (*a*) business firms
 (*b*) landowners
 (*c*) workers
 (*d*) consumers

3. To decide how to use its scarce resources to satisfy human wants pure capitalism relies on.
 (*a*) central planning
 (*b*) roundabout production

(c) a price system

(d) the coincidence of wants

4. In pure capitalism the role of government is best described as:

(a) nonexistent

(b) limited

(c) significant

(d) extensive

5. Which of the following is *not* a necessary consequence of specialization?

(a) people will use money

(b) people will engage in trade

(c) people will be dependent upon each other

(d) people will produce more of some things than they would produce in the absence of specialization

6. In an economy in which there are full employment and full production, constant amounts of resources, and unchanging technology:

(a) to increase the production of capital goods requires an increase in the production of consumer goods

(b) to decrease the production of capital goods necessitates a decrease in the production of consumer goods

(c) to increase the production of capital goods is impossible

(d) to increase the production of capital goods a decrease in the production of consumer goods is needed

7. Which of the following is *not* a characteristic of competition as the economist sees it?

(a) the widespread diffusion of economic power

(b) a large number of buyers in product markets

(c) just several sellers of all products

(d) the relatively easy entry into and exit of producers from industries

8. The two kinds of market found in the circular flow model are:

(a) the real and the money markets

(b) the real and the product markets

(c) the money and the resource markets

(d) the product and the resource markets

9. In the circular flow model businesses:

(a) demand both products and resources

(b) supply both products and resources

(c) demand products and supply resources

(d) supply products and demand resources

10. One of the limitations of the circular flow model found in this chapter is that:

(a) no mention is made of the role of government

(b) it is assumed households save some of their income

(c) too much attention is paid to how resource and produce prices are determined

(d) it "ensnares the viewer in a maze of detail"

■ **DISCUSSION QUESTIONS**

1. Explain the several elements—institutions and assumptions—embodied in pure capitalism.

2. What do each of the following seek if they pursue their own self-interest? Consumers, resource owners, and business firms.

3. Explain what economists mean by competition. Why is it important to have competition in an economy whose members are motivated by self-interest?

4. What are the advantages of "indirect" or "roundabout" production?

5. How does an economy benefit from specialization and the division of labor?

6. What disadvantages are there to specialization and the division of labor?

7. What are the principal disadvantages of barter?

8. What is money? What important function does it perform? Explain how money performs this function and how it overcomes the disadvantages associated with barter. Why are people willing to accept paper money in exchange for the goods and services which they sell?

9. In the circular-flow-of-income model:

(a) What two markets are involved?

(b) What roles do households play in each of these markets?

(c) What roles do businesses play in each of these markets?

(d) What two income flows are pictured in money terms? In real terms?

(e) What two expenditure flows are pictured in money terms? In real terms?

10. What are the five shortcomings of the circular-flow-of-income model?

11. Give several international examples of specialization and efficiency.

■ **ANSWERS**

CHAPTER 3 PURE CAPITALISM AND THE CIRCULAR FLOW

Fill-in questions

1. private property

2. enterprise, choice

3. do what is best for itself, competition

4. a. large numbers of independently acting buyers and sellers operating in the markets; b. freedom of buyers and sellers to enter or leave these markets

5. control (rig, affect)

6. markets, prices

7. a limited

8. the extensive use of capital, specialization, the use of money

9. efficient

10. interdependent, exchange (trade)

11. inefficient

12. medium of exchange

13. coincidence of wants

14. generally acceptable by sellers in exchange

15. *a.* product, resource; *b.* real, money (either order); *c.* cost, income

Problems and projects

1. *a.* goods and services; *b.* expenditures for goods and services; *c.* money income payments (wages, rent, interest, and profit); *d.* services or resources (land, labor, capital, and entrepreneurial ability)

Self-test

1. F; **2.** T; **3.** T; **4.** T; **5.** T; **6.** F; **7.** T; **8.** T; **9.** T; **10.** F; **11.** T; **12.** F; **13.** F; **14.** T; **15.** T

1. *b*; **2.** *a*; **3.** *c*; **4.** *b*; **5.** *a*; **6.** *d*; **7.** *c*; **8.** *d*; **9.** *d*; **10.** *a*

In the circular flow model, households supply the resource market with the four factors of production – land, labor, capital, & entrepreneurial ability. These then go as resources used into businesses, which are turned into production of goods & services in the product market. The product market then sells it to the households as goods & services. Households buy these goods & services. From the product market it goes to the businesses as revenues. Businesses incur these costs to the resource market, which in turn, pays for the land, labor, capital, entrepreneurial ability supplied by households.

① In the C.F.M., households supply r.m. which consists of 4 factors of production – land, labor, capital, & entrepreneurial ability to the businesses.

② Businesses use r.m. for the production of g & s required in the economy. Household buys the g & s produced in the product market which is called consumption expenditure.

③ Consumption expenditure is a revenue for businesses

④ Businesses pays to the r.m. the cost incurred for the production of g & s.

Understanding individual markets: demand and supply

Chapter 4 is an introduction to the most fundamental tools of economic analysis: demand and supply. If you are to progress successfully into the later chapters it is essential that you understand what is meant by demand and supply and how to use these powerful tools.

Demand and supply are simply "boxes" or categories into which all the forces and factors that affect the price and the quantity of a good bought and sold in a competitive market can conveniently be placed. Demand and supply determine price and quantity exchange and it is necessary to see *why* and *how* they do this.

Many students never do understand demand and supply because they never learn to *define* demand and supply *exactly* and because they never learn (1) what is meant by an increase or decrease in demand or supply, (2) the important distinctions between "demand" and "quantity demanded" and between "supply" and "quantity supplied," (3) the equally important distinctions between an increase (or decrease) in demand and an increase (or decrease) in quantity demanded and between an increase (or decrease) in supply and an increase (or decrease) in quantity supplied.

Having learned these, however, it is no great trick to comprehend the so-called "law of supply and demand." The equilibrium price—that is, the price which will tend to prevail in the market as long as demand and supply do not change—is simply the price at which *quantity demanded* and *quantity supplied* are equal. The quantity bought and sold in the market (the equilibrium quantity) is the quantity demanded and supplied at the equilibrium price. If you can determine the equilibrium price and quantity under one set of demand and supply conditions, you can determine them under any other set and so will be able to analyze for yourself the effects of changes in demand and supply upon equilibrium price and quantity.

The chapter includes a brief examination of the factors that determine demand and supply and of the ways in which changes in these determinants will affect and cause changes in demand and supply. A graphic method is employed in this analysis in order to facilitate an understanding of demand and supply, equilibrium price and quantity, changes in demand and supply, and the result-ing changes in equilibrium price and quantity. In addition to understanding the *specific* definitions of demand and supply, it is necessary to understand the two counterparts of demand and supply: the demand *curve* and the supply *curve*. These are simply graphic (or geometric) representations of the same data contained in the schedules of demand and supply.

If you wonder why an entire chapter has been devoted to demand and supply you will find the answer in the last major section of the chapter. Demand and supply have so many applications that they are the most important single tool in economics. The example given in the last section is the application of supply and demand to the foreign exchange market.

You will use supply and demand over and over again. It will turn out to be as important as jet propulsion is to the pilot of a Boeing 747: You can't get off the ground without it.

■ CHECKLIST

When you have studied this chapter you should be able to:
☐ Define a market.
☐ Define demand, quantity demanded, supply, and quantity supplied.
☐ Graph demand and supply when you are given demand and supply schedules.
☐ State the law of demand and the law of supply.
☐ List the major determinants of demand and of supply.
☐ Determine when you are given the demand for and the supply of a good what the equilibrium price and the equilibrium quantity will be.
☐ Explain why the price of a good and the amount of the good bought and sold in a competitive market will be the equilibrium price and the equilibrium quantity, respectively.
☐ Predict the effects of changes in demand and supply on equilibrium price and equilibrium quantity; and on the prices of substitute and complementary goods.

☐ Explain the meaning of the rationing function of prices.

☐ Demonstrate how supply and demand analysis applies to the foreign exchange market.

■ CHAPTER OUTLINE

1. A market is any institution or mechanism that brings together the buyers and the sellers of a particular good or service; and in this chapter it is assumed that markets are perfectly competitive.

2. Demand is a schedule of prices and the quantities which buyers would purchase at each of these prices during some period of time.

a. As price rises, other things being equal, buyers will purchase smaller quantities, and as price falls they will purchase larger quantities; this is the law of demand.

b. The demand curve is a graphic representation of demand and the law of demand.

c. Market (or total) demand for a good is a summation of the demands of all individuals in the market for that good.

d. The demand for a good depends upon the tastes, income, and expectations of buyers; the number of buyers in the market; and the prices of related goods.

e. A change (either an increase or a decrease) in demand is caused by a change in any of the factors (in *d*) which determine demand, and means that the demand schedule and demand curve have changed.

f. A change in demand and a change in the quantity demanded are *not* the same thing.

3. Supply is a schedule of prices and the quantities which sellers will offer to sell at each of these prices during some period of time.

a. The law of supply means, other things being equal, that as the price of the good rises larger quantities will be offered for sale, and that as the price of the good falls smaller quantities will be offered for sale.

b. The supply curve is a graphic representation of supply and the law of supply; the market supply of a good is the sum of the supplies of all sellers of the good.

c. The supply of a good depends upon the techniques used to produce it, the prices of the resources employed in its production, the extent to which it is taxed or subsidized, the prices of other goods which might be produced, the price expectations of sellers, and the number of sellers of the product.

d. Supply will change when any of these determinants of supply changes; a change in supply is a change in the entire supply schedule or curve.

e. A change in supply must be distinguished from a change in quantity supplied.

4. The market or equilibrium price of a commodity is that price at which quantity demanded and quantity supplied are equal; and the quantity exchanged in the market (the equilibrium quantity) is equal to the quantity demanded and supplied at the equilibrium price.

a. The rationing function of price is the elimination of shortages and surpluses of the commodity.

b. A change in demand, supply, or both changes both the equilibrium price and the equilibrium quantity in specific ways.

c. In resource markets suppliers are households and demanders are business firms, and in product markets suppliers are business firms and demanders are householders; and supply and demand are useful in the analysis of prices and quantities exchanged in both types of markets.

d. When demand and supply schedules (or curves) are drawn up it is assumed that all the nonprice determinants of demand and supply remain unchanged.

5. Understanding how demand and supply determine price and quantity in a competitive market is a powerful tool which:

a. has a large number of applications;

b. can be used to explain the market for foreign exchange.

■ IMPORTANT TERMS

Market

Demand schedule

Quantity demanded

Income effect

Substitution effect

Demand curve

Individual demand

Total or market demand

Nonprice determinant of demand

Increase (or decrease) in demand

Normal (superior) good

Inferior good

Substitute (competing) goods

Complementary goods

Independent goods

Supply schedule

Law of demand

Diminishing marginal utility

Diminishing marginal utility

Quantity supplied

Law of supply

Supply curve

Nonprice determinant of supply

Increase (or decrease) in supply

Equilibrium price

Equilibrium quantity

Rationing function of prices

Price-increasing (-decreasing) effect

Quantity-increasing (-decreasing) effect

Foreign exchange market

Depreciation and appreciation of the dollar

■ FILL-IN QUESTIONS

1. A market is the institution or mechanism that brings

together the _____ and the

_____ of a particular good or service.

  a. In resource markets prices are determined by the demand decisions of (business firms, households)

_____ and the supply decisions of

_____

  b. In product markets they are determined by _____

_____ and _____

2. The relationship between price and quantity in the demand schedule is a(n) (direct, inverse) _____

_____ relationship; in the supply schedule

the relationship is a(n) _____ one.

3. The added satisfaction or pleasure obtained by a consumer from additional units of a product decreases as her or his consumption of the product increases. This phenomenon is called _____

4. A consumer tends to buy more of a product as its price falls because:

  a. the purchasing power of the consumer is increased and the consumer tends to buy more of this product (and of other products); this is called the (income, substitution)

_____ effect;

  b. the product becomes less expensive relative to similar products and the consumer tends to buy more of this and less of the similar products; and this is called the

_____ effect.

5. When demand or supply is graphed, price is placed on

the (horizontal, vertical) _____ axis and

quantity on the _____ axis.

6. When a consumer demand schedule or curve is drawn up, it is assumed that five factors that determine demand are fixed and constant. These five determinants of consumer demand are:

  a. _____

  b. _____

  c. _____

  d. _____

  e. _____

7. A decrease in demand means that consumers will buy

(larger, smaller) _____ quantities at every

price or will pay (more, less) _____ for the same quantities.

8. A change in income or in the price of another product will result in a change in the (demand for, quantity demanded of) _____

_____

the given product, while a change in the price of the given

product will result in _____

_____

9. The fundamental factors which determine the supply of any commodity in the product market are:

  a. _____

  b. _____

  c. _____

  d. _____

  e. _____

  f. _____

10. The equilibrium price of a commodity is the price at

which _____

_____

11. If quantity demanded exceeds quantity supplied,

price is (above, below) _____ the
equilibrium price; and the (shortage, surplus)

_____ will cause the price to (rise, fall)

_____

12. In the spaces below each of the following, indicate the effect [*increase* (+), *decrease* (−), or *indeterminate* (?)] upon equilibrium price and equilibrium quantity of each of these changes in demand and/or supply.

  a. Increase in demand, supply constant   ____ ____

  b. Increase in supply, demand constant   ____ ____

  c. Decrease in demand, supply constant   ____ ____

  d. Decrease in supply, demand constant   ____ ____

  e. Increase in demand, increase in supply   ____ ____

  f. Increase in demand, decrease in supply   ____ ____

  g. Decrease in demand, decrease in supply   ____ ____

  h. Decrease in demand, increase in supply   ____ ____

13. If supply and demand establish a price for a good such that there is no shortage or surplus of the good, then price is successfully performing its _____

14. To assume that all the nonprice determinants of demand and supply do not change is to employ the _____ assumption.

15. When the dollar price of foreign currency increases, there has been a(n) _____ in the value of the dollar. When the dollar price of foreign currency decreases, there has been a(n) _____ in the value of the dollar.

Price	Quantity demanded, 1,000 bushels of soybeans
$7.20	10
7.00	15
6.80	20
6.60	25
6.40	30
6.20	35

a. Plot the supply schedule which follows on the same graph.

Price	Quantity supplied, 1,000 bushels of soybeans
$7.20	40
7.00	35
6.80	30
6.60	25
6.40	20
6.20	15

■ **PROBLEMS AND PROJECTS**

1. Using the demand schedule at the top of the next column, plot the demand curve on the graph below. Label the axes and indicate for each axis the units being used to measure price and quantity.

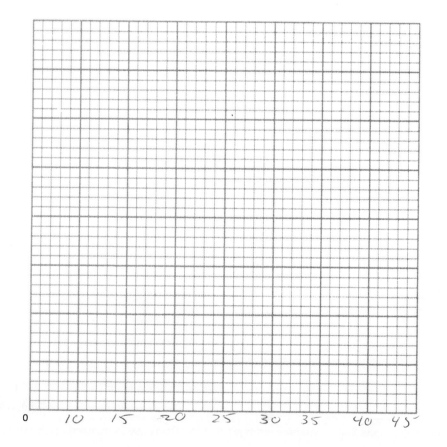

0   10   15   20   25   30   35   40   45

b. The equilibrium price of soybeans will be $_____

c. _____
thousand bushels of soybeans will be exchanged at this price.

d. Indicate clearly on the graph the equilibrium price and quantity by drawing lines from the intersection of the supply and demand curves to the price and quantity axes.

e. If the Federal government supported a price of $7.00 per bushel there would be a (shortage, surplus)

_____ of _____ bushels of soybeans.

2. The demand schedules of three individuals (Roberts, Charles, and Lynn) for loaves of bread are shown below. Assuming there are only three buyers of bread, draw up the total or market demand schedule for bread.

	Quantity demanded, loaves of bread			
Price	Roberts	Charles	Lynn	Total
$.40	1	4	0	2·0
.36	3	5	1	_____
.32	6	6	5	_____
.28	10	7	10	_____
.24	15	8	16	_____

3. Below is a demand schedule for bushels of apples. In columns 3 and 4 insert *any* new figures for quantity which represent in column 3 an increase in demand and in column 4 a decrease in demand.

(1) Price	(2) Quantity demanded	(3) Demand increases	(4) Demand decreases
$6.00	400	_____	_____
5.90	500	_____	_____
5.80	600	_____	_____
5.70	700	_____	_____
5.60	800	_____	_____
5.50	900	_____	_____

4. Assume that O'Rourke has, when his income is $100 per week, the demand schedule for good A shown in columns 1 and 2 of the table below and the demand schedule for good B shown in columns 4 and 5. Assume that the price of A and B are $.80 and $5, respectively.

Demand for A (per week)			Demand for B (per week)		
(1) Price	(2) Quantity demanded	(3) Quantity demanded	(4) Price	(5) Quantity demanded	(6) Quantity demanded
$.90	10	0	$5.00	4	7
.85	20	10	4.50	5	8
.80	30	20	4.00	6	9
.75	40	30	3.50	7	10
.70	50	40	3.00	8	11
.65	60	50	2.50	9	12
.60	70	60	2.00	10	13

a. How much A will O'Rourke buy? _____
How much B? _____

b. Suppose that, as a consequence of a $10 increase in O'Rourke's weekly income, the quantities demanded of A become those shown in column 3 and the quantities demanded of B become those shown in column 6.

(1) How much A will he now buy? _____
How much B? _____

(2) Good A is (normal, inferior) _____

(3) Good B is _____

5. The market demand for good X is shown in columns 1 and 2 of the next table. Assume the price of X to be $2 and constant.

(1) Price	(2) Quantity demanded	(3) Quantity demanded	(4) Quantity demanded
$2.40	1,600	1,500	1,700
2.30	1,650	1,550	1,750
2.20	1,750	1,650	1,850
2.10	1,900	1,800	2,000
2.00	2,100	2,000	2,200
1.90	2,350	2,250	2,450
1.80	2,650	2,550	2,750

a. If as the price of good Y rises from $1.25 to $1.35 the quantities demanded of good X become those shown in column 3, it can be concluded that X and Y are (substitute, complementary) _____ goods.

b. If as the price of good Y rises from $1.25 to $1.35 the quantities of good X become those shown in column 4, it can be concluded that X and Y are _____ goods.

6. In a local market for hamburger on a given date, each of 300 sellers of hamburger has the following supply schedule.

(1) Price	(2) Quantity supplied— one seller, lb.	(3) Quantity supplied— all sellers, lb.
$2.05	150	_____
2.00	110	_____
1.95	75	_____
1.90	45	_____
1.85	20	_____
1.80	0	_____

a. In column 3 construct the market supply schedule for hamburger.

b. Below is the market demand schedule for hamburger on the same date and in the same local market as that given above.

Price	Quantity demanded, lb.
$2.05	28,000
2.00	31,000
1.95	36,000
1.90	42,000
1.85	49,000
1.80	57,000

If the Federal government sets a price on hamburger at $1.90 a pound the result would be a (shortage, surplus) _____

of _____ pounds of hamburger in this market.

7. Each of the following events would tend to increase or decrease either the demand for or the supply of video games and, as a result, increase or decrease the price of these games. In the first blank indicate the effect upon demand or supply; and in the second indicate whether price would rise or fall.

a. It becomes known that a local department store is going to have a sale on these games three months from now. _____ ;

b. The workers who produce the games go on strike for over two months. _____ ;

c. The workers in the industry receive a 90-cent-an-hour wage increase. _____ ;

d. The average price of movie tickets increases. _____ ; _____

e. The firms producing the games undertake to produce a large volume of missile components for the Defense Department. _____ ;

f. It is announced by a private research institute that children who have taken to playing video games also improve their grades in school. _____ ;

g. Because of the use of mass-production techniques, the amount of labor necessary to produce a game decreases. _____ ;

h. The price of compact discs decreases. _____ ;

i. The average consumer believes that a shortage of games is developing in the economy. _____ ;

j. The Federal government imposes a $5 per game tax upon the manufacturers of video games. _____ ;

■ **SELF-TEST**

Circle the T if the statement is true, the F if it is false.

1. A market is any arrangement that brings the buyers and sellers of a particular good or service together. **T   F**

2. Demand is the amount of a commodity or service which a buyer will purchase at a particular price.   **T   F**

3. The law of demand states that as price increases, other things being equal, the quantity of the product demanded increases.   **T   F**

4. In graphing supply and demand schedules, supply is put on the horizontal axis and demand on the vertical axis.
T   F

5. If price falls, there will be an increase in demand. **T   F**

6. If the demand curve moves from D_1 to D_2 in the graph shown below, demand has increased. **T   F**

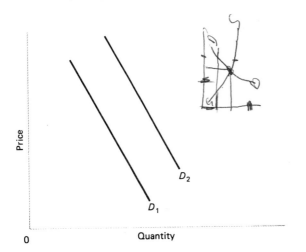

7. A fall in the price of a good will cause the demand for goods which are substitutes for it to increase. **T   F**

8. If two goods are complementary, an increase in the price of one will cause the demand for the other to increase. **T   F**

9. If the market price of a commodity is for a time below its equilibrium price, the market price will tend to rise because demand will decrease and supply will increase. **T   F**

10. The equilibrium price of a good is the price at which the demand and the supply of the good are equal. **T   F**

11. The rationing function of prices is the elimination of shortages and surpluses. **T   F**

12. The interaction of the demand for, and supply of, Japanese yen will establish the dollar price of Japanese yen. **T   F**

13. An increase in incomes in the United States would tend to cause the dollar price of the Japanese yen to fall. **T   F**

14. When the dollar price of another nation's currency increases, there has been an appreciation in the value of the dollar. **T   F**

15. When the dollar depreciates relative to the value of the currencies of the trading partners of the United States, then goods imported into the United States will tend to become more expensive. **T   F**

Circle the letter that corresponds to the best answer.

1. The markets examined in this chapter are:
(a) perfectly competitive markets
(b) markets for goods and services
(c) markets for products and resources
(d) all of the above

2. Which of the following could cause a decrease in consumer demand for product X?
(a) a decrease in consumer income
(b) an increase in the prices of goods which are good substitutes for product X
(c) an increase in the price which consumers expect will prevail for product X in the future
(d) a decrease in the supply of product X

3. If two goods are substitutes for each other, an increase in the price of one will necessarily:
(a) decrease the demand for the other
(b) increase the demand for the other
(c) decrease the quantity demanded of the other
(d) increase the quantity demanded of the other

4. The income of a consumer decreases and his/her demand for a particular good increases. It can be concluded that the good is:
(a) normal
(b) inferior
(c) a substitute
(d) a complement

5. If the supply curve moves from S_1 to S_2 on the graph below, there has been:
(a) an increase in supply
(b) a decrease in supply
(c) an increase in quantity supplied
(d) a decrease in quantity supplied

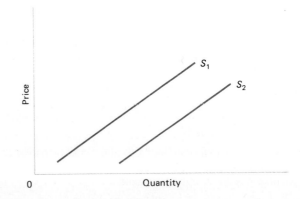

6. An increase in demand and a decrease in supply will:
(a) increase price and increase the quantity exchanged
(b) decrease price and decrease the quantity exchanged
(c) increase price and the effect upon quantity exchanged will be indeterminate
(d) decrease price and the effect upon quantity exchanged will be indeterminate

7. An increase in supply and an increase in demand will:
(a) increase price and increase the quantity exchanged
(b) decrease price and increase the quantity exchanged
(c) affect price in an indeterminate way and decrease the quantity exchanged
(d) affect price in an indeterminate way and increase the quantity exchanged

8. Which of the following could *not* cause an increase in the supply of cotton?
(a) an increase in the price of cotton
(b) improvements in the art of producing cotton
(c) a decrease in the price of the machinery and tools employed in cotton production
(d) a decrease in the price of corn

9. The law of supply states that other things being constant as price increases:
(a) supply increases
(b) supply decreases
(c) quantity supplied increases
(d) quantity supplied decreases

10. Demand and supply may be employed to explain how price is determined in:
(a) product markets
(b) resource markets
(c) markets for foreign currency
(d) all of the above markets

11. When government sets the price of a good and that price is below the equilibrium price the result will be:
(a) a surplus of the good
(b) a shortage of the good
(c) an increase in the demand for the good
(d) a decrease in the supply of the good

12. A decrease in supply and an increase in demand will:
(a) increase price and decrease the quantity exchanged
(b) decrease price and increase the quantity exchanged
(c) increase price and affect the quantity exchanged in an indeterminate way
(d) affect price in an indeterminate way and decrease the quantity exchanged

13. A decrease in the price of a product would most likely be caused by:
(a) an increase in business taxes
(b) an increase in consumer incomes
(c) a decrease in resource costs for production
(d) a decrease in the price of a complementary good

14. If the equilibrium exchange rate changes so that the dollar price of Japanese yen increases:
(a) the dollar has appreciated in value
(b) the dollar has depreciated in value
(c) Americans will be able to buy more Japanese goods
(d) Japanese will be able to buy fewer U.S. goods

15. A decrease in the United States demand for Japanese goods will:
(a) increase the demand for Japanese yen and increase the dollar price of yen
(b) increase the demand for Japanese yen but decrease the dollar price of yen
(c) decrease the demand for Japanese yen and decrease the dollar price of yen
(d) decrease the demand for Japanese yen but increase the dollar price of yen

■ **DISCUSSION QUESTIONS**

1. How is a market defined?

2. Carefully define demand and state the law of demand. Now define supply and state the law of supply.

3. Two decades ago the price of coffee in the United States rose as a result of bad weather in coffee-producing regions. Employ the income-effect and the substitution effect concepts to explain why the quantity of coffee demanded in the U.S. declined dramatically. A few years later when the weather became normal the price of coffee fell. Use the diminishing-marginal-utility notion to explain why the quantity of coffee demanded rose.

4. Explain the difference between an increase in demand and an increase in quantity demanded, and between a decrease in supply and a decrease in quantity supplied.

5. Neither demand nor supply remains constant for long because the factors which determine demand and supply do not long remain constant. What are these factors? How do changes in them affect demand and supply?

6. How are normal, inferior, substitute, complementary, and independent goods defined, and how can these concepts be used to predict the way in which a change in income or in the price of another good will affect the demand for a given good?

7. Given the demand for and the supply of a commodity, what price will be the equilibrium price of this commodity?

Explain why this price will tend to prevail in the market and why higher (lower) prices, if they do exist temporarily, will tend to fall (rise).

8. Analyze the following quotation and explain the fallacies contained in it. "An increase in demand will cause price to rise; with a rise in price, supply will increase and the increase in supply will push price down. Therefore, an increase in demand results in little change in price because supply will increase also."

9. What is meant by the "rationing function of prices"?

10. What is the difference between individual and market demand; and what is the relationship between these two types of demand? Does this distinction and relationship also apply to individual and market supply?

11. The interest rates received by those who lend money have in recent years been higher in the United States than in most foreign countries. This has led many foreigners to increase their purchases of American dollars (for which they pay with foreign money) and to lend these dollars in the United States. The price which foreigners have to pay to obtain an American dollar is the exchange rate for the dollar. What do you think has been the effect of higher interest rates in the United States on the exchange rate for the dollar—has it risen or fallen?

■ ANSWERS

CHAPTER 4 UNDERSTANDING INDIVIDUAL MARKETS: DEMAND AND SUPPLY

Fill-in questions

1. buyers (demanders), sellers (suppliers) (either order); *a.* business firms, households; *b.* demand decisions of households, supply decisions of business firms

2. inverse, direct

3. diminishing marginal utility

4. *a.* income; *b.* substitution

5. vertical, horizontal

6. *a.* the tastes or preferences of consumers; *b.* the number of consumers in the market; *c.* the money income of consumers; *d.* the prices of related goods; *e.* consumer expectations with respect to future prices and incomes

7. smaller, less

8. demand for, a change in the quantity demanded of the product

9. *a.* the technique of production; *b.* resource prices; *c.* taxes and subsidies; *d.* prices of other goods; *e.* price expectations; *f.* the number of sellers in the market

10. quantity demanded and quantity supplied are equal

11. below, shortage, rise

12. *a.* +, +; *b.* −, +; *c.* −, −; *d.* +, −; *e.* ?, +; *f.* +, ?; *g.* ?, −; *h.* −, ?

13. rationing function

14. other things being equal

15. depreciation, appreciation

Problems and projects

1. *b.* 6.60; *c.* 25; *e.* surplus, 20

2. Total: 5, 9, 17, 27, 39

3. Each quantity in column 3 is greater than in column 2, and each quantity in column 4 is less than in column 2.

4. *a.* 30, 4; *b.* (1) 20, 7; (2) inferior; (3) normal (superior)

5. *a.* complementary; *b.* substitute

6. *a.* 45,000; 33,000; 22,500; 13,500; 6,000; 0 *b.* shortage, 28,500

7. *a.* decrease demand, decrease price; *b.* decrease supply, increase price; *c.* decrease supply, increase price; *d.* increase demand, increase price; *e.* decrease supply, increase price; *f.* increase demand, increase price; *g.* increase supply, decrease price; *h.* decrease demand, decrease price, *i.* increase demand, increase price; *j.* decrease supply, increase price

Self-test

1. T; **2.** F; **3.** F; **4.** F; **5.** F; **6.** T; **7.** F; **8.** F; **9.** F; **10.** F; **11.** T; **12.** T; **13.** F; **14.** F; **15.** T

1. *d;* **2.** *a;* **3.** *b;* **4.** *b;* **5.** *a;* **6.** *c;* **7.** *d;* **8.** *a;* **9.** *c;* **10.** *d;* **11.** *b;* **12.** *c;* **13.** *c;* **14.** *b;* **15.** *c*

The market system and the five fundamental questions

In Chapters 2, 3, and 4 you examined the institutions and characteristics of pure capitalism and saw how supply and demand determine equilibrium prices and equilibrium quantities in resource and product markets. Chapter 5 draws these elements together into an explanation of the ways in which the market system finds answers to basic economic questions.

There are Five Fundamental Questions that any economic system must answer in attempting to use its scarce resources to satisfy its material wants. The five questions or problems are: (1) How much output is to be produced? (2) What is to be produced? (3) How is the output to be produced? (4) Who is to receive the output? (5) Can the economic system adapt to change? Only the last four questions will be discussed in this chapter. Answers to the first question will await the presentation of material on macroeconomics.

The explanation of how the market system finds answers to the last four of the Five Fundamental Questions is only an approximation—a simplified version or a model—of the methods actually employed by the American economy. Yet this simple model, like all good models, contains enough realism to be truthful and is general enough to be understandable.

The model is intentionally and specifically unrealistic because the economic role of government is ignored and because actual competition in the American economy is probably much less effective than is assumed in Chapter 5. These shortcomings, however, do not weaken the major points made in the chapter about the functioning of the price-market system; and the shortcomings are corrected in later chapters to make the model more realistic.

The first of the two major sections is entitled "Operation of the Market System" and is both the most important part of this chapter and the part you will find most difficult. If you will try to understand how the American system of prices and markets finds answers for each of the four basic questions by examining them *individually* and in the order in which they are presented, you will more easily understand how the market system as a whole operates. Actually the market system finds answers for all these questions simultaneously, but it is much simpler to consider them as if they were separate questions.

In addition to explaining how the market system operates, Chapter 5 also takes up the question of *how well* it operates. Here you will find the going much easier. It should be particularly noted, however, that the market system is a widely accepted method of allocating scarce resources because it is economically quite efficient in the allocation of resources. But even so, it, like every other economic system devised by humans, is not so efficient as it might be. The specific criticisms leveled against the market system are well worth noting because, as will be seen in Chapter 6, many of government's functions in the economy are directed toward the correction of the system's faults which have been pointed out by its critics; in fact, one of the reasons for ignoring the role of government in Chapter 5 is to emphasize the shortcomings of pure capitalism in the absence of government.

A few final words of advice to you. Be sure to understand the *importance* and *role* of each of the following in the operation of the market system: (1) the rationing and directing functions of prices, (2) the profit motive of business firms, (3) the entry into and exodus of firms from industries, (4) competition, and (5) consumer sovereignty.

■ CHECKLIST

When you have studied this chapter you should be able to:

□ Identify the Five Fundamental Questions.

□ Explain how a competitive market system determines what will be produced.

□ Distinguish between normal profit and economic profit.

□ Predict what will happen to the price charged by and the output of a prosperous and an unprosperous industry; and explain why these events will occur.

□ Explain how production is organized in a competitive market system.

☐ Find the least-cost combination of resources when you are given the technological data and the prices of the resources.

☐ Explain how a competitive market system determines the distribution of total output.

☐ List the three kinds of change to which an economy must be able to adapt itself if it is to remain efficient; and explain how a competitive market system both adjusts to and initiates desirable changes.

☐ Present the case for and the case against the market system.

☐ Identify the two basic differences between an ideal market system and the market system found in the United States.

■ **CHAPTER OUTLINE**

1. There are Five Fundamental Questions which must be answered by every economic system:

(1) How much output is to be produced?

(2) What is to be produced?

(3) How is output to be produced?

(4) Who is to receive the output?

(5) Can the economic system adapt to change?

2. The system of prices and markets and the choices of households and business firms furnish the economy with answers to the last four Fundamental Questions.

a. The demands of consumers for products and the desires of business firms to maximize their profits determine what and how much of each product is produced (and its price).

b. The desires of business firms to maximize profits by keeping their costs of production as low as possible guide them to employ the most efficient techniques of production and determine their demands for and prices of the various resources; competition forces them to use the most efficient techniques and ensures that only the most efficient will be able to stay in business.

c. With resource prices determined, the money income of each household is determined; and with product prices determined, the quantity of goods and services which these money incomes will buy is determined.

d. The market system is able to accommodate itself to changes in consumer tastes, technology, and resource supplies.

(1) The desires of business firms for maximum profits and competition lead the economy to make the appropriate adjustments in the way it uses its resources.

(2) Competition and the desire to increase profits promote both better techniques of production and capital accumulation.

e. Competition in the economy compels firms seeking to promote their own interests to promote (as though led by an "invisible hand") the best interest of society as a whole: an allocation of resources appropriate to consumer wants, production by the most efficient means, and the lowest possible prices.

3. The market system has been praised and damned because it has both merits and faults.

a. The major merits of the system are that it efficiently allocates scarce resources and allows individuals large amounts of personal freedom.

b. The chief faults are the decline in the competitiveness of markets and wasteful and inefficient production.

c. The analysis of the price system found in this chapter is only a rough approximation of how the American economy actually operates: competition is weakened in some markets because a few large firms dominate or there are barriers to entry; the economic role of government has been ignored.

■ **IMPORTANT TERMS**

Five Fundamental Questions	**Consumer sovereignty**
Normal profit	**Derived demand**
Economic cost	**Guiding function of prices**
Economic profit	**Self-limiting adjustment**
Expanding (prosperous) industry	**Invisible hand**
	Market failure
Declining (unprosperous) industry	**External (spillover) benefit**
Dollar votes	**External (spillover) cost**

■ **FILL-IN QUESTIONS**

1. List the Five Fundamental Questions which every economy must answer.

a. _____

b. _____

c. _____

d. _____

e. _____

2. The competitive market system is a mechanism for both _____ the decisions of producers and households and _____ these decisions.

3. A *normal* profit (is, is not) _____ an economic cost because it is a payment that (must, need not) _____ be paid to (workers, land-owners, suppliers of capital goods, entrepreneurs)

_____ ; but a *pure* (or ***economic***) profit (is, is not) _____ an economic cost because it (must, need not) _____ be paid to them to obtain and retain the services they provide to the firm.

4. Pure or economic profits are equal to the total _____ of a firm less its total _____

5. Business firms tend to produce those products from which they can obtain:

   a. at least a (pure, normal) _____ profit; and

   b. the maximum _____ profit.

6. If firms in an industry are obtaining economic profits, firms will (enter, leave) _____ the industry, the price of the industry's product will (rise, fall) _____ , the industry will employ (more, fewer) _____ resources, produce a (larger, smaller) _____ output, and the industry's economic profits will (increase, decrease) _____ until they are equal to _____

7. Consumers:

   a. vote with their _____ for the production of a good or service when they buy that good or service;
   b. are said, because firms are motivated by their desire for profits to produce the goods and services consumers vote for in this way, to be (dependent, sovereign) _____

   c. (restrict, expand) _____ the freedom of firms and resource suppliers.

8. Because firms are interested in obtaining the largest economic profits possible the technique they select to produce a product is the one that enables them to produce that product in the least _____ ly way.

9. In determining how the total output of the economy will be divided among its households the market system is involved in two ways:

   a. it determines the money _____ each of the households receives; and

   b. it determines the _____ they have to pay for each of the goods and services produced.

10. In industrial economies:
   a. the changes which occur almost continuously are changes in consumer _____ , in _____ , and in the supplies of _____ ;
   b. to make the adjustments in the way it uses its resources that are appropriate to these changes a market economy allows price to perform its _____ function.

11. The competitive market system tends to foster technological change.
   a. The incentive for a firm to be the first to employ a new and improved technique of production or to produce a new and better product is a greater economic _____ ;
   b. and the incentive for other firms to follow its lead is the avoidance of _____

12. The entrepreneur uses money which is obtained either from _____ or from _____ to acquire capital goods.

13. If the market system is competitive, there is an identity of _____ interests and the _____ interest: firms seem to be guided by an _____ to allocate the economy's resources efficiently.

14. The chief economic advantage of the market system, it is said, is that _____ _____ ;

its chief noneconomic advantage is that _____ _____ _____

15. Critics of the market system argue that:
   a. with the passage of time there is a weakening of _____

   b. the system is inefficient because

     (1) the distribution of income is _____
     (2) even competitive markets fail to recognize external _____ and _____

and to take into account the demand for _____ goods;

(3) it does not ensure the _____

of resources and stable _____

16. This chapter has been (intentionally) unrealistic because it has ignored the existence of a few dominant firms in some markets, barriers to _____ , the economic role of _____

■ **PROBLEMS AND PROJECTS**

1. Assume that a firm can produce *either* product A, product B, or product C with the resources it currently employs. These resources cost the firm a total of $50 per week. Assume, for the purposes of the problem, that the firm's employment of resources cannot be changed. The market prices of and the quantities of A, B, and C these resources will produce per week are given below. Compute the firm's profit when it produces A, B, or C; and enter these profits in the table below.

Product	Market price	Output	Economic profit
A	$7.00	8	$_____
B	4.50	10	_____
C	.25	240	_____

a. Which product will the firm produce? _____

b. If the price of A rose to $8, the firm would _____

_____

(Hint: You will have to recompute the firm's profit from the production of A.)

c. If the firm were producing A and selling it at a price of $8, what would tend to happen to the number of firms producing A?

_____

2. Suppose that a firm can produce 100 units of product X by combining labor, land, capital, and entrepreneurial ability in three different ways. If it can hire labor at $2 per unit, land at $3 per unit, capital at $5 per unit, and entrepreneurship at $10 per unit; and if the amounts of the resources required by the three methods of producing 100 units of product X are indicated in the table, answer the questions below it.

		Method	
Resource	1	2	3
Labor	8	13	10
Land	4	3	3
Capital	4	2	4
Entrepreneurship	1	1	1

a. Which method is the least expensive way of producing 100 units of X? _____

b. If X sells for 70 cents per unit, what is the economic profit of the firm? $_____

c. If the price of labor should rise from $2 to $3 per unit and if the price of X is 70 cents,

(1) the firm's use of:

Labor would change from _____ to _____

Land would change from _____ to _____

Capital would change from _____ to _____

Entrepreneurship would not change.

(2) The firm's economic profit would change from $_____ to $_____

■ **SELF-TEST**

Circle the T if the statement is true, the F if it is false.

1. Business firms try to maximize their normal profits.
T F

2. Industries in which economic profits are earned by the firms in the industry will attract the entry of new firms into the industry. **T F**

3. If firms have sufficient time to enter and leave industries, the economic profits of an industry will tend to disappear. **T F**

4. Business firms are really only free to produce whatever they want in any way they wish if they do not want to maximize profits or to minimize losses. **T F**

5. To say that the demand for a resource is a derived demand means that it depends upon the demands for the products the resource is used to produce. **T F**

6. Resources will tend to be used in those industries capable of earning normal or economic profits. **T F**

7. Economic efficiency requires that a given output of a good or service be produced in the least costly way. **T F**

8. If the market price of resource A increases, firms will tend to employ smaller quantities of resource A.   **T   F**

9. Changes in the tastes of consumers are reflected in changes in consumer demand for products.   **T   F**

10. The incentive which the market system provides to induce technological improvement is the opportunity for economic profits.   **T   F**

11. In a capitalistic economy it is from the entrepreneur that the demand for capital goods arises.   **T   F**

12. The tendency for individuals pursuing their own self-interests to bring about results which are in the best interest of society as a whole is often called the "invisible hand."   **T   F**

13. The basic economic argument for the market system is that it promotes an efficient allocation of resources.   **T   F**

14. Critics of the market system charge that it creates too much competition.   **T   F**

15. One of the Five Fundamental Questions is who will control the output.   **T   F**

Circle the letter that corresponds to the best answer.

1. The competitive market system is a method of:
 (a) communicating the decisions of consumers, producers, and resource suppliers
 (b) synchronizing these decisions
 (c) communicating and synchronizing these decisions
 (d) neither communicating nor synchronizing the decisions

2. Which of the following best defines economic costs?
 (a) total payments made to workers, landowners, suppliers of capital, and entrepreneurs
 (b) only total payments made to workers, landowners, suppliers of capital, and entrepreneurs which must be paid to obtain the services of their resources
 (c) total payments made to workers, landowners, suppliers of capital, and entrepreneurs less normal profits
 (d) total payments made to workers, landowners, suppliers of capital, and entrepreneurs plus normal profits

3. If less than normal profits are being earned by the firms in an industry, the consequences will be that:
 (a) lower-priced resources will be drawn into the industry
 (b) firms will leave the industry, causing the price of the industry's product to fall
 (c) the price of the industry's product will rise and fewer resources will be employed by the industry
 (d) the price of the industry's product will fall and thereby cause the demand for the product to increase

4. Which of the following would not necessarily result, sooner or later, from a decrease in consumer demand for a product?
 (a) a decrease in the profits of the industry producing the product
 (b) a decrease in the output of the industry
 (c) a decrease in the supply of the product
 (d) an increase in the prices of resources employed by the firms in the industry

5. If firm A does not employ the most "efficient" or least costly method of production, which of the following will *not* be a consequence?
 (a) firm A will fail to earn the greatest profit possible
 (b) other firms in the industry will be able to sell the product at lower prices
 (c) new firms will enter the industry and sell the product at a lower price than that at which firm A now sells it
 (d) firm A will be spending less on resources and hiring fewer resources than it otherwise would

6. Which of the following is *not* a factor in determining the share of the total output of the economy received by any household?
 (a) the price at which the household sells its resources
 (b) the quantities of resources which the household sells
 (c) the tastes of the household
 (d) the prices which the household must pay to buy products

7. If an increase in the demand for a product and the resulting rise in the price of the product cause the supply of the product, the size of the industry producing the product, and the amounts of resources devoted to its production to expand, price is successfully performing its:
 (a) guiding function
 (b) rationing function
 (c) medium-of-exchange function
 (d) standard-of-value function

8. In a capitalistic economy characterized by competition, if one firm introduces a new and better method of production, other firms will be forced to adopt the improved technique:
 (a) to avoid less-than-normal profits
 (b) to obtain economic profits
 (c) to prevent the price of the product from falling
 (d) to prevent the price of the product from rising

9. Which of the following would be an indication that competition does not exist in an industry?
 (a) less-than-normal profits in the industry
 (b) inability of the firms in the industry to expand
 (c) inability of firms to enter the industry
 (d) wages lower than the average wage in the economy paid to workers in the industry

10. Economic criticism of the price system is widespread and has pointed out many of the failures of the system. However, the chief economic virtue of the system remains that of:
(a) allowing extensive personal freedom
(b) efficiently allocating resources
(c) providing an equitable distribution of income
(d) eliminating the need for decision making

11. Which one of the following is **not** a part of the case *against* the price system?
(a) with the passage of time competition becomes excessive
(b) it distributes income unequally
(c) spillover costs and benefits are not registered in the marketplace
(d) it does not guarantee either full employment or price stability

12. This chapter is unrealistic because it ignores:
(a) the role of government in the economy
(b) the impact of large business corporations
(c) the existence of big labor unions
(d) all of the above

Answer the next two questions (13 and 14) on the basis of the following information.

Suppose 50 units of product X can be produced by employing just labor and capital in the four ways shown below. Assume the prices of labor and capital are $5 and $4 respectively.

	A	B	C	D
Labor	1	2	3	4
Capital	5	3	2	1

13. Which technique is economically most efficient in producing product X?
(a) A
(b) B
(c) C
(d) D

14. If the price of product X is $1.00, then the firm will realize:
(a) an economic profit of $28
(b) an economic profit of $27
(c) an economic profit of $26
(d) an economic profit of $25

15. An example of a spillover cost is:
(a) the bankruptcy of a firm
(b) environmental pollution from a factory

(c) a recreational lake created by a flood control project
(d) free vaccinations offered by a local government

16. This chapter is unrealistic because it ignores:
(a) the role of government in the economy
(b) the existence of barriers to entry in markets
(c) the influence of a few dominant firms on markets
(d) all of the above

■ DISCUSSION QUESTIONS

1. What are the Five Fundamental Questions?

2. In what way do the desires of entrepreneurs to obtain economic profits and to avoid losses make consumer sovereignty effective?

3. Why is the ability of firms to enter industries which are prosperous important to the effective functioning of competition?

4. Explain **in detail** how an increase in the consumer demand for a product will result in more of the product being produced and in more resources being allocated to its production.

5. To what extent are firms "free" to produce what they wish by methods which they choose? Do resource owners have freedom to use their resources as they wish?

6. What is meant when it is said that competition is the mechanism which "controls" the market system? How does competition do this? What do critics of the price system argue tends to happen to this controlling mechanism as time passes, and why do they so argue?

7. What are the two important functions of prices? Explain the difference between these two functions.

8. "An invisible hand operates to identify private and public interests." What are private interests and what is the public interest? What is it that leads the economy to operate as if it were directed by an invisible hand?

9. If the basic economic decisions are not made in a capitalistic economy by a central authority, how are they made?

10. Households use the dollars obtained by selling resource services to "vote" for the production of consumer goods and services. Who "votes" for the production of capital goods, why do they "vote" for capital-goods production, and where do they obtain the dollars needed to cast these "votes"?

11. What five arguments do critics of the market system advance to refute the contention that the market system allocates resources efficiently?

12. What are the two principal kinds of market failures? Include in your answer definitions of an external cost and an external benefit.

13. To what extent is this chapter unrealistic?

■ **ANSWERS**

CHAPTER 5 THE MARKET SYSTEM AND THE FIVE FUNDAMENTAL QUESTIONS

Fill-in questions

1. *a.* at what level to utilize resources in the productive process; *b.* what collection of goods and services best satisfies its wants; *c.* how to produce this total output; *d.* how to divide this output among the various economic units of the economy; *e.* how to make the responses required to remain efficient over time

2. communicating, synchronizing (coordinating)

3. is, must, entrepreneurs, is not, need not

4. revenues, costs

5. *a.* normal; *b.* pure (economic)

6. enter, fall, more, larger, decrease, zero

7. *a.* dollars; *b.* sovereign; *c.* restrict

8. cost

9. *a.* income; *b.* prices

10. *a.* preferences (tastes), technology, resources; *b.* guiding

11. *a.* profit; *b.* losses (bankruptcy)

12. profits, borrowed funds

13. private, public (social), invisible hand

14. it efficiently allocates resources, it emphasizes personal freedom

15. *a.* competition; *b.* (1) unequal, (2) costs, benefits, public, (3) full employment, prices

16. entry, government

Problems and projects

1. $6, −$5, $10; *a.* C; *b.* produce A and have an economic profit of $14; *c.* it would increase

2. *a.* method 2; *b.* 15; *c.* (1) 13, 8; 3, 4; 2, 4; (2) 15, 4

Self-test

1. F; **2.** T; **3.** T; **4.** T; **5.** T; **6.** T; **7.** T; **8.** T; **9.** T; **10.** T; **11.** T; **12.** T; **13.** T; **14.** F, **15.** F

1. *c;* **2.** *b;* **3.** *c;* **4.** *d;* **5.** *d;* **6.** *c;* **7.** *a;* **8.** *a;* **9.** *c;* **10.** *b;* **11.** *a;* **12.** *d;* **13.** *b;* **14.** *a;* **15.** *b;* **16.** *d*

CHAPTER 6

The economic functions of government

Chapter 6 introduces you to the five basic functions performed by the Federal, state, and local governments in America's mixed capitalistic economy. This is an examination of the actual role of government (the public sector) in an economy which is neither a purely planned nor a purely market-type economy. The discussion points out the degree and the ways in which government causes the American economy to differ from pure capitalism. The chapter does not attempt to list all the *specific* ways in which government affects the behavior of the economy. Instead it provides a *general* classification of the tasks performed by government.

The chapter begins by discussing the two major functions of government. First, the legal and social framework for the operation of the market system is provided by government. Second, government actions can be taken to maintain competition in the economy. In addition, the chapter explains how government influences the market system in three other ways by: redistributing wealth and income; altering the composition of national output; and stabilizing the economy.

The chapter ends by returning to the circular flow model that was first presented in Chapter 3. The model has now been modified to include government along with businesses and households. The addition of government changes the real and monetary flows in the model. The twelve linkages among the household, business, and government sectors in the model are described in detail in this last section of the chapter.

■ CHECKLIST

When you have studied this chapter you should be able to:

□ Explain in one or two sentences why the American economy is *mixed* rather than *pure* capitalism.

□ Enumerate the five economic functions of government in the United States; and explain the difference between the purpose of the first two and the purpose of the last three functions.

□ Define monopoly and explain why government wishes to prevent monopoly and to preserve competition in the economy.

□ Explain why government feels it should redistribute income and list the three principal policies it employs for this purpose.

□ Define a spillover cost and a spillover benefit; explain why a competitive market fails to allocate resources efficiently when there are spillovers; and list the things government may do to reduce spillovers and improve the allocation of resources.

□ Define a public good and a private good and explain how government goes about reallocating resources from the production of private to the production of public goods.

□ Draw a circular flow diagram that includes businesses, households, and government; label all the flows in the diagram; and use the diagram to explain how government alters the distribution of income, the allocation of resources, and the level of activity in the economy.

■ CHAPTER OUTLINE

1. The American economy is neither a pure market economy nor a purely planned economy. It is an example of mixed capitalism in which government affects the operation of the economy in important ways.

2. Government in the American economy performs five economic functions. The first two of these functions are designed to enable the market system to operate more effectively; and the other three functions are designed to eliminate the major shortcomings of a purely market-type economy.

3. The first of these functions is to provide the legal and social framework that makes the effective operation of the market system possible.

4. The second function is the maintenance of competition and the regulation of monopoly.

5. Government performs its third function when it redistributes income to reduce income inequality.

6. When government reallocates resources it performs its fourth function.

   a. It reallocates resources to take account of spillover costs and benefits.

   b. It also reallocates resources to provide society with public (social) goods and services.

   c. It levies taxes and uses the tax revenues to purchase or produce the public goods.

7. Its fifth function is stabilization of the price level and the maintenance of full employment.

8. A circular flow diagram that includes the public sector as well as business firms and households in the private sector of the economy reveals that government purchases public goods from private businesses, collects taxes from and makes transfer payments to these firms, purchases labor services from households, and collects taxes from and makes transfer payments to these households; and government can alter the distribution of income, reallocate resources, and change the level of economic activity by affecting the real and monetary flows in the diagram.

■ IMPORTANT TERMS

Market economy	**Subsidy**
Planned economy	**Public (social) good**
Mixed capitalism	**Private good**
Monopoly	**Exclusion principle**
Spillover (externality)	**Quasi-public good**
Spillover cost	**Free-rider problem**
Spillover benefit	

■ FILL-IN QUESTIONS

1. All actual economies are "mixed" because they combine elements of a _____ economy and a _____ economy.

2. List the five economic functions of government:

   a. _____

   b. _____

   c. _____

   d. _____

   e. _____

3. To control monopoly in the United States government has:

   a. created commissions to _____ the prices and the services of the _____ monopolies; and taken over at the local level the _____ of electric and water companies;

   b. enacted _____ laws to maintain competition.

4. The market system, because it is an impersonal mechanism, results in an (equal, unequal) _____ distribution of income. To redistribute income from the upper- to the lower-income groups the Federal government has:

   a. enacted _____ programs;

   b. engaged in _____ intervention;

   c. used the _____ tax to raise much of its revenues.

5. Government frequently reallocates resources when it finds instances of _____ failure; and the two major cases of such failure occur when the competitive price system either;

   a. _____

   b. or _____

6. Competitive markets bring about an optimum allocation of resources only if there are no _____ costs or benefits in the consumption and production of the good or service.

7. There is a spillover whenever some of the costs of producing a product or some of the benefits from consuming it accrue to _____

8. Whenever in a competitive market there are:

   a. spillover costs the result is an (over-, under-) _____ allocation of resources to the production of the good or service;

   b. spillover benefits the result is an _____ _____ allocation of resources to the production of the good or service.

9. What two things can government do to:
   a. Make the market reflect spillover costs?

     (1) _____

     (2) _____

   b. Make the market reflect spillover benefits?

(1) _____

(2) _____

10. Public (social) goods tend to be goods which are not subject to the _____ principle and which are (divisible, indivisible) _____ . Quasi-public goods are goods which could be subjected to the exclusion principle but which are provided by government because they have large spillover _____

11. To reallocate resources from the production of private to the production of public goods government reduces the demand for private goods by _____ consumers and firms and then _____ public goods.

12. To stabilize the economy, government:
a. when there is less than full employment (increases, decreases) _____ aggregate demand by (increasing, decreasing) _____ its expenditures for public goods and services and by (increasing, decreasing) _____ taxes.

b. when there are inflationary pressures _____ _____ aggregate demand by _____ its expenditures for public goods and services and by _____ taxes.

13. Throughout most of its history government in the United States has performed in some degree each of the five functions except that of _____

_____

■ **PROBLEMS AND PROJECTS**

1. Below is a list of various government activities. Indicate in the space to the right of each into which of the five classes of government functions the activity falls. If it falls under more than one of the functions, indicate this.

a. Maintaining an army *allocation of resources*
b. Providing for a system of unemployment compensation

stabilizing economy

c. Establishment of the Federal Reserve Banks _____

d. Insuring employees of business firms against industrial accidents _____
e. Establishment of an Antitrust Division in the Department of Justice _____
f. Making it a crime to sell stocks and bonds under false pretenses _____

g. Providing low-cost lunches to school children _____

h. Taxation of whisky and other spirits _____
i. Regulation of organized stock, bond, and commodity markets _____
j. Setting tax **rates** higher for larger incomes than for smaller ones _____

2. The circular flow diagram below includes business firms, households, and government (the public sector). Also shown are the product and resource markets.

a. Supply a label or an explanation for each of the twelve flows in the model:

(1) _____ *Costs* _____
(2) _____ *Resources* _____
(3) _____ *Revenue* _____
(4) _____ *Goods & services* _____
(5) _____ *Expenditures* _____
(6) _____ *Goods & services* _____
(7) _____ *Expenditures* _____
(8) _____ *Resources* _____
(9) _____ *Goods & services* _____

(10) _____ *Goods & services* _____

(11) _____ *Net Taxes* _____

(12) _____ *Net taxes* _____

b. If government wished to

(1) expand output and employment in the economy it would increase expenditure flows _____ or

_____ , decrease net tax flows

_____ or _____ , or do both;

(2) increase the production of public (social) goods and decrease the production of private goods in the economy

it would increase flows _____ and

_____ or _____ ;

(3) redistribute income from high-income to low-income households it would (increase, decrease)

_____ the net taxes (taxes minus transfers)

paid by the former and _____ the net taxes

paid by the latter in flow _____

3. On the following graph are the demand and supply curves for a product bought and sold in a competitive market. Assume that there are no spillover benefits or costs.

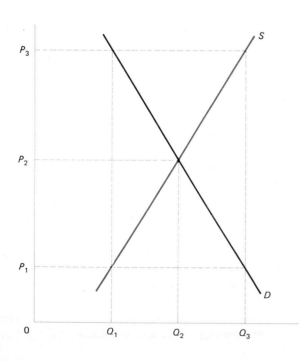

a. Were this market to produce an output of **Q₁** there

would be an (optimum, under, over) _____

allocation of resources to the production of this product.

b. Were this market to produce **Q₃** there would be an

_____ allocation of resources to this product.

c. The equilibrium output is _____

and at this output there is an _____

allocation of resources.

4. On two graphs that follow are product demand and supply curves that do **not** reflect either the spillover costs of producing the product or the spillover benefits obtained from its consumption.

a. On the first graph draw in another curve that reflects the inclusion of spillover costs.

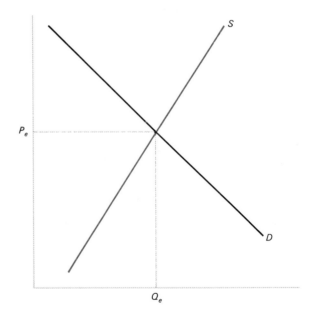

(1) Government might force the (demand for, supply

of) _____ the product to reflect the spillover costs of producing it by (taxing, subsidizing)

_____ the producers.

(2) The inclusion of spillover costs in the total cost of producing the product (increases, decreases)

_____ the output of the product and _____

its price.

b. On the next graph draw in a supply curve that reflects the inclusion of spillover *benefits*.

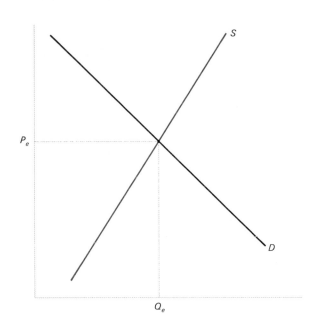

(1) Indicate on the graph the output that is optimum when spillover benefits are included.

(2) To bring about the production of this optimum output government might (tax, subsidize) _____ the producers of this product and this would (increase, decrease) _____ the supply of the product.

(3) This optimum output is (greater than, less than, equal to) _____ **Q_e**; and the price of the product is (above, below, equal to) _____ **P_e**.

■ **SELF-TEST**

Circle the T if the statement is true, the F if it is false.

1. The American economy cannot be called "capitalistic" because its operation involves some "planning."   **T   F**

2. When the Federal government provides for a monetary system, it is functioning to provide the economy with public goods and services.   **T   F**

3. An economy in which strong and effective competition is maintained will find no need for programs designed to redistribute income.   **T   F**

4. Competitive product markets ensure an optimal allocation of an economy's resources.   **T   F**

5. In a competitive product market and in the absence of spillover costs, the supply curve or schedule reflects the costs of producing the product.   **T   F**

6. If demand and supply reflected all the benefits and costs of a product, the equilibrium output of a competitive market would be identical with its optimum output.   **T   F**

The following graph should be used to answer true-false question 7 and multiple-choice question 3.

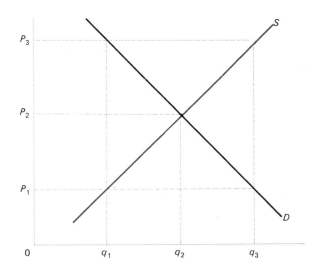

7. Assuming there are no spillover costs or benefits, the production of q_1 units of this product would result in an overallocation of resources to the production of the product.   **T   F**

8. The inclusion of the spillover benefits would increase the demand for a product.   **T   F**

9. When there are spillover costs involved in the production of a product, more resources are allocated to the production of that product and more of the product is produced than is optimal or most efficient.   **T   F**

10. Subsidizing the firms producing goods which provide spillover benefits will usually result in a better allocation of resources.   **T   F**

11. Governments have undertaken to provide lighthouse services because these services have social benefits and private producers of such services encounter the free-rider problem.   **T   F**

12. In performing its stabilization function when there is widespread unemployment and no inflation in the economy, government should decrease its spending for public goods and services and increase taxes.   **T   F**

13. Net taxes for businesses are taxes paid by business less a depreciation allowance.   **T   F**

14. Flood control projects are usually undertaken by government because of the free-rider problem.   **T   F**

15. When the Federal government takes actions to control unemployment or inflation it is performing the allocative function of government.   **T   F**

Circle the letter that corresponds to the best answer.

1. Which of the following is *not* one of the methods utilized by government to control monopoly?
  (*a*) the imposition of special taxes on monopolists
  (*b*) government ownership of monopolies
  (*c*) government regulation of monopolies
  (*d*) antitrust laws

2. One of the following is *not* employed by government to redistribute income. Which one?
  (*a*) the negative income tax
  (*b*) direct market intervention
  (*c*) income taxes which take a larger part of the incomes of the rich than the poor
  (*d*) public assistance programs

Use the graph on page 51 to answer the following question.

3. If there are neither spillover costs nor spillover benefits, the output which results in the optimum allocation of resources to the production of this product is
  (*a*) q_1
  (*b*) q_2
  (*c*) q_3
  (*d*) none of these outputs

4. When the production and consumption of a product entail *both* spillover costs and benefits, a competitive product market results in:
  (*a*) an underallocation of resources to the product
  (*b*) an overallocation of resources to the product
  (*c*) an optimum allocation of resources to the product
  (*d*) an allocation of resources that may or may not be optimum

5. Which of the following is the best example of a good or service providing the economy with spillover benefits?
  (*a*) an automobile
  (*b*) a drill press
  (*c*) a high school education
  (*d*) an operation for appendicitis

6. In the American economy the reallocation of resources needed to provide for the production of public goods is accomplished mainly by means of:

  (*a*) government subsidies to the producers of social goods
  (*b*) government purchases of social goods from producers
  (*c*) direct control of producers of both private and social goods
  (*d*) direct control of producers of social goods only

7. Which of the following is characteristic of public goods?
  (*a*) they are indivisible
  (*b*) they are sold in competitive markets
  (*c*) they are subject to the exclusion principle
  (*d*) they can be produced only if large spillover costs are incurred

8. Quasi-public goods are goods and services:
  (*a*) to which the exclusion principle could not be applied
  (*b*) which have large spillover benefits
  (*c*) which would not be produced by private producers through the market system
  (*d*) which are indivisible

9. To redistribute income from high-income to low-income households government might
  (*a*) increase transfer payments to high-income and decrease transfer payments to low-income households
  (*b*) increase the taxes paid by high-income and increase the transfer payments to low-income households
  (*c*) increase the taxes paid by low-income and decrease the taxes paid by high-income households
  (*d*) decrease the taxes paid by high-income and decrease the transfer payments to low-income households

10. To reallocate resources from the private to the public sector of the economy government should:
  (*a*) increase its expenditures for the goods it purchases from business firms
  (*b*) increase the transfer payments it makes to households
  (*c*) increase its expenditures for the labor services it purchases from households
  (*d*) do either or both *a* and *c*

11. To prevent or slow inflation in the economy government would most likely:
  (*a*) increase its expenditures for the goods and services it purchases from business firms and households
  (*b*) increase the transfer payments it makes to business firms and the public
  (*c*) increase the taxes it collects from business firms and the public
  (*d*) do either or both *a* and *c*

12. Which of the following is the best example of a good or service providing the economy with a spillover cost?
  (*a*) a textbook
  (*b*) an automobile

(c) a business suit
(d) an audit of a business firm's books

13. There is a "free-rider" problem when people:
(a) are willing to pay for what they want
(b) are not willing to pay for what they want
(c) benefit from a good without paying for its cost
(d) want to buy more than is available for purchase in the market

14. In the circular flow model, net taxes are;
(a) taxes minus depreciation
(b) taxes minus transfer payments
(c) subsidies minus transfer payments
(d) business receipts minus household expenditures

15. In the circular flow model, government provides goods and services and receives net taxes from:
(a) colleges and universities
(b) businesses and households
(c) resource and product markets
(d) foreign nations and corporations

■ DISCUSSION QUESTIONS

1. Why is it proper to refer to the United States economy as "mixed capitalism"?

2. What are the five economic functions of government in America's mixed capitalistic economy? Explain what the performance of each of these functions requires government to do.

3. Would you like to live in an economy in which government undertook only the first two functions listed in the text? What would be the advantages and disadvantages of living in such an economy?

4. Why does the market system provide some people with lower income than it provides others?

5. What is "market failure" and what are the two major kinds of such failures?

6. What is meant by a spillover in general and by spillover cost and spillover benefit in particular? How does the existence of such costs and benefits affect the allocation of resources and the prices of products? If a market could be required to take these costs and benefits into account, how would the allocation of resources and the price of the product bought and sold in that market be changed?

7. What methods do governments employ to
(a) redistribute income;
(b) reallocate resources to take account of spillover costs;
(c) reallocate resources to take account of spillover benefits?

8. Distinguish between a private and a public good. Include in your answer an explanation of the "exclusion principle" and the distinction between divisible and indivisible goods.

9. What basic method does government employ in the United States to reallocate resources away from the production of private goods and toward the production of social goods?

10. In a circular flow diagram that includes not only business firms and households but also government (or the public sector), what are the four flows of money into or out of the government sector of the economy? Using this diagram, explain how government redistributes income, reallocates resources from the private to the public sector, and stabilizes the economy.

■ ANSWERS

CHAPTER 6 THE ECONOMIC FUNCTIONS OF GOVERNMENT

Fill-in questions

1. market, centrally planned (either order)

2. a. provide legal foundation and social environment; b. maintain competition; c. redistribute income and wealth; d. reallocate resources; e. stabilize the economy

3. a. regulate, natural, ownership; b. antitrust (antimonopoly)

4. unequal; a. public assistance (welfare): b. market; c. income

5. market; a. produces the "wrong" amounts of certain goods and services; b. fails to allocate any resources to the production of certain goods and services whose production is economically justified

6. spillover

7. people other than the buyers and sellers (third parties)

8. a. over; b. under

9. a. (1) enact legislation, (2) pass special taxes; b. (1) subsidize production, (2) finance or take over the production of the product

10. exclusion, indivisible, benefits

11. taxing, spends the revenue to buy

12. a. increases, increasing, decreasing; b. decreases, decreasing, increasing

13. stabilizing the economy

Problems and projects

1. a. reallocates resources; b. redistributes income; c. provides a legal foundation and social environment *and* stabilizes the economy; d. reallocates resources; e. maintains competition; f. provides a legal foundation and social environment *and* maintains competition; g. redistributes income; h. reallocates resources; i. provides a legal foundation and social environment; j. redistributes income

2. *a.* (1) business pay costs for resources that becomes money income for households; (2) households provide resources to businesses; (3) household expenditures become receipts for businesses; (4) business provide goods and services to households; (5) government spends money in product market; (6) government receives goods and service from product market; (7) government spends money in resource market; (8) government receives resources from resource market; (9) government provides goods and services to households; (10) government provides goods and services to businesses; (11) business pays net taxes to government; (12) households pay net taxes to government; *b.* (1) 5, 7 (either order), 11, 12 (either order); (2) 9, 10, 11 (either order); (3) increase, decrease, 12

3. *a.* under; *b.* over; *c.* Q_2, optimum

4. *a.* (1) supply of, taxing, (2) decreases, increases; *b.* (2) subsidize, increase, (3) greater than, below

Self-test

1. F; **2.** F; **3.** F; **4.** F; **5.** T; **6.** T; **7.** F; **8.** T; **9.** T; **10.** T; **11.** T; **12.** F; **13.** F; **14.** T; **15.** F

1. *a;* **2.** *a;* **3.** *b;* **4.** *d;* **5.** *c;* **6.** *b;* **7.** *a;* **8.** *b;* **9.** *b;* **10.** *d;* **11.** *c;* **12.** *b;* **13.** *c;* **14.** *b;* **15.** *b*

The facts of American capitalism: the private sectors

In the American economy, there are private sectors and a public sector. This chapter discusses the private sectors: the 65 million households, the roughly 18 million business firms in the country, and our trade with other nations in the international sector. The next chapter deals with the public sector of the economy: the approximately 82,000 governments found in the United States. These two chapters will acquaint you with a few of the facts relevant to an understanding of our economy.

The first part of Chapter 7 examines the households of the economy, the distribution of income in the United States, and the uses to which the households put their incomes. Two different distributions of income are examined. American households earn five kinds of income and receive transfer payments. The way in which the total personal income received by all American households is divided among the five types of earned income and transfer payments is called the *functional distribution*. The way in which the total personal income received by all households is distributed among the various income classes is called the *personal* distribution of income. Attention should be concentrated on the *general* facts of income distribution (not the exact figures), the conclusions which are drawn from these general facts, and the definitions of the new terms employed. In the examination of the different uses households make of their incomes, several new terms and concepts are introduced; and figures are employed in the discussion. Again, attention should be paid to the generalizations and to the new terms.

The next part of the chapter is concerned with the business firms of the United States. It is apparent that what most characterizes American business is the differences among firms insofar as their size and legal form are concerned, as well as in the products they produce. You should note the distinctions between a proprietorship, a partnership, and a corporation and the advantages and disadvantages of each.

In the next section of the chapter you will find that the American economy can be divided into ten sectors or industry classes. The privately owned business firms are found in eight of these industry classes. These eight sectors are not equal in terms of the number of firms in the

class, the contribution to the national income made by the industry class, and the number of full-time workers employed by the sector. These facts serve as an introduction to two major observations. In the economy as a whole and in the manufacturing sector a relatively few firms produce a relatively large part of the output of that sector.

These two observations indicate that big business is an important characteristic of the American economy. The corollary of these observations is that the American economy also has a large number of small business firms. But the problems created by big business and the ways in which government deals with these problems are topics examined later in the text.

The last part of the chapter focuses on the international sector of the economy of the United States. The volume, patterns, and linkages of our trade with the rest of the world is described. In addition, our growing international trade has economic implications for our: (1) living standards; (2) ability to compete in a world economy; (3) banking and finance; and (4) macroeconomic instability and policy.

■ CHECKLIST

When you have studied this chapter you should be able to:

☐ Define and distinguish between a functional and a personal distribution of income.

☐ State the relative size of the five sources of personal income in the functional distribution.

☐ List the three uses to which households put their personal incomes and state the relative size of each.

☐ Distinguish among durable goods, nondurable goods, and services.

☐ Explain the difference between a plant, a firm, and an industry; and between limited and unlimited liability.

☐ State the advantages and disadvantages of the three legal forms of business enterprise.

☐ Report the relative importance of each of the legal forms of business enterprise in the American economy.

☐ State which two industry classes contain the largest

and the smallest number of privately owned business firms, produce the largest and the smallest percentages of the national income, and employ the greatest and the smallest number of full-time workers.

☐ Cite evidence to indicate that large corporations dominate the economy and some major American industries; and indicate in which industry classes big business is and is not a dominant force.

☐ Describe the main characteristics of our volume and pattern of trade with other nations.

☐ Explain four economic implications of our growing international trade.

■ **CHAPTER OUTLINE**

1. Households play a dual role in the economy. They supply the economy with resources, and they purchase the greatest share of the goods and services produced by the economy. They obtain their personal incomes in exchange for the resources they furnish the economy and from the transfer payments they receive from government.

a. The functional distribution of income indicates the way in which total personal income is divided among the five sources of earned income (wages and salaries, proprietors' income, corporate profits, interest, and rents) and transfer payments.

b. The personal distribution of income indicates the way in which total personal income is divided among households in different income classes.

2. Households use their incomes to purchase consumer goods, to pay taxes, and to accumulate savings.

a. Personal taxes constitute a deduction from a household's personal income; what remains after taxes can be either saved or spent.

b. Saving is what a household does not spend of its after-tax income.

c. Households spend for durable goods, nondurable goods, and services.

3. The business population of the American economy consists of many imperfectly defined and overlapping industries; business firms which operate one or more plants and produce one or more products are the components of these industries.

4. The three principal legal forms of organization of firms are the proprietorship, the partnership, and the corporation; each form has special characteristics, advantages, and disadvantages. The form of organization which any business firm should adopt depends primarily upon the amount of money capital it will require to carry on its business. Although the proprietorship is numerically dominant in the United States, the corporation accounts for the major portion of the economy's output.

5. An examination of the ten industry classes found in the American economy reveals at least four important facts and leads to the conclusion that large firms are a characteristic of the American economy and that many of its industries are dominated by big businesses.

6. The merchandise trade of the United States with other nations has increased in absolute terms and as a percentage of our national output. Our major trading partner is Canada, not Japan. In recent years, the United States has had trade deficits because our economy has imported more goods and services than it has exported to other nations. These large trade deficits are financed by borrowing from other nations.

7. International trade produces sizable economic benefits because there is more efficient use of world resources and it strengthens competition. The dramatic improvements in communications also mean that the banking industry and financial markets operate on a global basis. The one potential drawback of the increased trade is that the domestic economy is more vulnerable to influence from changes in the world economy. The involvement in a world economy becomes a potential source of macroeconomic instability in the domestic economy and can present new problems for economic policymakers.

■ **IMPORTANT TERMS**

Private sectors	**Industry**
Functional distribution of income	**Horizontal combination**
	Vertical combination
Personal distribution of income	**Conglomerate combination**
Personal consumption expenditures	**Sole proprietorship**
	Partnership
Durable good	**Corporation**
Nondurable good	**Unlimited liability**
Services	**Limited liability**
Personal taxes	**Double taxation**
Personal saving	**Separation of ownership and control**
Plant	
Firm	

■ **FILL-IN QUESTIONS**

1. The approximately _____ million households in the United States play a dual role in the economy because they _____

and _____

2. The largest single source of income in the United States is _____ and is equal to about _____ % of total income.

3. In the United States the poorest 20% of all American families receive about _____ % of total personal income and the richest 20% of these families receive about _____ % of total personal income.

4. The total income of households is disposed of in three ways: _____ ,

_____ ,

and _____

5. Households use about _____ % of their total income to pay personal taxes; and the greatest part of their personal taxes are the personal _____ taxes which they pay to the (Federal, state, local) _____ government.

6. Households save primarily in order to obtain _____ and for purposes of _____

7. Based on their durability, consumer spending is classified as spending for _____

_____ ,

_____ ,

and _____

8. There are today about _____ business firms in the United States. The legal form of the great majority of these firms is the _____ ; but the legal form that produces over one-half the output of the American economy is the _____

9. The liabilities of a sole proprietor and of partners are _____ but the liabilities of stockholders in a corporation are _____

10. Indicate in the spaces to the right of each of the following whether these business characteristics are associated with the proprietorship (PRO), partnership (PART), corporation (CORP), two of these, or all three of these legal forms.

a. Much red tape and legal expense in beginning the firm _____

b. Unlimited liability _____

c. No specialized management _____

d. Has a life independent of its owner(s) _____

e. Modest tax advantage if its profits are large _____

f. Greatest ability to acquire funds for the expansion of the firm _____

g. Permits some but not a great degree of specialized management _____

h. Possibility of an unresolved disagreement among owners over courses of action _____

i. Makes it possible for a businessman to avoid responsibility for illegal actions _____

11. Of the eight industry classes in which privately owned business firms are found:

a. The two which contain the greatest number of firms are _____ and _____

b. The two which make the largest contribution to the national income and employ the most full-time workers are _____ and _____ trade.

12. The public sector produces roughly one-_____ -th of all the goods and services produced in the American economy.

13. The United States is often called a big business economy because a relatively _____ firms produce a relatively _____ part of the output of the economy and of some industries.

14. The imports and exports of the United States are about _____ % of the national output.

15. Our major trading partner is _____

16. The United States incurred a $ _____billion trade (surplus, deficit) _____ in 1988.

17. List four economic implications of growing international trade and finance:

a. _____

b. _____

c. _____

d. _____

■ **PROBLEMS AND PROJECTS**

1. The table below shows the functional distribution of total income in the United States in 1988.

	Billions of dollars
Wages and salaries	$2373
Proprietors' income	242
Corporate profits	299
Interest	288
Rents	14
Total earnings	3216

Of the total earnings about _____ % were wages and salaries, and about _____ % were corporate profits.

2. Below are six numbers and each of them is a percentage. Match these six numbers with the six phrases that follow.

81	13
34	12
51	9

A. Percentage of U.S. merchandise exports going to developing countries. _____

B. Percentage of the national income which is contributed by the government sector of the economy. _____

C. Percentage of the privately owned business firms in the United States which are in the agriculture, forestry, and fishing sector of the economy. _____

D. Percentage of business firms in the United States which are partnerships. _____

E. Percentage of personal consumption expenditures which are for services. _____

F. Percentage of the income of consumers which is used for personal consumption expenditures. _____

3. Indicate to the best of your ability what you would call the industries in which the following firms operate:
 a. Sears, Roebuck and Company
 b. The General Electric Company
 c. A used-car dealer in your town
 d. Macy department stores
 e. Your local electric company
 f. A new-car dealer
 g. The Mars Candy Company
 h. The Aluminum Company of America
 i. The Revere Copper and Brass Company
 j. General Mills

4. Look at the list of firms in question 3 above.
 a. In which industry *class* would you put each of these firms?

■ **SELF-TEST**

Circle the T if the statement is true, the F if it is false.

1. The personal distribution of income describes the manner in which society's total personal income is divided among wages and salaries, corporate profits, proprietors' income, interest, and rents. **T F**

2. Limited liability refers to the fact that all members of a partnership are liable for the debts incurred by one another. **T F**

3. In both relative and absolute terms, personal taxes have exceeded personal saving in recent years. **T F**

4. Most of the personal saving in the American economy is done by those households in the top 10% of its income receivers. **T F**

5. *Dissaving* means that personal consumption expenditures exceed after-tax income. **T F**

6. A "durable good" is defined as a good which has an expected life of one year or more. **T F**

7. A plant is defined as a group of firms under a single management. **T F**

8. An industry is a group of firms that produce the same or nearly the same products. **T F**

9. The corporate form of organization is the least used by firms in the United States. **T F**

10. The corporation in the United States today always has a tax advantage over other legal forms of business organization. **T F**

11. Whether a business firm should incorporate or not depends chiefly upon the amount of money capital it must have to finance the enterprise. **T F**

12. The wholesale and retail trade and the service industries contain a relatively large number of firms but are not important sources of income and employment in the American economy. **T F**

13. Corporations produce over one-half the total output produced by privately owned business firms in the United States. **T F**

14. Increased international trade creates more macroeconomic stability for the United States. **T F**

15. Foreign competition gives consumers a greater variety of goods and services and forces domestic producers to be more efficient.   **T   F**

Circle the letter that corresponds to the best answer.

1. There are in the United States approximately how many households (families)?
(a) 65 million
(b) 75 million
(c) 80 million
(d) 85 million

2. The functional distribution for the United States shows that the largest part of the personal income is:
(a) wages and salaries
(b) proprietors' income
(c) corporate profits
(d) interest and rents

3. Expenditures for **nondurable** goods in recent years have amounted to approximately what percentage of personal consumption expenditures?
(a) 35%
(b) 40%
(c) 50%
(d) 65%

4. Which of the following is a true statement?
(a) the durable goods and service parts of personal consumption expenditures vary more over time than do the expenditures for nondurables
(b) expenditures for nondurables vary more than do the expenditures for durable goods and services
(c) expenditures for nondurables vary more than the expenditures for services and less than the expenditures for durables
(d) expenditures for nondurables vary more than the expenditures for durables and less than the expenditures for services

5. In recent years personal taxes have been approximately what percentage of total income?
(a) 16%
(b) 22%
(c) 24%
(d) 80%

6. If we include self-employed farmers and professional people, there are approximately how many million business firms in the United States?
(a) 5
(b) 8
(c) 18
(d) 20

7. A group of three plants which is owned and operated by a single firm and which consists of a farm growing wheat, a flour milling plant, and a plant which bakes and sells bakery products is an example of:
(a) a horizontal combination
(b) a vertical combination
(c) a conglomerate combination
(d) a corporation

8. Limited liability is associated with:
(a) only proprietorships
(b) only partnerships
(c) both proprietorships and partnerships
(d) only corporations

9. Which of the following forms of business organization can most effectively raise money capital?
(a) corporation
(b) partnership
(c) proprietorship
(d) vertical combination

10. Which of the following industry classes has the largest number of firms?
(a) agriculture, forestry, and fishing
(b) manufacturing
(c) wholesale and retail trade
(d) mining

11. About what percentage of the national income of the United States is produced by government?
(a) 3%
(b) 5%
(c) 10%
(d) 12%

12. The part of after-tax income which is not consumed is defined as:
(a) saving
(b) capital investment
(c) wages and salaries
(d) nondurable goods expenditure

13. A deficit in merchandise trade with other nations is produced when a nation's:
(a) exports are greater than imports
(b) imports are greater than exports
(c) imports are greater than currency appreciation
(d) exports are greater than currency appreciation

14. One of the major benefits of international trade and finance for the United States is:
(a) lower living standards
(b) less efficient use of world resources
(c) greater competition among businesses
(d) greater economic security for domestic banks and financial markets

15. If incomes increased significantly in the major industrial countries that trade with the United States, this development would most likely:
(*a*) increase United States exports
(*b*) decrease United States exports
(*c*) decrease United States imports of oil
(*d*) have no significant effect on the imports or exports of the United States

■ DISCUSSION QUESTIONS

1. Explain the difference between a functional and a personal distribution of income. Rank the five types of earned income in the order of their size.

2. Which would result in greater total saving and less consumption spending out of a national income of a given size: a more or less nearly equal distribution of income?

3. The purchase of what type of consumer goods is largely postponable? Why is this? How is it possible for a family's personal consumption expenditures to exceed its after-tax income?

4. What is the difference between a plant and a firm? Between a firm and an industry? Which of these three concepts is the most difficult to apply in practice? Why? Distinguish between a horizontal, a vertical, and a conglomerate combination.

5. What are the principal advantages and disadvantages of each type of the three legal forms of business organization? Which of the disadvantages of the proprietorship and partnership accounts for the employment of the corporate form among the big businesses of the American economy?

6. Explain what "separation of ownership and control" of the modern corporation means. What problems does this separation create for stockholders and the economy?

7. What figures can you cite to show that the typical firm engaged in agriculture is relatively small and that the average firm engaged in manufacturing is relatively large? Are firms engaged in wholesaling and retailing; mining; finance, insurance, and real estate; and services relatively large or relatively small?

8. Is the American economy and manufacturing in the United States dominated by big business? What evidence do you use to reach this conclusion?

9. Describe the merchandise trade import and export patterns for the United States. What percentage of our exports and imports are with

(*a*) industrial countries;
(*b*) OPEC countries;
(*c*) developing countries other than OPEC; and
(*d*) Eastern European countries?

10. Explain how increasing international trade for the United States affects
(*a*) living standards;
(*b*) competition;
(*c*) banking and finance; and
(*d*) macroeconomic stability and policy.

■ ANSWERS

CHAPTER 7 THE FACTS OF AMERICAN CAPITALISM: THE PRIVATE SECTORS

Fill-in questions

1. 65, furnish resources, buy the bulk of the total output of the economy

2. wages and salaries, 74

3. 5, 44

4. personal consumption, personal saving, personal taxes

5. 16, income, Federal

6. security, speculation

7. services, nondurable goods, durable goods

8. 17.6, sole proprietorship, corporation .

9. unlimited, limited

10. *a.* CORP; *b.* PRO and PART; *c.* PRO; *d.* CORP; *e.* CORP; *f.* CORP; *g.* PART: *h.* PART: *i.* CORP

11. *a.* agriculture, forestry, and fishing; services; *b.* manufacturing, wholesale and retail

12. eight

13. few, large

14. 12

15. Canada

16. 93, deficit

17. *a.* increased productive efficiency and living standards; *b.* increased worldwide competition; *c.* financial markets and banking industries operate globally; and *d.* more macroeconomic instability and possibly less effective domestic policy

Problems and projects

1. 74, 9

2. A. 34; B. 12; C. 13; D. 9; E. 51; F. 81

4. *a.* Firms *a, c, d,* and *f* are in wholesale and retail trade; firms *b, g, h, i,* and *j* are in manufacturing; firms *h* and *i* are in mining; firm *e* is in transportation, communications, and public utilities;

Self-test

1. F; **2.** T; **3.** T; **4.** T; **5.** T; **6.** T; **7.** F; **8.** T; **9.** F; **10.** F; **11.** T; **12.** F; **13.** T; **14.** F; **15.** T

1. *a;* **2.** *a;* **3.** *a;* **4.** *a;* **5.** *a;* **6.** *c;* **7.** *b;* **8.** *d;* **9.** *a;* **10.** *c;* **11.** *d;* **12.** *a;* **13.** *b;* **14.** *c;* **15.** *a*

The facts of American capitalism: the public sector

The facts of public-sector or government finance in the United States presented in Chapter 8 center on two questions: Where do governments get their incomes? On what do they spend these incomes?

The organization of the chapter is relatively simple. First, the trends which taxes collected and expenditures made by all levels of government—Federal, state, and local—have taken since 1929 and the causes of the increases in expenditures and taxes are examined briefly. Second, a closer look is taken at the major items upon which the Federal government spends its income, the principal taxes it levies to obtain its income, and the relative importance of these taxes. This section also includes a discussion of the changes brought about by the Tax Reform Act of 1986. Third, the chapter looks at the major expenditures of and the major taxes of the state and the local governments, and at fiscal federalism. Fourth, the chapter examines the principles applied in levying taxes, the way tax rates vary as personal incomes change, who really pays the taxes levied against various groups in the economy, and how much of their incomes Americans pay to government in the form of taxes. Finally, Chapter 8 takes a look at two controversial issues related to further reform of the American tax system.

What should you get out of this chapter? There are at least five important sets of facts: (1) the trends which taxes and government expenditures have taken in recent years and why; (2) the relative importance of the principal taxes and the relative importance of the various expenditure items in the budgets of the three levels of government; (3) the meaning of the benefits-received and the ability-to-pay principles; (4) the meaning of progressive, regressive, and proportional taxation, the shifting and incidence of taxes, and the incidence of the major types of taxes; and (5) estimates of the degree of progressiveness of the American tax system.

Avoid memorizing statistics. You should look instead for the trends and generalizations which these statistics illuminate. Spend your time, also, on the terms used, the classifications employed, and the conclusions which are drawn and which embody these terms and classifications.

■ CHECKLIST

When you have studied this chapter you should be able to:

☐ List the five causes of the historical expansion and the present size of government tax revenues and expenditures.

☐ Explain the differences between government purchases and transfer payments; and the effect of each of these two kinds of expenditures on the composition of the national output.

☐ Describe the three largest categories of expenditures and the two greatest sources of revenue of the Federal government.

☐ Explain the major changes made to the Federal personal income tax by the Tax Reform Act of 1986.

☐ Define and explain the difference between the marginal and the average tax rate.

☐ Describe how loopholes or tax evasion reduce the progressivity of the Federal personal income tax.

☐ List the two largest sources of tax revenue and the four largest types of expenditures of state governments; and the largest single source of tax revenue and the largest category of expenditures of local governments.

☐ Distinguish between the ability-to-pay principle and the benefits-received principle.

☐ Define and explain the differences among a regressive, proportional, and progressive tax; and identify the taxes levied in the American economy that fall into each of these categories.

☐ State the probable incidence of personal income, corporate income, sales and excise, and property taxes.

☐ Describe the estimates made about how the tax burden in the American economy is distributed among different income classes, the progressivity of the American tax system, and the effect of this tax system on the distribution of income in the United States.

☐ Explain two tax-related issues that have been paramount in recent years.

■ CHAPTER OUTLINE

1. Government's functions in the economy are felt most directly when it collects revenue by taxation and expends this revenue for goods and services; but there is an important difference between the voluntary transactions in the private and the compulsory transactions in the public sector of the economy.

2. In both absolute and relative terms, government tax collections and spending have increased during the past sixty or so years.

a. The increased tax collections and spending are the result of hot and cold wars, population increases, urbanization and the greater demand for social goods, pollution of the environment, egalitarianism, and inflation.

b. Government spending consists of purchases of goods and services and of transfer payments; but these two types of spending have different effects on the composition of the national output.

3. At the Federal level of government:

a. 40% of the total expenditure is for income security, about 28% is for national defense, and some 14% is for interest on the national debt;

b. the major sources of revenue are personal income, payroll, and corporate income taxes;

c. the Tax Reform Act of 1986 reduced the number of tax backets, lowered tax rates, and broadened the tax base of the Federal personal income tax.

d. deductions of interest on home mortgages, interest on state and local government bonds, and property taxes are tax loopholes for some persons.

e. illegal tax evasion may reduce personal income tax revenues by as much as 20%.

f. the personal income tax is "indexed" to the rate of inflation to prevent rising prices from pushing taxpayers into higher tax brackets.

4. At the other two levels of government:

a. state governments depend largely on sales and excise taxes and personal income taxes, and use a large part of their revenues for education and public welfare;

b. local governments rely heavily upon property taxes and spend the greatest part of their revenues for education;

c. tax revenues are less than expenditures and the Federal government shares some of its revenues with these governments by making grants to them.

5. Although the overall level of taxes is important to the economy, the question of who pays the tax bill is equally important.

a. The benefits-received principle and the ability-to-pay principle are widely employed to determine how the tax bill should be apportioned among the economy's citizens.

b. Taxes can be classified as progressive, regressive, or proportional according to the way in which the average tax *rate* changes as income increases.

c. A tax levied upon one person or group of persons may be shifted partially or completely to another person or group; and to the extent that a tax can be shifted or passed on through lower prices paid or higher prices received, its incidence is passed on. The incidence of the four major types of taxes is only probable and is not known for certain.

d. Because some taxes levied in the American economy are progressive and some are regressive it appears that the American tax system is only slightly progressive, has very little effect on the distribution of income in the United States, and has become less progressive over the past 20 years; but estimates of the progressivity of the tax system depend on the assumed incidence of the various taxes; and the transfer payments made by governments do reduce income inequality in the United States.

6. In recent years two tax-related issues have been debated in the United States.

a. How to "reindustrialize" the American economy by significantly increasing spending for modern machinery and equipment is the first of these issues; and it has been suggested that the corporate income tax be reduced and a value-added tax on consumer goods be levied.

b. Whether higher tax rates or new taxes are required to reduce large and persistent Federal budget deficits is the second tax-related issue.

■ IMPORTANT TERMS

Government purchase	**Average tax rate**
Government transfer payment	**Payroll tax**
Personal income tax	**Corporate income tax**
Tax Reform Act (TRA) of 1986	**Benefits-received principle**
Marginal tax rate	**Ability-to-pay principle**
Double taxation	**Progressive tax**
Sales tax	**Regressive tax**
Excise tax	**Proportional tax**
Capital gain	**Tax incidence**
Property tax	**Tax shifting**
Fiscal federalism	**Value-added tax (VAT)**

■ **FILL-IN QUESTIONS**

1. It is through the _____ it makes and the _____ it collects that the functions of government are most directly felt by the economy.

2. Transactions in the private sector of the economy are (voluntary, compulsory) _____ while those in the public sector, by and large, are _____ _____

3. An examination of the public sector of the American economy reveals that:
  a. between 1929 and 1988 government **purchases** of goods and services as a percentage of national output have tended to (increase, decrease, remain constant) _____ and since the early 1950s have been about (10, 20, 33) _____% of the GNP;
  b. but government **transfer payments** as a percentage of national output during the past 20 or so years have (increased, decreased, remained constant) _____
  c. and the tax revenues required to finance both government expenditures and transfer payments are today about (10, 20, 33) _____% of the GNP.

4. Government transfer payments are defined as _____ _____ and are a(n) (exhaustive, nonexhaustive) _____

5. When government raises $20 billion by taxation and uses it to purchase goods it shifts resources from the production of (private, public) _____ goods to the production of _____ goods; but when it uses the $20 billion to make transfer payments it changes the _____ of the output of private goods.

6. The most important source of revenue for the Federal government is the _____ tax; next in importance are the _____ taxes. The three largest categories of Federal expenditures are for _____, for _____, and for interest on the _____

7. The Federal government uses the personal income tax to obtain most of the _____ it requires to finance its expenditures. In fact, the personal income tax accounts for _____ % of Federal tax revenues. The Federal government also receives _____ % from payroll taxes and _____ % from corporate income taxes.

8. The Tax Reform Act of 1986 (increased, decreased) _____ the number of tax brackets, (raised, lowered) _____ tax rates, and (narrowed, broadened) _____ the tax base of the Federal personal income tax.

9. Two principal loopholes in the Federal tax system are the _____ securities of state and local governments and the deduction of interest on home _____

10. Illegal tax evasion is the result of activities in the "_____ economy" and the failure of individuals to report all of their incomes; and may cost the Federal government up to _____ % of personal income tax revenues.

11. The state governments rely primarily upon _____ and _____ taxes for their incomes which they spend mostly on _____ and _____

12. At local levels of government the single most important source of revenue is the _____ tax and the single most important expenditure is for _____

13. The amount by which the expenditures of state and local governments exceed their tax revenues is largely filled by grants from the _____ government; these grants account for _____ % to _____ % of all revenue received by state and local governments.

14. The two philosophies of apportioning the tax burden which are most evident in the American economy are the _____ principle and the _____ principle.

15. As income increases: if a tax is proportional the average tax rate _____; if it is progressive the average rate _____; and if it is regressive the average rate _____

16. Indicate in the space to the right of each of the following taxes whether that tax (as applied in the United States) is regressive (R) or progressive (P) or whether it is uncertain (U) which it is.

a. Personal income tax   _____

b. Sales tax   _____

c. Payroll tax   _____

d. Property tax   _____

e. Corporation income tax   _____

17. What is the probable incidence of each of the following taxes?

a. Personal income tax: _____

b. Sales and excise tax: _____

c. Corporate income tax: _____

d. Property tax: _____

18. The American tax structure is mildly (regressive, progressive) _____

a. As a result it has a (small, great) _____ effect on the distribution of income in the United States.
b. But these conclusions depend on the assumed _____ of the various taxes used in the American economy.
c. Over the last 20 years the American tax structure has become (more, less) _____ progressive.
d. Income inequality in the United States is, however, reduced by the system of _____ payments made by governments.

19. In recent years, two major issues related to taxes have been:

a. reindustrializing the U.S. economy and increasing the _____ of American workers.
  (1) This would require that consumption be (increased, decreased) _____ and investment be _____.

(2) This might be accomplished by lowering the (personal, corporate) _____ income tax and establishing a _____ tax on consumption;

b. whether there should be (higher, lower) _____ tax rates or new taxes to contain large and persistent Federal budget deficits. One option is to introduce _____ ; the other option is to increase the progressivity of the personal _____.

■ **PROBLEMS AND PROJECTS**

1. In the table below are several levels of taxable income and hypothetical marginal tax rates for each $1000 increase in income.

Taxable income	Marginal tax rate, %	Tax	Average tax rate, %
$1500		$300	20
2500	22	520	20.8
3500	25	_____	_____
4500	29	_____	_____
5500	34	_____	_____
6500	40	_____	_____

a. Compute at the four income levels the tax and the average tax rate.
b. As the marginal tax rate:
  (1) increases the average tax rate (increases, decreases, remains constant) _____

_____

  (2) decreases the average tax rate _____

_____

2. In the table below are five levels of taxable income and the amount that would be paid at each of the five levels under three tax laws: A, B, and C. Compute for each of the

	Tax A			Tax B			Tax C		
Income	Tax paid	Av. tax rate %		Tax paid	Av. tax rate %		Tax paid	Av. tax rate %	
$ 1,500	45.00	3	%	30.00	2	%	135.00	9	%
3,000	90.00	_____		90.00	_____		240.00	_____	
5,000	150.00	_____		150.00	_____		350.00	_____	
7,500	225.00	_____		187.50	_____		450.00	_____	
10,000	300.00	_____		200.00	_____		500.00	_____	
Type of tax:	_____			_____			_____		

three tax laws the **average** rate of taxation at each of the four remaining income levels and indicate whether the tax is regressive, proportional, progressive, or some combination thereof.

3. Assume a state government levies a 4% sales tax on all consumption expenditures. Consumption expenditures at six income levels are shown in the table below.

Income	Consumption expenditures	Sales tax paid	Average tax rate, %
$ 5,000	$5,000	$200	4.0
6,000	5,800	232	3.9
7,000	6,600	_____	_____
8,000	7,400	_____	_____
9,000	8,200	_____	_____
10,000	9,000	_____	_____

a. Compute the sales tax paid at the next four incomes.
b. Compute the average tax rate at these incomes.
c. Using income as the tax base, the sales tax is a

_____ tax.

■ **SELF-TEST**

Circle the T if the statement is true, the F if it is false.

1. Transactions in the public sector of the economy are largely compulsory and those in the private sector are voluntary. **T F**

2. Government purchases of goods and services are called **nonexhaustive** and government transfer payments are called **exhaustive** expenditures. **T F**

3. When a government levies taxes and uses the tax revenue to make transfer payments it shifts resources from the production of private goods to the production of public goods. **T F**

4. The level of Federal expenditures in 1987 was about $1,000 billion. **T F**

5. The chief source of revenue for the Federal government is the corporation income tax. **T F**

6. The Tax Reform Act of 1986 reduced the number of tax brackets, lowered tax rates, and broadened the tax base of the Federal personal income tax. **T F**

7. Personal income tax rates have been "indexed" to prevent inflation from pushing taxpayers into higher marginal tax brackets. **T F**

8. Because the marginal tax rate on all taxable corporate profits in excess of $100,000 is 34%, beyond $100,000 the Federal corporate income tax is proportional. **T F**

9. The Federal government levies sales taxes on tobacco and gasoline. **T F**

10. Evading taxes is legal, but avoiding taxes is illegal. **T F**

11. There is a major loophole in the Federal tax system because personal income tax rates are progressive. **T F**

12. One of the problems with the corporate income tax is double taxation. **T F**

13. Total taxes collected by the Federal government are approximately equal to the amount of taxes collected by all state and local governments. **T F**

14. The chief difficulty in applying the benefits-received principle of taxation is determining who receives the benefits of many of the goods and services which government supplies. **T F**

15. A sales tax generally turns out to be a proportional tax. **T F**

16. The state and Federal taxes on gasoline are good examples of taxes levied on the benefits-received principle. **T F**

17. Estimates of the overall structure of the American tax system depend on the assumed incidence of taxes. **T F**

18. A value-added tax is a tax on the difference between the value of goods sold by a firm and the value of the goods it purchased from other firms. **T F**

19. Advocates of "reindustrializing" the American economy have proposed increasing the tax rate imposed by the Federal government on corporate incomes to force corporations to be more efficient. **T F**

20. A value-added tax, its proponents argue, would tend to reduce consumption and increase saving in the economy and release resources for the production of more investment goods. **T F**

Circle the letter that corresponds to the best answer.

1. Today all government expenditures equal approximately what percentage of the American economy's total output?
(*a*) 10%
(*b*) 18%
(*c*) 23%
(*d*) 33%

2. Which of the following is **not** one of the causes of the present size of government expenditures in the United States?

(a) national defense
(b) double taxation
(c) population growth
(d) egalitarianism

3. Which of the following would **not** be a government transfer expenditure?
(a) contributions of employers to support the social security program
(b) social security payments to the aged
(c) unemployment compensation benefits
(d) payments to the widows of war veterans

4. Which of the following accounts for the largest percentage of all Federal expenditures?
(a) income security
(b) national defense
(c) interest on the public debt
(d) veterans' services

5. Which of the following is the largest source of the tax revenues of the Federal government?
(a) sales and excise taxes
(b) property taxes
(c) payroll taxes
(d) personal income taxes

6. The Tax Reform Act of 1986:
(a) raised the corporate income tax rate
(b) lowered the corporate income tax rate
(c) raised the personal income tax rate
(d) narrowed the tax base

7. Taxing people according the principle of ability-to-pay would be most characteristic of:
(a) a payroll tax
(b) a value-added tax
(c) a general sales tax
(d) a progressive income tax

8. Which of the following is **not** a loophole in the application of the Federal tax on personal income?
(a) exempting interest received by owners of bonds of state and local governments
(b) allowing interest payments on home mortgages to be deducted
(c) permitting general sales taxes to be deducted
(d) permitting property taxes to be deducted

9. A tax that would most likely alter consumer expenditures on a product would be:
(a) an excise tax
(b) a general sales tax
(c) a personal income tax
(d) a corporate income tax

10. Which of the following pairs represents the chief source of income and the most important type of expenditure of state governments?
(a) personal income tax and expenditures for education
(b) personal income tax and expenditures for highways
(c) sales and excise taxes and expenditures for public welfare
(d) sales and excise taxes and expenditures for education

11. Which of the following pairs represents the chief source of income and the most important type of expenditure of **local** governments?
(a) property tax and expenditures for highways
(b) property tax and expenditures for education
(c) sales and excise taxes and expenditures for public welfare
(d) sales and excise taxes and expenditures for police, fire, and general government

12. Which of the following is **not** true of the ability-to-pay principle as applied in the United States?
(a) it is more widely applied than the benefits-received principle
(b) income is generally taken as the measure of the ability to pay
(c) it is more widely applied by state and local than by the Federal government
(d) as the tax base increases, taxes paid increase both absolutely and relatively

13. When the income of a taxpayer increases and a tax is regressive, the amount of the tax paid by the taxpayer:
(a) increases
(b) decreases
(c) remains unchanged
(d) may do any of the above

14. Which of the following tends to be a progressive tax in the United States?
(a) income tax
(b) property tax
(c) sales tax
(d) payroll tax

15. Which of the following taxes can be least easily shifted?
(a) personal income tax
(b) corporation income tax
(c) sales tax
(d) business property tax

16. The Pechman study of the American tax structure shows it to be:
(a) very progressive
(b) slightly progressive
(c) slightly regressive
(d) very regressive

17. In recent reform of the Federal personal income tax:
(a) the average tax rate increases faster than the marginal tax rate
(b) the marginal tax rate increases faster than the average tax rate
(c) both the average and marginal tax rates increase at an equal rate
(d) the average tax rate remains constant across all income brackets

18. The advocates of "reindustrializing" the American economy argue that:
(a) the production of consumer goods must be increased
(b) the productivity of American workers must be improved
(c) corporate income taxes should be increased
(d) the production of investment goods needs to be reduced by a substantial amount

The next two questions (19 and 20) are based on the portion of the tax table given below:

Taxable income	Total tax
$ 0	$ 0
30,000	5,000
70,000	15,000
150,000	42,000

19. The marginal tax rate at the $70,000 level of taxable income is:
(a) 16.6
(b) 21.4
(c) 25.0
(d) 28.0

20. The average tax rate at the $150,000 level of taxable income is:
(a) 21.4
(b) 28.0
(c) 31.5
(d) 33.8

■ **DISCUSSION QUESTIONS**

1. How do transactions in the public sector differ from those in the private sector of the economy?

2. What are the causes of the historical growth and the present size of government spending and taxes in the American economy?

3. Government expenditures fall into two broad classes: expenditures for goods and services, and transfer payments. Explain the difference between these and give examples of expenditures which fall into each of the two classes.

4. Explain the difference between exhaustive and nonexhaustive government spending.

5. When government collects taxes and spends the tax revenues it affects the composition of the total output of the economy. What is the effect on the composition of total output if government uses the tax revenues to purchase goods and services? What is the effect if it uses them to make transfer payments?

6. Explain precisely the difference between the marginal tax rate and the average tax rate.

7. Explain how the Federal personal income tax enables the Federal government to perform three (of the five) economic functions discussed in Chapter 6 of the text.

8. What are the major features of the Tax Reform Act of 1986? How did it affect the personal income tax and the corporate income tax?

9. What is a tax "loophole"? What are the two loopholes in the Federal tax system? How do these loopholes affect the distribution of income?

10. What is the difference between avoiding taxes and evading them? How are taxes evaded in the United States and why is the Treasury so concerned by the evasion of taxes?

11. Explain in detail the differences that exist among Federal, state, and local governments in the taxes upon which they primarily rely for their revenues and the major purposes for which they use these revenues.

12. Why does the Federal government share its tax revenues with state and local governments? How has this fiscal federalism changed in recent years?

13. What are the two basic philosophies for apportioning the tax burden in the United States? Explain each. What are the difficulties encountered in putting these philosophies into practice?

14. Explain the differences among progressive, regressive, and proportional taxes. Which taxes fall into each of these three categories? What can be said about the progressivity or regressivity of the overall structure of the American tax system?

15. Which of the following taxes tends to be shifted?
(a) Personal income tax;
(b) corporate income tax;

(*c*) sales and excise taxes;
(*d*) property tax.
From whom is the tax shifted and upon whom is the tax incidence?

16. What does the term "reindustrialize" mean when applied to the American economy? Why do the proponents of reindustrialization feel the economy is in need of it and what steps would they take to accomplish it?

17. Why might higher tax rates or new taxes be needed for the Federal government? What options might be considered?

■ **ANSWERS**

**CHAPTER 8 THE FACTS OF AMERICAN CAPITALISM:
THE PUBLIC SECTOR**

Fill-in questions

1. expenditures, taxes

2. voluntary, compulsory

3. *a.* increase, 20; *b.* increased; *c.* 33

4. expenditures for which government currently receives no good or service in return, nonexhaustive

5. private, public, composition

6. personal income, payroll, income security, national defense, public debt

7. revenue, 46, 35, 10

8. decreased, lowered, broadened

9. tax-exempt, mortgages

10. underground, 20

11. sales and excise, personal income, education, public welfare

12. property, education

13. Federal, 15, 20

14. benefits-received, ability-to-pay

15. is constant, increases, decreases

16. *a.* P; *b.* R; *c.* R; *d.* U; *e.* P

17. *a.* the persons upon whom it is levied; *b.* those who buy the taxed product; *c.* either the firm or its customers; *d.* owners when they occupy their own residences, tenants who rent residences from the owners, consumers who buy the products produced on business property

18. progressive; *a.* small; *b.* incidence; *c.* less; *d.* transfer

19. *a.* productivity, (1) decreased, increased, (2) corporate, value-added; *b.* higher, VAT, income tax.

Problems and projects

1. *a.* tax: $770, 1,060, 1,400, 1,800; average tax rate: 22%, 23.6%, 25.5%, 27.7%; *b.* (1) increases, (2) decreases

2. Tax A: 3, 3, 3, 3, proportional; Tax B: 3, 3, 2.5, 2, combination; Tax C: 8, 7, 6, 5, regressive

3. *a.* $264, 296, 328, 360; *b.* 3.8, 3.7, 3.64, 3.6; *c.* regressive

Self-test

1. T; **2.** F; **3.** F; **4.** T; **5.** F; **6.** T; **7.** T; **8.** F; **9.** F; **10.** F; **11.** F; **12.** T; **13.** F; **14.** T; **15.** F; **16.** T; **17.** T; **18.** T; **19.** F; **20.** T

1. *d;* **2.** *b;* **3.** *a;* **4.** *a;* **5.** *d;* **6.** *b;* **7.** *d;* **8.** *c;* **9.** *a;* **10.** *d;* **11.** *b;* **12.** *c;* **13.** *d;* **14.** *a;* **15.** *a;* **16.** *b;* **17.** *b;* **18.** *b;* **19.** *c;* **20.** *b*

Measuring national output, national income, and the price level

The subject matter of Chapter 9 is national income (or social) accounting. This type of accounting measures or estimates the size of (1) the gross national product, (2) the net national product, (3) the national income, (4) the personal income, and (5) the disposable income of the economy.

National income (or social) accounting involves estimating output or income for the nation society as a whole, rather than for an individual business firm or family. Note that the terms "output" and "income" are interchangeable because the nation's output and its income are identical. The value of the nation's output equals the total expenditures for this output, and these expenditures become the income of those in the nation who have produced this output. Consequently, there are two equally acceptable methods, both discussed in the chapter, for obtaining each of the five income-output measures listed above. These two methods are the expenditures method and the income method.

Accounting is essentially an adding-up process. This chapter explains in detail and lists the items which must be added to obtain by both methods each of the five income-output measures. It is up to you to learn precisely *what* to add, i.e., how to compute GNP, NNP, NI, PI, and DI by both methods. This is a fairly difficult chapter, and the only way to learn the material is simply to sit down and learn it—memorize it if necessary! A careful reading of the chapter, however, will enable you to avoid the necessity of memorizing. You should first try to understand what each of the five income-output measures measures and the two alternative approaches to these measurements. Remembering the items to be added will then be much simpler.

In addition to explaining the two methods of computing the five income-output measures and each of the items used in the computation process, the chapter discusses the measurement of the price level in the economy. By measuring the price level, economists are able to determine how much inflation (an increase in the price level) or deflation (a decrease in the price level) has occurred in the economy. This information is important because income-output measures are expressed in monetary units,

so if accurate comparisons are to be made between years, these monetary measures must be adjusted to take account of changes in the price level. A simple example is presented to show how a GNP price index or deflator is constructed and then the index is used to adjust nominal GNP to determine real GNP for comparison purposes. But, as the last section of the chapter points out, it is especially dangerous to assume that GNP is a good measure of the welfare of the society.

Chapter 9 is the essential background for Parts 2 and 3, which explain the history of and the factors that determine the level of total output and income in the economy. This chapter is important because it explains the several methods used to measure the performance of the economy in a given year and make the adjustments necessary to ensure accurate measurements of performance over time.

■ CHECKLIST

When you have studied this chapter you should be able to:

☐ State the purposes of national income accounting.

☐ Define GNP; and compute it using either the expenditures or the income approach when you are given the necessary data.

☐ Explain: the difference between gross and net investment; why changes in inventories are investment; and the relation between net investment and economic growth.

☐ Define each of the following; and, when you are given the needed data, compute each by two different methods: NNP, NI, PI, and DI.

☐ Explain how the GNP price index or deflator is calculated and calculate an index number when given data.

☐ Adjust the nominal GNP when you are given the relevant price index, to find the real GNP.

☐ Present several reasons why GNP is not an index of social welfare.

■ **CHAPTER OUTLINE**

1. National income (or social) accounting consists of concepts which enable those who use them to measure the economy's output, to compare it with past outputs, to explain its size and the reasons for changes in its size, and to formulate policies designed to increase it.

2. The gross national product (GNP) is the market value of all final goods and services produced in the economy during a year.

  a. GNP is measured in dollar terms rather than in terms of physical units of output.

  b. To avoid double counting, GNP includes only *final* goods and services (goods and services that will not be processed further during the *current* year).

  c. Nonproductive transactions are not included in GNP; purely financial transactions and second-hand sales are, therefore, excluded.

  d. Measurement of GNP can be accomplished by either the expenditures or the income method but the same result is obtained by the two methods.

3. Computation of the GNP by the expenditures method requires the addition of the total amounts of the four types of spending for final goods and services.

  a. Personal consumption expenditures (**C**) are the expenditures of households for durable and nondurable goods and for services.

  b. Gross private domestic investment (I_g) is the sum of the spending by business firms for machinery, equipment, and tools; spending by firms and households for new buildings; and the changes in the inventories of business firms.

  (1) A change in inventories is included in investment because it is the part of output of the economy which was not sold during the year.

  (2) Investment does not include expenditures for stocks or bonds or for second-hand capital goods.

  (3) Gross investment exceeds net investment by the value of the capital goods worn out during the year.

  (4) An economy in which net investment is positive (zero, negative) is an expanding (a static, a declining) economy.

  c. Government purchases of goods and services (**G**) are the expenditures made by all governments in the economy for products produced by business firms and for resource services from households.

  d. Net exports (X_n) in an economy equal the expenditures made by foreigners for goods and services produced in the economy less the expenditures made by the consumers, governments, and investors of the economy for goods and services produced in foreign nations.

  e. In symbols, $\mathbf{C} + \mathbf{I_g} + \mathbf{G} + \mathbf{X_n} = \text{GNP}$

4. Computation of GNP by the income method requires the addition of the nine uses to which the income derived from the production and sales of final goods and services are put. These nine items are:

  a. Depreciation (capital consumption allowance).

  b. Indirect business taxes.

  c. Compensation of employees (the sum of wages and salaries *and* wage and salary supplements).

  d. Rents.

  e. Interest (only the interest payments made by business firms are included and the interest payments made by government are excluded).

  f. Proprietors' income (the profits or net income of unincorporated firms).

  g. Corporate profits which are subdivided into:

  (1) Corporate income taxes

  (2) Dividends

  (3) Undistributed corporate profits

5. In addition to GNP, four other national income measures are important in evaluating the performance of the economy. Each has a distinct definition and can be computed by making additions to or deductions from another measure.

  a. NNP is the annual output of final goods and services over and above the capital goods worn out during the year; and is equal to the GNP minus depreciation (capital consumption allowance).

  b. NI is the total income *earned* by owners of land and capital and by the suppliers of labor and entrepreneurial ability during the year; and equals NNP less indirect business taxes.

  c. PI is the total income *received*—whether it is earned or unearned—by the households of the economy before the payment of personal taxes; and is found by *adding* transfer payments to and *subtracting* social security contributions, corporate income taxes, and undistributed corporate profits from the NI.

  d. DI is the total income available to households after the payment of personal taxes; and is equal to PI less personal taxes and also equal to personal consumption expenditures plus personal saving.

  e. The relations among the five income-output measures are summarized for you in Table 9-5.

  f. Figure 9-2 is a more realistic and complex circular flow diagram that shows the flows of expenditures and incomes among the households, business firms, and governments in the economy.

6. Because price levels change from year to year it is necessary to adjust the nominal GNP (or money GNP) computed for any year to obtain the real GNP before year-to-year comparisons between the outputs of final goods and services can be made.

  a. The price level is stated as an index number that

measures the price ratio of a market basket of goods in a given year to a market basket of goods in a base year, and that ratio is multiplied by 100.

b. Although there are many price indexes, the GNP price index or deflator is used to adjust GNP measures for changes in the price level.

c. To adjust the GNP figures, divide the nominal GNP in any year by the price index for that year; the result is the adjusted or real GNP.

d. When the price index in a year is below (above) the 100 it was in the base year the nominal GNP figure for that year is inflated (deflated) by this adjustment.

7. The GNP is not, for the following reasons, a measure of social welfare in the economy.

a. It excludes the value of final goods and services not bought and sold in the markets of the economy.

b. It excludes the amount of leisure the citizens of the economy are able to have.

c. It does not record the improvements in the quality of products which occur over the years.

d. It does not measure changes in the composition and the distribution of the national output.

e. It is not a measure of per capita output because it does not take into account changes in the size of the economy's population.

f. It does not record the pollution costs to the environment of producing final goods and services.

g. It does not measure the market value of the final goods and services produced in the underground sector of the economy.

■ IMPORTANT TERMS

National income (social) accounting

Gross national product

Final goods

Intermediate goods

Double counting

Value added

Nonproductive transaction

Nonmarket transaction

Expenditures approach

Income approach

Personal consumption expenditures

Government purchases of goods and services

Gross private domestic investment

Noninvestment transaction

Net private domestic investment

Expanding economy

Static economy

Declining economy

Net exports

Nonincome charges

Capital consumption allowances (depreciation)

Indirect business taxes

Compensation of employees

Wage and salary supplements

Net national product

National income

Personal income

Disposable income

Personal saving

Nominal GNP

Real GNP

Price index

Base year

Given year

Inflating

Deflating

GNP deflator

■ FILL-IN QUESTIONS

1. Social accounting is valuable because it provides a means of keeping track of the level of _____ in the economy and the course it has followed over the long run; and the information required to devise and put into effect the public _____ that will improve the performance of the economy.

2. Gross national product is a monetary measure of all final goods and services produced during a year; to measure the value of these goods and services, the goods and services are valued at their _____

3. In measuring GNP only final goods and services are included; if intermediate goods and services were included, the accountant would be _____

4. A firm buys materials for $200 from other firms in the economy and produces from them a product which sells for $315. The $115 is the _____ by the firm.

5. The total value added to a product at all stages of production equals the _____ value of the _____ product; and the total value added to all products produced in the economy during a year is the _____ product.

6. Personal consumption expenditures are the expenditures of households for _____ and _____ goods and for _____

7. Gross private domestic investment basically includes _____ , _____ , and _____ . Net private domestic investment is less than gross private domestic investment by an amount equal to _____

_____

8. If gross private domestic investment is less than depreciation, net private domestic investment is (positive, zero, negative) _____ and the economy is (static, declining, expanding) _____

9. An economy's *net* exports equal its _____ _____ less its _____

10. In symbols, the GNP by the expenditures approach =

_____ + _____ + _____ + _____

11. The capital consumption allowance and indirect business taxes, by the income approach, are referred to as _____ charges or allocations.

12. The compensation of employees in the system of social accounting consists of actual wages and salaries *and* wage and salary _____

_____

The latter are the payments employers make to social _____ programs and to _____ pension, health, and welfare funds.

13. Corporate profits are disposed of in three ways: ____ _____, _____, and _____

14. Gross national product overstates the economy's net production because it fails to make allowance for that part of the output which replaces the _____ worn out or used up in producing the output. To compute the net national product it is, therefore, necessary to subtract the _____

_____

15. National income equals net national product minus

_____

16. Personal income:
  a. equals national income plus _____

and minus the sum of _____,

_____,

and _____;

b. also equals _____

plus _____

plus _____

17. Disposable income:
  a. equals personal income minus _____

_____;

  b. also equals _____

_____

18. In order to compare the real gross national product in two different years, it is necessary to adjust the nominal GNP because _____

_____

  a. A price index is the ratio of the price of a market basket of goods and services in a given year to

_____ in the base year, with the ratio being multiplied by 100.
  b. The price index used to adjust nominal GNP for changes in the price level is called _____
  c. Real GNP is calculated by dividing _____

_____ GNP by the _____ (in hundredths).

19. For several reasons the real GNP is not a measure of social welfare in an economy.

  a. It does not include the _____ transactions that result in the production of goods and services or the amount of _____ enjoyed by the citizens of the economy.
  b. It fails to record improvements in the _____ of the products produced, changes in the composition and distribution of the economy's total _____, the undesirable effects of producing the GNP upon the

_____ of the economy, and the goods and services produced in the _____ economy.
  c. And because it is a measure of the **total** output of the economy it does not measure the _____ output of the economy.

20. When the population of an economy grows at a more rapid rate than its real GNP grows, the standard of living in that economy (rises, falls, remains constant) _____

■ PROBLEMS AND PROJECTS

1. Below are social accounting figures for the United States.

	Billions of dollars
Exports	$ 367
Dividends	60
Capital consumption allowance	307
Wages and salaries	1442
Government purchases of goods and services	577
Rents	33
Indirect business taxes	255
Wage and salary supplements	280
Gross private domestic investment	437
Corporate income taxes	88
Transfer payments	320
Interest	201
Proprietors' income	132
Personal consumption expenditures	1810
Imports	338
Social security contributions	148
Undistributed corporate profits	55
Personal taxes	372

a. Compute each of the following.

(1) Compensation of employees: $_____

(2) Net exports: $_____

(3) Net private domestic investment: $_____

b. Use any of these figures and any of your computations in (*a*) above to prepare in the table below an Income Statement for the Economy similar to the one found in Table 9-4 (on page 138 of the text).

Receipts: Expenditures approach	Allocations: Income approach
$_____	$_____
$_____	$_____
$_____	$_____
$_____	$_____
	$_____
	$_____
	$_____
	$_____
	$_____
Gross national product $_____	Gross national product $_____

c. In this economy:

(1) Net national product is $_____

(2) National income is $_____

(3) Personal income is $_____

(4) Disposable income is $_____

2. A farmer who owns a plot of ground sells the right to pump crude oil from his land to a crude-oil producer. The crude-oil producer agrees to pay the farmer $20 a barrel for every barrel pumped from the farmer's land.

a. During one year 10,000 barrels are pumped.

(1) The farmer receives a payment of $_____ from the crude-oil producer.

(2) The value added by the farmer is $_____

b. The crude-oil producer sells the 10,000 barrels pumped to a petroleum refiner at a price of $25 a barrel.

(1) The crude-oil producer receives a payment of $_____ from the refiner.

(2) The value added by the crude-oil producer is $_____

c. The refiner employs a pipeline company to transport the crude oil from the farmer's land to the refinery and pays the pipeline company a fee of $1 a barrel for the oil transported.

(1) The pipeline company receives a payment of $_____ from the refiner.

(2) The value added by the pipeline company is $_____

d. From the 10,000 barrels of crude oil the refiner produces 315,000 gallons of gasoline and various by-products which are sold to distributors and gasoline service stations at an average price of $1 per gallon.

(1) The total payment received by the refiner from its customers is $_____

(2) The value added by the refiner is $_____

e. The distributors and service stations sell the 315,000 gallons of gasoline and by-products to consumers at an average price of $1.30 a gallon.

(1) The total payment received by distributors and service stations is $_____

(2) The value added by them is $_____

f. The total value added by the farmer, crude-oil producer, pipeline company, refiner, and distributors and service stations is $_____ and the market value of the gasoline and by-products (the final good) is $_____

3. Below is a list of items which may or may not be included in the five income-output measures. Indicate in the space to the right of each which of the income-output measures includes this item; it is possible for the item to be included in none, one, two, three, four, or all of the measures. If the item is included in none of the measures, indicate why it is not included.

a. Interest on the national debt _____

b The sale of a used computer _____

c. The production of shoes which are not sold by the manufacturer _____

d. The income of a bootlegger in a "dry" state _____

e. The purchase of a share of common stock on the New York Stock Exchange _____

f. The interest paid on the bonds of the General Motors Corporation _____

g. The labor performed by a homemaker _____

h. The labor performed by a paid baby-sitter _____

i. The monthly check received by an idler from his rich aunt _____

j. The purchase of a new tractor by a farmer _____

k. The labor performed by an assembly-line worker in repapering his own kitchen _____

l. The services of a lawyer _____

m. The purchase of shoes from their manufacturer by a shoe retailer _____

n. The monthly check received from the Social Security Administration by a college student whose father has died _____

o. The rent a homeowner would receive if he did not live in his own home _____

4. In the table below are nominal GNP figures for three years and the price indices for each of the three years. (The GNP figures are in billions.)

Year	Nominal GNP	Price index	Real GNP
1929	$104	121	$_____
1933	56	91	_____
1939	91	100	_____

a. Which of the three years appears to be the base year? _____

b. Between:
  (1) 1929 and 1933 the economy experienced (inflation, deflation) _____
  (2) 1933 and 1939 experienced _____
c. Use the price indices to compute the real GNP in each year. (You may round your answers to the nearest billion dollars.)
d. The nominal GNP figure:
  (1) for 1929 was (deflated, inflated, neither) _____
  _____
  (2) for 1933 was _____
  (3) for 1939 was _____
e. The price level:
  (1) fell by _____ % from 1929 to 1933.
  (2) rose by _____ % from 1933 to 1939.

■ **SELF-TEST**

Circle the T if the statement is true, the F if it is false.

1. Gross national product measures at their market values the total output of all goods and services produced in the economy during a year. **T F**

2. Both the nominal GNP and the real GNP of the American economy are measured in dollars. **T F**

3. The total market value of the wine produced in the United States during a year is equal to the number of bottles of wine produced in that year multiplied by the (average) price at which a bottle sold during that year. **T F**

4. The total value added to a product and the value of the final product are equal. **T F**

5. The two approaches to the measurement of the gross national product yield identical results because one approach measures the total amount spent on the products produced by business firms during a year while the second approach measures the total income of business firms during the year. **T F**

6. In computing gross national product, net national product, and national income by the expenditures approach, transfer payments are excluded because they do not represent payments for currently produced goods and services. **T F**

7. The expenditure made by a household to have a new home built for it is a personal consumption expenditure. **T F**

8. In national income accounting any increase in the inventories of business firms is included in gross private domestic investment.   **T F**

9. If gross private domestic investment is greater than capital consumption during a given year, the economy has declined during that year.   **T F**

10. The net exports of an economy equal its exports of goods and services less its imports of goods and services.   **T F**

The data in the following table should be used to answer true-false questions 11 through 14 and multiple-choice questions 8 through 14.

	Billions of dollars
Net private domestic investment	$ 32
Personal taxes	39
Transfer payments	19
Indirect business taxes	8
Corporate income taxes	11
Personal consumption expenditures C	217
Capital consumption allowance	7
United States exports	15
Dividends	15
Government purchases of goods and services G	51
Undistributed corporate profits	10
Social security contributions	4
United States imports	17

11. The stock of capital goods in the economy has expanded.   **T F**

12. Gross private domestic investment is equal to $25 billion.   **T F**

13. National income equals the net national product minus $8 billion.   **T F**

14. Disposable income is equal to $245 billion.   **T F**

15. Comparison of a gross national product with the gross national product of an earlier year when the price level has risen between the two years necessitates the "inflation" of the GNP figure in the later year.   **T F**

16. To adjust nominal gross national product for a given year so that a comparison between GNP in that year and in the base year can be made, it is necessary to divide nominal GNP in the given year by the price index—expressed in hundredths—for that year.   **T F**

17. The price index used to adjust nominal GNP to measure the real GNP is the consumer price index (CPI).   **T F**

18. The GNP is a measure of the social welfare of society.   **T F**

19. The productive services of a homemaker are included in GNP.   **T F**

20. The spillover costs from pollution and other activities associated with the production of the GNP are deducted from total output.   **T F**

Circle the letter that corresponds to the best answer.

1. Which of the following is *not* an important use to which social accounting is put?
(a) provides a basis for formulation and application of policies designed to improve the economy's performance
(b) permits measurement of the economic efficiency of the economy
(c) makes possible an estimate of the output of final goods and services in the economy
(d) enables the economist to chart the growth or decline of the economy over a period of time

2. To include the value of the parts used in producing the automobiles turned out during a year in gross national product for that year would be an example of:
(a) including a nonmarket transaction
(b) including a nonproductive transaction
(c) including a noninvestment transaction
(d) double counting

3. Which of the following is *not* a purely financial transaction?
(a) the sale of a used (second-hand) ironing board at a garage sale
(b) the sale of shares of stock in the United States Steel Corporation
(c) the payment of social-security benefits to a retired worker
(d) the birthday gift of a check for $5 sent by a grandmother to her grandchild

4. The sale in 1989 of an automobile produced in 1988 would not be included in the gross national product for 1989; doing so would involve:
(a) including a nonmarket transaction
(b) including a nonproductive transaction
(c) including a noninvestment transaction
(d) double counting

5. The service a baby-sitter performs when she stays at home with her baby brother while her parents are out and for which she receives no payment is not included in the gross national product because:
(a) this is a nonmarket transaction
(b) this is a nonproductive transaction
(c) this is a noninvestment transaction
(d) double counting would be involved

6. Which of the following does *not* represent investment?
(*a*) an increase in the quantity of shoes on the shelves of a shoe store
(*b*) the construction of a house which will be occupied by its owner
(*c*) the purchase of newly issued shares of stock in the General Motors Corporation
(*d*) the construction of a factory building using money borrowed from a bank

7. A refrigerator is produced by its manufacturer in 1988, sold during 1988 to a retailer, and sold by the retailer to a final consumer in 1989. The refrigerator is:
(*a*) counted as consumption in 1988
(*b*) counted as investment in 1989
(*c*) counted as investment in 1988 and consumption and disinvestment in 1989
(*d*) not included in the gross national product of 1988

Questions 8 through 14 use the national income accounting data given in the table in the true-false section.

8. The nonincome charges are equal to:
(*a*) $11 billion
(*b*) $15 billion
(*c*) $17 billion
(*d*) $19 billion

9. Corporate profits are equal to:
(*a*) $15 billion
(*b*) $25 billion
(*c*) $26 billion
(*d*) $36 billion

10. Net exports are equal to:
(*a*) −$2 billion
(*b*) $2 billion
(*c*) −$32 billion
(*d*) $32 billion

11. The gross national product is equal to:
(*a*) $298 billion
(*b*) $302 billion
(*c*) $317 billion
(*d*) $305 billion

12. The net national product is equal to:
(*a*) $298 billion
(*b*) $302 billion
(*c*) $317 billion
(*d*) $321 billion

13. National income exceeds personal income by:
(*a*) $6 billion
(*b*) $15 billion
(*c*) $21 billion
(*d*) $44 billion

14. Personal saving is equal to:
(*a*) −$28 billion
(*b*) −$8 billion
(*c*) $8 billion
(*d*) $28 billion

15. If both nominal gross national product and the level of prices are rising, it is evident that:
(*a*) real GNP is constant
(*b*) real GNP is rising but not so rapidly as prices
(*c*) real GNP is declining
(*d*) no conclusion can be drawn concerning the real GNP of the economy on the basis of this information

16. Suppose GNP rose from $500 billion to $600 billion while the GNP deflator increased from 125 to 150. The real GNP:
(*a*) remained constant
(*b*) increased
(*c*) decreased
(*d*) cannot be calculated from these figures

17. The GNP includes:
(*a*) the goods and services produced in the underground economy
(*b*) expenditures for equipment to reduce the pollution of the environment
(*c*) the value of the leisure enjoyed by citizens
(*d*) the goods and services produced but not bought and sold in the markets of the economy

18. Changes in the real GNP from one year to the next do *not* reflect:
(*a*) changes in the quality of the goods and services produced
(*b*) changes in the size of the population of the economy
(*c*) changes in the average length of the workweek
(*d*) any of the above changes

19. If nominal GNP was $3,774 billion in 1984 and the GNP deflator was 108 and nominal GNP was $3,989 in 1985 and the GNP deflator that year was 112, what was real GNP in 1984 and 1985, respectively?
(*a*) $3,494 billion and $3,562 billion
(*b*) $3,339 billion and $3,695 billion
(*c*) $3,595 billion and $3,725 billion
(*d*) $3,643 billion and $3,854 billion

20. A price index one year was 145 and the next year it was 167. What is the approximate percentage change in the price level from one year to the next as measured by that index?
(*a*) 12%
(*b*) 13%
(*c*) 14%
(*d*) 15%

■ DISCUSSION QUESTIONS

1. Of what use is national income accounting to the economist and to the policy makers in the economy?

2. Why are GNP, NNP, etc., monetary measures, and why is it necessary that they be monetary measures?

3. Why does GNP exclude nonproductive transactions? What are the two principal types of nonproductive transactions? List some examples of each.

4. Why are there two ways, both of which yield the same answers, of computing GNP, NNP, etc.?

5. Why are transfer payments excluded from GNP, NNP, and NI?

6. Is residential construction counted as investment or consumption? Why? Why is a change in inventories an investment?

7. How do you define a static, an expanding, and a declining economy? What is the relationship between gross private domestic investment and the capital consumption allowance in these three economies?

8. What is meant by a nonincome charge or allocation? What are the two principal nonincome charges included in GNP? Why are they excluded from NI?

9. What are the basic differences between the GNP deflator and the consumer price index (CPI)? Why do economists use the GNP deflator to adjust GNP figures?

10. Why do economists find it necessary to inflate and deflate GNP when comparing GNP in different years? How do they do this?

11. Why is GNP not a measure of the social welfare of society?

■ ANSWERS

CHAPTER 9 MEASURING NATIONAL OUTPUT, NATIONAL INCOME, AND THE PRICE LEVEL

Fill-in questions

1. production, policies

2. market prices

3. double counting

4. value added

5. market, final, gross national

6. durable, nondurable (either order), services

7. all final purchases of machinery, tools, and equipment by business firms; all construction; changes in inventories; the capital consumption allowance

8. negative, declining

9. exports, imports

10. C, I_g, G, X_n

11. nonincome

12. supplements, insurance, private

13. corporate income taxes, dividends, undistributed corporate profits

14. capital goods, capital consumption allowance

15. indirect business taxes

16. *a.* transfer payments, social security contributions, corporate income taxes, undistributed corporate profits; *b.* personal consumption expenditures, personal taxes, personal saving

17. *a.* personal taxes; *b.* personal consumption expenditures plus personal saving

18. the price level changes *a.* the price of the same market basket; *b.* GNP deflator; *c.* nominal, price index

19. *a.* nonmarket, leisure; *b.* quality, output, environment, underground; *c.* per capita

20. falls

Problems and projects

1. *a.* (1) 1722, (2) 29, (3) 130; *b.* see table below; *c.* (1) 2546, (2) 2291, (3) 2320, (4) 1948

Receipts: expenditures approach		Allocations: income approach	
Personal consumption expenditures	$1810	Capital consumption allowance	$ 307
Gross private domestic investment	437	Indirect business taxes	255
Government purchases of goods and services	577	Compensation of employees	1722
		Rents	33
		Interest	201
Net exports	29	Proprietors' income	132
		Corporate income taxes	88
		Dividends	60
		Undistributed corporate profit	55
Gross national product	2853	Gross national product	2853

2. *a.* (1) 200,000, (2) 200,000; *b.* (1) 250,000, (2) 50,000; *c.* (1) 10,000, (2) 10,000; *d.* (1) 315,000, (2) 55,000; *e.* (1) 409,500, (2) 94,500; *f.* 409,500, 409,500

3. *a.* personal income and disposable income, a public transfer payment; *b.* none; a second-hand sale; *c.* all, represents investment (additions to inventories); *d.* all, illegal production and incomes are included when known; *e.* none, a purely financial transaction; *f.* all; *g.* none, a nonmarket transaction; *h.* all; *i.* none, a private transfer payment; *j.* all; *k.* none, a nonmarket transaction; *l.* all; *m.* all, represents additions to the inventory of the retailer; *n.* personal income and disposable income, a public transfer payment; *o.* all; estimate of rental value of owner-occupied homes is included in rents as if it were income and in personal consumption expenditures as if it were payment for a service

4. *a.* 1939; *b.* (1) deflation, (2) inflation; *c.* 86, 62, 91; *d.* (1) deflated, (2) inflated, (3) neither; *e.* (1) 24.8 (2) 9.9

Self-test

1. F; **2.** T; **3.** T; **4.** T; **5.** F; **6.** T; **7.** F; **8.** T; **9.** F; **10.** T; **11.** T; **12.** F; **13.** T; **14.** T; **15.** F; **16.** T; **17.** F; **18.** F; **19.** F; **20.** F

1. *b;* **2.** *d;* **3.** *a;* **4.** *b;* **5.** *a;* **6.** *c;* **7.** *c;* **8.** *b;* **9.** *d;* **10.** *a;* **11.** *d;* **12.** *a;* **13.** *a;* **14.** *d;* **15.** *d;* **16.** *a;* **17.** *b;* **18.** *d;* **19.** *a;* **20.** *d*

Macroeconomic instability: unemployment and inflation

In the last chapter you learned how to define and how to compute the gross and net national product and national, personal, and disposable income in any year. This chapter begins the explanation of what determines how large each of these five income-output measures will tend to be. In the chapters that follow you will learn what causes the income and output of the economy to be what they are, what causes them to change, and how they might be controlled for the welfare of society.

Chapter 10 is concerned with the instability of the American economy or with what is commonly called the business cycle: the ups and downs in the employment of labor and the real output of the economy that occur over the years. That there have been expansions and contractions in economic (or business) activity since the end of the American Civil War is evident from even a casual look at American economic history. What is not immediately evident, however, is that these alternating and relatively short periods of prosperity and "hard times" have taken place over a longer period in which the trends in output, employment, and the standard of living have been upward. During this long history booms and busts have occurred quite irregularly; and their duration and intensity have been so varied that it is better to think of economic instability than of business cycles.

There are two principal problems that result from the instability of the economy—from the business cycle. After a brief look in the first major section of the chapter at the business cycle, its phases, and its impact on the production of different kinds of goods, Professors McConnell and Brue turn to the first of these two problems in the second major section. Here you will find an examination of the unemployment that accompanies a downturn in the level of economic activity in the economy. You will discover that there are three different kinds of unemployment, that full employment means about 5% to 6% of the labor force is unemployed, and that there are at least three problems encountered in measuring the percentage of the labor force actually unemployed at any time. That unemployment has an economic cost and that this cost is unequally distributed among different sectors of our society you will

also learn; and you probably won't be too surprised to discover that widespread unemployment can be the cause of other social problems.

The second of the two problems that result from economic instability is inflation and it is examined in the remainder of the chapter. Inflation is an increase in the general (or average) level of prices in an economy. It does not have a unique cause: it may result from increases in demand; increases in costs; or from both. But regardless of its cause, it works a real hardship on certain sectors within the economy. If it occurs at too rapid a rate it may bring about a severe breakdown in the economy.

One last word. The thing to keep your eye on when you consider economic fluctuations and unemployment and inflation in the American economy is the changes in aggregate expenditures which can occur because consumers, business firms, or the public sector decides to spend more or less for goods and services.

■ CHECKLIST

When you have finished this chapter you should be able to:

☐ Explain what is meant by the business cycle; describe the four phases of an idealized cycle; and identify the two types of noncyclical fluctuations.

☐ Identify the "immediate determinant" or cause of the levels of output and employment.

☐ Distinguish between the impact of cyclical fluctuations on industries producing capital and consumer durable goods and on those producing consumer nondurable goods; and on high- and low-concentration industries.

☐ Distinguish between frictional, structural, and cyclical unemployment, and explain the causes of these three kinds of unemployment.

☐ Define full employment and the full-employment unemployment rate (the natural rate of unemployment).

☐ Describe the process employed (by the Bureau of Labor Statistics) to measure the rate of unemployment; and list the three criticisms of the BLS data.

☐ Identify the economic cost of unemployment and three groups that bear the unequal burdens of unemployment.

☐ Define the GNP gap, and state Okun's law.

☐ Define inflation and the rate of inflation.

☐ Make international comparisons of inflation rate and unemployment rate data.

☐ Define demand-pull inflation and explain its effects in ranges 1, 2, and 3 of a price level and real national output graph.

☐ Define cost-push inflation and its relation to per unit production costs.

☐ Identify two types of cost-push or supply-side inflation.

☐ Distinguish between real and nominal income and calculate real income when given data on nominal income and the price level.

☐ List three groups that are hurt and two groups that benefit from unanticipated inflation.

☐ Describe how the redistributive effects of inflation are changed when it is anticipated.

☐ Present three scenarios that describe the possible effects of inflation on real output and employment.

■ **CHAPTER OUTLINE**

1. The history of the American economy is a record of exceptional economic growth.

a. But this growth has been accompanied by periods of inflation, of depression, and of both.

b. The business cycle means alternating periods of prosperity and depression. These recurrent periods of ups and downs in employment, output, and prices are irregular in their duration and intensity; but the typical pattern is peak, recession, trough, and recovery to another peak.

c. Changes in the levels of output and employment are largely the result of changes in the level of aggregate spending or demand in the economy.

d. Not all changes in employment and output which occur in the economy are cyclical; some are due to seasonal and secular influences.

e. The business cycle affects almost the entire economy, but it does not affect all parts in the same way and to the same degree: the production of capital and durable consumer goods fluctuates more than the production of consumer nondurable goods during the cycle because

(1) the purchase of capital and durable consumer goods can be postponed, and

(2) the industries producing these goods are largely dominated by a few large firms that hold prices constant and let output decline when demand falls.

2. Full employment does not mean that all workers in the labor force are employed and that there is no unemployment; some unemployment is normal.

a. There are at least three kinds of unemployment.

(1) There is always some frictional unemployment; and this kind of unemployment is generally desirable.

(2) And in addition there is the structural unemployment that is the result of changes in technology and in the types of goods and services consumers wish to buy.

(3) Cyclical unemployment is the result of insufficient aggregate demand in the economy.

b. Because some frictional and structural unemployment is unavoidable, the full-employment unemployment rate (the natural rate of unemployment) is the sum of frictional and structural unemployment; is achieved when cyclical unemployment is zero (the real output of the economy is equal to its potential output); and is about 5% to 6% of the labor force.

c. Surveying 60,000 households each month, the Bureau of Labor Statistics finds the unemployment rate by dividing the number of persons in the labor force who are unemployed by the number of persons in the labor force; but the figures collected in the survey have been criticized for at least three reasons.

d. Unemployment has an economic cost.

(1) The economic cost is the unproduced output (or the GNP gap), and Okun's law is that for every 1% the actual unemployment rate exceeds the natural rate of unemployment there is 2.5% GNP gap.

(2) This cost is unequally distributed among different groups of workers in the labor force.

e. Unemployment also leads to serious social problems.

3. Over its history the American economy has experienced not only periods of unemployment but periods of inflation.

a. Inflation is an increase in the general level of prices in the economy; and a decline in the level of prices is deflation.

b. The rate of inflation in any year is equal to the percentage change in the price index between that year and the preceding year; and the rule of 70 can be used to calculate the number of years it will take for the price level to double at any given rate of inflation.

c. There are at least two causes of inflation; and these two causes may operate separately or simultaneously to raise the price level.

(1) Demand-pull inflation is the result of excess aggregate demand in the economy; and while increases in aggregate demand do not increase the price level when the unemployment rate is high (in a depression) they do bring about inflation as the economy nears and reaches full employment.

(2) Cost-push or supply-side inflation is the result of factors that raise per unit production costs. This average cost is found by dividing the total cost of the resource inputs by the amount produced. There are two variants that explain this rise in costs: (a) excessive wage in-

creases that push up unit costs; and (*b*) a supply shock from an increase in the prices of resource inputs. With cost-push inflation, output and employment are declining as the price level rises.

4. Even if the total output of the economy did not change, inflation would arbitrarily redistribute real income and wealth; and would benefit some groups and hurt other groups in the economy.

a. Whether someone benefits or is hurt by inflation is measured by what happens to real income. Inflation injures those whose real income falls and benefits those whose real income rises.

(1) Real income is determined by dividing nominal income by the price level expressed in hundredths; and

(2) The percentage change in real income can be approximated by subtracting the percentage change in the price level from the percentage change in nominal income.

b. It also injures savers because it decreases the real value of any savings the money value of which is fixed.

c. And it benefits debtors and hurts creditors because it lowers the real value of debts.

d. But when the inflation is anticipated and people can adjust their nominal incomes to reflect the expected rise in the price level the redistribution of income and wealth is lessened.

e. Since World War II inflation in the United States has redistributed wealth from the household to the public sector of the economy.

f. In short, inflation acts to tax some groups and to subsidize other groups.

5. Inflation may also affect the total output of the economy but economists disagree over whether it is likely to expand or contract total output.

a. Mild demand-pull inflation seems likely to expand output and employment in the economy.

b. Cost-push inflation is apt to contract output and employment.

c. And hyperinflation may well lead to the breakdown of the economy.

■ IMPORTANT TERMS

Business cycle
Seasonal variation
Secular trend
Frictional unemployment
Structural unemployment
Cyclical unemployment
Full employment

Full-employment unemployment rate
Natural rate of unemployment
Potential output
Unemployment rate
Labor force

Discouraged workers
GNP gap
Okun's law
Inflation
Deflation
Rule of 70
Demand-pull inflation
Cost-push inflation
Per unit production cost

Nominal income
Real income
Cost-of-living adjustment (COLA)
Anticipated inflation
Unanticipated inflation
Nominal interest rate
Real interest rate
Hyperinflation

■ FILL-IN QUESTIONS

1. The history of the American economy is one of (steady, unsteady) _____ economic growth; and at times its growth has been accompanied by _____ and at other times its expansion has been interrupted by low levels of _____ and _____

2. The business cycle is a term which means the recurrent _____ and _____ in the level of business activity in the economy; and the four phases of a typical business cycle are peak, _____ _____, _____, and _____

3. The basic determinant of the levels of employment and output in an economy is the level of total _____ or aggregate _____ in the economy.

4. In addition to the changes brought about by the operation of the business cycle, changes in output and employment may be due to _____ variations and to a _____ trend.

5. Production and employment in the (durable, nondurable) _____ and (capital, consumer) _____ goods industries are affected to a greater extent by the expansion and contraction of the economy than they are in the _____ goods industries; and prices vary to a greater extent in the (low-, high-) _____ concentration industries.

6. The three types of unemployment are:

a. _____

b. _____

c. _____

7. The full-employment unemployment rate is:

a. sometimes called the _____ rate of unemployment;

b. equal to the total of the _____ and the _____ unemployment in the economy;

c. realized when the _____ unemployment in the economy is equal to zero and when the _____ output of the economy is equal to its _____ output; and

d. assumed in this chapter to be about _____ %.

8. When the economy achieves its natural rate of unemployment the number of job seekers is (greater than, less than, equal to) _____ the number of job vacancies; and the price level is (rising, falling, constant) _____

9. The unemployment *rate* is found by dividing _____ _____ by the _____

10. The GNP gap is equal to _____ GNP *minus* _____ GNP; and for every percentage point the unemployment rate rises above the natural rate of unemployment the GNP gap will, according to Okun's law, (increase, decrease) _____ by _____ %

11. The burdens of unemployment are borne more heavily by (black, white) _____, (adult, teenage) _____, and (white-collar, blue-collar) _____ workers; and the percentage of the labor force unemployed for 15 or more weeks is (greater, less) _____ than the unemployment rate.

12. Inflation means a _____ in the general level of _____ in the economy; and the rate

of inflation in year 1990 is equal to the price index for year _____ less the price index for year _____ all divided by the price index for year _____

13. The basic cause of:
a. demand-pull inflation is (an increase, a decrease) _____ in aggregate demand;
b. cost-push inflation is explained in terms of factors that raise _____. Two sources of cost-push inflation are increases in _____ and increases in _____
c. In practice, it is (easy, difficult) _____ to distinguish the two types of inflation.

14. The amount of goods and services one's nominal income can buy is called _____
a. If one's nominal income rises by 10% and the price level rose by 7%, the percentage increase in _____ would be _____
b. If nominal income was $30,000 and the price index, expressed in hundredths, was 1.06, then _____ would be _____

15. Inflation:
a. hurts those whose nominal incomes are relatively (fixed, flexible) _____
b. penalizes savers when the inflation is (expected, unexpected) _____
c. hurts (creditors, debtors) _____ and benefits _____
d. has since World War II shifted wealth from (the public sector, households) _____ _____ to _____

16. The redistributive effects of inflation are less severe when it is (anticipated, unanticipated) _____
a. Clauses in labor contracts that call for automatic adjustments of workers' income from the effects of inflation are called _____
b. The percentage increase in purchasing power that the lender receives from the borrower is the (real rate of interest, nominal rate of interest) _____,

the percentage increase in money that the lender receives

is the _____

17. Despite considerable disagreement and uncertainty among economists it seems that:

   a. demand-pull inflation, unless there is full employment

in the economy, will (increase, decrease) _____ total output and employment;

   b. cost-push inflation will _____ output and employment in the economy;

   c. hyperinflation may bring about an economic _____

_____

■ PROBLEMS AND PROJECTS

1. In the table below are statistics showing the labor force and total employment during year 1 and year 5. Make the computations necessary to complete the table. (Numbers of persons are in thousands.)

	Year 1	Year 5
Labor force	84,889	95,453
Employed	80,796	87,524
Unemployed	_____	_____
Unemployment rate	_____	_____

   a. How is it possible that **both** employment and unemployment increased? _____

_____

   b. In relative terms, if unemployment increases employment will decrease? Why? _____

_____

   c. Would you say that year 5 was a year of full employment? _____

   d. Why is the task of maintaining full employment over the years more than just a problem of finding jobs for those who happen to be employed at any given time?

_____

2. In the space below, indicate for each of the following situations the effects of an increase in total spending on **real GNP, nominal GNP,** the **unemployment rate,** and the **price level,** respectively, using the following symbols: A, little or no effect; B, increase; C, decrease; and D, sharp increase.

   a. Depression and widespread unemployment

_____ _____ _____ _____

   b. Prosperity, but moderate unemployment

_____ _____ _____ _____

   c. Prosperity and full employment

_____ _____ _____ _____

3. Indicate in the space to the right of each of the following the most likely effect—beneficial (B), detrimental (D), or indeterminate (I)—of unanticipated inflation on these persons:

   a. A retired business executive who now lives each month by spending a part of the amount that was saved and deposited in a savings and loan association.

_____

   b. A retired private-school teacher who lives on the dividends received from the shares of stock owned.

_____

   c. A farmer who (by mortgaging a farm) borrowed at the local bank $500,000 that must be repaid during the next

ten years. _____

   d. A retired couple whose sole source of income is the pension they receive from a former employer.

_____

   e. A widow whose income consists entirely of interest received from the corporate bonds she owns.

_____

   f. A public school teacher. _____

   g. A member of union who works for a firm that produces

computers. _____

4. Suppose that in 1990 the economy is at full employment, has a potential and actual real GNP of $3000 billion, and an unemployment rate of 6%.

   a. Compute the GNP gap in 1990 and enter it in the table below.

Year	Potential GNP	Actual GNP	GNP gap
1990	$3000	$3000	$_____
1991	3800	3705	_____
1992	4125	3712.5	_____

   b. The potential and actual real GNPs in 1991 and 1992 are also shown in the table. Compute and enter into the table the GNP gaps in these two years.

   c. In 1991 the actual real GNP is _____ % of the potential real GNP. (**Hint:** divide the actual real GNP by the potential real GNP.)

   (1) The actual real GNP is _____ % *less* than the potential real GNP.

(2) Using Okun's law, the unemployment rate will rise from 6% in 1990 and be _____ % in 1991.

d. In 1992 the actual real GNP is _____ % of the potential real GNP.

(1) The actual real GNP is _____% *less* than the potential real GNP.
(2) The unemployment rate, according to Okun's law, will be _____%.

5. The table below shows the price index in the economy at the end of four different years.

Year	Price index	Rate of inflation
1	100.00	
2	112.00	_____%
3	123.20	_____
4	129.36	_____

a. Compute and enter in the table the rates of inflation in years 2, 3, and 4.
b. Employing the "rule of 70," how many years would it take for the price level to double at each of these three inflation rates? _____

_____

c. If nominal income increased by 15% from year 1 to year 2, what was the approximate percentage change in real income? _____
d. If nominal income increased by 7% from year 2 to year 3, what was the approximate percentage change in real income? _____
e. If nominal income was $25,000 in year 2, what was real income that year? _____
f. If nominal income was $25,000 in year 3, what was real income that year? _____
g. If the nominal interest rate was 14% to borrow money from year 1 to year 2, what was the approximate real rate of interest over that period? _____
h. If the nominal interest rate was 8% to borrow money from year 3 to year 4, what was the approximate real rate of interest over that period? _____

6. On the two graphs in the next column the price *level* is measured along the vertical axis and real *national* output is measured along the horizontal axis. The demand for and the supply of national output are shown by the curves labeled *D* and *S*.
a. Applying the principles of dermand and supply which you learned in Chapter 4, the equilibrium price level is the price level at which the national output demanded and the

national output supplied are _____

and the equilibrium national output is _____

_____

b. Draw on the first graph a new demand curve which represents an *increase* in the demand for national output.

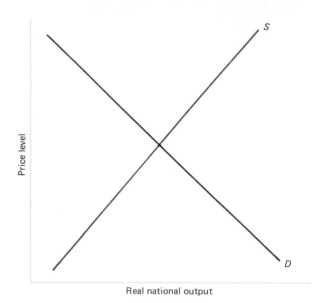

Real national output

(1) The effect of this increase in demand is a rise in the equilibrium price level and a(n) _____ in the equilibrium national output.

(2) This rise in the price level is an example of _____

_____ inflation.

c. On the graph below draw a new supply curve which represents a *decrease* in the supply of national output.

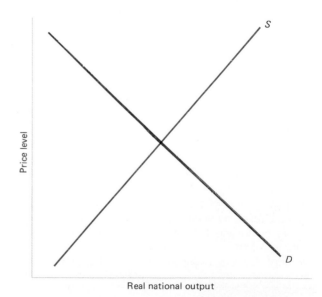

Real national output

(1) The effect of this decrease in supply is a _____

in the equilibrium price level and a _____
in the equilibrium national output.

(2) These effects are an example of _____

_____

■ SELF-TEST

Circle the T if the statement is true, the F if it is false.

1. The American economy has experienced a long period of substantial economic growth and shorter periods of inflation and of high unemployment. **T F**

2. The business cycle is best defined as alternating periods of increases and decreases in the rate of inflation in the economy. **T F**

3. Individual business cycles tend to be of roughly equal duration and intensity. **T F**

4. Not all changes which occur in output and employment in the economy are due to the business cycle. **T F**

5. Industries which are highly concentrated show small relative decreases in output and large relative decreases in prices during a downswing of the business cycle. **T F**

6. Frictional unemployment is not only inevitable but largely desirable. **T F**

7. The essential difference between frictionally and structurally unemployed workers is that the former do *not* have and the latter do have salable skills. **T F**

8. When the number of people seeking employment is less than the number of job vacancies in the economy the actual rate of unemployment is less than the natural rate of unemployment and the price level will tend to rise. **T F**

9. If unemployment in the economy is at its natural rate the actual and potential outputs of the economy are equal. **T F**

10. The natural rate of unemployment in the American economy is a constant 6% of the labor force. **T F**

11. An economy cannot produce an actual real GNP that exceeds its potential real GNP. **T F**

12. The unemployment rate is equal to the number of persons in the labor force divided by the number of people who are unemployed. **T F**

13. The percentage of the labor force unemployed for fifteen or more weeks is always less than the unemployment rate and tends to rise during a recession. **T F**

14. The economy's GNP gap is measured by deducting its actual GNP from its potential GNP. **T F**

15. The economic cost of cyclical unemployment is the goods and services that are not produced. **T F**

16. Inflation is defined as an increase in the total output of an economy. **T F**

17. Between 1984 and 1985 the consumer price index rose from 311.1 to 322.2. The rate of inflation was, therefore, 5.6%. **T F**

18. If the price level increases by 10% each year the price level will double every ten years. **T F**

19. With a moderate amount of unemployment in the economy, an increase in aggregate spending will generally increase both the price level and the output of the economy. **T F**

20. If the economy is operating at full employment a decrease in total spending can be expected to reduce both the price level and employment in the economy. **T F**

21. A person's real income is the amount of goods and services which the person's nominal (or money) income will enable him or her to purchase. **T F**

22. Whether inflation is anticipated or unanticipated, the effects of inflation on the distribution of income are much the same. **T F**

23. Suppose a household has $10,000 on deposit in a savings and loan association upon which it earns 7% interest during a year and the rate of inflation is 9% in that year. By the end of the year the purchasing power of the $10,000 and the interest it has earned will have decreased to about $9,817. **T F**

24. Unemployment and inflation rates vary greatly among major industrialized nations. **T F**

25. Inflation in the United States has transferred wealth from the public sector to the households of the economy. **T F**

Circle the letter that corresponds to the best answer.

1. Which one of the following is *not* one of the four phases of an idealized business cycle?
(*a*) inflation
(*b*) recession
(*c*) recovery
(*d*) trough

2. Most economists believe that the immediate determinant of the levels of national output and employment is:
(*a*) the price level
(*b*) the size of the civilian labor force

(c) the nation's stock of capital goods
(d) the level of aggregate spending

3. Total employment in December of this year was greater than total employment in December of 1928. This is no doubt due to the effect of:
(a) seasonal variations
(b) secular trend
(c) the business cycle
(d) business fluctuations

4. If employment in the agricultural sector of the American economy during last August and September was 112% of what it normally is in those months, this is probably a consequence of:
(a) seasonal variations
(b) secular trend
(c) the business cycle
(d) both seasonal variations and the business cycle

5. Production and employment in which of the following industries would be least affected by a depression?
(a) nondurable consumer goods
(b) durable consumer goods
(c) capital goods
(d) iron and steel

6. A worker who loses a job at a petroleum refinery because consumers and business firms switch from the use of oil to the burning of coal is an example of:
(a) frictional unemployment
(b) structural unemployment
(c) cyclical unemployment
(d) disguised unemployment

7. A worker who has quit one job and is taking two weeks off before reporting to a new job is an example of:
(a) frictional unemployment
(b) structural unemployment
(c) cyclical unemployment
(d) disguised unemployment

8. Insufficient aggregate demand results in:
(a) frictional unemployment
(b) structural unemployment
(c) cyclical unemployment
(d) disguised unemployment

9. The full-employment unemployment rate in the economy has been achieved when:
(a) frictional unemployment is zero
(b) structural unemployment is zero
(c) cyclical unemployment is zero
(d) the natural rate of unemployment is zero

10. Which of the following has increased the natural rate of unemployment in the United States?

(a) the increased participation of women in the American labor force
(b) the expansion of unemployment compensation
(c) having more young workers in the labor force
(d) all of the above

11. The labor force includes those who are:
(a) under sixteen years of age
(b) in mental institutions
(c) not seeking work
(d) employed

12. The data collected by the Bureau of Labor Statistics have been criticized because:
(a) part-time workers are not counted in the number of workers employed
(b) discouraged workers are treated as a part of the labor force
(c) some workers who are not looking for work are included in the labor force
(d) all of the above

13. Okun's law predicts that when the actual unemployment rate exceeds the natural rate of unemployment by two percentage points the GNP gap will equal:
(a) 2% of the potential GNP
(b) 3% of the potential GNP
(c) 4% of the potential GNP
(d) 5% of the potential GNP

14. If the GNP gap were equal to 7.5% of the potential GNP the actual unemployment rate would exceed the natural rate of unemployment by:
(a) two percentage points
(b) three percentage points
(c) four percentage points
(d) five percentage points

15. The burden of unemployment is *least* felt by:
(a) white-collar workers
(b) teenagers
(c) blacks
(d) males

16. If the resources of the economy are fully employed, an increase in aggregate spending will cause:
(a) output and employment to increase
(b) output and prices to increase
(c) nominal incomes and prices to increase
(d) employment and nominal incomes to increase

17. If the economy is experiencing a depression with substantial unemployment, an increase in total spending will cause:
(a) a decrease in the *real* income of the economy
(b) little or no increase in the level of prices

(*c*) an increase in the *real* income and a decrease in the *nominal* income of the economy

(*d*) proportionate increases in the price level, output, and income in the economy

18. If a person's nominal income increases by 8% while the price level increases by 10% the person's real income will have:
(*a*) increased by 2%
(*b*) increased by 18%
(*c*) decreased by 18%
(*d*) decreased by 2%

19. If no inflation were anticipated a bank would be willing to lend a business firm $10 million at an annual interest rate of 8%. If the rate of inflation were expected to be 6% the bank would charge the firm an annual interest rate of:
(*a*) 2%
(*b*) 6%
(*c*) 8%
(*d*) 14%

20. Which of the following would *not* be hurt by unanticipated inflation?
(*a*) those living on fixed nominal incomes
(*b*) those who find prices rising more rapidly than their nominal incomes
(*c*) those who have money savings
(*d*) those who became debtors when prices were lower

21. Mild demand-pull inflation, many economists argue, results in:
(*a*) rising output
(*b*) rising real income
(*c*) falling unemployment
(*d*) all of the above

22. Which of the following is *not* related to the cost-push theory of inflation?
(*a*) an increase in employment and output
(*b*) an increase in per unit production costs
(*c*) excessive wage gains
(*d*) supply-shocks

23. Which of the following is *not* associated with hyper-inflation?
(*a*) war or its aftermath
(*b*) rising output in the economy
(*c*) the hoarding of goods and speculation
(*d*) a halt to the use of money as both a medium of exchange and a standard of value

24. Inflation in the American economy has been caused by:
(*a*) increases in aggregate demand
(*b*) decreases in aggregate supply
(*c*) either *a* or *b*
(*d*) both *a* and *b*

25. Since 1983:
(*a*) both the rate of inflation and the unemployment rate have increased
(*b*) the rate of inflation has increased and the unemployment rate has decreased
(*c*) the rate of inflation has increased and the unemployment rate has decreased
(*d*) both the rate of inflation and the unemployment rate have decreased

■ **DISCUSSION QUESTIONS**

1. What is the historical record of American economy with respect to economic growth, full employment, and price-level stability?

2. Define the business cycle. Why do some economists prefer the term "business fluctuations" to "business cycle"? Describe the four phases of an idealized cycle.

3. What, in the opinion of most economists, is the immediate determinant or cause of the levels of output and employment in the economy?

4. The business cycle is only one of three general causes of changes in output and employment in the economy. What are the other influences which affect these variables?

5. Compare the manner in which the business cycle affects output and employment in the industries producing capital and durable goods with industries producing nondurable goods and services. What causes these differences?

6. Distinguish between frictional, structural, and cyclical unemployment.

7. When is there full employment in the American economy? (Answer in terms of the unemployment rate, the actual and potential output of the economy, and the markets for labor.)

8. How is the unemployment rate measured in the United States? What criticisms have been made of the method used by the Bureau of Labor Statistics to determine the unemployment rate?

9. What is the economic cost of unemployment and how is this cost measured? What is the quantitative relationship (called Okun's law) between the unemployment rate and the cost of unemployment?

10. What groups in the economy tend to bear the burdens of unemployment? How are women affected by unemployment and how is the percentage of the labor force unemployed fifteen or more weeks related to the unemployment rate in the economy?

11. What is inflation and how is the rate of inflation measured?

12. Compare and contrast demand-pull and cost-push inflation.

13. What groups benefit from and what groups are hurt by inflation and how has the public sector of the economy been affected by it?

14. What is the difference between the effects of unanticipated and the effects of anticipated inflation on the redistribution of real incomes in the economy?

15. Explain what will tend to happen to employment, output, money income, and the price level if total spending increases and the resources of the economy are: (*a*) widely unemployed, (*b*) moderately unemployed, (*c*) fully employed. If total spending *decreased* would the effects on employment, output, income, and the price level be just the opposite?

16. Write three scenarios that describe the effects of inflation on the national output.

17. How do the unemployment rate and inflation rate in the United States compare with those for other industrialized nations in recent years?

■ **ANSWERS**

CHAPTER 10 MACROECONOMIC INSTABILITY: UNEMPLOYMENT AND INFLATION

Fill-in questions

1. unsteady, inflation, output, employment

2. ups (increases), downs (decreases), recession, trough, recovery

3. spending, demand

4. seasonal, secular

5. durable, capital, nondurable, low-

6. *a.* frictional unemployment; *b.* structural unemployment; *c.* cyclical unemployment (any order)

7. *a.* natural; *b.* frictional, structural (either order); *c.* cyclical, actual, potential (either order); *d.* 5 to 6

8. equal to, constant

9. the number of unemployed persons, labor force

10. the potential, the actual, increase, 2.5

11. black, teenage, blue-collar, less

12. rise (increase), prices, 1990, 1989, 1989

13. *a.* an increase; *b.* per unit production costs, wages, nonwage inputs; *c.* difficult

14. real income; *a.* real income, 3; *b.* real income, $28,301.88

15. *a.* fixed; *b.* unexpected; *c.* creditors, debtors; *d.* households, the public sector

16. anticipated; *a.* Cost-of-Living Adjustments (COLA); *b.* real rate of interest, nominal rate of interest

17. *a.* increase; *b.* decrease; *c.* breakdown (collapse)

Problems and projects

1. year 1: 4,093, 4.8; year 5: 7,929, 8.3; *a.* the labor force increased more than employment increased; *b.* because unemployment and employment in relative terms are percentages of the labor force and *always* add to 100%, and if one increases the other must decrease; *c.* no economist would argue that the full-employment unemployment rate is as high as 8.3% and year 5 was not a year of full employment; *d.* the number of people looking for work expands

2. *a.* B, B, C, A; *b.* B, B, C, B; *c.* A, D, A, D

3. *a.* D; *b.* I; *c.* B; *d.* D; *e.* D; *f.* I; *g.* B

4. *a.* 0; *b.* 95, 412.5; *c.* 97.5, (1) 2.5, (2) 7; *d.* 90, (1) 10, (2) 10

5. *a.* 12, 10, 5; *b.* 5.83, 7, 14; *c.* 3; *d.* −3; *e.* $22,321; *f.* $20,292; *g.* 2; *h.* 3

6. *a.* equal, the national output demanded and supplied at the equilibrium price level; *b.* (1) increase, (2) demand-pull; *c.* (1) rise, fall, (2) cost-push inflation

Self-test

1. T; **2.** F; **3.** F; **4.** T; **5.** F; **6.** T; **7.** F; **8.** T; **9.** T; **10.** F; **11.** F; **12.** F; **13.** T; **14.** T; **15.** T; **16.** F; **17.** F; **18.** F; **19.** T; **20.** F; **21.** T; **22.** F; **23.** T; **24.** T; **25.** F

1. *a;* **2.** *d;* **3.** *b;* **4.** *c;* **5.** *a;* **6.** *b;* **7.** *a;* **8.** *c;* **9.** *c;* **10.** *d;* **11.** *d;* **12.** *c;* **13.** *d;* **14.** *b;* **15.** *a;* **16.** *c;* **17.** *b;* **18.** *d;* **19.** *d;* **20.** *d;* **21.** *d;* **22.** *a;* **23.** *b;* **24.** *d;* **25.** *d*

CHAPTER II

Macroeconomic analysis: aggregate demand and aggregate supply

You learned in Chapter 9 how the GNP and the NNP are measured and how to adjust them when the price level changes to find the real GNP and the real NNP. Then in Chapter 10 you found that over the years the American economy has at times suffered from unemployment, has at other times experienced inflation, and has at still other times had both unemployment and inflation.

In Chapter 11 you will begin learning what determines how large the real national output (the real GNP or NNP) and the price level at any time will be; what causes them to change; and what policies the Federal government can use to prevent unemployment and inflation.

The tools employed to explain what determines the economy's real output and price level are demand and supply. You first encountered these tools in Chapter 4 where they were used to explain what determines the output and the price of a particular product. These same tools are now employed in a slightly different way. To use these tools of aggregate demand and aggregate supply you will have to think not of the price of a particular good or service but of the price level in the economy. And instead of thinking about the quantity of a particular good or service demanded or supplied it is necessary to think about the total (the aggregate) quantity of all final goods and services demanded (purchased) and supplied (produced) in the economy. You will have no difficulty with the way demand and supply are used in this chapter once you adjust the way you think about them from a particular good or service and its price to all final goods and services and their average price.

Having made this adjustment in your way of thinking about demand and supply, the rest is not too difficult. The aggregate demand curve is downsloping because of the interest-rate, real-balances, and foreign-purchases effects of changes in the price level. With the downsloping aggregate demand, changes in the price level cause changes in the level of spending by domestic consumers, businesses, government, and foreign buyers that affect the amount of real national output, assuming **other things equal**. This change would be equivalent to a movement along an existing aggregate-demand curve: a lower price level increases the quantity of real national output and a higher price level decreases the quantity of real national output. But other things may not be equal and so the entire aggregate-demand curve can also shift due to a change in one of the nonprice level determinants of aggregate demand. You should pay attention to these "aggregate-demand shifters" that are outlined in Table 11–1.

The aggregate-supply curve differs from the shape of the aggregate-demand curve because it reflects what happens to per unit production costs as real national output increases or decreases. For the purposes of this analysis, it has three ranges: (1) at low level of real national output, the price level is relatively constant, so the aggregate-supply curve in this range is horizontal; (2) at high level of real national output, aggregate-supply curve is vertical; and (3) in the intermediate range, the level of real national output rises along with the price level, so the curve is upsloping.

You should remember that an assumption has also been made that other things are equal, when one moves along an aggregate-supply curve. When other things change, then the aggregate-supply curve can shift. The nonprice level determinants of aggregate supply include changes in input prices, changes in productivity, and changes in the legal and institutional environment for production.

Like the ordinary demand and supply curves of Chapter 4, the intersection of the aggregate demand and the aggregate supply curves determines equilibrium quantity and price: the equilibrium quantity is the equilibrium real national output and the equilibrium price is the equilibrium price level. With the knowledge of how aggregate demand and supply determine the real national output and the price level you have acquired the ability to explain the basic causes of inflation (an increase in demand or a decrease in supply), of a decrease in national output and employment (a decrease in demand or in supply).

Aggregate demand and aggregate supply are the skeleton upon which macroeconomic theory and policies are based. The next nine chapters "flesh-out" this skeleton. As you study these chapters you may forget the aggregate-demand-aggregate-supply framework. Don't!

■ CHECKLIST

When you have studied this chapter you should be able to:

☐ Define aggregate demand and aggregate supply.

☐ Explain why the aggregate-demand curve slopes downward.

☐ Identify the major nonprice level determinants of aggregate demand and explain how they shift the aggregate-demand curve.

☐ Describe the shape of the aggregate supply curve and name the three ranges on it.

☐ List the major nonprice level determinants of aggregate supply and describe how they shift the aggregate-supply curve.

☐ Explain what the real national output and price level will be in equilibrium and why the economy will tend to produce this output and price level (rather than another combination).

☐ State the effects on the real national output and on the price level of an increase in aggregate demand when the economy is in the Keynesian, classical, and intermediate ranges.

☐ Explain why a decrease in aggregate demand will not reduce the price level so much as an equal increase in aggregate demand would have raised it.

■ CHAPTER OUTLINE

1. Aggregate demand and aggregate supply determine the real national output and the price level of the economy; and are used in this chapter to explain why output and the price level fluctuate.

2. Aggregate demand is a curve which shows the total quantity of goods and services that will be purchased (demanded) at different price levels; and the curve slopes downward for three reasons.

a. With the supply of money fixed, an increase in the price level increases the demand for money, increases interest rates, and as a result reduces those expenditures (by consumers and business firms) which are sensitive to increased interest rates; and a decrease in the price level has the opposite effects.

b. An increase in the price level also decreases the purchasing power of financial assets with a fixed money value, and because those who own such assets are now poorer they spend less for goods and services; and a decrease in the price level has the opposite effects.

c. In addition, an increase in the price level (relative to foreign price levels) will reduce American exports, expand American imports, and decrease the quantity of goods and services demanded in the American economy; and a

decrease in the price level (relative to foreign price levels) will have opposite effects.

3. Spending by domestic consumers, businesses, government, and foreign buyers that is independent of changes in the price level shifts aggregate demand, as outlined in Table 11–1.

a. For domestic consumers, increases in wealth, improved expectations, reductions in indebtedness, or lower taxes can increase consumer spending and aggregate demand; decreases in consumer wealth, less positive expectations, increases in indebtedness, and higher taxes decrease consumer spending and aggregate demand.

b. For businesses, lower interest rates, improved profit expectations, lower taxes, improved technology, and less excess capacity may increase investment spending and aggregate demand; whereas higher interest rates, worse profit expectations, higher taxes, and more excess capacity may retard investment spending and aggregate demand.

c. More government spending tends to increase aggregate demand and less government spending will decrease it, assuming that tax collections and interest rates do not change as a result.

d. Net export spending and aggregate demand is increased by increases in the national incomes of other nations and by a dollar depreciation; declines in the incomes of foreign buyers and a dollar appreciation tend to reduce net exports and aggregate demand.

4. Aggregate supply is a curve that shows the total quantity of goods and services that will be produced (supplied) at different price levels; and the curve has three ranges.

a. In the Keynesian range (when the economy is in a severe recession or depression) the aggregate supply curve is horizontal; the price level need not rise to induce producers to supply larger quantities of goods and services.

b. In the classical range (when the economy is at full employment) the aggregate supply curve is vertical: a rise in the price level cannot result in an increase in the quantity of goods and services supplied.

c. Between these two ranges is the intermediate range in which the supply curve slopes upward: the price level must rise to induce producers to supply larger quantities of goods and services.

5. Factors that shift the aggregate-supply curve include changes in the prices of inputs for production, changes in productivity, and changes in the legal and institutional environment in the economy, as outlined in Table 11–2.

a. Lower prices for productive domestic resources (land, labor, capital, and entrepreneurial ability) and imported resources tend to reduce unit costs of production and increase aggregate supply, whereas higher input prices, which may be brought about by more market power on the part of resource suppliers, will tend to decrease aggregate supply.

b. As productivity improves, per unit production costs fall and aggregate supply increases; the converse occurs when productivity falls.

c. A decrease in the level of business taxation or reduced regulation of business may improve the business environment and increase aggregate supply; the opposite actions may reduce aggregate supply.

6. The equilibrium real national output and the equilibrium price level are at the intersection of the aggregate-demand and the aggregate-supply curves. Were the actual output greater (less) than the equilibrium output producers would find that their inventories were increasing (decreasing) and they would contract (expand) their output to the equilibrium output.

a. An increase in aggregate demand in:

(1) the Keynesian range would result in an increase in real output but the price level would remain unchanged;

(2) the classical range would result in an increase in the price level but the real national output would remain unchanged;

(3) the intermediate range would result in an increase in both real national output and the price level.

b. But a decrease in aggregate demand would not have the opposite effect on the price level because prices (for several reasons) tend to be inflexible (sticky) downward.

c. A decrease in aggregate supply means there will be a decrease in real national output (economic growth) and employment, and at the same time a rise in the price level, or cost-push inflation.

d. An increase in aggregate supply, however, has the beneficial effects of improving real national output and employment, while simultaneously reducing the price level.

■ IMPORTANT TERMS

Aggregation	**Classical range**
Aggregates	**Intermediate range**
Aggregate-demand curve	**Non-price-level determinants of aggregate supply**
Interest-rate effect	
Wealth or real balances effect	**Productivity**
Foreign-purchases effect	**Equilibrium price level**
Non-price-level determinants of aggregate demand	**Equilibrium real national output**
	Demand-pull inflation
Aggregate-supply curve	**Cost-push inflation**
Keynesian range	**Ratchet effect**

■ FILL-IN QUESTIONS

1. Aggregate demand and aggregate supply together determine the equilibrium real national _____ and the equilibrium price _____

2. The aggregate-demand curve shows the quantity of goods and services that will be _____ at various price _____

a. It slopes (upward, downward) _____

b. because of the _____,

the _____,

and the _____effects.

3. For the aggregate-demand curve:

a. An increase in the price level leads to a(n) (increase, decrease) _____ in the quantity of real national output;

b. whereas a decrease in the price level leads to a(n) _____ in the quantity of real national output,

c. assuming _____

4. When the price level changes:

a. there is a (movement along, change in) _____ _____ the aggregate-demand curve;

b. when the entire aggregate-demand curve shifts, there is a (change in the quantity of real output demanded, change in aggregate demand) _____,

c. and that change is caused by one or more of the _____ of aggregate demand.

5. List the nonprice level determinants of aggregate demand by type:

a. From changes in consumer spending due to changes in:

(1) _____

(2) _____

(3) _____

(4) _____

b. From changes in investment spending due to changes in:

(1) _____

(2) _____

(3) _____

(4) _____

(5) _____

c. From government due to changes in:

(1) _____

d. From net export spending due to changes in:

(1) _____

(2) _____

6. The aggregate-supply curve shows the quantity of goods and services that will be _____ at various price _____; and in the:

a. Keynesian range is (vertical, horizontal, upsloping)

_____

b. the intermediate range is _____

c. the classical range is _____

7. The basic cause of a decrease in aggregate supply is a(n) (increase, decrease) _____ in the per unit costs of producing goods and services; and the basic cause of an increase in aggregate supply is _____

_____ , all other things equal.

8. List the nonprice level determinants of aggregate supply:

a. From a change in input prices due to a change in:

(1) _____

(2) _____

(3) _____

b. From a change in _____

c. From a change in the legal and institutional environment due to a change in:

(1) _____

(2) _____

9. The equilibrium real national output and price level are found at the _____ of the aggregate-demand and the aggregate-supply curves.

a. At this price level the aggregate quantity of goods and services _____ is equal to the aggregate quantity of goods and services

_____

b. And at this real national output the prices producers

are willing to (pay, accept) _____ are equal to the prices buyers are willing to _____

10. Were the actual real national output:

a. greater than the equilibrium national output producers would find that their inventories are (increasing, decreasing) _____ and they would (expand, reduce) _____ their production;

b. less than the equilibrium national output producers would find that their inventories are _____ and they would _____ their production.

11. When the economy is producing in:

a. the Keynesian range an increase in aggregate demand will (increase, decrease, have no effect on) _____ real national output and will _____ the price level;

b. the intermediate range an increase in aggregate demand will _____ real national output and will _____ the price level;

c. the classical range an increase in aggregate demand will _____ real national output and will _____ the price level.

12. Were the economy operating in the intermediate or classical ranges and aggregate demand were to decrease, the price level would decline by (a larger, a smaller, the same) _____ amount as an equal increase in aggregate demand would have raised the price level; this is called the (interest-rate, real-balances, ratchet) _____ effect.

13. An increase in aggregate supply will not only (raise, lower) _____ real national output and (lead to, prevent) _____ inflation but will also (increase, decrease) _____ the full-employment level of national output; a decrease in aggregate supply will _____ real output and _____ the price level.

14. Demand-pull inflation is the result of a(n) (increase, decrease) _____ in aggregate demand and is accompanied by a (rise, fall) _____ in real output; but cost-push inflation is the result of a(n)

_____ in aggregate supply and is accompanied by a _____

■ **PROBLEMS AND PROJECTS**

1. In the table below is an aggregate-supply schedule.

Price level	Real national output supplied
250	2000
225	2000
200	1900
175	1700
150	1400
125	1000
125	500
125	0

a. The economy is in the:
(1) Keynesian range when the real national output is

between _____ and _____
(2) classical range when the real national output is

_____ and the price level is _____
or more
(3) intermediate range when the real national output is

between _____ and _____
b. Plot this aggregate-supply schedule on the graph below.

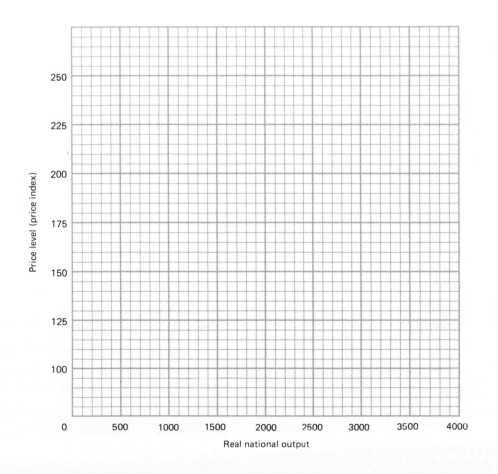

c. In the table below are three aggregate-demand schedules.

| | Real national output demanded | | |
Price level (1)	(2)	(3)	(4)
250	1400	1900	400
225	1500	2000	500
200	1600	2100	600
175	1700	2200	700
150	1800	2300	800
125	1900	2400	900
100	2000	2500	1000

(1) Plot the aggregate-demand curve shown in columns (1) and (2) on the graph on the previous page; and label this curve D_1. At this level of aggregate demand the equilibrium real national output is _____ and the equilibrium price level is _____

(2) On the same graph plot the aggregate-demand curve shown in columns (1) and (3); and label this curve D_2. The equilibrium real national output is _____ and the equilibrium price level is _____

(3) Now plot the aggregate-demand curve in columns (1) and (4) and label it D_3. The equilibrium real national output is _____ and the equilibrium price level is _____

2. In the diagram in the next column are an aggregate-supply curve and six aggregate demand curves.

a. The movements of the aggregate-demand curves from D_1 to D_2, from D_3 to D_4, and from D_5 to D_6 all portray (increases, decreases) _____ in aggregate demand.

(1) The movement from D_1 to D_2 increases the (real national output, price level) _____ but does not change the _____

(2) The movement from D_3 to D_4 will (raise, lower) _____ the price level and will (expand, contract) _____ the real national output.

(3) The movement from D_5 to D_6 will _____

b. The movements of the aggregate-demand curves to the left all portray (increases, decreases) _____ in aggregate demand.

(1) If prices are flexible in a downward direction, what effects will these changes in aggregate demand have upon the real national output and the price level? _____

(2) If prices are **not** flexible in a downward direction, what effects will these changes in aggregate demand have? _____

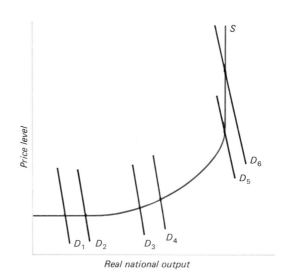

Real national output

3. In the diagram on the next page there are two aggregate-supply curves and three aggregate-demand curves.

a. The movement of the aggregate-supply curve from S_1 to S_2 represents a(n) (increase, decrease) _____ in aggregate supply.

(1) If the price level is flexible downward and upward, this change in aggregate supply in each of the three ranges along the aggregate supply curve will (raise, lower) _____ the price level and (expand, contract) _____ the real national output.

(2) But if prices are inflexible in a downward direction, this change in aggregate supply will (increase, decrease) _____ real national output but (will, will not) _____ affect the price level.

b. The movement of aggregate supply from S_2 to S_1 portrays a(n) _____ in aggregate supply and in each of the three ranges will _____ the price level and _____ the real national output.

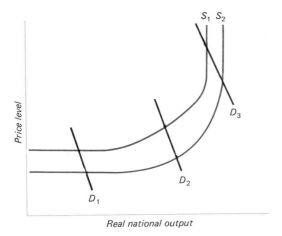

Real national output

■ **SELF-TEST**

Circle the T if the statement is true, the F if it is false.

1. The aggregate-demand curve slopes downward. **T   F**

2. A fall in the price level increases the real value of financial assets with fixed money values and, as a result, increases spending by the holders of these assets. **T   F**

3. A fall in the price level reduces the demand for money in the economy and drives interest rates upward. **T   F**

4. A rise in the price level of an economy (relative to foreign price levels) tends to increase that economy's exports and to reduce its imports of goods and services. **T   F**

5. The aggregate-supply curve is horizontal in the classical range. **T   F**

6. At the equilibrium price level the real national output purchased is equal to the real national output produced. **T   F**

7. In the intermediate range on the aggregate-supply curve an increase in aggregate demand will increase both the price level and the real national output. **T   F**

8. A decrease in aggregate demand will lower the price level by the same amount as an equal increase in aggregate demand would have raised it. **T   F**

9. An increase in aggregate supply increases both the equilibrium real national output and the full-employment output of the economy. **T   F**

10. A decrease in aggregate supply is "doubly good" because it increases the real national output and prevents inflation. **T   F**

11. Aggregation in macroeconomics is the process of combining all the prices of individual products and ser-

vices into a price level and merging all the equilibrium quantities into real national output. **T   F**

12. Per unit production cost is determined by dividing total input cost by units of output. **T   F**

13. A change in aggregate demand is caused by a change in the price level, **other things equal**. **T   F**

14. A fall in excess capacity, or unused existing capital goods, will retard the demand for new capital goods and therefore reduce aggregate demand. **T   F**

15. The wealth or real-balances effect is one of the non-price-level determinants of aggregate demand. **T   F**

16. A high level of consumer indebtedness will tend to increase consumption spending and aggregate demand. **T   F**

17. Appreciation of the dollar relative to foreign currencies will tend to lift net exports and aggregate demand. **T   F**

18. When the non-price-level determinants of aggregate supply change they alter the per unit production cost and thereby aggregate supply. **T   F**

19. Productivity is a measure of real output per unit of input. **T   F**

20. A change in the degree of market power or monopoly power held by sellers of resources can affect input prices and aggregate supply. **T   F**

Circle the letter that corresponds to the best answer.

1. The slope of the aggregate-demand curve is the result of:
  (*a*) the real balances effect
  (*b*) the interest-rate effect
  (*c*) the foreign-purchases effect
  (*d*) all of the above effects

2. The aggregate-demand curve is the relationship between the:
  (*a*) price level and the real national output purchased
  (*b*) price level and the real national output produced
  (*c*) price level which producers are willing to pay
  (*d*) real national output purchased and the real national output produced

3. The aggregate-supply curve is the relationship between the:
  (*a*) price level and the real national output purchased
  (*b*) price level and real national output produced
  (*c*) price level which producers are willing to accept and the price level purchasers are willing to pay
  (*d*) real national output purchased and the real national output produced

4. In the Keynesian range the aggregate-supply curve is:
(a) upsloping
(b) downsloping
(c) vertical
(d) horizontal

5. In the intermediate range the aggregate-supply curve is:
(a) upsloping
(b) downsloping
(c) vertical
(d) horizontal

6. An increase in aggregate supply will:
(a) reduce the price level and real national output
(b) reduce increases in the price level and increase the real national output
(c) increase the price level and real national output
(d) reduce increases in the price level and decrease the real national output

7. When the price level rises:
(a) holders of financial assets with fixed money values increase their spending
(b) the demand for money and interest rates rise
(c) spending which is sensitive to interest-rate changes increases
(d) holders of financial assets with fixed money values have more purchasing power

8. If the real national output is less than the equilibrium real national output producers find:
(a) their inventories decreasing and expand their production
(b) their inventories increasing and expand their production
(c) their inventories decreasing and contract their production
(d) their inventories increasing and contract their production

9. When the economy is in the Keynesian range an increase in aggregate demand will:
(a) increase the price level and have no effect on real national output
(b) increase the real national output and have no effect on the price level
(c) increase both real output and the price level
(d) increase the price level and decrease the real national output

10. The ratchet effect is the result of:
(a) a price level that is inflexible upward
(b) a price level that is inflexible downward
(c) a national output that cannot be increased
(d) a national output that cannot be decreased

11. If there were stagflation in the economy and aggregate supply were to increase:
(a) both the real national output and the price level would decrease
(b) the real national output would increase and rises in the price level would become smaller
(c) the real national output would decrease and the price level would rise
(d) both the real national output and rises in the price level would become greater

12. The aggregate-demand curve will tend to be increased by:
(a) a decrease in the price level
(b) an increase in the price level
(c) an increase in the excess capacity of factories
(d) a depreciation in the value of the United States dollar

13. A sharp decline in the real value of stock prices, which is independent of a change in the price level, would best be an example of:
(a) the wealth effect
(b) the real balance effect
(c) a change in real wealth
(d) a change in consumer indebtedness

Suppose that real national output in an economy is 50 units, the quantity of inputs is 10, and the price of each input is $2. Answer the next four questions (14, 15, 16, and 17) on the basis of this information.

14. The level of productivity in this economy is:
(a) 5
(b) 4
(c) 3
(d) 2

15. The per unit cost of production is:
(a) 0.40
(b) 0.50
(c) $2.50
(d) $3.50

16. If real national output in the economy rose to 60 units, then per unit production costs would:
(a) remain unchanged and aggregate supply would remain unchanged
(b) increase and aggregate supply would decrease
(c) decrease and aggregate supply would increase
(d) decrease and aggregate supply would decrease

17. All else equal, if the price of each input increases from $2 to $4, productivity would:
(a) decrease from $4 to $2 and aggregate supply would decrease
(b) decrease from $5 to $3 and aggregate supply would decrease
(c) increase from $4 to $2 and aggregate supply would increase

(d) remain unchanged and aggregate supply would remain unchanged

18. If the prices of imported resources increase, then this event would most likely:
(a) decrease aggregate supply
(b) increase aggregate supply
(c) increase aggregate demand
(d) decrease aggregate demand

19. If Congress passed much stricter laws to control the air pollution from business, then this action would tend to:
(a) increase per unit production costs and shift the aggregate-supply curve to the right
(b) increase per unit production costs and shift the aggregate-supply curve to the left
(c) increase per unit production costs and shift the aggregate-demand curve to the left
(d) decrease per unit production costs and shift the aggregate-supply curve to the left

20. An increase in business taxes will tend to:
(a) decrease aggregate demand but not change aggregate supply
(b) decrease aggregate supply but not change aggregate demand
(c) decrease aggregate demand and decrease aggregate supply
(d) decrease aggregate supply and increase aggregate demand

■ **DISCUSSION QUESTIONS**

1. What is an aggregate-demand and an aggregate supply curve?

2. Explain
(a) the interest-rate effect,
(b) the real-balances effect, and
(c) the foreign-purchases effect of change in the price level on the quantity of goods and services demanded in an economy.

3. The aggregate-supply curve is divided into three distinct ranges. Describe the slope of this curve in each of the three ranges. What conditions prevail in the economy in each of the ranges? Why is one range called the Keynesian and another called the classical range?

4. Why does the aggregate-supply curve slope upward in the intermediate range?

5. What real national output is the equilibrium real national output? Why will business firms that produce the national output reduce or expand their production when they find themselves producing more or less than the equilibrium output?

6. What are the effects on the real national output and the price level when aggregate demand increases in each of the three ranges along the aggregate-supply curve?

7. If prices were as flexible downward as they are upward, what would be the effects on real national output and the price level of a decrease in aggregate demand in each of the three ranges along the aggregate-supply curve?

8. Prices in the economy tend to be "sticky" or inflexible in a downward direction. Why? How does this downward inflexibility alter your answers to question 7 (above)?

9. What are the effects on the real national output and the price level of a decrease in aggregate supply? What are the effects of an increase in aggregate supply on the real national output, the price level, and the maximum real output the economy is able to produce?

10. Why is a decrease in aggregate supply "doubly bad" and an increase in aggregate supply "doubly good"?

11. Using the aggregate-demand and aggregate-supply concepts, explain the difference between demand-pull and cost-push inflation.

12. What roles do the expectations of consumers and businesses play in influencing aggregate demand?

13. Explain the difference between the "wealth effect" and "a change in the real value of consumer wealth" for the interpretation of aggregate demand.

14. Describe how changes in the international economy influence aggregate demand or aggregate supply.

15. How does an increase or decrease in per unit production costs change aggregate supply? Give examples.

16. Explain how a change in business taxes affects aggregate demand and aggregate supply.

17. How does the legal and institutional environment affect the price level and real national output? Give examples.

18. What is the relationship between the production possibilities curve and aggregate supply?

■ **ANSWERS**

CHAPTER 11 MACROECONOMIC ANALYSIS: AGGREGATE DEMAND AND AGGREGATE SUPPLY

Fill-in questions

1. Output, level

2. demanded (purchased), levels a. downward; b. wealth (real-balances), interest-rate, foreign-purchases (any order)

3. *a.* decrease; *b.* increase; *c.* other things equal

4. *a.* movement along; *b.* change in aggregate demand; *c.* non-price-level determinants

5. *a.* (1) consumer wealth, (2) consumer expectations, (3) consumer indebtedness, (4) personal taxes (any order); *b.* (1) interest rates, (2) profit expectations, (3) business taxes, (4) technology, (5) degree of excess capacity (any order); *c.* (1) government purchases; *d.* (1) national income of other nations; (2) exchange rates (any order)

6. supplied (produced), levels; *a.* horizontal; *b.* upsloping; *c.* vertical

7. increase, a decrease in the per unit costs of production

8. *a.* (1) domestic resource availability, (2) prices of imported resources, (3) market power (any order); *b.* productivity; *c.* (1) business taxes and subsidies, (2) government regulation (either order)

9. intersection; *a.* purchased (demanded), produced (supplied) (either order); *b.* accept, pay

10. *a.* increasing, reduce; *b.* decreasing, expand

11. *a.* increase, have no effect on; *b.* increase, increase; *c.* have no effect on, increase

12. smaller, ratchet

13. raise, prevent, increase; lower, raise

14. increase, rise, decrease, fall in real output

Problems and projects

1. *a.* (1) 0, 1000, (2) 2000, 225, (3) 1000, 2000; *c.* (1) 1700, 175, (2) 2000, 225, (3) 900, 125

2. *a.* increases, (1) real national output, price level, (2) raise, expand, (3) increase the price level but will not affect national output; *b.* decreases, (1) Decrease the price level in the classical and intermediate ranges and decrease national output in the intermediate and Keynesian ranges, (2) Decrease only output in the intermediate and Keynesian ranges

3. *a.* increase, (1) lower, expand, (2) increase, will not; *b.* decrease, increase, decrease

Self-test

1. T; **2.** T; **3.** F; **4.** F; **5.** F; **6.** T; **7.** T; **8.** F; **9.** T; **10.** F; **11.** T; **12.** T; **13.** F; **14.** F; **15.** F; **16.** F; **17.** F; **18.** T; **19.** T; **20.** T

1. *d;* **2.** *a;* **3.** *b;* **4.** *d;* **5.** *a;* **6.** *b;* **7.** *b;* **8.** *a;* **9.** *b;* **10.** *b;* **11.** *b;* **12.** *d;* **13.** *c;* **14.** *a;* **15.** *a;* **16.** *c;* **17.** *d;* **18.** *a;* **19.** *b;* **20.** *c*

Classical and Keynesian theories of employment

Chapters 12 and 13 are really one chapter which has been divided into two parts. They continue the explanation begun in the last chapter of how aggregate demand and aggregate supply determine the real national output and price level of the economy. In these two chapters you will learn what determines the total quantity of goods and services that will be purchased (or demanded) at various price levels: the focus in these chapters is on aggregate demand.

Most of the material contained in these two chapters deals with the Keynesian theory or explanation of what determines the demand for the real national output (the real NNP) and how the equilibrium level of output (and of employment) is determined. The Keynesian explanation is not the only possible explanation, however. It is with the alternative classical theory that the first part of Chapter 12 deals. The classical theory is described there for several reasons: to impress upon you the fact that an alternative theory does exist; to examine its assumptions and its "cures" for depression; and to prepare you for both Keynesian and "monetarist" macroeconomic theory.

The outstanding thing about the classical theory is its conclusion that the economy will *automatically* function to produce the maximum output it is capable of producing and to provide employment for all those who are willing and able to work. Compare this with the conclusion drawn by the exponents of the Keynesian theory that the economy functions in no such way, that both depression and inflation can prevail with no automatic tendency to be corrected, and that full employment and maximum output, when achieved, are accidental. Compare also the political philosophies of the proponents of the two theories. Those accepting the classical theory have advocated as little government interference with the economy as possible in the belief that such interference prevents the achievement of full employment and maximum output. Adherents of the Keynesian theory argue that government action is necessary to eliminate the periods of depression that occur. The basic proposition contained in the Keynesian theory is that the level of total or aggregate expenditures in the economy determines the location of the economy's aggregate-demand curve and, as a result, determines real output and employment and, as you learned in the last chapter, therefore determines the price level. The latter part of the chapter analyzes the economic factors which determine two principal components of aggregate expenditures—consumption expenditures and investment expenditures. You should pay particular attention to the relationships called the consumption schedule, the saving schedule, and their characteristics; to the four propensity concepts; and to the "non-income" determinants of consumption and saving.

Investment expenditures—that is, the purchase of capital goods—depend upon the rate of net profits which business firms **expect** to earn from an investment and upon the real rate of interest they have to pay for the use of money. Because firms are anxious to make profitable investments and to avoid unprofitable ones, they undertake all investments which have an expected rate of net profit greater than (or equal to) the real rate of interest and do not undertake an investment when the expected rate of net profit is less than the real interest rate. You should see that because business firms behave this way the lower the real rate of interest the larger will be the dollar amount invested; and that this relationship between the real interest rate and the level of investment spending, called the investment-demand schedule, is an inverse one. But you should not confuse the investment-demand schedule (or curve) with the investment schedule (or curve) which relates investment spending to the NNP and which may show investment is either unrelated to or directly related to the NNP. Five noninterest determinants of investment spending influence the profit expectations of business firms; and these are analyzed. You should learn how changes in these determinants affect investment; and why investment spending is unstable.

In the next chapter the tools and ideas developed and explained in Chapter 12 are put together to form a complete and coherent picture of how aggregate expenditures determine the level of NNP in the Keynesian theory.

■ **CHECKLIST**

When you have studied this chapter you should be able to:

☐ Contrast the views of classical and Keynesian economists on unemployment in a market (or capitalistic) economy and the type of policy government should pursue.

☐ List the three simplifying assumptions made in this and the next chapter and the two implications of these assumptions.

☐ State Say's Law and explain how classical economists were able to reason that all saving would be borrowed and spent for capital goods.

☐ Explain how classical economists were able to reason that price-wage flexibility would eliminate a recession and unemployment.

☐ Present three reasons why the rate of interest may not guarantee the quantity of saving and investment, and two reasons why price-wage flexibility may not guarantee full employment; and state the classical response to the latter Keynesian contention.

☐ Compare and contrast the classical and Keynesian views of the aggregate-demand curve and the aggregate-supply curve.

☐ State what determines the amount of goods and services produced and the level of employment in the Keynesian theory.

☐ Explain how consumption and saving are related to disposable income.

☐ Compute, when you are given the necessary data, the four propensities.

☐ Explain what happens to the size of the two average propensities as income increases.

☐ List five nonincome determinants of consumption and saving; and explain how a change in each of these determinants will affect the consumption and saving schedules.

☐ Explain the difference between a change in the amount consumed (or saved) and a change in the consumption (or saving) schedule.

☐ List the two basic determinants of investment; and explain when a firm will and will not invest.

☐ Compute, when given the appropriate data, the investment-demand schedule; and explain why the relationship between investment spending and the real rate of interest is inverse.

☐ List the five noninterest determinants of investment; and explain how a change in each of these determinants will affect the investment-demand curve.

☐ Explain the two variables found in an investment schedule; and the two kinds of relationships that might be found to exist between these two variables.

☐ List the four factors which explain why investment spending tends to be unstable.

■ **CHAPTER OUTLINE**

1. Classical economists contend that full employment is the norm in a market (or capitalistic) economy and laissez-faire is the best policy for government to pursue; but Keynesian economists argue that unemployment is typical of such economies and activist policies are required to eliminate it.

2. To simplify the explanation of Keynesian employment theory in this and the next chapter three assumptions are made: the economy is "closed," government neither spends nor collects taxes, and all saving is personal saving; and these assumptions have two important implications.

3. The classical theory of employment reached the conclusion that the economy would automatically tend to employ its resources fully and produce a full-employment level of output; this conclusion is based on Say's Law and the assumption that prices and wages are flexible.

a. Say's Law stated that the production of goods produced an equal demand for these goods because changes in the rate of interest would ensure that all income not spent (that is, income saved) by consumers would be lent to investors who would spend these borrowed funds for capital goods.

b. If there were an excess supply of goods or an excess supply of labor (unemployment), prices and wages would fall until the excesses were eliminated and full employment and maximum output again prevailed in the economy.

c. Believing that capitalism would automatically ensure a full-employment level of output, the classical economists saw no need for government interference with the operation of the economy.

4. J. M. Keynes, in *The General Theory of Employment, Interest, and Money,* denied that flexible interest rates, prices, and wages would automatically promote full employment; he set forth the theory that there was nothing automatic about full employment and that both depression and inflation might prevail without any tendency existing for them to be self-correcting.

a. According to Keynes, flexible interest rates do not guarantee that all income saved by consumers will be spent by investors for capital goods because savers and investors are different groups and are differently motivated and because saving is neither the only source of the funds to finance investment nor the only use to which consumers can put these funds.

b. Keynes also argued that prices and wages
(1) are not, in fact, flexible downward; and
(2) that even if they were a reduction in prices and wages would not reduce unemployment in the economy; but
(3) the defenders of classical theory responded that they would be flexible downward if it were not for government policies that prevented them from falling.

5. Classical and Keynesian economics can be compared by examining their aggregate demand-aggregate supply models of the economy.
a. In the classical model the aggregate-supply curve is vertical at the economy's full-employment output; and a decrease in aggregate demand will lower the equilibrium price level and have no effect on the real output of (or employment in) the economy because of Say's Law, flexible interest rates, and responsive prices and wages.
b. In the Keynesian model the aggregate-supply curve is horizontal at the current price level; and a decrease in aggregate demand will lower the real output of (and employment in) the economy and have no effect on the equilibrium price level because of the downward inflexibility of prices and wages.
c. In both the classical and Keynesian models the aggregate-demand curve slopes downward.
(1) In the classical model it slopes downward because (with a fixed money supply in the economy) a fall in the price level increases the purchasing power of money and enables consumers and business firms to purchase a larger real output; aggregate demand will be reasonably stable if the nation's monetary authorities maintain a constant supply of money.
(2) Keynesians view aggregate demand as being unstable over time, even if the supply of money is held constant, in part because of fluctuations in investment spending; and a decline in aggregate demand decreases real national output, but has no effect on the price level, thereby causing output to stay permanently below the full-employment level.

6. Aggregate output and employment in the Keynesian theory are directly related to the level of total or aggregate expenditures in the economy; and to understand what determines the level of total expenditures at any time it is necessary to explain the factors that determine the levels of consumption and investment expenditures.

7. Consumption is the largest component of aggregate expenditures; and saving is disposable income not spent for consumer goods.
a. Disposable income is the most important determinant of both consumption and saving; the relationships between income and consumption and between income and saving are both direct (positive) ones.
b. The consumption schedule shows the amounts that households plan to spend for consumer goods at various levels of income, given a price level.
c. The saving schedule indicates the amounts households plan to save at different income levels, given a price level.
d. The average propensities to consume and to save and the marginal propensities to consume and to save can be computed from the consumption and saving schedules.
(1) The APC and the APS are, respectively, the percentages of income spent for consumption and saved; and their sum is equal to 1.
(2) The MPC and the MPS are, respectively, the percentages of **additional** income spent for consumption and saved; and their sum is equal to 1.
e. In addition to income, there are several other important determinants of consumption and saving; and changes in these nonincome determinants will cause the consumption and saving **schedules** to change.
f. A change in the amount consumed (or saved) is not the same thing as a change in the consumption (or saving) schedule. If these schedules change they change in opposite directions; but the schedules are very stable.

8. The two important determinants of the level of net investment spending in the economy are the expected rate of net profits from the purchase of additional capital goods and the real rate of interest.
a. The expected rate of net profits is directly related to the net profits (revenues less operating costs) that are expected to result from an investment and inversely related to the cost of making the investment (purchasing capital goods).
b. The rate of interest is the price paid for the use of money. When the expected real rate of net profits is greater (less) than the real rate of interest a business will (will not) invest because the investment will be profitable (unprofitable).
c. For this reason, the lower (higher) the real rate of interest, the greater (smaller) will be the level of investment spending in the economy; and the investment-demand curve (schedule) indicates this inverse relationship between the real rate of interest and the level of spending for capital goods.
d. There are at least five noninterest determinants of investment demand; and a change in any of these determinants will shift the investment-demand curve (schedule).
e. Investment spending in the economy may also be either independent or directly related to the real NNP; and the investment schedule may show that investment either remains constant or increases as real NNP increases.
f. Because the five noninterest determinants of investment are subject to sudden changes, investment spending tends to be unstable.

■ **IMPORTANT TERMS**

Classical theory of employment

Say's Law

Rate of interest

Money market

Savings

Investment

Price-wage flexibility

Keynesian economics

Aggregate total expenditures

Dissaving

Consumption schedule

Saving schedule

Break-even income

Average propensity to consume

Average propensity to save

Marginal propensity to consume

Marginal propensity to save

Nonincome determinants of consumption and saving

Change in amount consumed (saved)

Change in the consumption (saving) schedule

Expected rate of net profits

Real rate of interest

Investment-demand schedule (curve)

Noninterest determinants of investment

Investment schedule (curve)

■ **FILL-IN QUESTIONS**

1. Classical economists believe a market (or capitalistic) economy will tend to produce an output at which its labor force is (fully, less than fully) _____ employed but Keynesian economists argue it will tend to produce an output at which its labor force is _____ employed; and for this reason the classical economists favor a(n) (activist, laissez faire) _____ government policy and the Keynesian economists favor a(n) _____ policy.

2. Three "simplifying assumptions" used throughout most of the chapter are that the economy is a(n) (open, closed) _____ economy, that all saving is (personal, business) _____ saving, and that government does not collect _____, make _____ payments, or _____ for goods and services. The implications of these assumptions are:

a. NNP = _____ =

_____ = _____

b. total spending = _____ +

3. Full employment, in the classical theory, was ensured by the operation of _____ Law and price-wage _____.

4. According to Say's Law, the production of goods and services creates an equal _____

5. Changes in _____, according to the classical economists, ensure that what is not spent on consumer goods is spent on capital goods.

6. In the classical theory, if saving is greater than investment the rate of interest will (rise, fall) _____; and if investment is greater than saving it will _____; and the rate of interest will move to the level at which _____ and _____ are equal.

7. According to the classical way of thinking, if the interest rate did not equate saving and investment, and if total output exceeded the level of spending, prices in the output markets would tend to (rise, fall) _____ because of competition among business firms; this would make some production unprofitable and temporarily cause _____ in labor markets; but competition among workers would tend to drive wage rates (upward, downward) _____ and (increase, decrease) _____ their employment. This process would continue until _____

8. According to the Keynesian theory of employment:
a. saving and investment are done by different _____ and for different _____
b. the funds to finance investment come not only from current saving but from the _____ of households and from _____
c. current saving may not be lent to investors in the money market but added to the money _____ of consumers or used to retire outstanding bank _____.

9. Keynes, in attacking the classical theory of employment, contended that in the modern economy prices and wages (do, do not) _____ fall when there is unemployment; and that wage reductions would lead to (smaller, larger) _____ money incomes, a (fall, rise) _____ in total spending, a(n) (increase, decrease) _____ in prices, and little or no change in total _____ in the economy.

10. Reasoning that if a price and wage-rate reduction would increase the output and employment of an individual firm, then a general reduction in prices and wages will increase output and employment in the economy as a whole is an example of the (**post hoc, ergo propter hoc** fallacy, fallacy of composition, fallacy of limited decisions)

_____

_____

11. The aggregate-supply curve of the classical economists is (horizontal, vertical) _____ and the aggregate-supply curve of the Keynesian economists is

_____ up to the full-employment level of output. Therefore, a decrease in aggregate demand will have no effect on the price level and will decrease output and employment in the (classical, Keynesian)

_____ model; but a decrease in aggregate demand will decrease the price level and have no effect on output and employment in the _____ model.

12. The views of classical and Keynesian economists also differ on the nature of the aggregate-demand curve.
 a. In the classical way of thinking, the money supply sets the basis for aggregate demand: if the price level falls and the money supply is constant, the purchasing power of

money will (rise, fall) _____ and consumers and

business firms will (expand, contract) _____ their expenditures for goods and services; aggregate demand will be reasonably stable if the nation's monetary authorities maintain a _____
 b. From the Keynesian perspective, aggregate demand

is (stable, unstable) _____, even if there are no changes in the supply of money, in part because

business investment tends to be _____

13. Keynes argued that:
 a. the national output and employment depend (directly,

inversely) _____ upon the level of aggre-

gate _____ in the economy;
 b. the most important determinant of consumption and

of saving in the economy is the economy's _____

 c. and that both consumption and saving are (directly,

inversely) _____ related to this determinant.

14. As disposable income falls, the average propensity to consume will (rise, fall) _____ and the

average propensity to save will _____

15. The most important determinants of consumption spending, other than the level of income, are:
 a. the wealth or the sum of the _____ and the

_____ assets households have accumulated

 b. _____

 c. _____

 d. _____

 e. _____

16. A change in the consumption (or saving) schedule

means that _____

_____

but a change in the amount consumed (or saved) means

that _____

17. Investment is defined as spending for additional

_____; and the total amount of investment spending in the economy depends upon:
 a. the _____ rate of net _____

 b. the real rate of _____

18. A business firm will invest in more capital if the expected rate of net profits on this investment is (greater,

less) _____ than the real rate of interest it must pay for the use of money.

19. The relation between the rate of interest and the total amount of investment in the economy is (direct, inverse)

_____

This means that if the real rate of interest:
 a. rises, investment will _____

 b. falls, investment will _____

20. Five noninterest determinants of investment demand are:
 a. _____

 b. _____

 c. _____

d. _____

e. _____

21. The consumption schedule and the saving schedule tend to be (stable or unstable) _____ while investment demand tends to be _____

_____

22. The demand for new capital goods tends to be unstable because of the _____ of capital goods, the _____ of innovation, and the _____ of actual and expected profits.

■ **PROBLEMS AND PROJECTS**

1. Below is a consumption schedule. Assume taxes and transfer payments are zero and that all saving is personal saving.

NNP	C	S	APC, %	APS, %
$1500	$1540	$_____	1.027	−.027
1600	1620	_____	1.025	−.025
1700	1700	_____	_____	_____
1800	1780	_____	.989	.011
1900	1860	_____	.979	.021
2000	1940	_____	_____	_____
2100	2020	_____	.962	.038
2200	2100	_____	_____	_____

a. Compute saving at each of the eight levels of NNP and the missing average propensities to consume and to save.
b. The break-even level of income (NNP) is $ _____
c. As NNP rises the marginal propensity to consume remains constant. Between each two NNPs the MPC can be found by dividing $ _____ by $ _____; and is equal to _____%
d. The marginal propensity to save also remains constant when the NNP rises. Between each two NNPs the MPS is equal to $ _____ divided by $ _____; or to _____%

e. Plot the consumption schedule, the saving schedule, and the 45° line on the graph on the next page.

2. Indicate in the space to the right of each of the following events whether the event will tend to increase (+) or decrease (−) the *saving* schedule.
a. Development of consumer expectations that prices will be higher in the future _____
b. Gradual shrinkage in the quantity of real assets owned by consumers _____
c. Increase in the volume of consumer indebtedness _____
d. Growing belief that disposable income will be lower in the future _____
e. Rumors that a current shortage of consumer goods will soon disappear _____
f. Rise in the actual level of disposable income _____
g. A build-up in the dollar size of the financial assets owned by consumers _____
h. Development of a belief by consumers that the Federal government can and will prevent depressions in the future _____

3. The schedule below has eight different rates of net profit and the dollar amounts of the investment projects expected to have each of these net profit rates.

Expected rate of net profit	Investment projects (billions)
18%	$ 0
16	10
14	20
12	30
10	40
8	50
6	60
4	70

a. If the real rate of interest in the economy were 18%, business firms would plan to spend $ _____ billion for investment; but if the real interest rate were 16% they would plan to spend $ _____ for investment.
b. Should the real interest rate be 14% they would still wish to make the investments they were willing to make at real interest rates of 18% and 16%; they would also plan to spend an additional $ _____ billion for investment; and their total investment would be $ _____ billion.
c. Were the real rate of interest 12% they would make all

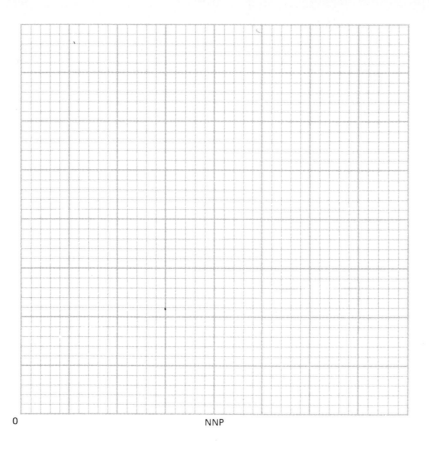

0   NNP

the investments they had planned to make at higher real interest rates plus an additional $ _____ billion; and their total investment spending would be $ _____ billion.

d. Complete the table below by computing the amount of planned investment at the four remaining real interest rates.

Real rate of interest	Amount of investment (billions)
18%	$ 0
16	10
14	30
12	60
10	_____
8	_____
6	_____
4	_____

e. Graph the schedule you completed on the graph on the next page. Plot the real rate of interest on the vertical axis and the amount of investment planned at each real rate of interest on the horizontal axis.

f. Both the graph and the table show that the relation between the real rate of interest and the amount of investment spending in the economy is _____
This means that when the real rate of interest:

(1) increases, investment will (increase, decrease)

_____

(2) decreases, investment will _____
g. It also means that should we wish to;

(1) increase investment, we would need to

_____ the real rate of interest
(2) decrease investment, we would have to

_____ the real rate of interest

h. This graph (or table) is the _____

_____ curve (or schedule).

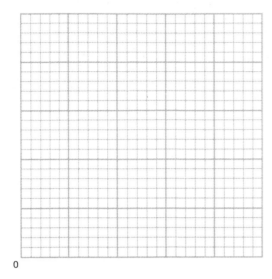

0

Schedule number 1		Schedule number 2	
NNP	I	NNP	I
$1850	$90	$1850	$ 75
1900	90	1900	80
1950	90	1950	85
2000	90	2000	90
2050	90	2050	95
2100	90	2100	100
2150	95	2150	105

a. Each of these schedules is an _____ schedule.

b. When such a schedule is drawn up it is assumed that

the real rate of interest is _____

c. In schedule:

 (1) number 1, NNP and *I* are (unrelated, directly re-

lated) _____

 (2) number 2, NNP and *I* are _____

d. Should the real rate of interest rise, investment spending at each NNP would (increase, decrease)

_____ and the curve relating NNP and investment

spending would shift (upward, downward) _____

4. Indicate in the space to the right of the following events whether the event would tend to increase (+) or decrease (−) investment expenditures.

a. Rising stock market prices ____

b. Development of expectations by businessmen that

business taxes will be higher in the future ____

c. Step-up in the rates at which new products and new

production processes are being introduced ____

d. Business belief that wage rates may be lower in the

future ____

e. A mild recession ____

f. A belief that business is "too good" and the economy

is due for a period of "slow" consumer demand ____

g. Rising costs in the construction industry ____

h. A rapid increase in the size of the economy's popula-

tion ____

i. A period of a high level of investment spending which has resulted in productive capacity in excess of the cur-

rent demand for goods and services ____

5. Below are two schedules showing several NNPs and the level of investment spending (*I*) at each NNP. (All figures are in billions of dollars.)

■ **SELF-TEST**

Circle the T if the statement is true, the F if it is false.

1. According to the classical economists, full employment is normal in market economies.   **T   F**

2. The classical economists believed that government assistance was *not* required to bring about full employ-ment and full production in the economy.   **T   F**

3. Say's Law states that demand for goods and services creates an equal supply of goods and services.   **T   F**

4. In both the classical and Keynesian theories of employ-ment saving is income not expended for consumer goods and services.   **T   F**

5. In the classical theory, if saving exceeds investment the rate of interest will rise until saving and investment are equal.   **T   F**

6. Keynesians contend that most saving is done by busi-ness firms and most investment is done by households in the economy.   **T   F**

7. Classical economists contend that prices and wages would be sufficiently flexible to assure full employment in the economy if it were not for the government policies that reduce their downward flexibility.　　　　T　F

8. The classical economists' view of aggregate demand is that if the money supply is constant a decrease in the price level will decrease the purchasing power of money and increase the quantities of goods and services demanded by consumers and business firms.　　T　F

9. The level of saving in the economy, according to the Keynesians, depends primarily upon the level of its disposable income.　　　　T　F

10. The consumption schedule which is employed as an analytical tool is also a historical record of the relationship of consumption to disposable income.　　T　F

11. Statistics show the economists tend to agree that the marginal propensity to consume rises and the marginal propensity to save falls as disposable income rises.　T　F

12. An increase in the price level will increase the consumption schedule (shift the consumption curve upward).　　　　T　F

13. An increase in the taxes paid by consumers will decrease both the amount they spend for consumption and the amount they save.　　　　T　F

14. Both the consumption schedule and the saving schedule tend to be relatively stable over time.　　T　F

15. The *real* interest rate is the nominal interest rate minus the rate of inflation.　　　　T　F

16. A business firm will purchase additional capital goods if the real rate of interest it must pay exceeds the expected rate of net profits from the investment.　　T　F

17. An increase in an economy's income may induce an increase in investment spending.　　　　T　F

18. The relationship between the rate of interest and the level of investment spending is called the investment schedule.　　　　T　F

19. The investment-demand schedule (or curve) tends to be relatively stable over time.　　　　T　F

20. The irregularity of innovations and the variability of business profits contribute to the instability of investment expenditures.　　　　T　F

Circle the letter that corresponds to the best answer.

1. Keynesian economists believe that:
(a) unemployment is characteristic of capitalistic economies and in activist government policies
(b) unemployment is characteristic of capitalistic economies and in a government policy of laissez-faire

(c) full employment is characteristic of capitalistic economies and in activist government policies
(d) full employment is characteristic of capitalistic economies and in a government policy of laissez-faire

2. If government neither taxes nor spends, and all saving done in the economy is personal saving:
(a) gross national product equals net national product
(b) gross national product equals national income
(c) net national product equals disposable income
(d) disposable income equals personal consumption expenditures

3. In the classical theory of employment, a decline in the rate of interest will:
(a) decrease saving and investment
(b) decrease saving and increase investment
(c) increase saving and decrease investment
(d) increase saving and investment

4. The classical theory predicts that an increase in the supply of savings will:
(a) lower interest rates and reduce investment
(b) raise interest rates and reduce investment
(c) lower interest rates and expand investment
(d) raise interest rates and expand investment

5. If the rate of interest did not equate saving and investment and total output was greater than total spending, the classical economists argued, competition would tend to force:
(a) product and resource prices down
(b) product prices up and resource prices down
(c) product prices up and resource prices up
(d) product prices down and resource prices up

6. Which of the following is *not* involved in Keynes's criticism of the classical theory of employment?
(a) a reduction in wage rates will lead only to a reduction in total spending, not to an increase in employment
(b) investment spending is not influenced by the rate of interest
(c) prices and wages are simply not flexible downward in modern capitalistic economies
(d) saving in modern economies depends largely upon the level of disposable income and is little influenced by the rate of interest

7. Keynesian economists argue the source of the funds which finance investment are:
(a) current saving
(b) the accumulated money balances of households
(c) commercial banks
(d) all of the above

8. The Keynesian economists also argue that saving is:
(a) used to finance investment expenditures

(b) added to the money balances of savers
(c) used to retire the loans made previously by banks
(d) utilized for all of the above

9. The Keynesian aggregate-supply curve:
(a) is horizontal
(b) slopes upward
(c) is vertical
(d) slopes downward

10. The aggregate-supply curve of classical economists:
(a) is horizontal
(b) slopes upward
(c) is vertical
(d) slopes downward

11. In the classical theory of employment a decrease in aggregate demand results in:
(a) a decrease in both the price level and national output
(b) a decrease in the price level and no change in national output
(c) no change in the price level and a decrease in national output
(d) no change in either the price level or national output

12. A decrease in aggregate demand, in the Keynesian theory of employment, results in:
(a) a decrease in both the price level and national output
(b) a decrease in the price level and no change in national output
(c) no change in the price level and a decrease in national output
(d) no change in either the price level or national output

13. In the Keynesian theory, output and employment in the economy depend:
(a) directly on the level of total expenditures
(b) inversely on the quantity of resources available to it
(c) directly on the level of disposable income
(d) directly on the rate of interest

14. As disposable income decreases, *ceteris paribus:*
(a) both consumption and saving increases
(b) consumption increases and saving decreases
(c) consumption decreases and saving increases
(d) both consumption and saving decrease

15. If consumption spending increases from $358 to $367 billion when disposable income increases from $412 to $427 billion, it can be concluded that the marginal propensity to consume is:
(a) 0.4
(b) 0.6
(c) 0.8
(d) 0.9

16. If when disposable income is $375 billion the average propensity to consume is 0.8, it can be concluded that:

(a) the marginal propensity to consume is also 0.8
(b) consumption is $325 billion
(c) saving is $75 billion
(d) the marginal propensity to save is 0.2

17. As the disposable income of the economy increases:
(a) both the APC and the APS rise
(b) the APC rises and the APS falls
(c) the APC falls and the APS rises
(d) both the APC and the APS fall

18. Which of the following would *not* cause the consumption schedule to increase (that is, cause the consumption curve to rise)?
(a) a decrease in the expected price level
(b) an increase in consumers' ownership of financial assets
(c) a decrease in the amount of consumers' indebtedness
(d) an increase in the income received by consumers

19. A decrease in the price level tends to:
(a) increase the amount consumed
(b) decrease the amount consumed
(c) shift the consumption schedule upward
(d) shift the consumption schedule downward

20. A decrease in the level of investment spending would be a consequence of:
(a) a decline in the rate of interest
(b) a decline in the level of wages paid
(c) a decline in business taxes
(d) a decline in stock market prices

21. Which of the following relationships is an inverse one?
(a) the relationship between consumption spending and disposable income
(b) the relationship between investment spending and the rate of interest
(c) the relationship between saving and the rate of interest
(d) the relationship between investment spending and net national product

22. The slope of the consumption schedule or line for a given economy is the:
(a) marginal propensity to consume
(b) average propensity to consume
(c) marginal propensity to save
(d) average propensity to save

23. According to the classical economists, aggregate demand will be reasonably stable if:
(a) aggregate supply is reasonably stable
(b) business investment does not fluctuate
(c) there is a constant supply of money
(d) interest rates are flexible

Answer the next two questions (24 and 25) on the basis of the following diagram.

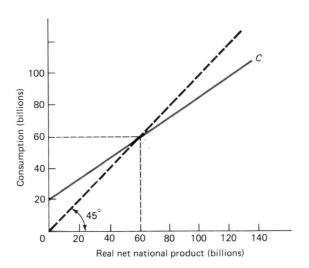

24. This diagram indicates that:

(a) consumption decreases after the $60 billion level of NNP

(b) the marginal propensity to consume decreases after the $60 billion level of NNP

(c) consumption decreases as a percentage of NNP as NNP increases

(d) consumption increases as NNP decreases

25. If the relevent saving schedule were constructed, one would find that:

(a) the marginal propensity to save is negative up to the $60 billion level of NNP

(b) the marginal propensity to save increases after the $60 billion level of NNP

(c) saving is zero at the $60 billion level of NNP

(d) saving is $20 billion at the $0 level of NNP

■ **DISCUSSION QUESTIONS**

1. How do the classical and Keynesian economists differ on

(a) the normal amount of unemployment that will prevail in a capitalistic (or market) economy; and

(b) the role they would assign to government in such an economy?

2. What are the three simplifying assumptions used in this chapter and what are the two implications of these assumptions?

3. According to the classical economists, what level of employment would tend to prevail in the economy? On

what two basic assumptions did their analysis of the level of employment rest?

4. What is Say's Law? How were the classical economists able to reason that whatever is saved is spent?

5. In the classical analysis Say's Law made it certain that whatever was produced would be sold. How did flexible prices, flexible wages, and competition drive the economy to full employment and maximum output?

6. On what grounds did J. M. Keynes argue that flexible interest rates would not assure the operation of Say's Law? What were his reasons for asserting that flexible prices and wages would not assure full employment; and what was the classical response to his assertion?

7. What is

(a) the difference between the classical and the Keynesian aggregate-supply curve; and

(b) the difference between the effects a decrease in aggregate demand would have on the price level and on the real national output in the two models? Why does the classical aggregate-demand curve have a negative (downward) slope?

8. "Savers and investors are largely different groups and are motivated by different factors." Explain in detail who these groups are and what motivates them. Does the rate of interest play any role in determining saving and investment?

9. Describe the relation between consumption and disposable income called the consumption schedule and the one between saving and disposable income known as the saving schedule; and then define the two average propensities and the two marginal propensities.

10. Explain briefly how the average propensity to consume and the average propensity to save vary as disposable income varies. Why do APC and APS behave this way? What happens to consumption and saving as disposable income varies?

11. Why do the sum of the APC and the APS and the sum of the MPC and the MPS always equal exactly one?

12. Explain briefly and explicitly **how** changes in the five nonincome determinants will affect the consumption schedule and the saving schedule and **why** such changes will affect consumption and saving in the way you have indicated.

13. Explain

(a) when a business firm will or will not purchase additional capital goods;

(b) how changes in the five noninterest determinants of investment spending will affect the investment-demand curve;

(c) why investment spending tends to rise when the rate of interest falls; and

(d) how changes in NNP might affect investment spending.

14. Why does the level of investment spending tend to be highly unstable?

15. Explain why the amount consumers spend and the amount investors spend matter all that much to the performance of the economy.

■ ANSWERS

CHAPTER 12 CLASSICAL AND KEYNESIAN THEORIES OF EMPLOYMENT

Fill-in questions

1. fully, less than fully, laissez faire, activist

2. closed, personal, taxes, transfer, spend; a. national income, personal income, disposable income; b. consumption, investment

3. Say's, flexibility

4. demand for these goods and services

5. the rate of interest

6. fall, rise, saving, investment

7. fall, unemployment, downward, increase, all who are willing to work at the going wage rate are employed and total output equals total spending

8. a. groups, reasons (motives); b. accumulated money balances, commercial banks; c. balances, loans (debts)

9. do not, smaller, fall, decrease, employment (output)

10. fallacy of composition

11. vertical, horizontal, Keynesian, classical

12. a. rise, expand, constant supply of money; b. unstable, unstable

13. a. directly, expenditures; b. disposable income; c. directly

14. rise, fall

15. a. real, financial (either order); b. the price level; c. expectations; d. consumer indebtedness; e. taxation of consumer income

16. the amount consumers plan to consume (save) will be different at every level of income, the level of income has changed and that consumers will change their planned consumption (saving) as a result

17. capital goods; a. expected, profits; b. interest

18. greater

19. inverse; a. decrease; b. increase

20. a. the cost of acquiring, maintaining, and operating the capital goods; b. business taxes; c. technological change; d. the stock of capital goods on hand; e. expectations

21. stable, unstable

22. durability, irregularity, variability

Problems and projects

1. a. S: − 40, −20, 0, 20, 40, 60, 80, 100; APC: 1.000, 0.970, 0.955; APS: 0.000, 0.030, 0.045; b. 1700; c. 80, 100, 80; d. 20, 100, 20

2. a. −; b. −; c. +; d. +; e. +; f. none; g. −; h. −

3. a. 0, 10; b. 20, 30; c. 30, 60; d. 100, 150, 210, 280; f. inverse, (1) decrease, (2) increase; g. (1) lower, (2) raise; h. investment-demand

4. a. +; b. −; c. +; d. +; e. −; f. −; g. −; h. +; i. −

5. a. investment; b. constant (given); c. (1) unrelated, (2) directly related; d. decrease, downward

Self-test

1. T; 2. T; 3. F; 4. T; 5. F; 6. F; 7. T; 8. F; 9. T; 10. F; 11. F; 12. F; 13. T; 14. T; 15. T; 16. F; 17. T; 18. F; 19. F; 20. T

1. a; 2. c; 3. b; 4. c; 5. a; 6. b; 7. d; 8. d; 9. a; 10. c; 11. b; 12. c; 13. a; 14. d; 15. b; 16. c; 17. c; 18. d; 19. c; 20. d; 21. b; 22. a; 23. c; 24. c; 25. c

Equilibrium national output in the Keynesian model

Chapter 13, building on the tools developed in the last chapter, continues the Keynesian explanation of what determines the equilibrium level of real NNP—the real NNP an economy will tend to produce. You **must** understand this chapter if you are to acquire an understanding of what causes the real NNP to rise and fall; of what causes unemployment, depression, inflation, and prosperity; and of what can be done to foster price stability, full· employment, and economic growth.

In the Keynesian model of the economy the equilibrium level of real NNP is determined **only** by the level of **aggregate expenditures** because it is assumed in this model that the economy is operating in the Keynesian (or depression) range of the aggregate-supply curve (and that the price level does not rise or fall). The two components of aggregate expenditures in an economy which is closed (neither exports nor imports goods and services) and in which governments do not spend or tax are consumption expenditures and net investment expenditures; and they were analyzed in the last chapter. In this chapter the equilibrium level of real NNP is explained with both tables and graphs, first by using the expenditures-output approach and then by employing the leakages-injections approach. These two approaches are complementary and are two different ways of analyzing the same process and of reaching the same conclusions. For each approach it is important for you to know, given the consumption (or saving) schedule and the level of net investment expenditures, **what** real NNP will tend to be produced and **why** this will be the real NNP which will be produced.

It is also important that you understand the significant distinction between **planned** investment and **actual** investment. Saving and actual net investment are always equal because they are defined in exactly the same way: the output of the economy minus its consumption. But saving and planned net investment are not, however, equal by definition. They are equal only when real NNP is at its equilibrium level. When real NNP is **not** at its equilibrium level, saving and planned net investment are **not** equal even though saving and actual investment are, as always, equal because the actual investment includes

unplanned investment or disinvestment. Remember: Equilibrium real NNP is achieved when saving and **planned** net investment—**not** saving and **actual** net investment—are equal.

The consumption (and the saving) schedule and the investment schedule—especially the latter—are subject to change, and when they change equilibrium real NNP will also change. The relationship between an initial change in the investment or consumption schedules and a change in equilibrium real NNP is called the multiplier. Three things to note here are: **how** the multiplier is defined, **why** there is a multiplier effect, and upon **what** the size of the multiplier depends. Because of the multiplier, the paradoxical consequence of an attempt by the economy to save more is either no increase or a decrease in the level of saving in the economy. The explanation of this paradox will be evident to you when you understand the equilibrium real NNP and the multiplier effect.

It is important to be aware that the equilibrium real NNP is not necessarily the real NNP at which full employment with inflationary pressures is achieved. Aggregate expenditures may be greater or less than the full-employment noninflationary real NNP; if they are greater there is an inflationary gap, and if they are less there exists a recessionary gap. Be sure that you know how to measure the size of each of these gaps: the amount by which the aggregate-expenditures schedule (or curve) must change to bring the economy to its full-employment real NNP without there being inflation in the economy.

The Keynesian model of the economy can be extended by adding the **net** exports of an economy to the aggregate-expenditures schedule. Net exports are nothing more than the economy's exports less its imports of goods and services. Like investment, the exports of a nation are an injection into its circular flow of income; and they increase the flow. But imports are, like saving, a leakage from the circular flow, and decrease the flow.

The generalization used to find the equilibrium real NNP in an open economy (one that exports and imports) is the same one as for a closed economy: the economy will tend to produce a real NNP which is equal to aggregate expenditures. The only difference is that the aggregate expenditures include not only consumption and planned net investment expenditures but the expenditures for net exports. So the equilibrium real NNP will equal $C + I_n + X_n$ (when X_n is the symbol used for net exports).

An increase in X_n, like an increase in I_n, will increase the equilibrium real NNP; and a decrease in X_n will decrease the equilibrium real NNP. And like a change in I_n, a change in X_n has a multiplier effect on real NNP.

The price level in the Keynesian model, as noted above, is assumed to be constant; but in the aggregate demand-aggregate supply model (examined in Chapter 11) the price level can rise or fall. These two models do not, however, contradict each other; and the last section of the chapter reconciles them. The important thing to understand is that prices can be constant at different levels. The price index in the economy, for example, might be constant at 100, at 75, or at 120. The AD curve is derived from the Keynesian model by letting prices be *constant at different levels.* Once you realize that it is no great problem to see that the lower (the higher) the level at which prices are constant in the Keynesian model the larger (the smaller) will be the equilibrium real NNP in that model of the economy; and that the AD curve slopes downward.

The AD curve derived in this way from the Keynesian model and the AS curve together determine the price level and the equilibrium real NNP in the aggregate demand-aggregate supply model. But aggregate demand can increase (or decrease); and when it does both the price level and the equilibrium real NNP may be changed. How the price level and real NNP are affected depends upon the range on the aggregate-supply curve in which the economy is initially operating. Here the important thing to see is that because the change in AD may also affect the price level in the economy, the change in AD may not have its *full* multiplier effect on the real NNP of the economy.

The next chapter deals with the fiscal policies that can be employed by government to eliminate recessionary and inflationary gaps in the economy. Chapter 13 has purposely ignored government and assumed an economy in which government neither taxes nor spends. But Chapter 14 does not ignore the role of government in the economy and discusses fiscal policies and their effects upon the equilibrium real NNP and the price level.

■ CHECKLIST

When you have studied this chapter you should be able to:

□ State the range along the aggregate supply in which the economy is assumed to operate and the assumption made about the price level in the Keynesian model.

□ Find the equilibrium real NNP, when you are given the necessary tabular or graphical data, by employing either the aggregate expenditures-national output or the leakages-injections approach.

□ Explain why the economy will tend to produce its equilibrium real NNP rather than some smaller or larger real NNP.

□ State the difference between planned investment and actual investment; and explain how it is possible for saving and actual investment to be equal when saving and planned investment are not equal.

□ Determine the economy's new equilibrium real NNP when there is a change in the consumption (or saving) schedule or in the investment schedule.

□ Find the value of the multiplier when you are given the needed information; and cite the two facts upon which the multiplier effect (a multiplier greater than one) is based.

▣ Draw a graph to explain the paradox of thrift.

□ Distinguish between the equilibrium real NNP and the full-employment noninflationary level of real NNP.

□ Find the recessionary and the inflationary gaps when you are provided the relevant data.

□ Use the concept of net exports to define aggregate expenditures in an open economy.

□ Explain what the equilibrium real NNP in an open economy will be when net exports are positive and when net exports are negative.

□ Find the equilibrium real NNP in an open economy when you are given the appropriate data.

□ Give examples of how circumstances or policies abroad can affect domestic NNP.

□ Contrast the Keynesian expenditures-output and the aggregate demand-aggregate supply models by comparing the variability of the price level and real NNP in the two models in the three ranges along the aggregate-supply curve.

□ Derive the aggregate-demand curve (or schedule) from the Keynesian model; and explain the effect of a change in aggregate expenditures (in the Keynesian model) on the aggregate-demand curve (or schedule).

□ Predict the effects of a change in aggregate demand on the price level and the equilibrium real NNP in the three ranges along the aggregate-supply curve; and explain what determines how large the multiplier effect on the equilibrium real NNP will be in the aggregate demand-aggregate supply model.

■ CHAPTER OUTLINE

1. In this chapter it is assumed (unless otherwise explicitly specified) that the economy is operating within the Keynesian range of the aggregate-supply curve and the price level is, therefore, constant; two approaches are used to explain what *real* national output (or NNP) the economy will tend to produce; but both approaches yield the same conclusion.

2. Employing the aggregate expenditures-national output approach, the equilibrium real NNP is the real NNP at which:

a. aggregate expenditures (consumption plus planned net investment) equal the real NNP; or

b. in graphical terms, the aggregate-expenditures curve crosses the 45-degree line.

3. Using the leakages-injections approach, the equilibrium real NNP is the real NNP at which:

a. saving and planned net investment are equal; or

b. in graphical terms, the saving curve crosses the planned net investment curve

4. The net investment schedule indicates what investors *plan* to do; and when saving is greater (less) than planned net investment,

a. *un*planned net investment (disinvestment) in inventories will occur; and

b. producers will reduce (expand) their production and the real NNP will fall (rise) until there is no unplanned net investment (disinvestment); but the *actual* net investment and saving are always equal because the former includes unplanned investment or disinvestment.

5. Changes in planned net investment (or in the consumption and saving schedules) will cause the equilibrium real NNP to change in the same direction by an amount greater than the initial change in investment (or consumption).

a. This is called the multiplier effect; and the multiplier is equal to the ratio of the change in the real NNP to the initial change in spending.

(1) The multiplier effect occurs because a change in the dollars spent by one person alters the income of another person in the same direction and because any change in the income of one person will change the person's consumption and saving in the same direction by a fraction of the change in income.

(2) The value of the simple multiplier is equal to the reciprocal of the marginal propensity to save.

(3) The significance of the multiplier is that relatively small changes in the spending plans of business firms or households bring about large changes in the equilibrium real NNP.

(4) The simple multiplier has this value only in an economy in which the only leakage is saving; and the complex multiplier takes into account such other leakages as taxes and imports.

b. The paradox of thrift is that an increase in the saving schedule results in no increase, and may result in a decrease, in saving: the increase in the saving schedule causes a multiple contraction in real NNP and at the lower

real NNP the same amount or even less saving takes place; but saving is not socially undesirable if it limits demand-pull inflation or if it leads to more investment and growth in the economy.

6. The equilibrium level of real NNP may turn out to be an equilibrium at less than full employment, at full employment, or at full employment with inflation.

a. If the equilibrium real NNP is *less* than the real NNP consistent with full employment, there exists a recessionary gap; the size of the recessionary gap equals the amount by which the aggregate-expenditures schedule must increase (shift upward) to increase the real NNP to its full-employment noninflationary level.

b. If equilibrium real NNP is *greater* than the real NNP consistent with stable prices there is an inflationary gap. The size of the inflationary gap equals the amount by which the aggregate-expenditures schedule must decrease (shift downward) if the economy is to achieve full employment without inflation.

c. It is, however, likely that a full-employment noninflationary real NNP is unattainable in the real world; and this likelihood complicates the elimination of an inflationary gap.

7. In an open economy the exports (*X*) of a nation increase and its imports (*M*) decrease aggregate expenditures in that economy; and aggregate expenditures are equal to the sum of consumption spending, planned net investment spending, and net exports (X_n) when X_n is defined as *X* minus *M.*

a. The equilibrium real NNP in an open economy is the real NNP equal to consumption plus planned net investment plus net exports; and

b. any increase (decrease) in its X_n will increase (decrease) its equilibrium real NNP with a multiplier effect.

c. In an open economy model, circumstances and policies abroad, such as a change in the level of national incomes of trading partners, changes in tariffs or quotas, or changes in exchange rates can affect domestic NNP.

8. The Keynesian expenditures-output model and the aggregate demand-aggregate supply model are reconciled by recalling that the price level is assumed to be constant in the former and is a variable (can rise or fall) in the latter model.

a. The AD curve is derived from the intersections of the aggregate-expenditures curves and the 45-degree curve: as the price level falls (rises) the aggregate-expenditures curve shifts upward (downward) and the equilibrium real NNP increases (decreases); and this inverse relationship between the price level and the equilibrium real NNP is the AD schedule (or curve).

As the price level falls (rises):

(1) the consumption curve shifts upward (downward) because of the **real balances** or **wealth** effect;

(2) the investment curve shifts upward (downward) because of the *interest-rate* effect; and

(3) the net export curve shifts upward (downward) because of the *foreign purchases* effect.

b. If the price level is constant, any change in the non-price level determinants of consumption and planned investment that shifts the aggregate-expenditures curve upward (downward) will increase (decrease) the equilibrium real NNP and shift the AD curve to the right (left) by an amount equal to the increase (decrease) in aggregate expenditures times the multiplier.

c. If the economy is operating along the

(1) Keynesian range of the AS curve an increase in AD will have no effect on the price level and the increase in the equilibrium real NNP will equal the full multiplier effect of the increase in aggregate expenditures;

(2) intermediate range the increase in AD will increase the price level and the increase in the equilibrium real NNP will be less than the full multiplier effect of the increase in aggregate expenditures;

(3) classical range the increase in AD will increase the price level and have no effect on the equilibrium real NNP.

d. The Keynesian expenditures-output model is expanded in the appendix to this chapter (by adding the effects of an economy's exports and imports on its real NNP); and in the next chapter (by including the effects of government expenditures and tax collections on real NNP).

■ IMPORTANT TERMS

Real national output (NNP)	Injection
Nominal national output (NNP)	Actual investment
	Unplanned investment
Aggregate expenditures-national output approach	Multiplier effect
	Multiplier
Leakages-injections approach	Simple multiplier
Aggregate expenditures	Complex multiplier
Aggregate-expenditures schedule (curve)	Paradox of thrift
	Recessionary gap
Planned investment	Inflationary gap
Equilibrium (real) NNP	Open economy
45-degree line	Closed economy
Leakage	Net exports

■ FILL-IN QUESTIONS

1. In this chapter (unless explicitly indicated to the contrary),

a. it is assumed that the economy is operating within the (Keynesian, classical) _____ range of the aggregate supply and the price level is (variable, constant) _____;

b. the explanation is in terms of the (real, nominal) _____ national output or (GNP, NNP) _____

2. Two complementary approaches which are employed to explain the equilibrium level of real national output are the _____ approach and the _____ approach.

3. Assuming a private and closed economy, the equilibrium level of real NNP is the real NNP at which:

a. aggregate _____ equal real national _____

b. real NNP equals _____ plus _____

c. the aggregate-expenditures schedule or curve intersects the _____ line.

4. When the leakages-injections approach is used:

a. In this chapter the only leakage considered is _____ and the only injection considered is _____

b. Later the two additional:

(1) leakages considered are _____ and _____

(2) injections considered are _____ and _____

5. If:

a. Aggregate expenditures are greater than the real national output, saving is (greater, less) _____ than planned net investment, there is unplanned (investment, disinvestment) _____ in inventories, and the real NNP will (rise, fall) _____

b. Aggregate expenditures are less than the real national output, saving is _____ than planned net investment, there is unplanned _____ in inventories, and the real NNP will _____

c. Aggregate expenditures are equal to the real national output, saving is _____ planned net investment, unplanned investment in inventories is _____, and the real NNP will _____

6. At every level of real NNP saving is equal to (planned, actual) _____ net investment.
  a. But if planned net investment is greater than saving by $10:
    (1) there is $10 of unplanned (investment, disinvestment) _____

    (2) the real NNP will (rise, fall) _____
  b. And if planned net investment is less than saving by $5:

    (1) there is $5 of unplanned _____

    (2) the real NNP will _____

7. The multiplier:
  a. is the ratio of the change in _____ to an initial change in spending in the economy;
  b. has a value equal to the one divided by the

_____
which is the same thing as one divided by the quantity of

one minus _____

8. The multiplier effect is based on two facts:
  a. an initial increase in spending by business firms or

consumers will increase the _____ of the households in the economy; and
  b. the latter increase will expand the (consumption, investment) _____ spending of the households by an amount equal to the increase in income times the

_____

9. When planned net investment spending increases the

equilibrium real NNP (increases, decreases) _____

_____ and when planned net investment spending

decreases the equilibrium real NNP _____
  a. The changes in the equilibrium real NNP are (greater,

less) _____ than the changes in planned net investment spending.
  b. The size of the multiplier varies (directly, inversely)

_____ with the size of the marginal propensity to consume.

10. If the economy decides to save more (consume less) at every level of NNP, the equilibrium real NNP will (increase, decrease) _____ and the equilibrium

level of saving in the economy will either remain the same or (increase, decrease) _____
This consequence of an increased desire to save is called

the _____

11. A recessionary gap exists when equilibrium real NNP

is (greater, less) _____ than the full-employment real NNP; to bring real NNP to the full-employment level, the aggregate-expenditures schedule must

(increase, decrease) _____ by an amount equal to the difference between the equilibrium and the full-employment noninflationary real NNP divided by the

_____

12. When equilibrium *money* NNP is greater than the full-employment real NNP at which prices are stable, there is

a(n) _____ gap; to eliminate this gap

_____ must decrease by _____
divided by the multiplier.

13. When a nation is able to export and import goods and services:
  a. Its net exports equal its _____

minus its _____
  b. In an open economy:
    (1) Aggregate expenditures are equal to consumption

plus planned net investment plus _____
    (2) The equilibrium real NNP is the real NNP which is

equal to _____

14. What would be the effect—increase (+) or decrease (−)—of each of the following upon an open economy's equilibrium real NNP?
  a. An increase in its imports   _____
  b. An increase in its exports   _____
  c. A decrease in its imports   _____
  d. A decrease in its exports   _____
  e. An increasing level of national income among trading

partners   _____
  f. An increase in trade barriers imposed by trading part-

ners   _____
  g. A depreciation in the value of the economy's currency

_____

15. In the aggregate demand-aggregate supply model

the price level is a (constant, variable) _____;
in the Keynesian expenditures-output model it is a

_____

a. But if the price level were lower in the Keynesian
model the _____ effect would (raise, lower)
_____ the consumption investment, net
exports, and aggregate-expenditures curves; and the

equilibrium real NNP would (rise, fall) _____
b. And if the price level were higher in the Keynesian

model this effect would _____ the consumption investment, net exports, and aggregate-expenditures curves; and the equilibrium real NNP would

_____

c. This (direct, inverse) _____ relationship between the price level and the equilibrium real
NNP in the Keynesian model is the aggregate (demand,

supply) _____ curve (or schedule).

16. If the price level were a constant, a(n)
a. increase in the aggregate-expenditures curve would
shift the aggregate-demand curve to the (right, left)

_____ by an amount equal to the upward shift in

aggregate expenditures times the _____
b. decrease in the aggregate-expenditures curve would

shift the aggregate-demand curve to the _____

by an amount equal to the _____

17. Were aggregate demand to increase,
a. the flatter the aggregate-supply curve, the (greater,

smaller) _____ is the multiplier effect on

the real equilibrium NNP and the _____ is
the effect on the equilibrium price level; and

b. the steeper the aggregate-supply curve, the _____
is the multiplier effect on the equilibrium real NNP and

the _____ is the effect on the equilibrium
price level.

■ **PROBLEMS AND PROJECTS**

1. The table in the next column shows consumption and
saving at various levels of real NNP. Assume the price
level is constant, the economy is closed, and government
neither taxes nor spends.

Real NNP	C	S	I	C + I	UI
$1300	$1290	$10	$22	$1312	−12
1310	1298	12	22	1320	−10
1320	1306	14	___	___	___
1330	1314	16	___	___	___
1340	1322	18	___	___	___
1350	1330	20	___	___	___
1360	1338	22	___	___	___
1370	1346	24	___	___	___
1380	1354	26	___	___	___
1390	1362	28	22	1384	+6
1400	1370	30	22	1392	+8

a. The next table is an investment-demand schedule
which shows the net amounts investors plan to invest at
different rates of interest (*i*). Assume the rate of interest is
6% and complete the net investment, the consumption-
plus-investment, and the unplanned investment (*UI*) columns—showing unplanned investment with a + and unplanned disinvestment with a −.

i	*I*
10%	$ 0
9	7
8	13
7	18
6	22
5	25
4	27
3	28

b. The equilibrium real NNP will be $ _____
c. The value of the marginal propensity to consume in

this problem is _____ and the value of the

marginal propensity to save is _____

d. The value of the simple multiplier is _____
e. If the rate of interest should fall from 6% to 5%,
planned net investment would (increase, decrease)

_____ by $ _____; and the
equilibrium real NNP would, as a result, (increase, de-

crease) _____ by $ _____
f. Suppose the rate of interest were to rise from 6% to

7%. Planned investment would _____ by

$ _____; and the equilibrium real NNP would _____

by $ _____

g. Assume the rate of interest is 6%. .

(1) On the following graph, plot **C, C** + **I,** and the 45-degree line, and indicate the equilibrium real NNP.

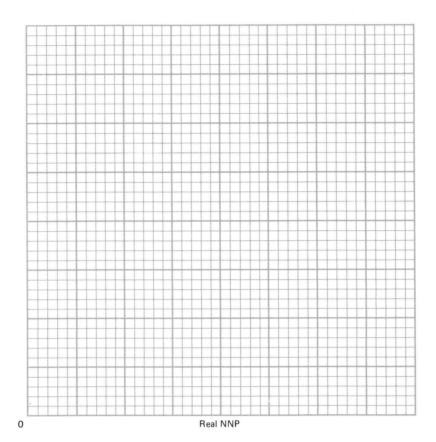

0   Real NNP

(2) On the graph at the right, plot **S** and **I** and indicate the equilibrium real NNP.

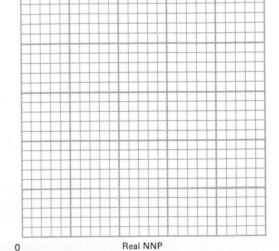

0   Real NNP

2. Assume the marginal propensity to consume is 0.8 and the change in net planned investment is $10. Complete the table on the next page, modeled after Table 13–2 in the textbook.

	Change in income	Change in consumption	Change in saving
Increase in net investment of $10	$ + 10	$ _____	$ _____
Second round	_____	_____	_____
Third round	_____	_____	_____
Fourth round	_____	_____	_____
Fifth round	_____	_____	_____
All other rounds	16.38	13.10	3.28
Totals	_____	_____	_____

3. Below are a saving schedule and an investment schedule (I_a) indicating that planned investment is constant.

Real NNP	S	I_a
$300	$ 5	$15
310	7	15
320	9	15
330	11	15
340	13	15
350	15	15
360	17	15
370	19	15
380	21	15
390	23	15
400	25	15

a. The equilibrium real NNP is $ _____ and saving and planned investment are both $ _____

b. The marginal propensity to save is _____ and the simple multiplier is _____

c. A $2 rise in the I_a **schedule** will cause real NNP to rise by $ _____

d. Use the investment schedule given in the table and assume a $2 increase in the saving schedule in the table—that is, saving at every real NNP increases by $2.

(1) Equilibrium real NNP will _____ to $ _____ and at this real NNP saving will be $ _____

(2) The effect of the increase in the saving schedule is to _____ equilibrium real NNP; this is called the _____

(3) The amount by which real NNP changes depends upon the size of the change in the saving schedule and the size of _____

4. In the next table are consumption and saving schedules for a closed economy. Assume that the level of real NNP at which full employment without inflation is achieved is $590.

Real NNP	C	S
$550	$520	$30
560	526	34
570	532	38
580	538	42
590	544	46
600	550	50
610	556	54
620	562	58
630	568	62

a. The value of the multiplier is _____

b. If planned net investment is $58, the equilibrium money NNP is $ _____ and exceeds the full-employment noninflationary real NNP by $ _____. There is a(n) _____ gap of $ _____

c. If planned investment is $38, the equilibrium real NNP is $ _____ and is less than full-employment real NNP by $ _____ There is a(n) _____ gap of $ _____

5. Next is a schedule showing what aggregate expenditures (consumption plus planned net investment) would be at various levels of real net national product in a closed economy.

Possible levels of real NNP (billions)	Aggregate expenditures, closed economy (billions)	Exports (billions)	Imports (billions)	Net Exports (billions)	Aggregate expenditures, open economy (billions)
$ 750	$ 776	$90	$86	$_____	$_____
800	816	90	86	_____	_____
850	856	90	86	_____	_____
900	896	90	86	_____	_____
950	936	90	86	_____	_____
1,000	976	90	86	_____	_____
1,050	1,016	90	86	_____	_____

a. Were this economy to become an open economy the volume of exports would be a constant $90 billion; and the volume of imports would be a constant $86 billion. At each of the seven levels of real NNP, net exports would be

$ _____ billion.

b. Compute aggregate expenditures in this open economy at the seven real NNP levels and enter them in the table.

c. The equilibrium real NNP in this open economy would

be $ _____ billion.

d. The value of the multiplier in this open economy is

equal to _____

e. A $10 billion increase in:

(1) exports would (increase, decrease) _____

the equilibrium real NNP by $ _____ billion.

(2) imports would (increase, decrease) _____

the equilibrium real NNP by $ _____ billion.

6. The real NNP an economy might produce is shown in column (1) below.

a. If the price level in this economy were $1.20 the aggregate expenditures (AE) at each real NNP would be those shown in column (2) and the equilibrium real NNP

would be $ _____

b. But if the price level were $1.00 the aggregate expenditures at each real NNP would be those shown in column

(3) and the equilibrium real NNP would be $ _____

c. And if the price level were $0.80 the aggregate expenditures at each real NNP would be those shown in column

(4) and the equilibrium real NNP would be $ _____

d. Show in the schedule below the equilibrium real NNP at each of the three price levels.

Price level	Equilibrium real NNP
$1.20	$_____
1.00	_____
.80	_____

(1) This schedule is the _____ schedule and

(2) in it the equilibrium real NNP is _____ related to the price level.

7. Columns (1) and (2) in the table on the next page are the aggregate-supply schedule of an economy.

(1) Real NNP	(2) AE$_{1.20}$	(3) AE$_{1.00}$	(4) AE$_{0.80}$
$2100	$2110	$2130	$2150
2200	2200	2220	2240
2300	2290	2310	2330
2400	2380	2400	2420
2500	2470	2490	2510
2600	2560	2580	2600

(1) Price level	(2) Real NNP	(3) AQD$_1$	(4) AQD$_2$	(5) AQD$_3$	(6) AQD$_4$	(7) AQD$_5$	(8) AQD$_6$
$2.60	$2390	$ 840	$ 940	$1900	$2000	$2190	$2290
2.40	2390	940	1040	2000	2100	2290	2390
2.20	2390	1040	1140	2100	2200	2390	2490
2.00	2390	1140	1240	2200	2300	2490	2590
1.90	2350	1190	1290	2250	2350	2540	2640
1.80	2300	1240	1340	2300	2400	2590	2690
1.60	2200	1340	1440	2400	2500	2690	2790
1.40	2090	1440	1540	2500	2600	2790	2890
1.20	1970	1540	1640	2600	2700	2890	2990
1.00	1840	1640	1740	2700	2800	2990	3090
1.00	1740	1640	1740	2700	2800	2990	3090
1.00	1640	1640	1740	2700	2800	2990	3090

a. The economy is in the

(1) classical range when its real NNP is $ _____ and the price level is $ _____ or higher;

(2) Keynesian range when its real NNP is $ _____ or less and its price level is $ _____

b. If the aggregate demand in the economy were columns (1) and (3) the equilibrium real NNP would be

$ _____ and the equilibrium price level would be

$ _____; and if aggregate demand should increase by $100 to that shown in columns (1) and (4) the

equilibrium real NNP would increase by $ _____

and the price level would _____

c. Should aggregate demand be that shown in columns (1) and (5) the equilibrium real NNP would be

$ _____ and the equilibrium price would be

$ _____; and if aggregate demand should increase by $100 to that shown in columns (1) and (6) the

equilibrium real NNP would increase by $ _____

and the price level would rise to $ _____

d. And if aggregate demand were that shown in columns (1) and (7) the equilibrium real NNP would be

$ _____ and the equilibrium price level would be

$ _____; but if aggregate demand increased by $100 to that shown in columns (1) and (8) the price level

would rise to $ _____ and the equilibrium real

NNP would _____

■ SELF-TEST

Circle the T if the statement is true, the F if it is false.

1. In the Keynesian model of the economy the price level is constant. **T F**

Questions 2 and 3 are based on the data supplied in the following table.

Real NNP	C
$200	$200
240	228
280	256
320	284
360	312
400	340
440	368
480	396

2. If saving at each level of real NNP decreased by $5 and if planned net investment remained constant at $24, equilibrium real NNP would decrease by $16⅔ and saving in the economy would decrease by $5. **T F**

3. If consumption spending at each level of real NNP increased by $10, the equilibrium level of real NNP would tend to rise by $30. **T F**

4. The investment schedule is a schedule of planned investment rather than a schedule of actual investment. **T F**

5. Saving and actual net investment are always equal. **T F**

6. Saving at any level of real NNP equals planned net investment plus unplanned investment (or minus unplanned disinvestment). **T F**

7. If real NNP were to decline by $40, consumers would reduce their consumption expenditures by an amount less than $40. **T F**

8. A decrease in the rate of interest will, other things remaining the same, result in a decrease in the equilibrium real NNP. **T F**

9. The larger the marginal propensity to consume, the larger the size of the multiplier. **T F**

10. The equilibrium real NNP is the real NNP at which there is full employment in the economy. **T F**

11. The existence of a recessionary gap in the economy is characterized by the full employment of labor. **T F**

12. The net exports of an economy equal the sum of its exports and its imports of goods and services. **T F**

13. An increase in the volume of a nation's exports, other things being equal, will expand the nation's real NNP. **T F**

14. An increase in the imports of a nation will increase the exports of other nations. **T F**

15. The higher the level at which the price level is constant in the Keynesian model of the economy the smaller are the real balances of consumers and the lower is the consumption schedule (curve). **T F**

16. An increase in the price level will shift the aggregate-demand curve to the right. **T F**

17. In the Keynesian range on the aggregate-supply curve an increase in aggregate demand will have no effect on the real equilibrium NNP of the economy and will raise its price level. **T F**

18. The greater the increase in the price level that results from an increase in aggregate demand the greater will be the increase in the equilibrium real NNP. **T F**

19. The Keynesian model of the economy does not adequately predict the effects of changes in aggregate expenditures on the equilibrium real NNP if the price level is not constant. **T F**

20. Inflation has no effect on the strength of the multiplier. **T F**

Circle the letter that corresponds to the best answer.

1. The range of the aggregate-supply curve to which the Keynesian model is relevant is:
(a) the horizontal range

(b) the intermediate range
(c) the vertical range
(d) both the intermediate and the vertical range

2. In the Keynesian model in this chapter the equilibrium real NNP is:
(a) the real NNP at which saving and planned net investment are equal
(b) the real NNP at which national output and aggregate expenditures are equal
(c) the real NNP which is equal to consumption plus planned net investment
(d) all of the above

Questions 3 and 4 below are based on the consumption schedule preceding true-false questions 2 and 3.

3. If planned net investment is $60, the equilibrium level of real NNP will be:
(a) $320
(b) $360
(c) $400
(d) $440

4. If planned investment were to increase by $5, the equilibrium real NNP would increase by:
(a) $5
(b) $7½
(c) $15
(d) $16⅔

5. When the economy's real NNP exceeds its equilibrium real NNP:
(a) there is unplanned real investment in the economy
(b) planned net investment exceeds saving
(c) the aggregate expenditures exceed the real national output
(d) there is an inflationary gap

6. If real NNP is $275 billion, consumption $250 billion, and planned investment $30 billion, real NNP:
(a) will tend to remain constant
(b) will tend to increase
(c) will tend to decrease
(d) equals aggregate expenditures

7. Which of the following is an injection?
(a) investment
(b) saving
(c) taxes
(d) imports

8. If saving is greater than planned net investment:
(a) businesses will be motivated to increase their investments
(b) aggregate expenditures will be greater than the real national output

(c) real NNP will be greater than planned net investment plus consumption

(d) saving will tend to increase

9. On a graph the equilibrium real NNP is found at the intersection of the 45-degree line and

(a) the consumption curve

(b) the investment-demand curve

(c) the saving curve

(d) the aggregate-expenditures curve

10. If the value of the marginal propensity to consume is 0.6 and real NNP falls by $25, this was caused by a decrease in the aggregate-expenditures schedule of:

(a) $10

(b) $15

(c) $16⅔

(d) $20

11. If the marginal propensity to consume is 0.6⅔ and if both planned net investment and the saving schedule increase by $25, real NNP will:

(a) increase by $75

(b) not change

(c) decrease by $75

(d) increase by $25

12. The paradox of thrift means that:

(a) an increase in saving lowers the level of real NNP

(b) an increase in the average propensity to save lowers or leaves unchanged the level of savings

(c) an increase in the marginal propensity to save lowers the value of the multiplier

(d) an increase in real NNP increases investment demand

13. If the economy's full-employment noninflationary real NNP is $1200 and its equilibrium real NNP is $1100 there is a recessionary gap of:

(a) $100

(b) $100 divided by the multiplier

(c) $100 multiplied by the multiplier

(d) $100 times the reciprocal of the marginal propensity to consume

14. To eliminate an inflationary gap of $50 in an economy in which the marginal propensity to save is 0.1, it will be necessary to:

(a) decrease the aggregate-expenditures schedule by $50

(b) decrease the aggregate-expenditures schedule by $5

(c) increase the aggregate-expenditures schedule by $50

(d) increase the aggregate-expenditures schedule by $5

Use the data in the table at the top of the next column to answer questions 15, 16, and 17.

Real NNP	C + I	Net exports
$ 900	$ 913	$3
920	929	3
940	945	3
960	961	3
980	977	3
1,000	993	3
1,020	1,009	3

15. The equilibrium real NNP is:

(a) $960

(b) $980

(c) $1,000

(d) $1,020

16. If net exports are increased by $4 billion at each level of NNP, the equilibrium real NNP would be:

(a) $960

(b) $980

(c) $1,000

(d) $1,020

17. If the marginal propensity to save in this economy is 0.2, a $10 increase in its net exports would increase its equilibrium real NNP by:

(a) $40

(b) $50

(c) $100

(d) $200

18. Other things remaining constant, which of the following would *not* increase an economy's real NNP and employment?

(a) the imposition of tarriffs on goods imported from abroad

(b) a decrease in the level of national income among the trading partners for this economy

(c) a decrease in the exchange rates for foreign currencies

(d) an increase in the exchange rate for foreign currencies

19. An increase in the real NNP of an economy will, other things remaining constant:

(a) increase its imports and the real NNPs in other economies

(b) increase its imports and decrease the real NNPs in other economies

(c) decrease its imports and increase the real NNPs in other economies

(d) decrease its imports and the real NNPs in other economies.

20. If the price level in the Keynesian model were lower the consumption and aggregate-expenditures curves would be:

(*a*) lower and the equilibrium real NNP would be smaller
(*b*) lower and the equilibrium real NNP would be larger
(*c*) higher and the equilibrium real NNP would be larger
(*d*) higher and the equilibrium real NNP would be smaller

21. An increase in aggregate expenditures in the Keynesian model shifts the aggregate-demand curve to the:
(*a*) right by the amount of the increase in aggregate expenditures
(*b*) right by the amount of the increase in aggregate expenditures times the multiplier
(*c*) left by the amount of the increase in aggregate expenditures
(*d*) left by the amount of the increase in aggregate expenditures times the multiplier

22. An increase in aggregate demand will increase the equilibrium real NNP if the economy is operating in the:
(*a*) Keynesian range
(*b*) intermediate range
(*c*) Keynesian or intermediate ranges
(*d*) classical range

23. An increase in aggregate demand will increase both the equilibrium real NNP and the price level if the economy is operating in the:
(*a*) Keynesian range
(*b*) intermediate range
(*c*) intermediate or classical ranges
(*d*) classical range

24. A decrease in the price level will shift the:
(*a*) consumption, investment, and net exports curves downward
(*b*) consumption, investment, and net exports curves upward
(*c*) consumption and investment curves upward, but the net exports curve upward
(*d*) consumption and net export curves upward, but the investment curve downward

25. In the aggregate-demand and aggregate-supply model, an increase in the price level will:
(*a*) increase the marginal propensity to consume
(*b*) increase the strength of the multiplier
(*c*) decrease the strength of the multiplier
(*d*) have no effect on the strength of the multiplier

■ **DISCUSSION QUESTIONS**

1. Why is the price level in the Keynesian model assumed to be constant? How does this Keynesian-model assumption differ from the assumption used in the aggregate demand-aggregate supply model?

2. Why is the equilibrium level of real NNP that level of real NNP at which national output equals aggregate expenditures and at which saving equals planned net investment? What will cause real NNP to rise if it is below this level and what will cause it to fall if it is above this level?

3. Explain what is meant by a leakage and by an injection. What are the three major leakages and the three major injections in the flow of income in the American economy? Which leakage and which injection are considered in this chapter? Why is the equilibrium real NNP the real NNP at which the leakages equal the injections?

4. What is meant by "the distinction between saving and investment plans and the actual amounts which households manage to save and businesses to invest"? Is the net investment schedule planned or actual investment? What adjustment causes planned and actual net investment to become equal?

5. What is the multiplier effect? **Why** does there tend to be a multiplier effect (that is, on what basic economic facts does the multiplier effect depend)? What determines how large the simple multiplier effect will be?

6. What is meant by the paradox of thrift?

7. What relationship is there between the equilibrium level of real NNP and the level of real NNP at which full employment without inflation is achieved?

8. Explain what is meant by a recessionary gap and an inflationary gap. What economic conditions are present in the economy when each of these gaps exists? How is the size of each of these gaps measured?

9. How do exports and how do imports affect aggregate expenditures within a nation?
  To what is the equilibrium real NNP equal in an open economy (in the Keynesian model)? How does a change in the volume of exports and in the volume of imports affect real NNP and employment in a nation?

10. What are some examples of international economic linkages affecting the domestic level of NNP?

11. How is the aggregate-demand curve used in the aggregate demand-aggregate supply model of the economy derived from the Keynesian model?

12. What is the effect of an increase in aggregate expenditures in the Keynesian model (*a*) on the aggregate demand curve; (*b*) on the equilibrium real NNP and price level in the Keynesian, intermediate, and classical ranges of the aggregate-supply curve; and *c*) on the size of the multiplier effect on real NNP in each of these three ranges? What is the relationship between the effect of an increase in aggregate expenditures on real NNP and the rise in the price level that accompanies it?

■ ANSWERS

CHAPTER 13 EQUILIBRIUM NATIONAL OUTPUT IN THE KEYNESIAN MODEL

Fill-in questions

1. *a.* Keynesian, constant; *b.* real, NNP

2. (aggregate) expenditures-(national) output, leakages-injections

3. *a.* expenditures, output; *b.* consumption, planned net investment; *c.* 45-degree

4. *a.* saving, net investment; *b.* (1) taxes, imports; (2) government expenditures, exports

5. *a.* less, disinvestment, rise; *b.* greater, investment, fall; *c.* equal to, zero, neither rise nor fall

6. actual; *a.* (1) disinvestment, (2) rise; *b.* (1) investment, (2) fall

7. *a.* the equilibrium real NNP; *b.* marginal propensity to save, the marginal propensity to consume

8. *a.* income; *b.* consumption, marginal propensity to consume

9. increases, decreases; *a.* greater; *b.* directly

10. decrease, decrease; paradox of thrift

11. less, increase, multiplier

12. inflationary, the aggregate-expenditures schedule, the amount by which equilibrium money NNP exceeds the full-employment noninflationary real NNP

13. *a.* exports, imports; *b.* (1) net exports, (2) aggregate expenditures

14. *a.* −; *b.* +; *c.* +; *d.* −; *e.* +; *f.* −; *g.* +

15. variable, constant; *a.* real-balances, raise, rise; *b.* lower, fall; *c.* inverse, demand

16. *a.* right, multiplier; *b.* left, downward shift in aggregate expenditures times the multiplier

17. *a.* greater, smaller; *b.* smaller, greater

Problems and projects

1. *a. I:* 22, 22, 22, 22, 22, 22, 22; *C + I:* 1328, 1336, 1344, 1352, 1360, 1368, 1376; *UI:* −8, −6, −4, −2, 0, +2, +4; *b.* 1360; *c.* 0.8, 0.2; *d.* 5; *e.* increase, 3, increase, 15; *f.* decrease, 4, decrease, 20

2. change in income: 8.00, 6.40, 5.12, 4.10, 50,000; change in consumption: 8.00, 6.40, 5.12, 4.10, 3.28, 40.00; change in saving: 2.00, 1.60, 1.28, 1.02, 0.82, 10.00

3. *a.* 350, 15; *b.* 0.20, 5; *c.* 10; *d.* (1) decrease, 340, 15; (2) decrease, paradox of thrift; (3) the multiplier

4. *a.* 2½; *b.* 620, 30, inflationary, 12; *c.* 570, 20, recessionary, 8

5. *a.* $4; *b.* $780, 820, 860, 900, 940, 980, 1,020; *c.* $900; *d.* 5; *e.* (1) increase, $50, (2) decrease, $50

6. *a.* 2200; *b.* 2400; *c.* 2600; *d.* 2200, 2400, 2600, (1) aggregate-demand, (2) inversely

7. *a.* (1) 2390, 2.00, (2) 1840, 1.00; *b.* 1640, 1.00, 100, remain constant; *c.* 2300, 1.80, 2350, 1.90; *d.* 2390, 2.20, 2.40, remain constant

Self-test

1. T; **2.** F; **3.** F; **4.** T; **5.** T; **6.** T; **7.** T; **8.** F; **9.** T; **10.** F; **11.** F; **12.** F; **13.** T; **14.** T; **15.** T; **16.** F; **17.** F; **18.** F; **19.** T; **20.** F

1. *a;* **2.** *d;* **3.** *c;* **4.** *d;* **5.** *a;* **6.** *b;* **7.** *a;* **8.** *c;* **9.** *d;* **10.** *a;* **11.** *b;* **12.** *b;* **13.** *b;* **14.** *a;* **15.** *b;* **16.** *c;* **17.** *b;* **18.** *c;* **19.** *a;* **20.** *c;* **21.** *b;* **22.** *c;* **23.** *b;* **24.** *b;* **25.** *c*

Fiscal policy

Chapter 14 is really a continuation of the two preceding chapters and is concerned with the chief practical application of the principles discussed in those chapters.

It is worth recalling that principles of economics are generalizations about the way the economy works; and that these principles are studied in order that policies may be devised to solve real problems. Over the past one hundred or so years the most serious problems encountered by the American economy have been those problems that resulted from the business cycle. Learning what determines the real output and price levels of an economy and what causes them to fluctuate will make it possible to discover ways to bring about full employment, maximum output, and stable prices. Economic principles, in short, suggest the policies that will lessen both recession and inflation.

Government spending and taxing have a strong influence on the economy's output and employment and its price level. Federal expenditure and taxation policies designed to expand total production and employment or reduce the rate of inflation are called fiscal policies. (The Federal Reserve Banks are also able to affect these variables by applying monetary policy; but the study of monetary policy must wait until the effect of banks on the operation of the economy is examined in Chapters 15, 16, and 17.)

The brief first section of the chapter makes it clear that Congress in the Employment Act of 1946 committed the Federal government to using fiscal (and monetary) policy to achieve a trio of economic goals—economic growth, stable prices, and full employment. This act also established the Council of Economic Advisers to advise the President and the Joint Economic Committee to advise Congress on matters pertaining to national economic policy.

The section entitled "Discretionary Fiscal Policy" is, however, the crucial part of Chapter 14. It introduces government taxing and spending into the analysis of equilibrium real NNP. It is important to note that government purchases of goods and services add to aggregate demand; and that taxation reduces the disposable income of con-

sumers, and thereby reduces both the amount of consumption and the amount of saving that will take place at any level of real NNP. Both "approaches" are again employed, and you are warned that you must know *what* real NNP will tend to be produced and *why.* Special attention should be directed to the exact effect taxes have upon the consumption and saving schedules and to the multiplier effects of changes in government purchases and taxes.

Once you learn how government purchases and taxing affect the equilibrium real NNP it is fairly easy to understand what fiscal policies will be expansionary and reduce unemployment and what fiscal policies will be contractionary and lessen inflation. In addition to this, you should be aware (1) that if the government has a budget deficit or surplus there are several ways of financing the deficit or disposing of the surplus, and the way the deficit or surplus is handled can affect the economy's operation as much as the size of the deficit or surplus; and (2) that the Federal government has the option of changing its expenditures or altering the taxes it collects when it applies fiscal policy to reduce unemployment or lessen inflation in the economy.

Discretionary fiscal policy requires that Congress take action to change tax rates, transfer payment programs, or purchases of goods and services. *Non*discretionary fiscal policy does not require Congress to take any action; and is a built-in stabilizer of the economy. You should be sure that you understand *why* net taxes increase when the NNP rises and decrease when the NNP falls and *how* this tends to stabilize the economy.

Unfortunately, nondiscretionary fiscal policy by itself may not able to eliminate any recessionary or inflationary gap that might develop; and discretionary fiscal policy may be necessary if the economy is to produce its full-employment NNP and avoid inflation. And the built-in stabilizers make it more difficult to use discretionary fiscal policy to achieve this goal because they create the illusion that the Federal government's policy is expansionary or contractionary when in fact its policy is just the opposite. Because of the illusions created by the built-in stabilizers, economists developed the full-employment budget and distinguished between a cyclical and structural deficit to enable them to discover whether Federal fiscal policy was actually expansionary or contractionary and to determine what policy should have been followed to move the economy toward full employment or slow the rate of inflation.

In addition to the problems of timing and the political problems encountered in using fiscal problems in the real world, you will discover in the last major section of the chapter that many economists and other people are concerned by three other important complications. They fear, first of all, that all expansionary fiscal policy which requires the Federal government to borrow in the money market will raise the level of interest rates in the economy and reduce (or crowd out) investment spending; this is called the crowding-out effect and if it is large it will reduce the effect of the expansionary fiscal policy on real NNP and unemployment. The second complication arises from the connection of the domestic economy to a world economy; aggregate demand shocks from abroad or a net export effect may increase or decrease the effectiveness of a given fiscal policy. The third fear is that an expansionary fiscal policy, if the economy is operating in the intermediate range along the aggregate-supply curve, will drive up the price level and have only a small effect on real output and employment. But all is not gloom. The supply-side economists argue that a reduction in tax rates will not only increase aggregate demand but will also (for a number of reasons explained in the text) expand aggregate supply. In this way, they contend, the real equilibrium NNP of the economy can be increased with little or no rise in the price level. This viewpoint will be dealt with in more detail in Chapter 19.

■ CHECKLIST

When you have studied this chapter you should be able to:

☐ State the responsibility imposed on the Federal government by the Employment Act of 1946 and the roles of the CEA and JEC in fulfilling this responsibility.

☐ Find the equilibrium real NNP in an economy in which government purchases goods and services and levies net taxes when you are given the necessary data.

☐ Determine the effect on the equilibrium real NNP of a change in government purchases of goods and services and in net taxes.

☐ Explain why the balanced-budget multiplier is equal to one.

☐ Explain when government should pursue an expansionary and a contractionary fiscal policy; what each of these policies might entail; and the effect of each upon the Federal budget.

☐ Describe the best way to finance a government deficit and to dispose of a surplus.

☐ Distinguish between discretionary and nondiscretionary fiscal policy.

☐ Indicate how the built-in stabilizers help to eliminate recession and inflationary pressures.

☐ Distinguish between the actual budget and the full-employment budget, and between cylical deficits and structural deficits as indicators of the government's fiscal policy.

☐ Outline the timing and political problems encountered in applying fiscal policy in the real world.

☐ Describe the crowding-out effect of an expansionary fiscal policy and how it may lessen the impact of an expansionary fiscal policy on real output and employment.

☐ Explain two ways that interdependency with the world economy influences the effectiveness of domestic fiscal policy.

☐ Distinguish between the effects of an expansionary fiscal policy in the Keynesian and intermediate ranges of the aggregate-supply curve; and explain how the impact of such a policy is reduced when the economy is in the latter range.

☐ State the effects supply-side economists argue a reduction in tax rates would have on aggregate supply, real NNP, and the price level; and explain why they believe it would have these effects.

■ CHAPTER OUTLINE

1. Fiscal policy is the manipulation by the Federal government of its expenditures and tax receipts in order to expand or contract aggregate expenditures in the economy; and by doing so either increase its real output (and employment) or decrease its rate of inflation.

2. The Employment Act of 1946 set the goals of American fiscal policy and provided for a Council of Economic Advisers to the President and the Joint Economic Committee; and in 1978 the Humphrey-Hawkins Act required the Federal government to develop a plan to reach specific economic goals.

3. Discretionary fiscal policy involves deliberate changes in tax rates and government spending to offset cyclical fluctuations and to increase economic growth.

a. Six assumptions are made in order to simplify the explanation of the effects of government spending and taxes on the equilibrium real NNP.

b. Government purchases of goods and services add to the aggregate-expenditures schedule and increase equilibrium real NNP; and an increase in these purchases has a multiplier effect upon equilibrium real NNP.

c. Taxes decrease consumption and the aggregate-expenditures schedule by the amount of the tax times the MPC (and decrease saving by the amount of the tax times the MPS); and an increase in taxes has a negative multiplier effect on the equilibrium real NNP. When government both taxes and purchases goods and services, the equilibrium NNP is the NNP at which

(1) aggregate expenditures (consumption + planned net investment + net exports + government purchases of goods and services) = the real national output (consumption + saving + taxes); or

(2) using the leakages-injections approach, at which planned net investment + exports + government purchases of goods and services = saving + imports + taxes.

d. Equal increases (decreases) in taxes and in government purchases increase (decrease) equilibrium real NNP by the amount of the change in taxes (or in expenditures).

e. The elimination of the inflation (recession) is accomplished by contractionary (expansionary) fiscal policy and by increasing (decreasing) taxes, decreasing (increasing) purchases, and incurring budget surpluses (deficits).

f. In addition to the size of the deficit or surplus, the manner in which government finances its deficit or disposes of its surplus affects the level of total spending in the economy.

g. Whether government purchases or taxes should be altered to reduce recession and inflation depends to a large extent upon whether an expansion or a contraction of the public sector is desired.

4. In the United States economy net tax revenues (tax revenues minus government transfer payments) are not a fixed amount or lump sum; they increase as the NNP rises and decrease as the NNP falls.

a. This net tax system serves as a built-in stabilizer of the economy because it reduces purchasing power during periods of inflation and expands purchasing power during periods of recession; but Keynesian economists contend that built-in stabilizers can only reduce and cannot eliminate economic fluctuations.

b. The full-employment budget is a better index than the actual budget of the direction of government fiscal policy because it indicates what the Federal budget deficit or surplus would be if the economy were to operate at full employment. In the case of a budget deficit, the full employment budget:

(1) removes the cyclical portion that is produced by swings in the business cycle; and

(2) reveals the size of the structural deficit, indicating how expansionary fiscal policy was that year.

5. Certain problems and complications arise in enacting and applying fiscal policy.

a. There will be problems of timing because it requires time to recognize the need for fiscal policy; to take the appropriate steps in the Congress; and for the action taken there to affect output and employment, and the rate of inflation in the economy.

b. There will also be political problems because:

(1) the economy has goals other than full employment and stable prices;

(2) there is an expansionary bias (for budget deficits and against surpluses);

(3) there may be a political business cycle (if politicians lower taxes and increase expenditures before and then do the opposite after elections).

c. An expansionary fiscal policy may, by raising the level of interest rates in the economy, reduce (or crowd out) investment spending and weaken the effect of the policy on real NNP; but this crowding-out effect may be small and can be offset by an expansion in the nation's money supply.

d. The effect of an expansionary fiscal policy on the real NNP will also be weakened to the extent that it results in a rise in the price level (inflation).

e. Aggregate demand and aggregate supply curves can be used to show how crowding out and inflation weaken the effects of an expansionary fiscal policy on real NNP.

f. The connection of the domestic economy to a world economy means that fiscal policy may be inappropriate or less effective because of aggregate-demand shocks from the world economy or a net export effect that counteracts or reinforces domestic fiscal policy.

g. But an expansionary fiscal policy that includes a reduction in taxes (tax rates) may, by increasing aggregate supply in the economy, expand real NNP (and employment), and reduce inflation.

■ **IMPORTANT TERMS**

Fiscal policy
Employment Act of 1946
Council of Economic Advisers
Joint Economic Committee
Humphrey-Hawkins Act of 1978
Discretionary fiscal policy
Lump-sum tax
Balanced-budget multiplier
Expansionary fiscal policy
Contractionary fiscal policy

Nondiscretionary fiscal policy
Net taxes
Built-in stability
Actual budget
Full-employment budget
Cyclical deficit
Structural deficit
Political business cycle
Crowding-out effect
Net export effect
Supply-side fiscal policy

■ **FILL-IN QUESTIONS**

1. The use of monetary and fiscal policy to reduce inflation and recession became national economic policy in

the _____ Act of 1946.

a. This act also established the Council of _____ to the President and the _____ Committee in Congress.

b. And in 1978 the _____ Act required the Federal government to establish five-year _____ for the economy and a _____ to achieve them.

2. Taxes tend to reduce consumption at each level of real NNP by an amount equal to the taxes multiplied by the _____; saving will decrease by an amount equal to the taxes multiplied by the _____ _____

3. In an economy in which government both taxes and purchases goods and services, the equilibrium level of real NNP is the real NNP at which:

a. aggregate _____ equal the national _____;

b. NNP is equal to _____ plus _____ plus _____ plus _____;

c. In the leakages-injection approach _____ plus _____ plus _____ **equals** _____ plus _____ plus _____.

4. Equal reductions in taxes and government purchases will (increase, decrease) _____ real NNP by an amount equal to _____ _____

5. In order to increase real NNP during a recession, taxes should be (increased, decreased) _____ and government purchases should be _____; to decrease the rise in the price level during a period of inflation taxes should be _____ and government purchases should be _____

6. If fiscal policy is to have a countercyclical effect, it will probably be necessary for the Federal government to incur a budget (surplus, deficit) _____ during a recession and a budget _____ during inflation.

7. The two principal means available to the Federal government for financing budget deficits are _____ and _____; and the (former, latter) _____ is more expansionary.

8. Those who wish to expand the public sector of the economy would during a period of *inflation* advocate a(n) (increase, decrease) _____ in (government purchases, taxes) _____; and those who wish to contract the public sector during a *recession* would advocate a(n) _____ in _____

9. Net taxes:

a. equal _____ minus _____

b. in the United States will (increase, decrease) _____ as the NNP rises and will _____ as the NNP falls.

10. When net tax receipts are directly related to the NNP the economy has some _____ stability because:

a. when the NNP rises, leakages (increase, decrease) _____ and the budget surplus will (increase, decrease) _____ (or the budget deficit will _____);

b. when the NNP falls, leakages _____ and the budget deficit will _____ (or the budget surplus will _____)

11. The full-employment budget:

a. indicates what the Federal _____ would have been if the economy had operated at _____ during the year;

b. tells us whether the Federal budget was in fact _____ or _____

c. A deficit produced by swings in the business cycle is (structural, cyclical) _____, whereas a deficit produced through government taxation and spending decisions is _____. The full-employment budget indicates the size of the _____ deficit.

12. There is a problem of timing in the use of discretionary fiscal policy because of the _____, _____, and _____ lags.

13. Political problems arise in the application of discretionary fiscal policy to stabilize the economy because government has _____ goals; because voters have a bias in favor of budget (surpluses, deficits) _____; and because politicians use fiscal policies in a way that creates a _____ business cycle.

14. When the Federal government employs an expansionary fiscal policy to increase real NNP and employment in the economy it usually has a budget (surplus, deficit) _____ and (lends, borrows) _____ in the money market.

  a. This will (raise, lower) _____ interest rates in the economy and (contract, expand) _____ investment spending.

  b. This change in investment spending is the _____ effect of the expansionary fiscal policy and it tends to (weaken, strengthen) _____ the impact of the expansionary fiscal policy on real NNP and employment.

15. Fiscal policy is subject to further complications from _____ with the world economy.

  a. The economy can be influenced by _____ shocks that might reinforce or retard fiscal policy; or

  b. from a _____ effect that results from an expansionary or contractionary fiscal policy:

  (1) When fiscal policy is expansionary, it tends to (increase, decrease) _____ interest rates, which in turn tends to _____ the value of the dollar, and _____ net exports.

  (2) When fiscal policy is contractionary, it tends to (increase, decrease) _____ interest rates, which in turn tends to _____ the value of the dollar, and _____ net exports.

16. An expansionary fiscal policy when the economy is operating in the intermediate range of the aggregate-supply curve will increase the real NNP and employment in the economy and (raise, lower) _____ the price level.

  a. This change in the price level will (weaken, strengthen) _____ the impact of the expansionary fiscal policy on output and employment in the economy.

  b. But if the expansionary fiscal policy is the result of reduction in taxes, the supply-side effects of the policy may be to (increase, decrease) _____ aggregate supply, to _____ productivity capacity of the economy, to _____ real NNP and employment, to _____ the rate of inflation, and to (weaken, strengthen) _____ the impact of the fiscal policy on output and employment.

■ **PROBLEMS AND PROJECTS**

1. Consumption and saving schedules are shown in the following table.

Real NNP	C	S	C_a	S_a	$S_a + M + T$	$I + X + G$	$C_a + I + X_n + G$
$1500	$1250	$250	$___	$___	$___	$___	$___
1600	1340	260	___	___	___	___	___
1700	1430	270	___	___	___	___	___
1800	1520	280	___	___	___	___	___
1900	1610	290	___	___	___	___	___
2000	1700	300	___	___	___	___	___
2100	1790	310	___	___	___	___	___

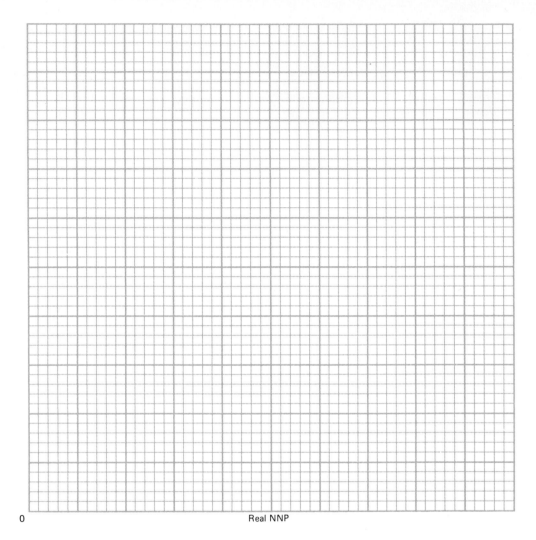

0   Real NNP

a. Assume government levies a lump-sum tax of $100. Also assume that imports are $5.

(1) Because the marginal propensity to consume in this problem is _____, the imposition of this tax will reduce consumption at all levels of real NNP by $_____. Complete the C_a column to show consumption at each real NNP after the levying of this tax.

(2) Because the marginal propensity to save in this problem is _____, this tax will reduce saving at all levels of real NNP by $_____ _____. Complete the S_a column to show saving at each real NNP after this tax has been levied.

b. Compute the (after-tax) saving-plus-imports-plus-taxes at each real NNP and put them in the $S_a + M + T$ column.

c. Suppose that planned net investment is $150, exports are $5, and government purchases of goods and services equal $200. Complete the investment-plus-exports-plus-government-purchases column $(I + X + G)$ and the (after-tax) consumption-plus-investment-plus-net-exports-plus-government-purchases column $(C_a + I + X_n + G)$.

d. The equilibrium real NNP is $ _____

e. On the graphs on pages 132 and 133 plot:

(1) C_a, $I + X_n + G$, $C_a + I + X_n + G$, and the 45-degree line. Show the equilibrium real NNP.

(2) $S_a + M + T$ and $I + X + G$. Show the real equilibrium NNP. (To answer the questions below it is *not* necessary to recompute C, S, $S + M + T$, $I + X + G$, or $C + I + X_n + G$. They can be answered by using the multipliers.)

f. If taxes remained at $100 and government purchases rose by $10, the equilibrium real NNP would (rise, fall) _____ by $ _____

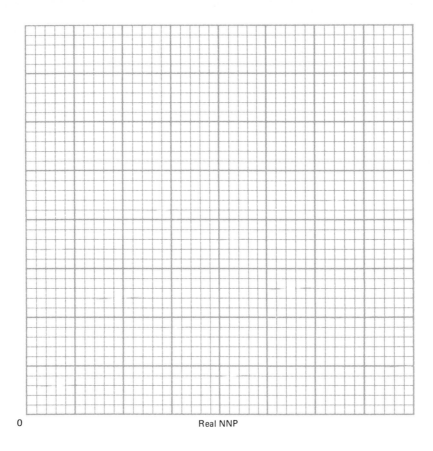

0   Real NNP

g. If government purchases remained at $200 and the lump-sum tax increased by $10, the equilibrium real NNP would _____ by $ _____

h. The combined effect of a $10 increase in government purchases **and** a $10 increase in taxes is to _____ real NNP by $ _____

2. In the table below are seven real NNPs and the net tax revenues of government at each real NNP.

Real NNP	Net tax revenues	Government purchases	Government deficit/surplus
$ 850	$170	$_____	$_____
900	180	_____	_____
950	190	_____	_____
1000	200	_____	_____
1050	210	_____	_____
1100	220	_____	_____
1150	230	_____	_____

a. Looking at the two columns on the left of the table, it can be seen that:

(1) when real NNP increases by $50, net tax revenues (increase, decrease) _____ by $ _____

(2) when real NNP decreases by $100, net tax revenues _____ by $ _____

(3) the relation between real NNP and net tax revenues is (direct, inverse) _____

b. Assume the investment multiplier has a value of 10 and that investment spending in the economy decreases by $10.

(1) **If** net tax revenues remained constant, the equilibrium real NNP would decrease by $ _____

(2) But when real NNP decreases, net tax revenues also decrease; and this decrease in net tax revenues will tend to (increase, decrease) _____ the equilibrium real NNP.

(3) And, therefore, the decrease in real NNP brought about by the $10 decrease in investment spending will be (more, less) _____ than $100.

(4) The direct relationship between net tax revenues and real NNP has (lessened, expanded) _____

the impact of the $10 decrease in investment spending on real NNP.

c. Suppose the government purchases multiplier is also 10 and government wishes to increase the equilibrium real NNP by $50.

(1) *If* net tax revenues remained constant, government would have to increase its purchases of goods and services by $ _____

(2) But when real NNP rises, net tax revenues also rise; and this rise in net tax revenues will tend to (increase, decrease) _____ the equilibrium real NNP.

(3) The effect, therefore, of the $5 increase in government purchases will also be to increase the equilibrium real NNP by (more, less) _____ than $50.

(4) The direct relation between net tax revenues and real NNP has (lessened, expanded) _____ the effect of the $5 increase in government purchases; and to raise the equilibrium real NNP by $50 government will have to increase its purchases by (more, less) _____ than $5.

d. Imagine that the full-employment real NNP of the economy is $1150 and that government purchases of goods and services are $200.

(1) Complete the table on page 133 by entering the government purchases and by computing the budget deficit or surplus at each of the real NNPs. (Show a government deficit by placing a minus sign in front of the amount by which expenditures exceed net tax revenues.)

(2) The full-employment surplus equals $ _____

(3) Were the economy in a recession and producing a real NNP of $900, the budget would show a (surplus, deficit) _____ of $ _____

(4) This budget deficit or surplus makes it appear that government is pursuing a(n) (expansionary, contractionary) _____ fiscal policy; but this deficit or surplus is not the result of countercyclical fiscal policy but the result of the _____

(5) If government did not change its net tax *rates* it could increase the equilibrium real NNP from $900 to the full-employment real NNP of $1150 by increasing its purchases by (approximately) $70. At the full-employment real NNP the budget would show a (surplus, deficit) _____ of $ _____

(6) If government did not change its purchases it would increase the equilibrium real NNP from $900 to the full-employment real NNP of $1150 by decreasing net tax revenues at all real NNPs by a lump sum of (approximately) $80. The full-employment budget would have a (surplus, deficit) _____ of $ _____

3. Columns (1) and (2) in the table below are the aggregate-supply schedule and columns (1) and (3) are the aggregate-demand schedule.

(1) Price level	(2) Real NNP_1	(3) AD_1	(4) AD_2	(5) Real NNP_2
220	2390	2100	2200	2490
200	2390	2200	2340	2490
190	2350	2250	2350	2450
180	2300	2300	2400	2400
160	2200	2400	2500	2300

a. The equilibrium real NNP is $ _____ and the price level is _____

b. Suppose that an expansionary fiscal policy increases aggregate demand from that shown in columns (1) and (3) to that shown in columns (1) and (4).

(1) If the price level remained constant the equilibrium real NNP would increase to $ _____

(2) But the increase in aggregate demand does raise the price level to _____; and this rise in the price level results in real NNP increasing to only $ _____

c. If the expansionary fiscal policy that increased aggregate demand also has supply-side effects and increased aggregate supply from that shown in columns (1) and (2) to that shown in columns (1) and (5):

(1) The equilibrium real NNP would increase to $ _____; and

(2) the price level would _____

■ **SELF-TEST**

Circle the T if the statement is true, the F if it is false.

1. The Employment Act of 1946 committed the Federal government to using monetary and fiscal policy to achieve economic stability.   **T   F**

2. The purposes of discretionary fiscal policy are reduced inflation, the elimination of unemployment, and the stimulation of economic growth.   **T   F**

3. If the MPS were 0.3 and taxes were levied by the government so that consumers paid $20 in taxes at each level of real NNP, consumption expenditures at each level of real NNP would be $14 less.   **T   F**

4. If taxes only are reduced by $10 at all levels of real NNP and the marginal propensity to save is 0.4, equilibrium real NNP will rise by $25. **T F**

5. Even a balanced budget can be a weapon in fighting depression and inflation. **T F**

6. A governmental deficit is contractionary. **T F**

7. A reduction in taxes during a recession would tend to contract the public sector of the economy. **T F**

8. Built-in stabilizers are not sufficiently strong to prevent recession or inflation, but they can reduce the severity of a recession or inflation. **T F**

9. The automatic (or built-in) stabilizers also increase the sizes of the government expenditures and investment multipliers. **T F**

10. The full-employment budget indicates how much government must spend and tax if there is to be full employment in the economy. **T F**

11. A cyclical deficit is the result of countercylical actions by government to stimulate the economy. **T F**

12. If an economy had achieved a full-employment level of output, but tax revenues were less than government expenditures, then a structural deficit is created. **T F**

13. Recognition, administrative, and operational lags in the timing of Federal fiscal policy make fiscal policies more effective in reducing the rate of inflation and decreasing unemployment in the economy. **T F**

14. The fiscal policies of state and local governments have tended to assist and reinforce the efforts of the Federal government to mitigate depression and inflation. **T F**

15. The spending and taxing policies of the Federal government are designed solely to reduce unemployment and limit inflation in the economy. **T F**

16. It is generally easier to induce U.S. Senators and Representatives to vote for decreases in tax rates and for increases in government purchases than for increased taxes and decreased purchases. **T F**

17. Economists who see evidence of a political business cycle argue that members of Congress tend to increase taxes and reduce expenditures before and to reduce taxes and increase expenditures after elections. **T F**

18. For a domestic economy, there are gains from specialization and trade but also complications from the interdependency with the world economy. **T F**

19. A net export effect may partially offset an expansionary fiscal policy. **T F**

20. Supply-side economists maintain that reductions in tax rates decrease aggregate supply and are, therefore, inflationary. **T F**

Circle the letter that corresponds to the best answer.

1. Which of the following established unemployment-rate and inflation-rate goals for the American economy?
(*a*) the Employment Act of 1946
(*b*) the Humphrey-Hawkins Act of 1978
(*c*) the Economic Recovery Act of 1981
(*d*) the Balanced Budget Amendment of 1983

The next four questions (2,3,4, and 5) are based on the consumption schedule below. Investment figures are for planned investment.

Real NNP	C
$300	$290
310	298
320	306
330	314
340	322
350	330
360	338

2. If taxes were zero, government purchases of goods and services $10, and investment $6, and net exports are zero, equilibrium real NNP would be:
(*a*) $310
(*b*) $320
(*c*) $330
(*d*) $340

3. If taxes were $5, government purchases of goods and services $10, and investment $6, and net exports are zero, equilibrium real NNP would be:
(*a*) $300
(*b*) $310
(*c*) $320
(*d*) $330

4. Assume investment is $42, taxes $40, and net exports are zero, government purchases of goods and services zero. If the full-employment level of real NNP is $340, the gap can be eliminated by reducing taxes by:
(*a*) $8
(*b*) $10
(*c*) $13
(*d*) $40

5. Assume that investment is zero, that taxes are zero, net exports are zero, and the government purchases of goods and services are $20. If the full-employment-with-

out-inflation level of real NNP is $330, the gap can be eliminated by decreasing government expenditures by:
(a) $4
(b) $5
(c) $10
(d) $20

6. If the marginal propensity to consume is 0.67 and both taxes and government purchases of goods and services increase by $25, real NNP will:
(a) fall by $25
(b) rise by $25
(c) fall by $75
(d) rise by $75

7. Which of the following policies would do the **most** to reduce inflation?
(a) increase taxes by $5 billion
(b) reduce government purchases of goods and services by $5 billion
(c) increase taxes and government expenditures by $5 billion
(d) reduce both taxes and government purchases by $5 billion

8. If APS is .2 and MPS is .10, a simultaneous increase in both taxes and government spending of $30 billion will:
(a) reduce consumption by $27 billion, increase government spending by $30 billion, and increase NNP by $30 billion
(b) reduce consumption by $27 billion, increase government spending by $27 billion, and increase NNP by $27 billion
(c) reduce consumption by $24 billion, increase government spending by $30 billion, and increase NNP by $30 billion
(d) reduce consumption by $24 billion, increase government spending by $24 billion, and increase NNP by $24 billion

Answer the next two questions (9 and 10) on the basis of the following diagram:

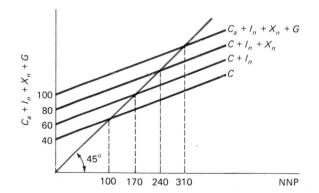

9. The size of the multiplier associated with changes in government spending in this economy is approximately:
(a) .29
(b) 1.50
(c) 2.50
(d) 3.50

10. If this was an open economy without a government sector, the level of NNP would be:
(a) $100
(b) $170
(c) $240
(d) $310

11. In which of the following situations for an open mixed economy will the level of NNP contract?
(a) when $C_a + S + M$ is less than $I_n + X + T$
(b) when $I + M + T$ is less than $C + X + S$
(c) when $S_a + M + T$ is less than $I + X + G$
(d) when $I_n + X + G$ is less than $S_a + M + T$

12. If the government wishes to increase the level of real NNP, it might:
(a) reduce taxes
(b) reduce its purchases of goods and services
(c) reduce transfer payments
(d) reduce the size of the budget deficit

13. Which of the following by itself is the most expansionary (least contractionary)?
(a) redemption of government bonds held by the public
(b) borrowing from the public to finance a budget deficit
(c) a build-up in the size of the government's checking account in the central banks
(d) issuing new money to finance a budget deficit

14. Which of the following by itself is the most contractionary (least expansionary)?
(a) redemption of government bonds held by the public
(b) borrowing from the public to finance a budget deficit
(c) a build-up in the size of the government's checking account in the central banks
(d) issuing new money to finance a budget deficit

15. If the economy is to have built-in stability, when real NNP falls:
(a) tax revenues and government transfer payments should fall
(b) tax revenues and government transfer payments should rise
(c) tax revenues should fall and government transfer payments should rise
(d) tax revenues should rise and government transfer payments should fall

16. A direct relation between net tax revenues and real NNP:

(a) automatically produces budget surpluses during a recession

(b) makes it easier for discretionary fiscal policy to move the economy out of a recession and toward full employment

(c) makes it easier to maintain full employment in a growing economy

(d) reduces the effect of a change in planned investment spending upon the national output and employment

Answer the next three questions (17, 18, and 19) on the basis of the following diagram:

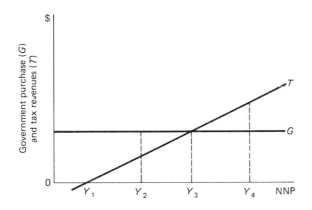

17. If the slope of the line **T** was steeper, there would be:

(a) more in-built stability for the economy

(b) less in-built stability for the economy

(c) no change in the in-built stability for the economy

(d) the need for more emphasis on discretionary fiscal policy

18. If the slope of the line **T** was flatter, there would be:

(a) larger cyclical deficits produced as NNP moved from Y_3 to Y_2

(b) smaller cyclical deficits produced as NNP moved from Y_3 to Y_2

(c) larger structural deficits produced as NNP moved from Y_3 to Y_2

(d) smaller structural deficits produced as NNP moved from Y_3 to Y_2

19. Actions by the Federal government to "index" personal income taxes and lower marginal tax rates would tend to:

(a) flatten the slope of line **T** and increase in-built stability

(b) flatten the slope of line **T** and decrease in-built stability

(d) steepen the slope of line **T** and increase in-built stability

(d) steepen the slope of line **T** and decrease in-built stability

20. The length of time it takes for the fiscal action taken by Congress to affect output, employment, or the price level is referred to as the:

(a) administrative lag

(b) operational lag

(c) recognition lag

(d) fiscal lag

21. The crowding-out effect of an expansionary (deficit) fiscal policy is the result of government borrowing in the money market which:

(a) increases interest rates and net investment spending in the economy

(b) increases interest rates and decreases net investment spending

(c) decreases interest rates and increases net investment spending

(d) decreases interest rates and net investment spending

22. Suppose that the economies of trading partners for the United States improved substantially and at the same time the United States had adopted an expansionary fiscal policy. What would most likely happen in the United States?

(a) there would a rise net exports, a rise in aggregate demand, and the potential for demand-pull inflation

(b) there would be a fall in interest rates, a rise in aggregate demand, and the potential for a recession

(c) there would be a rise in the incomes of trading partners, less demand for United States goods, and the potential for recession

(d) there would be a rise in the employment in other nations, a fall in net exports, and the potential for demand-pull inflation

23. If the United States pursued a contractionary fiscal policy, then what would be the likely effects?

(a) there would be a lower domestic interest rate and an increase in the demand for dollars that would partially offset the policy

(b) there would be a depreciation in the value of the dollar and a decrease in net exports that would partially reinforce the policy

(c) there would be an increase in net exports and an increase in aggregate demand that would partially offset the policy

(d) there would be a decrease in net exports and a decrease in aggregate demand that would partially reinforce the policy

24. The effect of an expansionary (deficit) fiscal policy on the real NNP of an economy operating in the Keynesian range on the aggregate-supply curve is lessened by:

(a) increases in aggregate supply

(b) the crowding-out effect

(c) increases in the price level
(d) both b and c

25. The effect of an expansionary (deficit) fiscal policy on the real NNP of an economy operating in the intermediate range on the aggregate-supply curve is lessened by:
(a) increases in aggregate supply
(b) the crowding-out effect
(c) increases in the price level
(d) both b and c

■ **DISCUSSION QUESTIONS**

1. What is meant by fiscal policy?

2. In the Employment Act of 1946, (a) what responsibility was given to the Federal government; (b) what tasks were assigned to the Council of Economic Advisers and the Joint Economic Committee; and (c) what specific kinds of policy were to be used to achieve the goals established by the act? What did the Humphrey-Hawkins Act require the Federal government to do?

3. What is the exact effect which taxes will have on the consumption schedule? On the saving schedule?

4. Explain why, with government taxing and spending, the equilibrium real NNP is the real NNP at which real NNP equals consumption plus planned investment plus net exports plus government purchases of goods and services; and saving plus imports plus taxes equals planned investment plus exports plus government purchases. What will cause NNP to move to its equilibrium level?

5. If both taxes and government purchases increase by equal amounts, real NNP will increase by that amount. Why?

6. What three things might the Federal government do if its fiscal policy were to be (a) expansionary and if it were to be (b) contractionary? When would it invoke each of these two kinds of policy and what would be their effects on the Federal budget?

7. What are the alternative means of financing deficits and disposing of surpluses available to the Federal government? What is the difference between these methods insofar as their expansionary and contractionary effect is concerned?

8. Explain the fiscal policy that would be advocated during a recession and during a period of inflation (a) by those who wish to expand the public sector and (b) by those who wish to contract the public sector.

9. What is the difference between discretionary and non-discretionary fiscal policy? How do the built-in stabilizers work to reduce rises and falls in the level of money NNP?

10. Explain why a tax system in which net tax revenues vary directly with the level of money NNP makes it difficult to achieve and sustain full employment.

11. What is the full-employment budget? What was the problem which the use of the full-employment budget was designed to solve?

12. Explain the distinction between a cyclical deficit and structural deficit. Which type of deficit provides the best indication of the direction of fiscal policy? Why?

13. Explain the three kinds of time lags that make it difficult to use fiscal policy to stabilize the economy.

14. What are three political problems that complicate the use of fiscal policy to stabilize the economy?

15. How do (a) crowding out and (b) inflation reduce the effect of an expansionary (deficit) fiscal policy on real NNP and employment?

16. What complications for fiscal policy arise from interdependency with the world economy? Explain how aggregate demand shocks from abroad and the net export effect influence fiscal policy.

17. What might be the supply-side effects of a reduction in tax rates on the capacity output of the economy, the equilibrium levels of real NNP and employment, and the price level?

■ **ANSWERS**

CHAPTER 14 FISCAL POLICY

Fill-in questions

1. Employment; a. Economic Advisers, Joint Economic; b. Humphrey-Hawkins (Full Employment and Balanced Growth), goals, plan (program)

2. marginal propensity to consume, marginal propensity to save

3. a. expenditures, output; b. consumption, planned net investment, net exports, government purchases of goods and services; c. planned net investment, exports, government purchases of goods and services, saving, imports, net taxes

4. decrease; the decreases in taxes and government purchases

5. decreased, increased, increased, decreased

6. deficit, surplus

7. borrowing from the public, creating new money, latter

8. increase, taxes, decrease, taxes

9. a. taxes, transfer payments; b. increase, decrease

10. built-in; a. increase, increase, decrease; b. decrease, increase, decrease

11. a. budget surplus or deficit, full employment; b. expansionary, contractionary; c. cyclical, structural, structural

12. recognition, administrative, operational

13. other, deficits, political

14. deficit, borrows; *a.* raise, contract; *b.* crowding-out, weaken

15. mutual interdependency; *a.* aggregate demand; *b.* net export, (1) increase, increase, decrease, (2) decrease, decrease, increase

16. raise; *a.* weaken; *b.* increase, increase, increase, decrease, strengthen

Problems and projects

1. *a.* (1) 0.9, 90, C_a: 1160, 1250, 1340, 1430, 1520, 1610, 1700, (2) 0.1, 10, S_a: 240, 250, 260, 270, 280, 290, 300; *b.* $S_a + M + T$: 345, 355, 365, 375, 385, 395, 405; *c.* $I + X + G$: 355, 355, 355, 355, 355, 355, 355; $C_a + I + X_n + G$: 1510, 1600, 1690, 1780, 1870, 1960, 2050; *d.* 1600; *f.* rise, 100; *g.* fall, 90; *h.* raise, 10

2. *a.* (1) increase, $10, (2) decrease, $20, (3) direct; *b.* (1) $100, (2) increase, (3) less, (4) lessened; *c.* (1) $5, (2) decrease, (3) less, (4) lessened, more; *d.* (1) government expenditures are $200 at all NNPs, government surplus or deficit: -30, -20, -10, 0, 10, 20, 30, (2) $30, (3) deficit, $20, (4) expansionary, recession, (5) deficit, $40, (6) deficit, $50

3. *a.* 2300, 180; *b.* (1) 2400, (2) 190, 2350; *c.* (1) 2400, (2) remain constant

Self-test

1. T; **2.** T; **3.** T; **4.** F; **5.** T; **6.** F; **7.** F; **8.** T; **9.** F; **10.** F; **11.** F; **12.** T; **13.** F; **14.** F; **15.** F; **16.** T; **17.** F; **18.** T; **19.** T; **20.** F

1. *b;* **2.** *c;* **3.** *b;* **4.** *b;* **5.** *a;* **6.** *b;* **7.** *b;* **8.** *a;* **9.** *d;* **10.** *c;* **11.** *d;* **12.** *a;* **13.** *d;* **14.** *c;* **15.** *c;* **16.** *d;* **17.** *a;* **18.** *b;* **19.** *b;* **20.** *b;* **21.** *b;* **22.** *a;* **23.** *c;* **24.** *b;* **25.** *d*

Money and banking

By and large, Chapter 15 is descriptive and factual. It contains only a brief explanation of how the financial system affects the operation of the economy. The purpose of this chapter is, however, to prepare you for a more detailed explanation (in Chapters 16 and 17).

Of special importance in this chapter are the many terms and definitions which will be new to you. These must be learned if the following two chapters and their analysis of how the financial system affects performance of the economy are to be understood. Chapter 15 also contains a factual description of the institutions which compose the American financial system—the Board of Governors of the Federal Reserve System, the Federal Reserve Banks, the commercial banks, and the "thrifts"—and the functions of these four institutions.

You will do well to pay particular attention to the following: (1) what money is and the functions it performs, what types of money exist in the American economy and their relative importance, and how the three measures of the money supply (*M*1, *M*2, and *M*3) are defined; (2) what gives value to or "backs" American money; (3) why people want to have money in their possession and what determines how much money they want to have on hand at any time; (4) how the total demand for money and the money supply together determine the equilibrium rate of interest; and (5) the four principal institutions of the American financial system and their functions.

Several points are worth repeating here because so much depends upon their being fully understood. First, money is whatever performs the three functions of money, and in the United States money consists largely of the debts (promises to pay) of the Federal Reserve Banks and depository institutions. In the United States, this money is "backed" by the goods and services for which its owners can exchange it and not by gold.

Second, because money is used as a medium of exchange, consumers and business firms wish to have money on hand to use for transaction purposes; and the quantity of money they demand for this purpose is directly related to the size of the economy's nominal (or money) gross national product. This means that when either the price level or the real gross national product increases they will want to have more money on hand to use for transactions. But money is also used as a store of value: consumers and firms who own assets may choose to have some of their assets in the form of money (rather than in stocks, bonds, goods, or property). There is, therefore, also an asset demand for money. Holding money, however, imposes a cost on those who hold it. This cost is the interest they lose when they own money rather than (say) bonds. This means that people will demand less money for asset purposes when the rate of interest (the cost of holding money) is high and more when the rate of interest is low: the quantity of money demanded for this purpose is inversely related to the interest rate. The total demand for money is the sum of the transactions demand and the asset demand and, therefore, depends upon the nominal GNP and the rate of interest. This total demand and the money supply determine interest rates in the economy.

Third, the central bank in the United States is the twelve Federal Reserve Banks and the Board of Governors of the Federal Reserve System which oversees their operation. These banks, while privately owned by the commercial banks, are operated more or less as an agency of the Federal government not for profit, but primarily to regulate the nation's money supply in the best interests of the economy as a whole and secondarily to perform other services for the banks, the government, and the economy. They are able to perform their primary function because they are bankers' banks where depository institutions (commercial banks and the "thrifts") can deposit and borrow money. They do not deal directly with the public.

Fourth, these depository institutions accept deposits and make loans, but they also are literally able to create money by lending checkable deposits. Because they are able to do this, they have a strong influence on the size of the money supply and the value of money. The Federal Reserve Banks exist primarily to regulate the money supply and its value by influencing and controlling the amount of money depository institutions create.

■ **CHECKLIST**

When you have studied this chapter you should be able to:
☐ List the three functions of money; and explain the meaning of each function.
☐ Define the money supply, *M*1.
☐ Identify the four kinds of checkable deposits; and the principal kinds of depository institutions.
☐ Explain the meaning of near-money and identify the principal near-monies; and then define *M*2 and *M*3.
☐ Present three reasons why near-monies are important.
☐ Explain why money in the American economy is debt; and whose debts paper money and checkable deposits are.
☐ Present three reasons why currency and checkable deposits are money and have value.
☐ Indicate the precise relationship between the value of money and the price level.
☐ Explain what is meant by stabilizing the value of money and enumerate the two devices government utilizes to try to stabilize its value.
☐ Identify the two demands for money and the determinant of each of these demands; and explain the relationship between each demand and its determinant.
☐ Explain what determines the equilibrium rate of interest; and how changes in the money GNP and in the money supply will affect this interest rate.
☐ Explain how disequilibrium in the money market is corrected through changes in bond prices.
☐ Describe the structure of the American financial system.
☐ Explain why the Federal Reserve Banks are central, quasi-public, bankers' banks.
☐ Enumerate the five functions of the Federal Reserve System; explain the meaning of each of these functions; and indicate which is the most important.

■ **CHAPTER OUTLINE**

1. Money is whatever performs the three basic functions of money: a medium of exchange, a measure of value, and a store of value.

2. In the American economy money is whatever is generally used as a medium of exchange; and consists of the debts of the Federal government and of commercial banks and other financial institutions.
 a. The narrowly defined money supply is called *M*1 and has two principal components.
   (1) The smaller component is currency: coins which are token money and paper money largely in the form of Federal Reserve Notes.

   (2) The larger and more important component is checkable deposits in commercial banks and savings institutions.
   (3) These checkable deposits include demand deposits (checking accounts) and ATS accounts in commercial banks; and other deposits against which checks may be written (NOW accounts and share drafts) in such savings institutions as savings and loan associations, mutual savings banks, and credit unions.
   (4) Currency and checkable deposits owned by the Federal government, commercial banks and savings institutions, and the Federal Reserve Banks are not, however, included in *M*1 or any of the more broadly defined money supplies.
 b. *M*2 and *M*3 are the more broadly defined money supplies; and include not only the currency and checkable deposits in *M*1 but such near-monies as noncheckable savings deposits and time deposits in commercial banks and savings institutions.
 c. The amount of these near-monies held by the public is important for at least three reasons.
 d. Credit cards are not money but are a device by which the cardholders obtain a loan (credit) from the issuer of the card.

3. In the United States:
 a. Money is the promise of a commercial bank, a savings (thrift) institution, or a Federal Reserve Bank to pay; but these debts cannot be redeemed for anything tangible.
 b. Money has value only because people can exchange it for desirable goods and services.
 c. The value of money is inversely related to the price level.
 d. Money is "backed" by the confidence which the public has that the value of money will remain stable; and the Federal government can use monetary and fiscal policy to keep the value of money relatively stable.

4. Business firms and households wish to hold and, therefore, demand money for two reasons.
 a. Because they use money as a medium of exchange they have a transactions demand which is directly related to the nominal gross national product of the economy.
 b. Because they also use money as a store of value they have an asset demand which is inversely related to the rate of interest.
 c. Their total demand for money is the sum of the transactions and asset demands.
 d. This total demand for money along with the supply of money determine the equilibrium interest rate in the money market of the economy.
 e. Disequilibrium in the money market is corrected through changes in bond prices:
   (1) lower bond prices increase interest rates; and
   (2) higher bond prices decrease interest rates.

5. The financial sector of the American economy has changed dramatically in recent years; and the Depository Institutions Deregulation and Monetary Control Act of 1980 narrowed the earlier differences between a commercial bank and the various thrift institutions.

a. But, despite the trend toward deregulation, the financial system remains centralized and regulated by government because the absence of centralization in the past led to an inappropriate supply of money, a multitude of different kinds of money, and a mismanagement of the money supply.

b. In the Federal Reserve System:

(1) The Board of Governors exercises control over the supply of money and the banking system.

(2) The Federal Reserve Banks are central, quasi-public, bankers' banks.

(3) About 14,000 commercial banks exist in the American financial system; and some of them are state banks and some are national banks. But since 1980 the distinctions between state and national banks and between commercial banks and thrift institutions have all but been eliminated.

(4) The thrift institutions, like all commercial banks, are subject to the reserve requirements imposed by and may borrow from the Federal Reserve Banks; but they are also subject to the rules imposed upon them by other regulatory agencies. Both they and the commercial banks by performing the two essential functions of holding deposits and making loans expand the supply of money.

c. The Board of Governors and the Federal Reserve Banks perform five functions aimed at providing certain essential services, supervision of the member commercial banks, and the regulation of the supply of money.

■ IMPORTANT TERMS

Medium of exchange

Measure of value

Store of value

Money supply

*M*1

Currency

Paper money

Checkable deposit

Commercial bank

Thrift (savings) institution

Token money

Intrinsic value

Face value

Federal Reserve Note

Checking account

Demand deposit

Savings and loan association

Mutual savings bank

Credit union

NOW account

Share draft account

ATS account

Near-money

*M*2

*M*3

Noncheckable savings account

Time deposit

Legal tender

Value of money

Federal Deposit Insurance Corporation

Federal Savings and Loan Insurance Corporation

Transactions demand for money

Asset demand for money

Total demand for money

Money market

Bonds

Depository Institutions Deregulation and Monetary Control Act

Depository institution

Board of Governors

Federal Open Market Committee

Federal Advisory Committee

Federal Reserve Bank

Central bank

Quasi-public bank

Bankers' bank

Commercial bank

State bank

National bank

Member bank

■ FILL-IN QUESTIONS

1. Three functions of money are:

a. _____

b. _____

c. _____

2. *M*1 is the sum of:

a. _____ which consists of _____ and paper _____;

b. and (time, checkable) _____ deposits in (commercial banks, thrift institutions, depository institutions) _____

_____

c. not owned by depository institutions, the _____ Banks, or the _____ government.

3. In addition to:

a. commercial banks, the principal depository institutions in the American economy are _____ associations, _____ banks, and _____ unions.

b. checkable deposits include demand deposits, _____ and _____ accounts and _____ drafts.

4. In the American economy:

a. **M**2 is equal to **M**1 plus

(1) (checkable, noncheckable) _____

_____ savings deposits

(2) and (small, large) _____ time deposits

b. **M**3 is equal to **M**2 plus (small, large) _____ time deposits

c. Large time deposits are mainly _____ of deposits which have a face value of $ _____ or more

5. Near-money in the United States includes not only noncheckable savings and time deposits:

a. but such government securities as _____ bills and U.S. government savings _____

b. all of which can be easily converted into _____ or _____ deposits without the risk of financial _____

6. List three reasons why the existence of near-money is important.

a. _____

b. _____

c. _____

7. Money in the United States consists largely of the debts of _____ institutions and the _____ Banks.

8. In the United States currency and checkable deposits:

a. (are, are not) _____ "backed" by gold and silver;

b. are money because they are used as a medium of _____, they are in some cases _____ tender, and they are relatively (abundant, scarce) _____

_____

9. Money has value because it can be exchanged for _____ and its value varies (directly, inversely) _____ with changes in the _____ level.

10. The total demand for money is the sum of:

a. the transactions demand which depends (directly, inversely) _____ upon the _____

b. and the asset demand which depends _____ upon the _____

11. The total demand for money and the _____ of money determine the equilibrium _____ rate in the _____ market.

a. When the quantity of money demanded exceeds the quantity of money supplied, bond prices (increase, decrease) _____ and interest rates _____

b. When the quantity of money demanded is less than the quantity of money supplied, bond prices (increase, decrease) _____ and interest rates _____

12. Two groups which help the Board of Governors of the Federal Reserve System to formulate its policies are _____ and the _____

13. The three principal characteristics of the Federal Reserve Banks are:

a. _____

b. _____

c. _____

14. If a bank is a bankers' bank it means that it accepts the _____ of and makes _____ to (households, business firms, depository institutions, the public sector)_____

15. Both commercial banks and thrift institutions perform two essential functions for the economy: they hold the _____ of and make _____ to the public; and in performing these functions they (increase, decrease) _____ money supply.

16. The five major functions of the Federal Reserve Banks are:

a. _____

b. _____

c. _____

d. _____

e. _____

The most important of the functions which the Federal Reserve Banks perform is that of _____

_____

■ PROBLEMS AND PROJECTS

1. From the figures in the table below it can be concluded that:

	Billions of dollars
Small time deposits	1,630
Large time deposits	645
Checkable deposits	448
Noncheckable savings deposits	300
Currency	170

a. M1 is equal to the sum of $ _____

and $ _____; and totals $ _____ billion.

b. M2 is equal to M1 plus $ _____

and $ _____; and totals $ _____ billion.

c. M3 is equal to M2 plus $ _____ and

totals $ _____ billion.

2. If the price level:
a. Fell by 20%, the value of money would _____

by _____%.

b. Rose by 10%, the value of money would _____

by _____%.

3. The total demand for money is equal to the transaction plus the asset demand for money.
a. Assume each dollar held for transaction purposes is spent (on the average) four times per year to buy final goods and services.
(1) This means that transaction demand for money will

be equal to (what fraction or percent) _____ of the nominal GNP; and
(2) If the nominal GNP is $2000 billion, the transaction

demand will be $ _____ billion.
b. The next schedule shows the number of dollars demanded for asset purposes at each rate of interest.

Rate of interest	Amount of money demanded (billions)	
	For asset purposes	Total
16%	$ 20	$ _____
14	40	_____
12	60	_____
10	80	_____
8	100	_____
6	120	_____
4	140	_____

(1) Given the transactions demand for money in (*a*), complete the table.
(2) On the graph on the next page plot the *total* demand for money (D_m) at each rate of interest.
c. Assume the money supply (S_m) is $580 billion.
(1) Plot this money supply on the graph which you drew on page 146.
(2) Using either the graph or the table, the equilibrium

rate of interest is _____%.
d. Should the money supply:
(1) increase to $600 billion the equilibrium interest rate

would (rise, fall) _____ to _____%.
(2) decrease to $540 billion the equilibrium interest rate

would _____ to _____%.
e. If the nominal GNP:
(1) increased by $80 billion, the total demand for

money would (increase, decrease) _____

by $ _____ billion at each rate of interest and the equilibrium rate of interest would (rise, fall)

_____ by _____%.
(2) decreased by $120 billion, the total demand for

money would _____ by $ _____ billion at each rate of interest and the equilibrium interest

rate would _____ by _____%.

■ SELF-TEST

Circle the T if the statement is true, the F if it is false.

1. The money supply designated M1 is the sum of currency and noncheckable deposits. **T F**

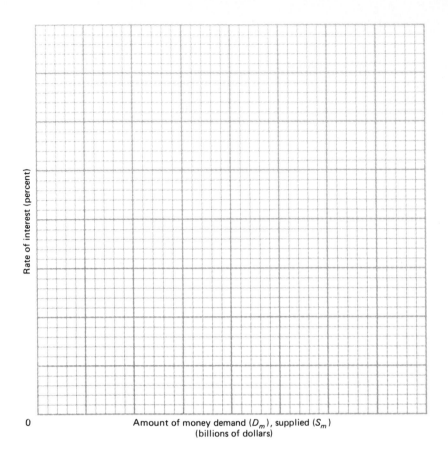

Rate of interest (percent)

0   Amount of money demand (D_m), supplied (S_m)
(billions of dollars)

2. The currency component of *M*1 includes both coins and paper money.   **T   F**

3. If a coin is "token money," its face value is less than its intrinsic value.   **T   F**

4. Both commercial banks and thrift institutions accept checkable deposits.   **T   F**

5. The checkable deposits of the Federal government at the Federal Reserve Banks are a component of *M*1. **T   F**

6. *M*2 exceeds *M*1 by the amount of noncheckable savings and small time deposits.   **T   F**

7. A *small* time deposit is one that is less than $100,000.   **T   F**

8. *M*2 is less than *M*3 by the amount of small time deposits in depository institutions.   **T   F**

9. Economists and public officials are in general agreement on how to define the money supply in the United States.   **T   F**

10. A near-money is a medium of exchange.   **T   F**

11. The larger the volume of near-monies owned by consumers, the larger will be their average propensity to save.   **T   F**

12. Currency and checkable deposits are money because they are acceptable to sellers in exchange for goods and services.   **T   F**

13. If money is to have a fairly stable value, its supply must be limited relative to the demand for it.   **T   F**

14. There is a transactions demand for money because households and business firms use money as a store of value.   **T   F**

15. An increase in the price level would, *ceteris paribus*, increase the transactions demand for money.   **T   F**

16. An increase in the nominal GNP, other things remaining the same, will increase both the total demand for money and the equilibrium rate of interest in the economy.   **T   F**

17. The Board of Governors of the Federal Reserve System is appointed by the President of the United States and confirmed by the Senate.   **T   F**

18. The Federal Reserve Banks are owned and operated by the United States government.   **T   F**

19. Federal Reserve Banks are bankers' banks because they make loans to and accept deposits from depository institutions.   **T   F**

20. The most important function of the Federal Reserve Banks is the control of the size of the economy's money supply.   **T   F**

Circle the letter that corresponds to the best answer.

1. Which of the following is *not* one of the functions of money?
(*a*) a factor of production
(*b*) a medium of exchange
(*c*) a store of value
(*d*) a measure of value

2. Checkable deposits are:
(*a*) all deposits in commercial banks
(*b*) demand deposits in commercial banks
(*c*) deposits in thrift institutions on which checks may be written
(*d*) the sum of *b* and *c* above

3. The largest element of the currency component of *M*1 is:
(*a*) coins
(*b*) United States Notes
(*c*) silver certificates
(*d*) Federal Reserve Notes

4. Which of the following constitutes the largest element in the *M*1 money supply?
(*a*) currency
(*b*) Federal Reserve Notes
(*c*) time deposits
(*d*) checkable deposits

5. Checkable deposits are money because they are:
(*a*) legal tender
(*b*) fiat money
(*c*) a medium of exchange
(*d*) token money

6. Which of the following is *not* called a thrift institution?
(*a*) a commercial bank
(*b*) a savings and loan association
(*c*) a credit union
(*d*) a mutual savings bank

7. Which of the following is *not* a checkable deposit?
(*a*) a NOW account
(*b*) a time deposit

(*c*) an ATS account
(*d*) a share draft

8. The supply of money *M*1 consists almost entirely of the debts of:
(*a*) the Federal government
(*b*) the Federal Reserve Banks
(*c*) depository institutions
(*d*) the Federal Reserve Banks and depository institutions

9. Which of the following is *not* a near-money?
(*a*) a noncheckable savings account
(*b*) a time deposit
(*c*) a credit card
(*d*) a certificate of deposit

10. Which of the following *best* describes the "backing" of money in the United States?
(*a*) the gold bullion stored at Fort Knox, Kentucky
(*b*) the belief of holders of money that it can be exchanged for desirable goods and services
(*c*) the willingness of banks and the government to surrender something of value in exchange for money
(*d*) the faith and confidence of the public in the ability of government to pay its debts

11. If the price level increases 20%, the value of money decreases:
(*a*) 14½%
(*b*) 16⅔%
(*c*) 20%
(*d*) 25%

12. To keep the value of money fairly constant the Federal government and Federal Reserve:
(*a*) utilize price and wage controls
(*b*) employ fiscal policy
(*c*) control the money supply
(*d*) do both *b* and *c* above

13. The total quantity of money demanded is:
(*a*) directly related to nominal GNP and the rate of interest
(*b*) directly related to nominal GNP and inversely related to the rate of interest
(*c*) inversely related to nominal GNP and directly related to the rate of interest
(*d*) inversely related to nominal GNP and the rate of interest

14. There is an asset demand for money because money is:
(*a*) a medium of exchange
(*b*) a measure of value
(*c*) a store of value
(*d*) a standard of deferred payment

15. If the dollars held for transactions purposes are, on the average, spent five times a year for final goods and services, then the quantity of money people will wish to hold for transactions is equal to:
(a) five times the nominal GNP
(b) 20% of the nominal GNP
(c) five divided by the nominal GNP
(d) 20% divided by the nominal GNP

16. An increase in the rate of interest would increase:
(a) the opportunity cost of holding money
(b) the transactions demand for money
(c) the asset demand for money
(d) the prices of bonds

17. Suppose the transactions demand for money is equal to 10% of the nominal GNP, the supply of money is $450 billion, and the asset demand for money is that shown in the table below. If the nominal GNP is $3,000 billion, the equilibrium interest rate is:
(a) 14%
(b) 13%
(c) 12%
(d) 11%

Interest rate (%)	Asset demand (billions)
14	$100
13	150
12	200
11	250

18. Using the information in multiple-choice question 17, if the nominal GNP remains constant an increase in the money supply from $450 billion to $500 billion would cause the equilibrium interest rate to:
(a) rise to 14%
(b) fall to 11%
(c) fall to 12%
(d) remain unchanged

19. The stock of money is determined by the Federal Reserve System and does not change when the interest rate changes, so therefore the:
(a) supply of money curve is downward sloping
(b) demand for money curve is downward sloping
(c) supply of money curve is upward sloping
(d) supply of money curve is vertical

20. If the legal ceiling on the interest rate was set below equilibrium, then the:
(a) quantity of money demanded would be greater than the quantity of money supplied

(b) quantity of money demanded would be less than the quantity of money supplied
(c) supply of money would increase and the demand for money would decrease
(d) demand for money would increase and the supply of money would decrease

21. Which one of the following points would be true?
(a) bond prices and the interest rate are directly related
(b) a lower interest rate raises the opportunity cost of holding money
(c) the supply of money is directly related to the interest rate
(d) the total demand for money is inversely related to the interest rate

Answer the next two questions (22 and 23) on the basis of the following information: Bond price = $10,000; bond fixed annual interest payment = $1,000; bond annual rate of interest = 10%.

22. If the price of this bond decreases by $2,500, the interest rate in effect will:
(a) decrease by 1.1 percentage points
(b) decrease by 1.9 percentage points
(c) increase by 2.6 percentage points
(d) increase by 3.3 percentage points

23. If the price of this bond increases by $2000, the interest rate in effect will:
(a) decrease by 1.7 percentage points
(b) decrease by 2.4 percentage points
(c) increase by 1.1 percentage points
(d) increase by 2.9 percentage points

24. Since the passage of the DIDMC Act in 1980:
(a) both nonmember commercial banks and thrift institutions have been subject to the reserve requirements set by the Federal Banks
(b) the thrift institutions have been allowed to accept checkable deposits
(c) nonmember commercial banks and the thrifts have been allowed to borrow at the Federal Reserve Banks
(d) all of the above

25. Both commercial banks and thrift institutions:
(a) accept the checkable deposits of the public
(b) make loans to the public
(c) expand the money supply
(d) do all of the above

■ **DISCUSSION QUESTIONS**

1. How would you define money? What are the components of the **M**1 supply of money in the United States? Which of these components is the larger?

2. What is (*a*) a checkable deposit; (*b*) a noncheckable deposit; (*c*) a thrift (or savings) institution; (*d*) a depository institution?

3. What is a near-money? What are the more important near-monies in the American economy? Define **M**2 and **M**3 and explain why the existence of near-monies is important.

4. For what reasons are checkable deposits included in the money supply?

5. What "backs" the money used in the United States? What determines the value of money? Explain the relationship between the value of money and the price level.

6. What must government do if it is to stabilize the value of money?

7. What are the two reasons people wish to hold money? How are these two reasons related to the "functions" of money?

8. Explain the determinant of each of the two demands for money and how a change in the size of these determinants will affect the amount of money people wish to hold.

9. The rate of interest is a price. Of what good or service is it the price? Explain how demand and supply determine this price.

10. Describe how changes in bond prices correct disequilibrium in the money market. What is the relationship between bond prices and interest rates?

11. Outline the structure of the Federal Reserve System and explain the chief functions of each of the four parts of the system.

12. As briefly as possible outline the three characteristics of the Federal Reserve Banks and explain the meaning of these characteristics.

13. What are the chief functions which the Federal Reserve Banks perform? Explain briefly the meaning of each of these functions. Which of the chief functions is the most important?

3. *a.* savings and loan, mutual savings, credit; *b.* NOW, ATS (either order), share

4. *a.* (1) noncheckable, (2) small; *b.* large; *c.* certificates, 100,000

5. *a.* Treasury, bonds; *b.* currency, checkable, loss

6. *a.* their existence influences consuming-saving habits; *b.* conversion from near-money to money or from money to near-money may affect the stability of the economy; *c.* important when monetary policy is to be employed

7. depository, Federal Reserve

8. *a.* are not; *b.* exchange, legal, scarce

9. desirable goods and services, inversely, price

10. *a.* directly, nominal GNP; *b.* inversely, rate of interest

11. supply, interest, money; *a.* decrease, increase; *b.* increase, decrease

12. Federal Open Market Committee, Federal Advisory Council

13. *a.* they are central banks; *b.* they are quasi-public banks; *c.* they are bankers' banks

14. deposits, loans, depository institutions

15. deposits, loans, increase

16. *a.* holding the deposits (reserves) of banks and thrifts; *b.* providing for the collection of checks; *c.* acting as fiscal agents for the Federal government; *d.* supervising member banks; *e.* regulating the money supply; regulating the money supply

Problems and projects

1. *a.* 170, 448 (either order), 618; *b.* 300, 1,630 (either order), 2,548; *c.* 645, 3,193

2. *a.* rise, 25; *b.* fall, 9.

3. *a.* (1) ¼ (25%), (2) 500; *b.* (1) 520, 540, 560, 580, 600, 620, 640; *c.* (2) 10; *d.* (1) fall, 8, (2) rise, 14; *e.* (1) increase, 20, rise, 2, (2) decrease, 30, fall, 3

■ **ANSWERS**

CHAPTER 15 MONEY AND BANKING

Fill-in questions

1. *a.* medium of exchange; *b.* measure of value; *c.* store of value

2. *a.* currency, coins, money; *b.* checkable, depository institutions; *c.* Federal Reserve, Federal

Self-test

1. F; **2.** T; **3.** F; **4.** T; **5.** F; **6.** T; **7.** T; **8.** F; **9.** F; **10.** F; **11.** F; **12.** T; **13.** T; **14.** F; **15.** T; **16.** T; **17.** T; **18.** F; **19.** T; **20.** T

1. *a;* **2.** *d;* **3.** *d;* **4.** *d;* **5.** *c;* **6.** *a;* **7.** *b;* **8.** *d;* **9.** *c;* **10.** *b;* **11.** *b;* **12.** *d;* **13.** *b;* **14.** *c;* **15.** *b;* **16.** *a;* **17.** *b;* **18.** *c;* **19.** *d;* **20.** *a;* **21.** *d;* **22.** *d;* **23.** *a;* **24.** *d;* **25.** *d*

How banks create money

Chapter 15 explained the institutional structure of banking in the United States today, the functions which banks and the other depository institutions and money perform, and the composition of the money supply. Chapter 16 explains how banks literally create money—checking account money—and the factors which determine and limit the money-creating ability of commercial banks. Even though the other depository institutions also create checkable deposits, this chapter focuses its attention on the commercial banks because they have and will continue to create a very large part of the total amount of money created by all depository institutions in the United States. But where the term *commercial bank* (or bank) appears it is legitimate to substitute depository *institution;* and it is permissible to substitute *checkable deposit* for *demand deposit* (or checking account).

The device (and a most convenient and simple device it is) employed to explain commercial banking operations and money creation is the balance sheet. All banking transactions affect this balance sheet, and the first step to understanding how money is created is to understand how various simple and typical transactions affect the commercial bank balance sheet.

In reading this chapter you must analyze for yourself the effect upon the balance sheet of each and every banking transaction discussed. The important items in the balance sheet are demand deposits and reserves, because demand deposits *are* money, and the ability of a bank to create new demand deposits is determined by the amount of reserves the bank has. Expansion of the money supply depends upon the possession by commercial banks of excess reserves. Excess reserves do not appear explicitly in the balance sheet but do appear there implicitly because excess reserves are the difference between the actual reserves and the required reserves of commercial banks.

Two cases—the single commercial bank and the banking system—are presented in order to help you build an understanding of banking and money creation. It is important here to understand that the money-creating potential of a single commercial bank differs in an important way from the money-creating potential of the entire banking system; it is equally important to understand how the money-creating ability of many single commercial banks is *multiplied* and results in the money-creating ability of the banking system as a whole.

Certain assumptions are used throughout most of the chapter to analyze money-creating ability; in certain instances these assumptions may not be completely realistic and may need to be modified. The chapter concludes with a discussion of how the earlier analysis must be modified—but not changed in its essentials—to take account of these slightly unrealistic assumptions.

■ CHECKLIST

When you have studied this chapter you should be able to:

☐ Recount the story of how goldsmiths came to issue paper money and became bankers who created money and held fractional reserves.

☐ Explain the effects of the deposit of currency in a checking account on the composition and size of the money supply.

☐ Compute a bank's required and excess reserves when you are given the needed balance-sheet figures.

☐ Explain why a commercial bank is required to maintain a reserve; and why this reserve is not sufficient to protect the depositors from losses.

☐ Indicate how the deposit of a check drawn on one commercial bank in a second commercial bank will affect the reserves and excess reserves of the two banks.

☐ Show what happens to the money supply when a commercial bank makes a loan (or buys securities); and what happens to the money supply when a loan is repaid (or a bank sells securities).

☐ Explain what happens to a commercial bank's reserves and demand deposits after it has made a loan, a check has been written on the newly created demand deposit, deposited in another commercial bank and cleared; and what happens to the reserves and demand deposits of the commercial bank in which the check was deposited.

☐ Describe what would happen to a commercial bank's reserves if it made loans (or bought securities) in an amount that exceeded its excess reserves.

☐ State the money-creating potential of a commercial bank (the amount of money a commercial bank can safely create by lending or buying securities).

☐ State the money-creating potential of the banking system; and explain how it is possible for the banking system to create an amount of money which is a multiple of its excess reserves when no individual commercial bank ever creates money in an amount greater than its excess reserve.

☐ Compute the size of the monetary multiplier and the money-creating potential of the banking system when you are provided with the necessary data.

☐ List the two leakages which reduce the money-creating potential of the banking system.

☐ Explain why the size of the money supply needs to be controlled.

■ CHAPTER OUTLINE

1. The balance sheet of the commercial bank is a statement of the assets, liabilities, and net worth (capital stock) of the bank at a specific time; and in the balance sheet the bank's assets equal its liabilities plus its net worth.

2. The history of the early goldsmiths illustrates how paper money came into being, how they became bankers when they began to make loans and issue money in excess of their gold holdings, and how the presently used fractional reserve system with its two significant characteristics was developed.

3. By examining the ways in which the balance sheet of the commercial bank is affected by various transactions, it is possible to understand how a single commercial bank in a multibank system can create money.

a. Once a commercial bank has been founded,

(1) by selling shares of stock and obtaining cash in return;

(2) and acquired the property and equipment needed to carry on the banking business;

(3) the deposit of cash in the bank does not affect the total money supply; it only changes its composition by substituting demand deposits for currency in circulation;

(4) three reserve concepts are vital to an understanding of the money-creating potential of a commercial bank:

(a) The **legal reserve deposit** (required reserve) which

a bank **must** maintain at its Federal Reserve Bank (or as vault cash—which can be ignored) equals the reserve ratio multiplied by the deposit liabilities of the commercial bank;

(b) the **actual reserves** of a commercial bank are its deposits at the Federal Reserve Bank (plus the vault cash which is ignored);

(c) the **excess reserves** equal to the actual reserves less the required reserve;

(5) the writing of a check upon the bank and its deposit in a second bank results in a loss of reserves and deposits for the first and a gain in reserves and deposits for the second bank.

b. When a single commercial bank lends or buys government securities it increases its own deposit liabilities and, therefore, the supply of money by the amount of the loan or security purchase. But the bank only lends or buys securities in an amount equal to its excess reserves because it fears the loss of reserves to other commercial banks in the economy.

c. When a single commercial bank receives loan repayments or sells government securities, its deposit liabilities and, therefore, the supply of money are decreased by the amount of the loan repayments or securities sale.

d. An individual commercial bank balances its desire for profits (which result from the making of loans and the purchase of securities) with its desire for liquidity or safety (which it achieves by having excess reserves or vault cash).

4. The ability of a banking system composed of many individual commercial banks to lend and to create money is a multiple (greater than one) of its excess reserves; and is equal to the excess reserves of the banking system multiplied by the demand-deposit (or monetary) multiplier.

a. The banking system as a whole can do this even though no single commercial bank ever lends an amount greater than its excess reserve because the banking system, unlike a single commercial bank, does not lose reserves.

b. The monetary (or demand-deposit) multiplier is equal to the reciprocal of the required reserve ratio for demand deposits; and the maximum expansion of demand deposits is equal to the excess reserves in the banking system times the monetary multiplier.

c. The potential lending ability of the banking system may not be fully achieved if there are leakages because borrowers choose to have additional currency or bankers choose to have excess reserves.

d. If bankers lend as much as they are able during periods of prosperity and less than they are able during recessions, they add to the instability of the economy; and to reduce this instability the Federal Reserve Banks must control the size of the money supply.

■ IMPORTANT TERMS

Balance sheet

Fractional reserve system of banking

Vault cash (till money)

Legal (required) reserve (deposit)

Reserve ratio

Fractional reserve

Actual reserve

Excess reserve

Federal Deposit Insurance Corporation

The lending potential of an individual commercial bank

Commercial banking system

Monetary (demand-deposit) multiplier

The lending potential of the banking system

Leakage

■ FILL-IN QUESTIONS

1. The balance sheet of a commercial bank is a statement of the bank's _____,

_____,

and _____
at some specific point in time.

2. The coins and paper money which a bank has in its possession are called _____ cash or _____ money.

3. When a person deposits cash in a commercial bank and receives a demand deposit in return, the size of the money supply has (increased, decreased, not changed)

_____

4. The legal reserve deposit of a commercial bank (ignoring vault cash) must be kept at the _____ and must equal (at least) its _____ multiplied by the _____

5. The excess reserves of a commercial bank equal its _____ less its _____

6. If commercial banks are allowed to accept (or create) deposits in excess of their reserves, the banking system is operating under a system of _____ reserves.

7. When a check is drawn upon bank X, deposited in bank Y, and cleared, the reserves of bank X are (in-

creased, decreased, not changed) _____ and the reserves of bank Y are _____; deposits in bank X are _____ and deposits in bank Y are _____

8. A single commercial bank in a multibank system can safely make loans or buy government securities equal in amount to the _____ of that commercial bank.

9. When a commercial bank makes a new loan of $10,000, it (increases, decreases) _____ the supply of money by $_____; but when this loan is repaid, the supply of money _____ by $_____

10. When a commercial bank sells a $2000 government bond to a securities dealer the supply of money (increases, decreases) _____ by $_____; but when a commercial bank buys a $2000 government bond from a securities dealer the supply of money _____ by $_____

11. A bank ordinarily pursues two conflicting goals; they are _____ and _____

12. The banking system can make loans (or buy government securities) and create money in an amount equal to its excess reserves multiplied by the _____

_____.
Its lending potential per dollar of excess reserves is greater than the lending potential of a single commercial bank because it does not lose _____ to other banks.

13. The greater the reserve ratio is, the (larger, smaller) _____ is the monetary multiplier.

14. If the required reserve ratio is 16⅔%, the banking system is $6 million short of reserves, and the banking system is unable to increase its reserves, the banking system must _____ the money supply by $ _____

15. The money-creating potential of the commercial banking system is lessened by the withdrawal of

_____ from banks and by the decisions
of bankers to keep _____ reserves.

16. Commercial banks in the past:

a. have kept considerable excess reserves during periods of (prosperity, recession) _____ and have kept few or no excess reserves during periods of

_____

b. and by behaving in this way have made the economy (more, less) _____ unstable.

		(a)	(b)	(c)	(d)
Assets:					
Cash	$100	$___	$___	$___	$___
Reserves	200	___	___	___	___
Loans	500	___	___	___	___
Securities	200	___	___	___	___
Liabilities and net worth:					
Demand deposits	900	___	___	___	___
Capital stock	100	100	100	100	100

■ PROBLEMS AND PROJECTS

1. At the top of the next column is the simplified balance sheet of a commercial bank. Assume that the figures given show the bank's assets and demand-deposit liabilities *prior to each of the following four transactions.* Draw up the balance sheet as it would appear after each of these transactions is completed and place the balance-sheet figures in the appropriate column. *Do not* use the figures you place in columns a, b, or c when you work the next part of the problem: start all parts of the problem with the printed figures.

a. A check for $50 is drawn by one of the depositors of the bank, given to a person who deposits it in another bank, and cleared (column a).

b. A depositor withdraws $50 in cash from the bank, and the bank restores its vault cash by obtaining $50 in additional cash from its Federal Reserve Bank (column b).

c. A check for $60 drawn on another bank is deposited in this bank and cleared (column c).

d. The bank sells $100 in government bonds to the Federal Reserve Bank in its district (column d).

2. Below are five balance sheets for a single commercial bank (columns 1a–5a). The required reserve ratio is 20%.

a. Compute the required reserves (A); ignoring vault cash, the excess reserves (B) of the bank (if the bank is short of reserves and must reduce its loans or obtain additional reserves, show this by placing a minus sign in front of the amounts by which it is short of reserves); and the amount of new loans it can extend (C).

	(1a)	(2a)	(3a)	(4a)	(5a)
Assets:					
Cash	$ 10	$ 20	$ 20	$ 20	$ 15
Reserves	40	40	25	40	45
Loans	100	100	100	100	150
Securities	50	60	30	70	60
Liabilities and net worth:					
Demand deposits	175	200	150	180	220
Capital stock	25	20	25	50	50
A. Required reserve	$___	$___	$___	$___	$___
B. Excess reserve	___	___	___	___	___
C. New loans	___	___	___	___	___

b. Draw up for the individual bank the five balance sheets as they appear after the bank has made the new *loans* that it is capable of making (columns 1b–5b).

	(1b)	(2b)	(3b)	(4b)	(5b)
Assets:					
Cash	$___	$___	$___	$___	$___
Reserves	___	___	___	___	___
Loans	___	___	___	___	___
Securities	___	___	___	___	___
Liabilities and net worth:					
Demand deposits	___	___	___	___	___
Capital stock	___	___	___	___	___

3. In the table at the top of the next column are several reserve ratios. Compute the monetary multiplier for each of the reserve ratios and enter the figures in column 2. In column 3 show the maximum amount by which a single commercial bank can increase its loans for each dollar's worth of excess reserves it possesses. In column 4 indicate the maximum amount by which the banking system can increase its leans for each dollar's worth of excess reserves in the system.

	(1)	(2)	(3)	(4)
12½%	___	$___	$___	
16⅔%	___	___	___	
20%	___	___	___	
25%	___	___	___	
30%	___	___	___	
33⅓%	___	___	___	

4. Shown below is the simplified consolidated balance sheet for *all* commercial banks in the economy. Assume that the figures given show the banks' assets and liabilities *prior to each of the following three transactions;* and that the reserve ratio is 20%. *Do not* use the figures you placed in columns 2 and 4 when you begin parts *b* and *c* of the problem: start parts *a, b,* and *c* of the problem with the printed figures.

a. The public deposits $5 in cash in the banks and the banks send the $5 to the Federal Reserve, where it is added to their reserves. Fill in column 1. If the banking system extends the new loans it is capable of extending, show in column 2 the balance sheet as it would then appear.

b. The banking system sells $8 worth of securities to the Federal Reserve. Complete column 3. Assuming the system extends the maximum amount of credit of which it is capable, fill in column 4.

c. The Federal Reserve lends $10 to the commercial banks; complete column 5. Complete column 6 showing the condition of the banks after the maximum amount of new loans which the banks are capable of making is granted.

	(1)	(2)	(3)	(4)	(5)	(6)
Assets:						
Cash	$ 50	$___	$___	$___	$___	$___	$___
Reserves	100	___	___	___	___	___	___
Loans	200	___	___	___	___	___	___
Securities	200	___	___	___	___	___	___
Liabilities and net worth:						
Demand deposits	500	___	___	___	___	___	___
Capital stock	50	50	50	50	50	50	50
Loans from Federal Reserve	0	___	___	___	___	___	___
Excess reserves		___	___	___	___	___	___
Maximum possible expansion of the money supply		___	___	___	___	___	___

■ **SELF-TEST**

Circle the T if the statement is true, the F if it is false.

1. The balance sheet of a commercial bank shows the transactions in which the bank has engaged during a given period of time.   **T   F**

2. A commercial bank's assets plus its net worth equal the bank's liabilities.   **T   F**

3. Goldsmiths increased the money supply when they accepted deposits of gold and issued paper receipts to the depositors.   **T   F**

4. Roberta Lynn, the dancing star, deposits a $30,000 check in a commercial bank and receives a demand deposit in return; an hour later the Manfred Iron and Coal Company borrows $30,000 from the same bank. The money supply has increased $30,000 as a result of the two transactions.   **T   F**

5. A commercial bank may maintain its legal reserve either as a deposit in its Federal Reserve Bank or as government bonds in its own vault.   **T   F**

6. The legal reserve which a commercial bank maintains must equal at least its own deposit liabilities multiplied by the required reserve ratio.   **T   F**

7. The actual reserves of a commercial bank equal excess reserves plus required reserves.   **T   F**

8. The reserve of a commercial bank in the Federal Reserve Bank is an asset of the Federal Reserve Bank.   **T   F**

9. A check for $1000 drawn on bank X by a depositor and deposited in bank Y will increase the excess reserves of bank Y by $1000.   **T   F**

10. A single commercial bank can safely lend an amount equal to its excess reserves multiplied by the required reserve ratio.   **T   F**

11. When a borrower repays a loan of $500, either in cash or by check, the supply of money is reduced by $500.   **T   F**

12. The granting of a $5000 loan and the purchase of a $5000 government bond from a securities dealer by a commercial bank have the same effect on the money supply.   **T   F**

13. A commercial bank seeks both profits and liquidity; but these are conflicting goals.   **T   F**

14. If the banking system has $10 million in excess reserves and if the reserve ratio is 25%, it can increase its loans by $40 million.   **T   F**

15. While a single commercial bank can increase its loans only by an amount equal to its excess reserves, the entire banking system can increase its loans by an amount equal to its excess reserves multiplied by the reciprocal of the reserve ratio.   **T   F**

16. When borrowers from a commercial bank wish to have cash rather than demand deposits, the money-creating potential of the banking system is increased.   **T   F**

17. The FSLIC insures deposit liabilities of commercial banks up to $100,000 per account, while the FDIC insures deposit liabilities of savings and loan institutions up to $100,000 per account.   **T   F**

18. Modern banking systems use gold as the basis for the fractional reserve system.   **T   F**

19. The selling of a government bond by a commercial bank will increase the money supply.   **T   F**

20. There is a need for the Federal Reserve System to control the money supply because profit-seeking banks tend to make changes in the money supply that are procyclical.   **T   F**

Circle the letter that corresponds to the best answer.

1. The goldsmiths became bankers when:
 (*a*) they accepted deposits of gold for safe storage
 (*b*) they issued receipts for the gold stored with them
 (*c*) their receipts for deposited gold were used as paper money
 (*d*) they issued paper money in excess of the amount of gold stored with them

2. When cash is deposited in a demand-deposit account in a commercial bank there is:
 (*a*) a decrease in the money supply
 (*b*) an increase in the money supply
 (*c*) no change in the composition of the money supply
 (*d*) a change in the composition of the money supply

3. A commercial bank has actual reserves of $9000 and deposit liabilities of $30,000; and the required reserve ratio is 20%. The excess reserves of the bank are:
 (*a*) $3000
 (*b*) $6000
 (*c*) $7500
 (*d*) $9000

4. A commercial bank is required to have a deposit at its Federal Reserve Bank in order:
 (*a*) to protect the deposits in the commercial bank against losses
 (*b*) to provide the means by which checks drawn on the commercial bank and deposited in other commercial banks can be collected

(c) to add to the liquidity of the commercial bank and protect it against a "run" on the bank

(d) to provide the Board of Governors of the Federal Reserve System with a means of controlling the lending ability of the commercial bank

5. A depositor places $750 in cash in a commercial bank, and the reserve ratio in 33⅓%; the bank sends the $750 to the Federal Reserve Bank. As a result, the *reserves* and the *excess reserves* of the bank have been increased, respectively, by:

(a) $750 and $250
(b) $750 and $500
(c) $750 and $750
(d) $500 and $500

6. A commercial bank has no excess reserves, but then a depositor places $600 in cash in the bank, and the bank adds the $600 to its reserves by sending it to the Federal Reserve Bank. The commercial bank then lends $300 to a borrower. As a consequence of these transactions the size of the money supply has:

(a) not been affected
(b) increased by $300
(c) increased by $600
(d) increased by $900

7. A commercial bank has excess reserves of $500 and a required reserve ratio of 20%; it grants a loan of $1000 to a borrower. If the borrower writes a check for $1000 which is deposited in another commercial bank, the first bank will be short of reserves, after the check has been cleared, in the amount of:

(a) $200
(b) $500
(c) $700
(d) $1000

8. A commercial bank sells a $1000 government security to a securities dealer. The dealer pays for the bond in cash, which the bank adds to its vault cash. The money supply has:

(a) not been affected
(b) decreased by $1000
(c) increased by $1000
(d) increased by $1000 multiplied by the reciprocal of the required reserve ratio

9. A commercial bank has deposit liabilities of $100,000, reserves of $37,000, and a required reserve ratio of 25%. The amount by which a **single commercial bank** and the amount by which the **banking system** can increase loans are, respectively:

(a) $12,000 and $48,000
(b) $17,000 and $68,000
(c) $12,000 and $60,000
(d) $17,000 and $85,000

10. If the required reserve ratio were 12½% the value of the monetary multiplier would be:

(a) 5
(b) 6
(c) 7
(d) 8

11. The commercial banking system has excess reserves of $700 and makes new loans of $2100 and is just meeting its reserve requirements. The required reserve ratio is:

(a) 20%
(b) 25%
(c) 30%
(d) 33⅓%

12. The commercial banking system, because of a recent change in the required reserve ratio from 20% to 30%, finds that it is $60 million short of reserves. If it is unable to obtain any additional reserves it must decrease the money supply by:

(a) $60 million
(b) $180 million
(c) $200 million
(d) $300 million

13. Only one commercial bank in the banking system has an excess reserve, and its excess reserve is $100,000. This bank makes a new loan of $80,000 and keeps an excess reserve of $20,000. If the required reserve ratio for all banks is 20%, the potential expansion of the money supply is:

(a) $80,000
(b) $100,000
(c) $400,000
(d) $500,000

14. The money-creating potential of the banking system is reduced when:

(a) bankers choose to have excess reserves
(b) borrowers choose to hold none of the funds they have borrowed in currency
(c) the Federal Reserve lowers the required reserve ratio
(d) bankers borrow from the Federal Reserve

15. The excess reserves held by banks tend to:

(a) rise during periods of prosperity
(b) fall during periods of recession
(c) rise during periods of recession
(d) fall when interest rates in the economy fall

16. Unless controlled, the money supply will:

(a) fall during periods of prosperity
(b) rise during periods of recession
(c) change in a procyclical fashion
(d) change in an anticyclical fashion

Use the following balance sheet for the First National Bank in answering the next five questions (17, 18, 19, 20, and 21). Assume the required reserve ratio is 20%.

Assets		Liabilities and Net Worth	
Reserves	$ 50,000	Demand Deposits	$150,000
Loans	70,000	Capital Stock	100,000
Securities	30,000		
Property	100,000		

17. This commercial bank has excess reserves of:
(a) $10,000
(b) $20,000
(c) $30,000
(d) $40,000

18. This bank can safely expand its loans by a maximum of:
(a) $50,000
(b) $40,000
(c) $30,000
(d) $20,000

19. Using the original bank balance sheet, assume that the bank makes a loan of $10,000 and has a check cleared against it for the amount of the loan, then its reserves and demand deposits will now be:
(a) $40,000 and $140,000
(b) $40,000 and $150,000
(c) $30,000 and $150,000
(d) $60,000 and $140,000

20. Using the original bank balance sheet, assume that the bank makes a loan of $15,000 and has a check cleared against it for the amount of the loan, then it will have excess reserves of:
(a) $5,000
(b) $10,000
(c) $15,000
(d) $20,000

21. If the original bank balance sheet was for the commercial banking *system,* rather than a single bank, loans and deposits could have been expanded by a maximum of:
(a) $50,000
(b) $100,000
(c) $150,000
(d) $200,000

22. The claims of the owners of the bank against the bank assets is the bank's:
(a) net worth
(b) liabilities

(c) balance sheet
(d) fractional reserves

23. The selling of government bonds by commercial banks is most similar to the:
(a) making of loans by banks because both actions increase the money supply
(b) making of loans by banks because both actions decrease the money supply
(c) repayment of loans to banks because both actions decrease the money supply
(d) repayment of loan to banks because both actions increase the money supply

Answer the next two questions (24 and 25) on the basis of the following consolidated balance sheet for the commercial banking system. All figures are in billions. Assume that the required reserve ratio is 12.5%.

Assets		Liabilities and Net Worth	
Reserves	$ 40	Demand Deposits	$200
Loans	80	Capital Stock	120
Securities	100		
Property	200		

24. The maximum amount by which this commercial banking system can expand the supply of money by lending is:
(a) $120 billion
(b) $240 billion
(c) $350 billion
(d) $440 billion

25. If there is a deposit of $20 billion of new currency into checking accounts in the banking system, excess reserves will increase by:
(a) $16.5 billion
(b) $17.0 billion
(c) $17.5 billion
(d) $18.5 billion

■ **DISCUSSION QUESTIONS**

1. How did the early goldsmiths come to issue paper money and then become bankers? Explain the difference between a 100% and a fractional reserve system of banking and why the latter system is subject to "runs" and requires public regulation.

2. Commercial banks seek both profits and safety. Explain how the balance sheet of the commercial banks reflects the desires of bankers for income and for liquidity.

3. Do the reserves held by commercial banks satisfactorily protect the bank's depositors? Are the reserves of commercial banks needed? Explain your answers.

4. Explain why the granting of a loan by a commercial bank increases the supply of money. Why does the repayment of a loan decrease the supply of money?

5. How does the buying or selling of government securities by commercial banks influence the money supply?

6. The owner of a sporting goods store writes a check on his account in a Kent, Ohio, bank and sends it to one of his suppliers who deposits it in his bank in Cleveland, Ohio. How does the Cleveland bank obtain payment from the Kent bank? If the two banks were in Kent and New York City, how would one bank pay the other? How are the excess reserves of the two banks affected?

7. Why is a single commercial bank able to lend safely only an amount equal to its excess reserves?

8. No one commercial bank ever lends an amount greater than its excess reserve, but the banking system as a whole is able to extend loans and expand the money supply by an amount equal to the system's excess reserves multiplied by the reciprocal of the reserve ratio. Explain why this is possible and how the multiple expansion of deposits and money takes place.

9. On the basis of a given amount of excess reserves and a given reserve ratio, a certain expansion of the money supply may be possible. What are two reasons why the potential expansion of the money supply may not be fully achieved?

10. Why is there a "need for monetary control" in the American economy?

■ **ANSWERS**

CHAPTER 16 HOW BANKS CREATE MONEY

Fill-in questions

1. assets, liabilities, net worth (capital)
2. vault, till
3. not changed
4. Federal Reserve Bank in its district, deposit liabilities, reserve ratio
5. actual reserves, required reserves
6. fractional
7. decreased, increased, decreased, increased
8. excess reserves
9. increases, 10,000, decreases, 10,000
10. decreases, 2000, increases, 2000
11. profits, liquidity (safety)
12. monetary multiplier (reciprocal of the reserve ratio), reserves
13. smaller
14. decrease, 36 million
15. currency (cash), excess
16. a. recession, prosperity; b. more

Problems and projects

1.

	(a)	(b)	(c)	(d)
Assets:				
Cash	$100	$100	$100	$100
Reserves	150	150	260	300
Loans	500	500	500	500
Securities	200	200	200	100
Liabilities and net worth:				
Demand deposits	850	850	960	900
Capital stock	100	100	100	100

2.

a.

	(1a)	(2a)	(3a)	(4a)	(5a)
A. Required reserve	$35	$40	$30	$36	$44
B. Excess reserve	5	0	−5	4	1
C. New loans	5	0	*	4	1

b.

	(1b)	(2b)	(3b)	(4b)	(5b)
Assets:					
Cash	$ 10	$ 20	$20	$ 20	$ 15
Reserves	40	40	25	40	45
Loans	105	100	*	104	151
Securities	50	60	30	70	60
Liabilities and net worth:					
Demand deposits	180	200	*	184	221
Capital stock	25	20	25	50	50

* If an individual bank is $5 short of reserves it must either obtain additional reserves of $5 by selling loans, securities, or its own IOUs to the reserve bank or contract its loans by $25.

3. column 2: 8, 6, 5, 4, 3⅓, 3; column 3: 1,1,1,1,1,1; column 4: 8, 6, 5, 4, 3⅓, 3

4.

	(1)	(2)	(3)	(4)	(5)	(6)
Assets:						
Cash	$ 50	$ 50	$ 50	$ 50	$ 50	$ 50
Reserves	105	105	108	108	110	110
Loans	200	220	200	240	200	250
Securities	200	200	192	192	200	200
Liabilities and net worth:						
Demand deposits	505	525	500	540	500	550
Capital stock	50	50	50	50	50	50
Loans from Federal						
Reserve	0	0	0	0	10	10
Excess reserves	4	0	8	0	10	0
Maximum possible expansion						
of the money supply	20	0	40	0	50	0

Self-test

1. F; **2.** F; **3.** F; **4.** T; **5.** F; **6.** T; **7.** T; **8.** F; **9.** F; **10.** F; **11.** T; **12.** T; **13.** T; **14.** T; **15.** T; **16.** F; **17.** F; **18.** F; **19.** F; **20.** T

1. *d;* **2.** *d;* **3.** *a;* **4.** *d;* **5.** *b;* **6.** *b;* **7.** *b;* **8.** *b;* **9.** *a;* **10.** *d;* **11.** *d;* **12.** *c;* **13.** *c;* **14.** *a;* **15.** *c;* **16.** *c;* **17.** *b;* **18.** *d;* **19.** *b;* **20.** *a;* **21.** *b;* **22.** *a;* **23.** *c;* **24.** *a;* **25.** *c*

The Federal Reserve Banks and monetary policy

Chapter 17 is the third chapter dealing with money and banking. It explains how the Board of Governors of the Federal Reserve System and the Federal Reserve Banks affect output, income, employment, and the price level of the economy. Central-bank policies designed to affect these variables are called monetary policies, the goal of which is full employment without inflation.

You should have little difficulty with this chapter if you have understood the material in Chapter 16. In the first half of Chapter 17 attention should be concentrated on the following: (1) the important items on the balance sheet of the Federal Reserve Banks; (2) the three major controls available to the Federal Reserve Banks, and how the employment of these controls can affect the reserves, excess reserves, the actual money supply, and the money-creating potential of the banking system; (3) the actions the Federal Reserve would take if it were pursuing a tight money policy to curb inflation, and the actions it would take if it were pursuing an easy money policy to reduce unemployment; (4) the relative importance of the three major controls; and (5) the three minor selective controls which the Federal Reserve Banks use or have used to influence the economy.

In order to acquire a thorough knowledge of the manner in which each of the Federal Reserve transactions affects reserves, excess reserves, the actual money supply, and the potential money supply, you must study very carefully each of the sets of balance sheets which are used to explain these transactions. On these balance sheets the items to watch are again reserves and demand deposits! Be sure that you know why each of the balance sheet changes is made and are able, **on your own,** to make the appropriate balance-sheet entries to trace through the effects of any transaction.

Following the examination of "The Tools of Monetary Policy" Professors McConnell and Brue explain how the demand for and the supply of money determine the interest rate (in the "money market"); how the interest rate and the investment-demand schedule determine the level of

planned investment in the economy; and how planned investment and the saving schedule together determine the equilibrium NNP. How an easy money policy and a tight money policy work through this cause-effect chain is illustrated with examples and summarized in Table 17–3, which you should study.

This explanation of the Keynesian view of monetary policy makes it clear that the effect of a change in the money supply depends upon just how steep or flat the down sloping demand-for-money and investment-demand curves are. Professors McConnell and Brue also use the aggregate-supply and the aggregate-demand curves to show you how changes in the money supply affect national output and the price level in the three stages along the aggregate-supply curve.

The strengths and shortcomings of monetary policy in reducing unemployment (and expanding national output) and in reducing inflation are examined in the next-to-last major section of the chapter. Here you will also encounter the dilemma faced by the Fed: it cannot simultaneously control both the money supply and the level of interest rates in the economy. You will also learn that monetary policy is further complicated by linkages with the international economy.

The last section of Chapter 17 is a summary of Chapters 9 through 17. It will restate for you the main outline of the Keynesian theory of employment and the principal public policies that may be used to promote full employment without creating inflation. They will help you to see that the various principles discussed in the previous chapters are *not* separate theories but are, in fact, connected parts of the one Keynesian theory; and that the public policies discussed in earlier chapters are *not* really separate policies but are alternative means of achieving the goal of economic stabilization.

This one theory of employment and the alternative means of achieving this one goal are summarized for you in Figure 17–4. This is probably the single most important figure in the textbook.

■ CHECKLIST

When you have studied this chapter you should be able to:

☐ State the fundamental objective of monetary policy.

☐ List the important assets and liabilities of the Federal Reserve Banks.

☐ Identify the three tools of monetary policy; and explain how each may be employed by the Federal Reserve to expand and to contract the money supply.

☐ Prescribe the three specific monetary policies the Federal Reserve should utilize to reduce unemployment; and the three specific policies it should employ to reduce inflationary pressures in the economy.

☐ State which of the three monetary-policy tools is the most effective.

☐ Identify three selective controls; and explain how each is used to promote economic stability.

☐ Draw the demand-for-money and the supply-of-money curves and use them to show how a change in the supply of money will affect the interest rate; draw an investment-demand curve to explain the effects of changes in the interest rate on investment spending; and construct a leakages-injections graph to show the effects of a change in planned investment on the equilibrium NNP.

☐ Explain, using the Keynesian cause-effect chain, the links between a change in the money supply and a change in the equilibrium NNP when there is an easy money policy and when there is a tight money policy.

☐ State precisely how the steepness of the demand-for-money and of the investment-demand curves affects the impact of a change in the money supply on the equilibrium NNP.

☐ Use the aggregate-demand and aggregate-supply curves to show the effects of changes in the money supply on national output and the price level in the Keynesian, classical, and intermediate ranges.

☐ List three strengths and three shortcomings of monetary policy.

☐ State the target (or policy) dilemma confronted by the Fed; and explain why it faces this dilemma.

☐ Describe how the effectiveness of an easy money policy or a tight money policy is influenced by net exports and how these policies affect international trade deficits.

☐ Summarize the Keynesian theory of employment and the policies that may be utilized to promote a full-employment noninflationary NNP.

■ CHAPTER OUTLINE

1. The objective of monetary policy is full employment without inflation. The Federal Reserve Banks can accomplish this objective by exercising control over the amount of excess reserves held by commercial banks and thereby influencing the size of the money supply and the level of aggregate expenditures.

2. By examining the consolidated balance sheet and the principal assets and liabilities of the Federal Reserve Banks, an understanding of the ways in which the Federal Reserve can control and influence the reserves of commercial banks and the money supply can be obtained.

a. The principal assets of the Federal Reserve Banks (in order of size) are U.S. government securities and loans to commercial banks.

b. Their principal liabilities are Federal Reserve Notes, the reserve deposits of commercial banks and U.S. Treasury deposits.

3. The Federal Reserve Banks employ three principal tools (techniques or instruments) to control the reserves of banks and the size of the money supply.

a. The Federal Reserve can buy and sell government securities in the open market.

(1) Buying securities in the open market from either banks or the public increases the reserves of banks.

(2) Selling securities in the open market to either banks or the public decreases the reserves of banks.

b. It can raise or lower the reserve ratio.

(1) Raising the reserve ratio decreases the excess reserves of banks and the size of the monetary (demand-deposit) multiplier.

(2) Lowering the reserve ratio increases the excess reserves of banks and the size of the monetary multiplier.

c. And it can also lower the discount rate to encourage banks to borrow reserves from the Fed and raise it to discourage them from borrowing reserves from the Fed.

d. A tight (easy) money policy involves increasing (decreasing) the reserve ratio, selling (buying) bonds in the open market, and increasing (decreasing) the discount rate.

e. Open-market operations are the most effective device for controlling the money supply.

f. The Federal Reserve may also employ selective controls to affect the availability of credit; and these controls are the setting of margin requirements, the setting of the terms of credit available to purchasers of durable consumer goods, and moral suasion.

4. To state the effects of monetary policy on the equilibrium NNP from the Keynesian view:

a. In the money market the demand-for- and the supply-of-money curves determine the real interest rate; the investment-demand curve and this rate of interest determine planned investment; and planned investment along with the saving curve determine the equilibrium NNP.

b. If unemployment and deflation is the problem, the Federal Reserve takes policy actions to increase the money supply, causing the interest rate to fall and investment spending to increase, thereby increasing real NNP by a multiple of the increase in investment.

c. But if inflation is the problem, the Federal Reserve uses its tools to decrease the money supply, causing the interest rate to rise and investment spending to decrease, and thereby reducing inflation.

d. There are refinements and feedback effects to monetary policy that must be considered:

(1) The steeper the demand-for-money curve and the flatter the investment-demand curve the greater will be the effect on the equilibrium NNP of a change in the money supply.

(2) Changes in the equilibrium NNP that result from a change in the money supply will alter the demand for money and dampen the effect of the change in the money supply on the NNP.

e. Stated in terms of the aggregate demand-aggregate supply model: the flatter (steeper) the aggregate-supply curve is, the greater (smaller) is the effect of a change in the money supply on real national output and employment and the smaller (greater) is the effect on the price level.

5. Whether monetary policy is effective in promoting full employment without inflation is a debatable question because monetary policy has both strengths and shortcomings in fighting recession and inflation.

a. Its strengths are that it can be more quickly changed than fiscal policy; it is more isolated from political pressure than fiscal policy; and (some economists believe) it is the key determinant of economic activity and, therefore, more effective than fiscal policy.

b. Its weaknesses are that it is more effective in fighting inflation than it is in curbing recession; it can be offset by changes in the velocity of money; and it may not have a significant impact on investment spending in the economy.

c. A most difficult problem for the Fed is its inability to control both the money supply and the level of interest rates at the same time.

(1) If the Fed's policy target is the stabilization of interest rates, an increase in the money GNP (and the resulting increase in the demand for money) will require it to increase the money supply; and if its policy target is the stabilization of the money supply, an increase in the money GNP (and the demand for money) will force interest rates upward.

(2) Controversy surrounds the issue of which of these two policy targets is preferable. The Fed switched from stabilizing interest rates to stabilizing the money supply in October of 1979, and from stabilizing the money supply to a middle-of-the-road policy in October of 1982. This flexible policy has been used by the Federal Reserve to deal with the stock market crash of 1987 and with changes in the measurement of money supply targets.

6. There are international linkages to monetary policy:

a. An easy money policy to bring the economy out of recession or slow growth will tend to lower domestic interest rates and cause the dollar to depreciate. In this situation, net exports will increase, thus increasing aggregate demand and reinforcing the effect of the easy money policy.

b. A tight money policy to reduce inflation will tend to raise domestic interest rates and cause the dollar to appreciate. These events will decrease net exports and reduce aggregate demand, thereby strengthening the tight money policy.

c. An easy policy is compatible with the goal of correcting a balance of trade deficit, but a tight money policy conflicts with this economic goal.

7. The income, employment, output, and prices of an economy are in Keynesian theory positively related to the level of aggregate expenditures which has four principal components.

a. These four components are consumption spending which depends upon the stable consumption schedule and the income of the economy; investment spending which is more unstable; government spending which depends partly on the level of spending needed to achieve full employment and price stability; and net exports which are influenced by exchange rates and the levels of domestic and foreign NNP.

b. To achieve economic stability, government employs both fiscal and monetary policy; but to be effective these two types of policy must be coordinated.

■ **IMPORTANT TERMS**

Monetary policy	**Margin requirement**
Open-market operations	**Money market**
Discount rate	**Feedback effects**
Easy money policy	**Velocity of money**
Tight money policy	**Target dilemma**
Selective control	**Net export effect**
Moral suasion	

■ **FILL-IN QUESTIONS**

1. The objective of monetary policy in the United States is

a _____ level of total output. Responsibility for these monetary policies rests with the

_____ of the Federal Reserve System; and they are put into effect by the twelve Federal Reserve

_____

2. The two important assets of the Federal Reserve Banks are _____ and _____. Their three major liabilities are _____, _____, and _____

3. The three tools (or instruments) employed by the monetary authority to control the money supply are _____, changing _____, and changing _____

4. The Federal Reserve Banks buy and sell government securities in the open market in order to change the amount of new _____ commercial banks are able to create and the rate of _____ in the economy.

5. If the Federal Reserve Banks were to sell $10 million in government bonds to the **public** and the reserve ratio were 25%, the supply of money would immediately be reduced by $_____, the reserves of commercial banks would be reduced by $_____, and the excess reserves of the banks would be reduced by $_____. But if these bonds were sold to the commercial banks, the supply of money would immediately be reduced by $_____, the reserves of the bank would be reduced by $_____, and the excess reserves of the banks would be reduced by $_____

6. Changes in the reserve ratio affect the ability of commercial banks to create money in two ways: they affect the amount of _____ held by the commercial banks; and the size of the monetary _____

7. If the Federal Reserve Banks were to lower the discount rate commercial banks would tend to borrow (more, less) _____ from them; and this would (increase, decrease) _____ their excess reserves.

8. To increase the supply of money, the Federal Reserve Banks should (raise, lower) _____ the reserve ratio, (buy, sell) _____ securities in the open market, and/or (increase, decrease) _____ the discount rate.

9. The most effective monetary control is _____ _____

10. The three selective controls are changes in _____ _____ and in _____ and the use of _____

11. Graphically, in an economy in which government neither purchases goods and services nor collects net taxes and which neither exports nor imports goods and services:

  a. the equilibrium real interest rate is determined by the demand-for- and the supply-of-_____ curves;

  b. this equilibrium interest rate and the _____ curve determine the level of planned investment;

  c. and the level of planned investment, using the leakages-injections approach, and the _____ curve determine the equilibrium NNP;

  d. but when the supply-of-money curve increases (shifts to the right), the real interest rate will (increase, decrease) _____, planned investment will _____, and the equilibrium NNP will _____

12. To eliminate inflationary pressures in the economy Keynesians argue that the monetary authority should seek to (increase, decrease) _____ the reserves of commercial banks; this would tend to _____ the money supply and to _____ the rate of interest; and this in turn would cause investment spending, aggregate expenditures, and NNP to _____. This action by monetary authorities would be considered a(n) _____ policy.

13. If there was a serious problem with unemployment in the economy, Keynesians would argue that the Federal Reserve should pursue a(n) _____ policy, in which case the Federal Reserve would (buy, sell) _____ government bonds as a way of (increasing, decreasing) _____ the money supply, and thereby _____ interest rates; these events would have the effect of _____ investment spending and thus _____ real NNP.

14. The effect of a $1 billion increase or decrease in the money supply upon the equilibrium NNP is greater the (flatter, steeper) _____ the demand-for-money curve and the _____ the invest-ment-demand curve.

15. An increase in the money supply will shift the aggre-gate (supply, demand) _____ curve to the (right, left) _____

  a. In the Keynesian (or depression) range along the aggregate-supply curve this increase in the money supply will have a (small, large) _____ effect on real national output and a _____ effect on the price level.

  b. In the classical range along the aggregate supply curve this increase in the money supply will have a _____ effect on real national output and a _____ effect on the price level.

  c. In the intermediate range along the aggregate-supply curve the effect of an increase in the money supply on the real national output is greater the (steeper, flatter) _____ the aggregate-supply curve, and the effect on the price level is greater the _____ the aggregate-supply curve.

16. The:

  a. strengths of monetary policy are that it is more _____, more isolated from _____, and (in the view of the monetarists) more _____ than fiscal policy;

  b. weaknesses of monetary policy are that it is more effective in curbing (recession, inflation) _____ than _____, can be ineffective if the _____ of money changes in the (same, opposite) _____ direction as the money supply, and will not be effective if changes in the interest rate have little or no effect on _____ spending in the economy.

17. The target dilemma faced by the Fed is that it is (able, unable) _____ to control both the money supply and the level of interest rates simul-taneously.

  a. If it is to stabilize the interest rate it must (increase, decrease) _____ the money supply when the nominal GNP rises.

  b. And if it stabilizes the money supply it must allow the interest rate to _____ when the nominal GNP rises.

18. An easy money policy (increases, decreases) _____ net exports; a tight money policy _____ net exports. The net export effect from an easy money policy thus (strengthens, weakens) _____ domestic monetary policy and a tight money policy _____ it. Also, an easy money policy is (compatible, incompatible) _____ with the economic goal of reducing a balance of trade deficit, but a tight money policy is _____ with this eco-nomic goal.

19. In the Keynesian theory the levels of output, employ-ment, income, and prices depend on the level of aggre-gate _____ which in turn depend upon the amounts of _____, _____, _____, and _____ spend-ing in the economy.

20. Government seeks to bring about a full-employment noninflationary NNP by employing both _____ and _____ policies.

■ **PROBLEMS AND PROJECTS**

1. Assume that the consolidated balance sheet below is for all commercial banks. Assume also that the required reserve ratio is 25% and that cash is **not** a part of the commercial banks' legal reserve.

Assets		Liabilities	
Cash	$ 50	Demand Deposits	$400
Reserves	100	Loans from Federal	
Loans	150	Reserve	25
Securities	200	Net worth	75
	$500		$500

  a. To *increase* the supply of money by $100, the Federal Reserve Banks could **either:**

  (1) (increase, decrease) _____ the re-serve ratio to _____ %;

(2) *or* (buy, sell) _____ securities worth

$_____ in the open market.

b. To **reduce** the supply of money by $50, the Federal Reserve Banks could **either:**

(1) _____ the reserve ratio to _____%

(2) *or* _____ securities worth

$_____ in the open market.

2. Shown below are the consolidated balance sheets of the Federal Reserve and of the commercial banks. Assume that the reserve ratio for commercial banks is 25%, that cash is **not** a part of a bank's legal reserve, and that the figures in column 1 show the balance sheets of the Federal Reserve and the commercial banks **prior to each of the following five transactions.** Place the new balance-sheet figures in the appropriate columns and complete A, B, C, D, and E in these columns. **Do not** use the figures you place in columns (2) through (5) when you work the next part of the problem; start all parts of the problem with the printed figures in column (1).

	(1)	(2)	(3)	(4)	(5)	(6)
			Federal Reserve Banks			
Assets:						
Gold certificates	$ 25	$____	$____	$____	$____	$____
Securities	30	____	____	____	____	____
Loans to commercial banks	10	____	____	____	____	____
Liabilities						
Reserves of commercial banks	50	____	____	____	____	____
Treasury deposits	5	____	____	____	____	____
Federal Reserve Notes	10	____	____	____	____	____
			Commercial Banks			
Assets:						
Reserves	$ 50	$____	$____	$____	$____	$____
Securities	70	____	____	____	____	____
Loans	90	____	____	____	____	____
Liabilities						
Demand deposits	200	____	____	____	____	____
Loans from Federal Reserve	10	____	____	____	____	____
A. Required reserves		____	____	____	____	____
B. Excess reserves		____	____	____	____	____
C. How much has the money supply changed?		____	____	____	____	____
D. How much *more* can the money supply change?		____	____	____	____	____
E. What is the total of C and D?		____	____	____	____	____

a. The Federal Reserve Banks sell $3 in securities to the public which pays by check (column 2).

b. The Federal Reserve Banks buy $4 in securities from the commercial banks (column 3).

c. The Federal Reserve Banks lower the required reserve ratio for commercial banks to 20% (column 4).

d. The U.S. Treasury buys $5 worth of goods from American manufacturers and pays the manufacturers by checks drawn on its accounts at the Federal Reserve Banks (column 5).

e. Because the Federal Reserve Banks have raised the discount rate, commercial banks repay $6 which they owe to the Federal Reserve (column 6).

3. On the graph below is the demand-for-money curve which shows the amounts of money consumers and firms wish to hold at various rates of interest (when the money NNP in the economy is given).

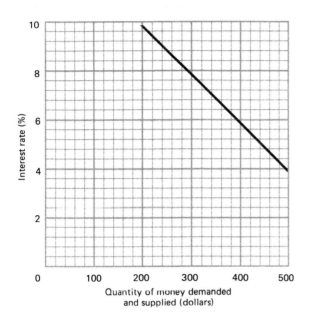

a. Suppose the supply of money is equal to $300.

(1) Draw on this graph the supply-of-money curve.

(2) The equilibrium rate of interest in the economy is

_____%.

b. On the next graph is an investment-demand curve which shows the amounts of planned investment at vari-

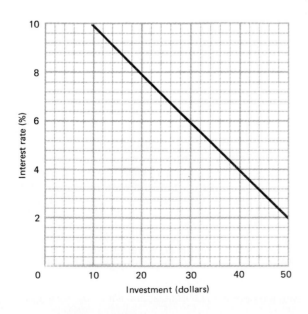

ous rates of interest. Given your answer to (2) above, how much will investors plan to spend for capital

goods? $_____

c. On the graph below is the saving curve is an economy in which the only leakage from the NNP is saving. (There are no taxes collected and no imports of goods and services.)

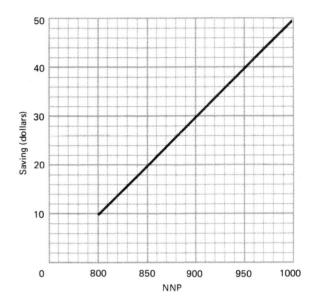

(1) On this graph plot the investment curve when planned investment is the amount given by you in your answer to (*b*) above.

(2) If the only injection into this economy is investment spending (that is, if there is no government spending for and no exports of goods and services), the equilibrium

NNP will be $_____

d. Assume the money supply increases to $400. On the first graph plot the new supply-of-money curve. The new:

(1) Equilibrium interest rate is _____%;

(2) Level of planned investment is $_____;

(3) Equilibrium NNP is $_____

e. Suppose the full-employment noninflationary NNP in this economy is $875.

(1) At this NNP saving would be $_____

(2) For this NNP to be the equilibrium NNP, investment

would have to be equal to $ _____

(3) For investment to be at this level the rate of interest

would have to be _____%.

(4) And for the interest rate to be at this level the supply of money would have to be equal to $_____

f. In this economy:

(1) the marginal propensity to save is equal to _____ and the multiplier has, therefore, a value equal to _____;

(2) a one percentage point decrease in the interest rate will (increase, decrease) _____ planned investment by $_____ and will, therefore, (increase, decrease) _____ the equilibrium NNP by $_____;

(3) but for the interest rate to decrease by one percentage point the money supply must (increase, decrease) _____ by $_____

4. Columns (1) and (2) of the table below are the aggregate-supply schedule. (The price level is a price index and real national output is measured in billions of dollars.)

(1) Price level	(2) Real national output	(3) AE$_1$	(4) AE$_2$	(5) AE$_3$	(6) AE$_4$	(7) AE$_5$	(8) AE$_6$
.30	$1500	$1600	$1700	$2070	$2400	$2920	$3020
.30	1600	1600	1700	2070	2400	2920	3020
.30	1700	1600	1700	2070	2400	2920	3020
.40	1790	1500	1600	1970	2300	2820	2920
.50	1870	1400	1500	1870	2200	2720	2820
.60	1940	1300	1400	1770	2100	2620	2720
.70	2000	1200	1300	1670	2000	2520	2620
.80	2050	1100	1200	1570	1900	2420	2520
.90	2090	1000	1100	1470	1800	2320	2420
1.00	2120	900	1000	1370	1700	2220	2320
1.10	2120	800	900	1270	1600	2120	2220
1.20	2120	700	800	1170	1500	2020	2120

a. The Keynesian range on this aggregate-supply schedule is from a real national output of zero to $_____ billion.

b. The classical range on this aggregate-supply curve is at the real national output of $_____ billion.

c. If the aggregate-demand schedule were that shown in columns (1) and (3) the equilibrium real national output would be $_____ billion and the price level would be _____

d. If the aggregate-demand schedule increased from that shown in columns (1) and (3) to the one shown in columns (1) and (4) the equilibrium real national output would _____ and the price level would _____

e. If the aggregate-demand schedule increased from that shown in columns (1) and (5) to the one shown in columns (1) and (6) the equilibrium real national output would _____ and the price level would _____

f. And if the aggregate-demand schedule increased from that shown in columns (1) and (7) to the one shown in columns (1) and (8) the equilibrium real national output would _____ and the price level would _____

5. Columns (1) and (2) in the following table show the money supply and column (3) shows the demand for money. (Dollar figures are in billions and the interest rate is a percentage.)

(1) Supply of money	(2) Interest rate	(3) Demand for money	(4) Demand for money
$400	.08	$100	$200
400	.07	200	300
400	.06	300	400
400	.05	400	500
400	.04	500	600
400	.03	600	700
400	.02	700	800

a. The equilibrium interest rate is _____%.

b. Suppose the Fed wishes to stabilize the interest rate at this level; but the nominal GNP produced by the economy increases, and as a result the demand for money in the economy increases from that shown in column (3) to that shown in column (4). The Fed will have to (increase, decrease) _____ the supply of money to $_____ billion.

c. But if the Fed stabilizes the supply of money at $400 billion and the nominal GNP increases to increase the demand for money from that shown in column (3) to that shown in column (4) the interest rate will (rise, fall) _____ to _____%.

d. If the Fed stabilizes the interest rate it must (increase, decrease) _____ the supply of money when the nominal GNP rises and _____ it when the nominal GNP falls; and if it holds the supply of money constant the interest rate will (rise, fall) _____ when the nominal GNP increases and _____ when the nominal GNP decreases.

■ SELF-TEST

Circle the T if the statement is true, the F if it is false.

1. The fundamental goal of monetary policy is to stabilize interest rates.　**T F**

2. The securities owned by the Federal Reserve Banks are almost entirely U.S. government bonds.　**T F**

3. If the Federal Reserve Banks buy $15 in government securities from the public in the open market, the effect will be to increase the excess reserves of commercial banks by $15.　**T F**

4. When the Federal Reserve sells bonds in the open market, the price of these bonds falls.　**T F**

5. A change in the reserve ratio will affect the multiple by which the banking system can create money, but it will not affect the actual or excess reserves of member banks.　**T F**

6. If the reserve ratio is lowered, some required reserves are turned into excess reserves.　**T F**

7. When commercial banks borrow from the Federal Reserve Banks they increase their excess reserves and their money-creating potential.　**T F**

8. If the monetary authority wished to follow a tight money policy, it would seek to reduce the reserves of commercial banks.　**T F**

9. An increase in the required reserve ratio tends to reduce the profits of banks.　**T F**

10. The equilibrium rate of interest is found at the intersection of the demand-for-money and the supply-of-money curves.　**T F**

11. An increase in the equilibrium NNP will shift the demand-for-money curve to the left and increase the equilibrium interest rate.　**T F**

12. Consumer spending is more sensitive to changes in the rate of interest than is investment demand.　**T F**

13. Monetary policy is more effective in fighting depression than it is in curbing inflation.　**T F**

14. In an economy in which the GNP is either rising or falling the Fed is unable to control both the money supply and interest rates.　**T F**

15. When the economy is at or near full employment an increase in the money supply tends to be inflationary.　**T F**

16. It is generally agreed that fiscal policy is more effective than monetary policy in controlling the business cycle because fiscal policy is more flexible.　**T F**

17. Since 1982 the policy target of the Federal Reserve was simply to control the money supply.　**T F**

18. An easy money policy decreases net exports.　**T F**

19. A tight money policy will tend to cause the dollar to appreciate.　**T F**

20. A tight money policy is compatible with the goal of correcting a trade deficit.　**T F**

Circle the letter that corresponds to the best answer.

1. The agency directly responsible for monetary policy in the United States is:
 (a) the twelve Federal Reserve Banks
 (b) the Board of Governors of the Federal Reserve System
 (c) the Congress of the United States
 (d) the U.S. Treasury

2. The largest single asset in the Federal Reserve Banks' consolidated balance sheet is:
 (a) securities
 (b) the reserves of commercial banks
 (c) Federal Reserve Notes
 (d) loans to commercial banks

3. The largest single liability of the Federal Reserve Banks is:
 (a) securities
 (b) the reserves of commercial banks
 (c) Federal Reserve Notes
 (d) loans to commercial banks

4. Assuming that the Federal Reserve Banks sell $20 million in government securities to commercial banks and the reserve ratio is 20%, then the effect will be:
 (a) to reduce the actual supply of money by $20 million
 (b) to reduce the actual supply of money by $4 million
 (c) to reduce the potential money supply by $20 million
 (d) to reduce the potential money supply by $100 million

5. Which of the following acts would **not** have the same general effect upon the economy as the other three?
 (a) the Federal Reserve Banks sell bonds in the open market

(b) The Federal Reserve increases the discount rate

(c) the Federal Reserve eases credit for the purchase of consumer durables

(d) the Federal Reserve raises the reserve ratio.

6. Which of the following is the most important control used by the Federal Reserve Banks to regulate the money supply?

(a) changing the reserve ratio

(b) open-market operations

(c) changing the discount rate

(d) changing the margin requirements

7. Which of the following is *not* one of the selective controls which have been employed by the Federal Reserve?

(a) setting tariff rates

(b) moral suasion

(c) setting margin requirements

(d) setting credit terms for consumer durable goods

8. A change in the money supply has the *least* effect on the equilibrium NNP when:

(a) both the demand-for-money and investment-demand curves are steep

(b) both the demand-for-money and investment-demand curves are flat

(c) the demand-for-money curve is flat and the investment-demand curve is steep

(d) the demand-for-money curve is steep and the investment-demand curve is flat

9. An increase in the money supply will have little or no effect on the real national output and employment in:

(a) the Keynesian range on the aggregate-supply curve

(b) the intermediate range along the aggregate-supply curve

(c) the classical range on the aggregate-supply curve

(d) any of the three ranges on the aggregate-supply curve

10. In the Keynesian chain of cause and effect between changes in the excess reserves of commercial banks and the resulting changes in output and employment in the economy:

(a) an increase in excess reserves will decrease the money supply

(b) a decrease in the money supply will increase the rate of interest

(c) an increase in the rate of interest will increase aggregate expenditures

(d) an increase in aggregate expenditures will decrease output and employment

11. Which of the following is most likely to be affected by changes in the rate of interest?

(a) consumer spending;

(b) investment spending

(c) the spending of the Federal government

(d) the exports of the economy

12. An increase in the money supply will have little or no effect on the price level in:

(a) the Keynesian range

(b) the intermediate range

(c) the classical range

(d) any of the three ranges

13. An increase in the money supply is *least* effective in stimulating aggregate expenditures when the velocity of money:

(a) falls as the money supply increases

(b) remains constant

(c) rises as the money supply increases

(d) is equal to 5

14. The Fed:

(a) can stabilize both the interest rate and the money supply

(b) cannot stabilize the interest rate

(c) cannot stabilize the money supply

(d) cannot stabilize both the interest rate and the money supply

15. Between October of 1979 and October of 1982 the Fed attempted to:

(a) stabilize interest rates and allowed the money supply to fluctuate

(b) stabilize the money supply and allowed interest rates to fluctuate

(c) stabilize neither the money supply nor interest rates

(d) stabilize both the money supply and interest rates

16. Which of the following are coordinated policies?

(a) an increase in government expenditures and in the money supply

(b) a decrease in personal tax rates and in the money supply

(c) an increase in transfer payments and a decrease in the money supply

(d) an increase in corporate tax rates and in the money supply

17. When the Federal Reserve Banks decide to buy government bonds, the demand for government bonds will:

(a) decrease, bond prices will decrease, and the interest rate will decrease

(b) increase, bond prices will increase, and the interest rate will decrease

(c) increase, bond prices will increase, and the interest rate will increase

(d) decrease, bond prices will increase, and the interest rate will decrease

18. A tight money policy in the United States is most likely to:

(a) increase domestic interest rates and cause the value of the dollar to depreciate.

(b) decrease domestic interest rates and cause the value of the dollar to appreciate

(c) increase domestic interest rates and cause the value of the dollar to appreciate

(d) decrease domestic interest rates and cause the value of the dollar to depreciate

19. Which policy combination would tend to reduce net exports?

(a) tight money policy and expansionary fiscal policy

(b) easy money policy and expansionary fiscal policy

(c) tight money policy and contractionary fiscal policy

(d) easy money policy and contractionary fiscal policy

20. A tight money policy that is used to reduce inflation in the domestic economy:

(a) is best conducted by reducing the required reserve ratios at commercial banks

(b) tends to increase net exports, thereby reducing the effectiveness of the policy

(c) conflicts with the economic goal of correcting a trade deficit

(d) causes the dollar to depreciate

■ DISCUSSION QUESTIONS

1. What is the basic goal of monetary policy? What actions are taken to achieve this goal during recession or during a period of high inflation?

2. What are the important assets and liabilities of the Federal Reserve Banks?

3. Explain how the monetary-policy tools of the Federal Reserve Banks would be used to contract the supply of money. How would they be used to expand the supply of money?

4. What is the difference between the effects of the Federal Reserve's buying (selling) government securities in the open market from (to) commercial banks and from (to) the public?

5. Which of the monetary-policy tools available to the Federal Reserve is most effective? Why is it more effective than other tools?

6. How do the selective controls differ from general or monetary controls? What are the principal selective controls? Explain how the Federal Reserve would use these controls in following a tight and an easy money policy.

7. Using the Keynesian theory and three graphs, explain what determines (a) the equilibrium interest rate; (b) planned investment; and (c) the equilibrium NNP. Now

employ these three graphs to show the effects of a decrease in the money supply upon the equilibrium NNP.

8. Utilizing your answers to the question above, (a) what determines how large the effect of the decrease in the money supply on the equilibrium NNP will be; and (b) how would the change in the equilibrium NNP affect the demand-for-money curve, the interest rate, planned investment, and the NNP itself?

9. Explain from a Keynesian viewpoint how the Board of Governors and the Federal Reserve Banks can influence income, output, employment, and the price level. In your explanation, employ the following concepts: reserves, excess reserves, the supply of money, the availability of bank credit, and the rate of interest.

10. Why are changes in the rate of interest more likely to affect investment spending than consumption and saving?

11. How does a change in the money supply affect the aggregate-demand curve? How will a change in the money supply and the resulting shift in the aggregate-demand curve affect the real national output and the price level in (a) the Keynesian range, (b) the classical range, and (c) the intermediate range along the aggregate-supply curve?

12. What are the strengths and shortcomings of monetary policy?

13. Why is monetary policy more effective in controlling inflation than in reducing unemployment?

14. What is the target (or policy) dilemma of the Fed? What target did the Fed set (a) before October of 1979; (b) between October of 1979 and October of 1982; and (c) after October of 1982?

15. How has the focus for measuring monetary growth changed from 1988? Why was this change made?

16. Suppose the nominal GNP in the American economy is increasing or decreasing. Why is the Federal Reserve unable to keep both interest rates and the size of the money supply from changing?

17. Explain how the net export effect influences the effectiveness of a tight or an easy money policy.

18. What type of monetary policy would you recommend to correct a balance of trade deficit? Why?

19. Explain as briefly as possible what Keynesians believe determines the level of national output in the American economy.

20. Distinguish between fiscal and monetary policy and explain how we may use each of them to achieve reasonably full employment and relatively stable prices.

■ ANSWERS

CHAPTER 17 THE FEDERAL RESERVE BANKS AND MONETARY POLICY

Fill-in questions

1. full-employment noninflationary, Board of Governors, Banks

2. securities, loans to commercial banks (either order), reserves of commercial banks, Treasury deposits, Federal Reserve Notes (any order)

3. open-market operations, reserve ratio, the discount rate (any order)

4. money, interest

5. 10 million, 10 million, 7.5 million, 0, 10 million, 10 million

6. excess reserves, multiplier

7. more, increase

8. lower, buy, decrease

9. open-market operations

10. margin requirements, the terms of credit available for consumer durable c   .s, moral suasion

11. *a.* money; *b.* investment-demand; *c.* saving; *d.* decrease, increase, increase

12. decrease, decrease, increase, decrease, tight money

13. easy money, buy, increasing, decreasing, increasing, increasing

14. steeper, flatter

15. demand, right; *a.* large, small; *b.* small, large; *c.* flatter, steeper

16. *a.* flexible, political pressure, effective; *b.* inflation, recession, velocity, opposite, investment

17. unable; *a.* increase; *b.* increase

18. increases, decreases, strengthens, strengthens, compatible, incompatible

19. expenditures, consumption, investment, government, net export

20. fiscal, monetary (either order)

Problems and projects

1. *a.* (1) decrease, 20, (2) buy, 25; *b.* (1) increase, 28⅘, (2) sell, 12½

2.

	(2)	(3)	(4)	(5)	(6)
		Federal Reserve Banks			
Assets:					
Gold certificates	$ 25	$ 25	$ 25	$ 25	$ 25
Securities	27	34	30	30	30
Loans to commercial banks	10	10	10	10	4
Liabilities:					
Reserves of commercial banks	47	54	50	55	44
Treasury deposits	5	5	5	0	5
Federal Reserve Notes	10	10	10	10	10
		Commercial Banks			
Assets:					
Reserves	$ 47	$ 54	$ 50	$ 55	$ 44
Securities	$ 70	66	70	70	70
Loans	90	90	90	90	90
Liabilities:					
Demand deposits	197	200	200	205	200
Loans from Federal Reserve	10	10	10	10	4
A. Required reserves	49.25	50	40	51.25	50
B. Excess reserves	− 2.25	4	10	3.75	− 6
C. How much has the money supply changed?	− 3	0	0	+ 5	0
D. How much more can the money supply change?	− 9	+ 16	+ 50	+ 15	− 24
E. What is the total of C and D?	− 12	+ 16	+ 50	+ 20.25	− 24

3. *a.* (2) 8: *b.* 20; *c.* (2) 850; *d.* (1) 6, (2) 30, (3) 900; *e.* (1) 25, (2) 25, (3) 7, (4) 350; *f.* (1) 0.20, 5, (2) increase, 5, increase, 25, (3) increase, 50

4. *a.* 1700; *b.* 2120; *c.* 1600, .30; *d.* rise to $1700 billion, remain constant; *e.* rise from $1870 billion to $2000 billion, rise from .50 to .70; *f.* remain constant at $2120 billion, rise from 1.10 to 1.20

5. *a.* 5; *b.* increase, 500; *c.* rise, 6; *d.* increase, decrease, rise, fall

Self-test

1. F; **2.** T; **3.** F; **4.** T; **5.** F; **6.** T; **7.** T; **8.** T; **9.** T; **10.** T; **11.** F; **12.** F; **13.** F; **14.** T; **15.** T; **16.** F; **17.** F; **18.** F; **19.** T; **20.** F

1. *b;* **2.** *a;* **3.** *c;* **4.** *d;* **5.** *c;* **6.** *b;* **7.** *a;* **8.** *c;* **9.** *c;* **10.** *b;* **11.** *b;* **12.** *a;* **13.** *a;* **14.** *d;* **15.** *b;* **16.** *a;* **17.** *b;* **18.** *c;* **19.** *a;* **20.** *c*

Alternative views: monetarism and rational expectations

Now that you understand the basic ideas behind fiscal and monetary policy from the Keynesian perspective you are ready to learn about different theories of how the economy functions and you are prepared to explore controversial issues to expand your understanding of macroeconomics. Chapter 18, therefore, begins a first of a four-chapter section of the text that examines "Problems and Controversies in Macroeconomics." This chapter focuses on alternative views to the Keynesian position on monetary policy and stabilization policy for the economy. Chapter 19 explores reasons for the simultaneous occurrence of inflation and unemployment in the economy and discusses supply-side economics. In Chapter 20, the problems with the Federal budget deficit and the national debt are examined. Finally, Chapter 21 deals with the topic of economic growth and the long-term performance of the economy.

Economics has always been an arena in which conflicting theories and policies opposed each other. This field of intellectual combat, in major engagements, has seen Adam Smith do battle with the defenders of a regulated economy. It witnessed the opposition of Karl Marx to the orthodox economics of his day. In more recent times it saw Keynes in conflict with the classical economists. Around the major engagements have been countless minor skirmishes between opposing viewpoints. Out of these major and minor confrontations have emerged not winners and losers but the advancement of economic theory and the improvement of economic policy.

Monetarism and (more recently) rational-expectations theory are the latest challengers to enter this intellectual arena. The opponent is the reigning champion, Keynesianism, which bested classical economics in the same arena during the 1940s. Monetarists and rational-expectations theorists wish to free the economy from what they see as the destabilizing effects of discretionary fiscal and monetary policies. They view the Keynesians as the proponents of government intervention and see themselves as the defenders of *laissez faire*.

Chapter 18 examines both monetarism and rational-expectations theory; but it directs most of its attention toward monetarism. But this chapter is more than a comparison of the attitudes of Keynesians and monetarists toward the role of government in the economy. And it is more than a comparison of the basic equations of the two schools of thought. The basic equation of the Keynesians and the equation of exchange of the monetarists say pretty much the same thing. The equation of exchange ($MV = PQ$) is another way of saying that the economy will produce the NNP which is equal to the aggregate quantity of goods and services demanded.

The issue is whether the velocity of money—the V in the equation of exchange—is stable or unstable. If it is stable, as the monetarists contend, then the only kind of policy that can be used to control (to increase or decrease) nominal NNP is monetary policy; and fiscal policy cannot expand or contract nominal NNP. But if V is unstable, as the Keynesians argue, then fiscal policy is the only effective means and monetary policy is an ineffective means of controlling nominal NNP. The issue of whether V is stable or unstable becomes an issue of whether the size of the money supply matters very much or very little. Monetarists argue that the M in the equation of exchange is the only thing that matters and their Keynesian rivals contend that it doesn't matter very much.

The emphasis in Chapter 18 is on monetarism because earlier chapters have emphasized Keynesianism. You are not expected, however, to determine which of the two groups is correct. But you should see that monetarism is an alternative to Keynesianism; that the economic issue is the stability of V; and that the political issue is, therefore, whether monetary or fiscal policy is more effective.

Rational-expectations theorists take a more extreme position in the debate over the relative effectiveness of monetary and fiscal policies. Their position is that the economy tends to produce its full-employment output and that neither of the two types of policy can expand real output and employment in either the short run or the long run: the only effect on the economy of an expansionary monetary or fiscal policy is inflation. They are modern-day (or the new) classical economists who argue that neither the size of the money supply nor the fiscal policies of government has any effect on real output and employment. While this extreme position will be strange to those who have come to believe government can bring about full employment without inflation in the economy, advocates of the rational-expectations theory are careful to explain how they reach these conclusions; and you should be sure you understand the assumptions they make in order to reach their unusual conclusions before you dismiss their extreme position.

Out of the debate among Keynesians, monetarists, and rational-expectationists, as out of the confrontations of the past, will eventually come better economic theory and the policies that solve economic problems. In the meantime, you can adopt an eclectic position: neither the Keynesians, monetarists, nor rational-expectations theorists are entirely correct and none of them are wholly wrong.

■ CHECKLIST

When you have studied this chapter you should be able to:

☐ Compare the positions of Keynesian and monetarist economists on the competitiveness of a capitalistic economy and its inherent stability and on the role government should play in stabilizing it.

☐ Write the equation of exchange and define each of the four terms in the equation.

☐ Show how the basic Keynesian equation is "translated" into the equation of exchange.

☐ Compare the monetarist and Keynesian views on the functions of money; on why households and firms demand money; and on what determines the quantity of money demanded.

☐ Explain why the monetarists believe nominal NNP is directly and predictably linked to M.

☐ Write a brief scenario which explains what monetarists believe will happen to change the nominal NNP and to V when M is increased.

☐ Construct a scenario which explains what Keynesians believe will happen to the interest rate and to V and nominal NNP if M is increased.

☐ Explain why Keynesians favor and monetarists reject the use of fiscal policy to stabilize the economy.

☐ State the monetary rule of the monetarists, and the two reasons why they propose a rule instead of discretionary monetary policy.

☐ Use the aggregate demand–aggregate supply models of the Keynesians and the monetarists to compare and contrast the effects of an expansionary monetary or fiscal policy on the real national output and the price level.

☐ Clarify the debate over the monetarist call for a monetary rule using the aggregate demand–aggregate supply model.

☐ State the two basic assumptions of the rational-expectations theory (RET).

☐ Explain how RET advocates believe firms, workers, and consumers react to the announcement of an expansionary monetary or fiscal policy to frustrate the achievement of the goal of the policy.

☐ Use aggregate demand and aggregate supply to show the effects of an expansionary monetary or fiscal policy on real output and the price level in the RET.

☐ Write a brief scenario to explain why rational-expectations theorists believe discretionary monetary and fiscal policies are procyclical; and state what type of government policy is advocated by these theorists.

☐ Present three criticisms of the RET.

☐ Offer a perspective on the continuing debate in macroeconomics.

■ CHAPTER OUTLINE

1. Monetarism and rational-expectations theory (RET) are alternatives to the Keynesian macroeconomic theory and policy recommendations; and while this chapter examines both of these alternatives, it stresses monetarism.

2. Keynesians and monetarists differ over the inherent stability of capitalistic economies and ideologically over the role government should play in the economy.

  a. Keynesians believe that, because many markets in a capitalistic economy are noncompetitive, it is unstable, that government should intervene to stabilize the economy, and that fiscal policy is a more effective stabilizer than monetary policy.

  b. Monetarists believe that because markets in a capitalistic economy are competitive the economy would be stable if it were not for government interference, that government intervention destabilizes the economy, and that government should not use either discretionary fiscal or monetary policy to try to stabilize it.

3. In the Keynesian model the equilibrium output of the economy is the output at which

$$C_a + I_n + X_n + G = \text{NNP}$$

  a. In the monetarist model the basic equation is the equation of exchange.

$$MV = PQ$$

but because MV (total spending) $= C_a + I_n + X_n + G$ and $PQ = \text{NNP}$, the equations are different ways of stating the same relationship.

  b. While Keynesians assign a secondary role to money because they believe the links in the cause-effect chain are loose ones, monetarists, believing V in the equation of exchange is stable, find that while a change in M may affect Q in the short run it will in the long run affect only P. These competing views of the monetary transmission mechanism are illustrated for you in Figure 18–1 of the textbook.

4. Whether **V** in the equation of exchange is stable or unstable is a critical question because if it is stable **PQ** is closely linked to **M**; and if it is unstable the link between **PQ** and **M** is loose and uncertain.

a. Reasoning that people have a stable desire to hold money relative to holding other assets or to making purchases, monetarists conclude that the quantity of money demanded is a stable percentage of NNP (that NNP/**M** is constant); that an increase (a decrease) in **M** will leave firms and households with more (less) money than they wish to have; that they will, therefore, increase (decrease) spending for consumer and capital goods; and that this will cause the NNP and the amount of money they wish to hold for transactions purposes to rise (fall) until their demand for money is equal to **M** and NNP/**M** = **V**.

b. But Keynesians argue that consumers and business firms also have an asset demand for money as well as a transactions demand for money; that this asset demand for money is inversely related to the rate of interest; and that an increase (a decrease) in **M** will decrease (increase) the interest rate, increase (decrease) the amount of money people wish to hold as an asset, lower (raise) **V**, and leave the effect on NNP uncertain.

c. Empirical evidence confirms neither the contention of the monetarists that **V** is stable nor the contention of the Keynesians that it is variable (or unstable).

5. Because their theories (their views on the stability of **V**) differ, Keynesians and monetarists disagree over the effectiveness of fiscal and monetary policies in stabilizing the economy.

a. Keynesians favor the use of fiscal policy to stabilize the economy because they believe it is a more powerful stabilizer; but the monetarists argue that the use of fiscal policy is both harmful and ineffective because of the crowding-out effect it has on investment expenditures in the economy.

b. Arguing that discretionary changes in **M** have produced monetary mismanagement and macroeconomic instability, the monetarists have proposed the monetary rule that **M** be increased at the same annual rate as the potential annual rate of increase in the real GNP.

c. In the aggregate demand-aggregate supply model the monetarists see an aggregate-supply curve that is very steep (or vertical) and in which an increase in aggregate demand has little (or no) effect on real national output and increases the price level by a relatively large amount; but the Keynesians see an aggregate-supply curve that is nearly flat (or horizontal) and in which an increase in aggregate demand has little (or no) effect on the price level and increases the real national output by a relatively large amount. At the full employment level of output, where the aggregate-supply curve is vertical, both Keynesians and monetarists would agree that expansionary policies would lead to demand-pull inflation.

d. The debate over the call for a monetary rule by the monetarist is also illustrated in the aggregate demand–aggregate supply model.

(1) From the monetarist perspective, a monetary rule would shift aggregate demand rightward to match a shift in the aggregate-supply curve because of economic growth, thus keeping the price level stable.

(2) From the Keynesian view, the loose link between changes in money and aggregate demand mean that a monetary rule might produce too great a shift in aggregate demand (and demand-pull inflation) or too small a shift (and deflation) to match the shift in aggregate supply, and therefore such a rule would contribute to price instability.

6. The RET, developed since the mid-1970s and called the new classical economics, is an alternative to Keynesian economics and to monetarism.

a. Economists who advocate the RET make two basic assumptions:

(1) business firms, consumers, and workers understand how the economy works so that they can anticipate the effect on the economy of an economic event or a change in economic policy, and use all available information to make decisions in a way to further their own self-interests; and

(2) all markets in the economy are so competitive that equilibrium prices and quantities quickly adjust to these events and changes in public policy.

b. From these assumptions the proponents of the RET conclude that the response of the public to the expected inflationary effect of an expansionary monetary (or fiscal) policy will cancel the intended effect on output and employment in the economy.

c. In an aggregate demand-aggregate supply model of the RET the aggregate supply curve is vertical; and any monetary or fiscal policy that increases or decreases aggregate demand affects only the price level, and has no effect on real output or employment, real wages, or real interest rates in either the short or the long run.

d. Rational-expectations theorists argue that discretionary monetary and fiscal policies are pro- (rather than counter-) cyclical; and would (like the monetarists) replace discretionary policies with rules.

e. The appeal of the RET comes from the inability of Keynesian economics to explain and to develop policies to correct simultaneous inflation and unemployment, and from the long-sought connection between micro- and macroeconomics; but RET has been subjected to three basic criticisms.

(1) One criticism is that people are not so well informed on the workings of the economy and the effect of economic policy on it as the rational-expectations theorists assume.

(2) A second criticism is that many markets in the economy are not so competitive as assumed in the RET, and

do not, therefore, adjust their prices as rapidly as assumed.

3) And the third criticism is that monetary and fiscal policies have worked in the past to expand real output and employment in the economy.

f. The debate among Keynesians, monetarists, and rational-expectationists will continue into the future; and three concluding comments put this debate into perspective.

■ **IMPORTANT TERMS**

Keynesianism   Crowding-out effect

Monetarism   Monetary rule

Equation of exchange   Rational-expectations theory

Income (or circuit)
velocity of money

■ **FILL-IN QUESTIONS**

1. Keynesians believe that capitalism is inherently (stable, unstable) _____ because many of its markets are (competitive, noncompetitive) _____, advocate (government intervention, laissez faire) _____ , and favor (monetary, fiscal) _____ over _____ policy.

2. Monetarists argue that capitalism is inherently _____ because most of its markets are _____ , advocate _____ and favor the use of (discretionary, nondiscretionary) _____ (monetary, fiscal) _____ policy.

3. The basic equation of the monetarists is _____ = _____

a. This equation is called the _____

b. Indicate below what each of the four letters in this equation represents.

    (1) *M*: _____

    (2) *V*: _____

    (3) *P*: _____

    (4) *Q*: _____

4. The basic equation of the Keynesians is $C_a + I_n + X_n + G$ = NNP.

a. $C_a + I_n + X_n + G$ is _____ and in the equation of exchange is equal to _____

b. Nominal NNP is equal to _____ in the equation of exchange.

5. Monetarists argue that

a. any increase in *M* will (increase, decrease) _____ *PQ*;

b. in the **short run** any increase in *M* may (increase, decrease) _____ both *P* and *Q*; but

c. in the **long run** any increase in *M* will (increase, decrease) _____ only (*P*, *Q*) _____

6. In the debate on the stability of *V*:

a. monetarists argue that people have a (stable, unstable) _____ desire to hold money relative to holding other assets or to making purchases, that the amount of money people will want to hold will depend on the level of _____ and that *V* is, therefore, _____

b. Keynesians contend that, in addition to a transactions demand for money, there is also a(n) _____ demand for money, that this demand is inversely related to the _____, and that *V* is, therefore, _____

7. An increase in *M*:

a. to the monetarist's way of thinking will

    (1) leave the public with (more, less) _____ money than it wishes to have,

    (2) induce the public to (increase, decrease) _____ its spending for consumer and capital goods,

    (3) which will result in a(n) _____ in nominal NNP

    (4) until the nominal NNP (or *MV*) is equal to _____ times _____

b. to the Keynesian's way of thinking it will

    (1) result in a(n) _____ in the rate of interest,

    (2) which will _____ the demand for money

(3) and _____ **V**
(4) and the effect on nominal NNP will be

_____

8. It is, in short, the view of the:
 a. monetarists that **V** (in the equation of exchange) is stable and that there is a direct relationship between

_____ and _____

 b. Keynesians that **V** is (directly, inversely) _____ related to the interest rate; that the interest rate (increases, decreases) _____ when **M** increases; and that, therefore, **M** and **V** are (directly, inversely)

_____ related to each other.

9. In the debate on the use of fiscal policy:
 a. the Keynesians contend that the more effective tool for stabilizing the economy is (fiscal, monetary)

_____ policy; but
 b. the monetarists reply that government borrowing to

finance a budget deficit will (raise, lower) _____

the rate of interest and have a _____
effect on investment spending.

10. Monetarists would have the supply of money increase at the same annual rate as the potential rate of growth

of _____ and this is a rate of from

_____ to _____ %.

11. Monetarists proposed the adoption of the "Monetary Rule" because they believe that discretionary monetary

policy tends to (stabilize, destabilize) _____
the economy.

12. In the:
 a. Keynesian model of the economy the aggregate supply curve is relatively (steep, flat) _____ and an increase in aggregate demand will have a relatively (large, small) _____ effect on the

price level and a relatively _____ effect on the real national output.
 b. monetarist model the aggregate-supply curve is relatively

_____ and an increase in aggregate

demand will have a relatively _____ effect

on price level and a relatively _____ effect on real national output.
 c. From the monetarist perspective, a monetary rule would keep the price level (stable, unstable) _____

_____ because a rightward shift in the aggregate supply from economic growth would be (greater

than, less than, or equal to) _____ the rightward shift of aggregate demand, but Keynesians would argue that the shift in aggregate demand with a

monetary rule might be _____ or _____ the shift in aggregate supply, therefore making the price

level (stable, unstable) _____

13. In the rational-expectations theory:
 a. Individuals correctly anticipate the effects of any economic event or a change in public policy on the economy and make decisions based on their anticipations to max-

imize their own _____;
 b. the markets in the economy are (noncompetitive,

purely competitive) _____ and prices in these markets are perfectly (inflexible, flexible)

_____; and as a result,
 c. an expansionary monetary or fiscal policy will lead

the public to expect (inflation, a recession) _____

_____ and they will react in a way that results in (an increase, a decrease, no change)

_____ in the real output of the economy

and _____ in the price level.

14. The aggregate supply curve in the RET is (vertical,

horizontal) _____ and a change in aggregate demand brings about a change in (the price level,

the real output) _____ and no change

in _____ of the economy.

15. Proponents of the RET:
 a. contend that discretionary monetary and fiscal pol-

icies are (pro-, counter-) _____ cyclical; and
 b. like the monetarists, favor (policy rules, discretionary

policy) _____

16. The critics of the RET maintain that people are (less

well, better) _____ informed than assumed in the theory; markets are (more, less)

_____ competitive than assumed in the theory and prices are, therefore, (sticky, flexible)

_____ ; and monetary and fiscal policies have been employed in the past to (stabilize, destabilize) _____ the economy and to expand its (real, nominal) _____ output.

■ PROBLEMS AND PROJECTS

1. You must imagine that you are a monetarist in this problem and assume that **V** is stable and equal to 4. In the table below is the aggregate supply schedule: the real output **Q** which producers will offer for sale at seven different price levels **P**.

P	Q	PQ	MV
$1.00	100	$_____	$_____
2.00	110	_____	_____
3.00	120	_____	_____
4.00	130	_____	_____
5.00	140	_____	_____
6.00	150	_____	_____
7.00	160	_____	_____

a. Compute and enter in the table above the seven values of **PQ**.

b. Assume **M** is $90. Enter the values of **MV** on each of the seven lines in the table. The equilibrium

(1) nominal national output (**PQ** or **MV**) is $_____

(2) price level is $_____

(3) real national output (**Q**) is $_____

c. When **M** increases to $175, **MV** at each price level is $_____; and the equilibrium

(1) nominal national output is $_____

(2) price level is $_____

(3) real national output is $_____

2. In this problem you are a Keynesian. The left side of the following table shows the amounts of money firms and households wish to have for transactions at different levels of nominal NNP. The right side of the table shows the amounts of money they want to have as assets at different rates of interest.

a. Suppose the nominal NNP is $500, the interest is 7%, and the supply of money is $125.

Money NNP	Transactions demand	Interest rate	Asset demand
$ 500	$ 50	7.0%	$ 75
600	60	6.8	80
700	70	6.6	85
800	80	6.4	90
900	90	6.2	95
1000	100	6.0	100

(1) The amount of money demanded for transactions is $_____

(2) The amount of money demanded as an asset is $_____

(3) The total amount of money demanded for both purposes is $_____

(4) The amount of money firms and households wish to have is (greater than, less than, equal to) _____ the amount of money they actually have.

(5) The velocity of money (equal to nominal NNP divided by the supply of money) is _____

b. Assume the Federal Reserve Banks expand the supply of money to $160 by purchasing securities in the open market; and that as a result the rate of interest falls to 6% and the nominal NNP rises to $600.

(1) The amount of money demanded for transactions is now $_____ and the amount demanded as an asset is now $_____

(2) The total amount of money demanded is $_____ and the amount of money the public wishes to have is _____ the amount of money they actually have.

(3) The velocity of money is _____

c. Suppose the Federal government pursues an expansionary fiscal policy which raises the money NNP from $600 to $800 and the interest rate from 6% to 6.8%, and the money supply remains at $160.

(1) The transactions demand for money is $_____ , the asset demand is $_____ , and the total demand is $_____

(2) The velocity of money is _____

d. The effect of the easy money policy was to (increase, decrease) _____ the velocity of money and the effect of the expansionary fiscal policy was to _____ it.

3. On the graph below are three aggregate-supply curves: S_1, S_2, and S_3.

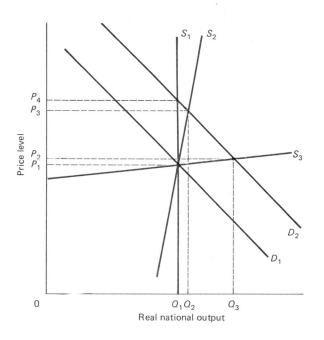

a. S_1 is the (Keynesian, monetarist, rational-expectations) _____ supply curve, S_2 is the _____ supply curve, and S_3 is the _____ supply curve.

b. Regardless of which is the economy's supply curve, if the aggregate-demand curve is D_1, the equilibrium real national output is _____ and the equilibrium price level is _____

c. Should aggregate demand increase from D_1 to D_2 in the

(1) monetarist model the equilibrium real national output would (increase, decrease, remain constant) _____ to (at) _____ and the equilibrium price level would (increase, decrease, remain constant) _____ to (at) _____;

(2) Keynesian model the equilibrium real national output would _____ to (at) _____ and the equilibrium price level

would _____ to (at) _____;

(3) rational-expectations model the equilibrium real national output would _____ to (at) _____ and the equilibrium price level would _____ to (at)

_____

■ **SELF-TEST**

Circle the T if the statement is true, the F if it is false.

1. The chief exponent of the monetarist position is Milton Friedman.　　　　　　**T　F**

2. The basic equations of the Keynesians and the monetarists are no more than two different ways of stating the same relationship.　　　　**T　F**

3. Most monetarists believe that an increase in the money supply will have no effect on real output and employment in either the short run or the long run.　　**T　F**

4. Keynesians contend that changes in the money supply will have little or no effect on the rate of interest.　**T　F**

5. Keynesians also maintain that relatively small changes in the interest rate have relatively large effects on investment spending.　　　　**T　F**

6. Monetarists argue that V in the equation of exchange is stable and that a change in M will bring about a direct and proportional change in P.　　　**T　F**

7. In the monetarists' analysis the demand for money is directly related to nominal NNP.　　　**T　F**

8. From the monetarist viewpoint, the economy is in equilibrium when the amount of money firms and households want to hold is equal to the money supply.　**T　F**

9. Keynesians contend that the velocity of money is unstable.　　　　　　**T　F**

10. In the Keynesians' analysis the demand for money is directly related to the rate of interest.　　**T　F**

11. Keynesians argue that a decrease in the rate of interest will decrease the velocity of money.　　**T　F**

12. Statistical evidence reveals that the velocity of money has remained almost constant from one year to the next.　　　　　　**T　F**

13. An expansionary fiscal policy will, the Keynesians contend, decrease the velocity of money.　　**T　F**

14. Monetarists conclude that discretionary monetary policy has resulted in macroeconomic instability.   **T   F**

15. Monetarists and Keynesians would agree that expansionary stabilization policies will produce demand-pull inflation in the classical range of the aggregate-supply curve.   **T   F**

16. According to Keynesians, a monetary rule would help promote price stability in the economy.   **T   F**

17. Rational-expectations theory assumes that both product and resource markets are uncompetitive and that wages and prices are "sticky."   **T   F**

18. Economists who have advanced the rational-expectations theory argue that discretionary fiscal and monetary policies have helped to stabilize the economy.   **T   F**

19. Most economists are proponents of the rational-expectations theory.   **T   F**

20. A legacy of new classical economics is that economists and policy makers are more sensitive about how expectations might affect the outcome of a policy change.   **T   F**

Circle the letter that corresponds to the best answer.

1. Keynesians:
 (*a*) believe capitalism is inherently stable
 (*b*) believe the markets in a capitalistic economy are highly competitive
 (*c*) argue against the use of discretionary monetary policy
 (*d*) contend that government intervention in the economy is desirable

2. Monetarists:
 (*a*) argue for the use of discretionary monetary policy
 (*b*) contend that government policies have reduced the stability of the economy
 (*c*) believe a capitalistic economy is inherently unstable
 (*d*) believe the markets in a capitalistic economy are largely noncompetitive

3. Which of the following is *not* true?
 (*a*) *MV* is total spending
 (*b*) *PQ* is the real NNP
 (*c*) *PQ* is nominal NNP
 (*d*) $MV = C_a + I_n + G$

4. If *V* in the equation of exchange is constant, an increase in *M* will necessarily increase:
 (*a*) *P*
 (*b*) *Q*
 (*c*) both *P* and *Q*
 (*d*) *P* times *Q*

5. Monetarists argue that velocity is stable and that the amount of money the public will want to hold depends primarily on the level of:
 (*a*) nominal NNP
 (*b*) investment
 (*c*) consumption
 (*d*) prices

6. From the monetarist viewpoint, an increase in the supply of money will:
 (*a*) raise the rate of interest
 (*b*) increase spending for consumer and capital goods
 (*c*) increase the asset demand for money
 (*d*) increase the demand for government securities

7. Keynesians argue that:
 (*a*) the only demand for money is the asset demand
 (*b*) the only demand for money is the transactions demand
 (*c*) there is no transactions demand
 (*d*) there is both a transactions and an asset demand for money

8. From the Keynesian viewpoint, an increase in supply of money will:
 (*a*) raise the rate of interest
 (*b*) decrease spending for consumer and capital goods
 (*c*) increase the asset demand for money
 (*d*) decrease the demand for government securities

9. The crowding-out-effect is the effect of borrowing funds to finance a government deficit on:
 (*a*) imports into the economy
 (*b*) the money supply
 (*c*) investment spending
 (*d*) consumer expenditures

10. Keynesians contend that borrowing to finance a government deficit incurred in order to increase employment and output in the economy will:
 (*a*) have little or no effect on the rate of interest
 (*b*) have little or no effect on investment spending
 (*c*) have a significant effect on *Q* in the equation of exchange
 (*d*) have all of the above effects

11. The rule suggested by the monetarists is that the money supply increases at the same rate as:
 (*a*) the price level
 (*b*) the interest rate
 (*c*) the velocity of money
 (*d*) the potential growth in real GNP

12. In the classical model:
 (*a*) the aggregate-supply curve is very steep and an increase in aggregate demand will have little or no effect on the price level

(b) the aggregate-supply curve is nearly flat and an increase in aggregate demand will have little or no effect on the price level

(c) the aggregate-supply curve is very steep and an increase in aggregate demand will have a large effect on the price level

(d) the aggregate-supply curve is nearly flat and an increase in aggregate demand will have a large effect on the price level

13. In the Keynesian model:

(a) the aggregate-supply curve is very steep and an increase in aggregate demand will have a large effect on real national output

(b) the aggregate-supply curve is nearly flat and an increase in aggregate demand will have a large effect on real national output

(c) the aggregate-supply curve is very steep and an increase in aggregate demand will have little or no effect on real national output

(d) the aggregate-supply curve is nearly flat and an increase in aggregate demand will have littlé or no effect on real national output

14. In the rational-expectations theory:

(a) individuals understand how the economy works and can correctly anticipate the effects of an event or a change in public policy on the economy

(b) the markets in the economy are purely competitive

(c) individuals to maximize their own self-interests respond to any expansionary fiscal or monetary policy in a way that prevents an increase in real output and fosters an increase in the price level

(d) all of the above are true

15. In the model of the rational-expectations theorists an increase in aggregate demand will:

(a) increase the price level and have no effect on real national output

(b) increase real national output and have no effect on the price level

(c) increase both the price level and the real national output

(d) have none of the above effects

16. To stabilize the economy rational-expectations theorists favor the use of:

(a) price controls

(b) discretionary fiscal policy

(c) discretionary monetary policy

(d) policy rules

17. The contention that changes in the money supply cause direct changes in aggregate demand and therefore changes in nominal NNP would be most closely associated with the view of:

(a) Keynesians

(b) monetarists

(c) new classical economists

(d) rational-expectations economists

18. Proponents of rational expectations argue that people:

(a) are not as rational as they are assumed to be by monetarists

(b) tend to make perfect forecasts which frustrates policy makers

(c) do not consistently make forecasting errors which can be exploited by policy makers

(d) do not respond quickly to changes in wages and prices, causing a misallocation of resources in the economy

19. The idea that the Federal Reserve should follow a monetary rule would find the most support from which combination?

(a) Keynesians and monetarists

(b) RET economists and Keynesians

(c) RET economists and monetarists

(d) classical economists and Keynesians

20. A distinguishing feature of the rational expectations in the aggregate demand–aggregate supply model would be an aggregate:

(a) demand curve that is downward sloping

(b) demand curve that is vertical

(c) supply curve that is vertical

(d) supply curve that is horizontal

■ **DISCUSSION QUESTIONS**

1. How do the views of Keynesians and monetarists on the competitiveness of capitalistic economies, their stability, and the need for government intervention in the economy differ?

2. What is the basic equation of the Keynesians and the basic equation of the monetarists? Define all terms in both equations and explain how the Keynesian equation can be converted to the monetarist equation.

3. Why do Keynesians believe that monetary policy is an "uncertain, unreliable and weak stabilization tool as compared to fiscal policy"?

4. Explain how a change in **M** in the equation of exchange will, to the monetarist way of thinking, affect

(a) **P** times **Q**,

(b) **P** and **Q** in the short run, and

(c) **P** and **Q** in the long run.

5. Explain the differences between the monetarist and Keynesian views on why firms and households demand money (or liquid balances); on what determines the demand for money; and the stability, therefore, of the velocity of money.

6. Suppose firms and households, because of an increase in the money supply, find themselves with more money than they wish to have. What do the monetarists believe they will do with this excess money? What effect will this have on the velocity of money and nominal NNP?

7. Suppose the supply of money increases. What do Keynesians believe will happen to the rate of interest, the amount of money firms and households will wish to hold, planned investment spending, and to the nominal NNP?

8. What empirical evidence is there to support the Keynesian contention that *V* is unstable or the monetarist contention that it is relatively stable?

9. Why do the Keynesians advocate and the monetarists reject the use of fiscal policy to stabilize the economy?

10. What is the monetary rule? Why do monetarists suggest this rule to replace discretionary monetary policy?

11. How do the aggregate demand-aggregate supply models of the Keynesians and monetarists differ? What effect will an expansionary monetary or fiscal policy have upon real national output and the price level in each of these models?

12. Use the aggregate demand–aggregate supply model to explain monetarist and Keynesian views of the use of a monetary rule for an expanding economy.

13. In as few words as possible, explain how and why rational-expectations theorists believe firms, workers, and consumers will respond to an expansionary monetary or fiscal policy; and how these responses make the policy ineffective and promote economic instability.

14. How will an expansionary monetary or fiscal policy affect real national output and the price level in the rational-expectations theorists' aggregate demand-aggregate supply model? Why does it have these effects?

15. What criticisms have been made of the RET by its opponents?

16. Why has the debate among Keynesians, monetarists, and rational-expectationists been "healthy"?

■ ANSWERS

CHAPTER 18 ALTERNATIVE VIEWS: MONETARISM AND RATIONAL EXPECTATIONS

Fill-in questions

1. unstable, noncompetitive, government intervention, fiscal, monetary

2. stable, competitive, laissez faire, nondiscretionary, monetary

3. $MV = PQ$; *a.* equation of exchange; *b.* (1) the money supply, (2) the (income or circuit) velocity of money, (3) the average price of each unit of physical output, (4) the physical volume of goods and services produced

4. *a.* total spending (aggregate demand), MV; *b.* PQ

5. *a.* increase; *b.* increase; (c) increase, P

6. *a.* stable, nominal NNP, stable; *b.* asset, interest rate, unstable

7. *a.* (1) more, (2) increase, (3) increase, (4) P, Q; *b.* (1) decrease, (2) increase, (3) decrease, (4) uncertain

8. *a.* M, PQ; *b.* directly, decreases, inversely

9. *a.* fiscal; *b.* raise, crowding-out

10. real GNP, 3, 5

11. destabilize

12. *a.* flat, small, large; *b.* steep, large, small; *c.* stable, equal to, less than, greater than (either order), unstable

13. *a.* self-interests; *b.* purely competitive, flexible; *c.* inflation, no change, an increase

14. vertical, the price level, the real output

15. *a.* pro-; *b.* policy rules

16. less well, less, sticky, stabilize, real

Problems and projects

1. *a.* 100, 220, 360, 520, 700, 900, 1120; *b.* 360, 360, 360, 360, 360, 360, 360, (1) 360, (2) 3.00, (3) 130; *c.* 700, (1) 700, (2) 5.00, (3) 140

2. *a.* (1) 50, (2) 75, (3) 125, (4) equal to, (5) 4; *b.* (1) 60, 100, (2) 160, equal to, (3) 3.75; *c.* (1) 80, 80, 160, (2) 5; *d.* decrease, increase

3. *a.* rational-expectations, classical, Keynesian; *b.* Q_1, P_1; *c.* (1) increase, Q_2, increase, P_3, (2) increase, Q_3, increase, P_2, (3) remain constant, Q_1, increase, P_4

Self-test

1. T; **2.** T; **3.** F; **4.** T; **5.** F; **6.** F; **7.** T; **8.** T; **9.** T; **10.** F; **11.** T; **12.** F; **13.** F; **14.** F; **15.** T; **16.** F; **17.** F; **18.** F; **19.** F; **20.** T

1. *d*; **2.** *b*; **3.** *b*; **4.** *d*; **5.** *a*; **6.** *b*; **7.** *d*; **8.** *c*; **9.** *c*; **10.** *d*; **11.** *d*; **12.** *c*; **13.** *b*; **14.** *d*; **15.** *a*; **16.** *d*; **17.** *b*; **18.** *c*; **19.** *c*; **20.** *c*

The inflation–unemployment relationship: Keynesian, new classical, and supply-side views

This chapter continues the discussion of alternative perspectives of macroeconomic theory and policy by examining the explanations for the simultaneous presence of unemployment and inflation in the United States economy. The mainstream or Keynesian views of the relationship between unemployment and inflation during the past three decades as embodied in the Phillips Curve are contrasted with new classical economics, with its the natural rate hypothesis and the distinction made between the short-run and long-run aggregate supply curve. The chapter aso presents other policy options for dealing with inflation and unemployment and introduces the perspective of supply-side economics.

In the early 1960s most economists believed that it was possible for the American economy to have both full employment and stable prices. This belief was based on the assumption that the price level would not rise until the labor force was fully employed. All that was necessary for full employment without inflation was just the right level of aggregate expenditures. Fiscal and monetary policy, thought Keynesian economists, could be used to assume that aggregate demand was adequate but not excessive.

But the assumption underlying this simplest Keynesian model was not realistic. The price level can rise before full employment is achieved; and the closer the economy moves to full employment the greater the rate at which prices rise. This observation became the basis for the concept of an unemployment-inflation rate tradeoff and its menu of policy choices as described in the supposedly stable Phillips Curve. According to Keynesians, the reason for inflation before full employment and for the Phillips Curve is that some types of labor become fully employed before other types of labor, and possibly also the market power of businesses and unions to raise prices and wages.

While this apparent unemployment–inflation rate tradeoff created a policy dilemma for economists of the 1960s, the situation and the problem became much more complicated in the 1970s and early 1980s. The problem was stagflation, with rising prices and rising unemployment rates. Keynesians explained stagflation of the period by citing events that produced aggregate supply shocks, de-creasing the aggregate supply curve and driving up the price level and reducing real output and employment. The leftward shift in the aggregate supply curve caused the Phillips Curve to move to the right; hence the occurrence of both rising prices and unemployment. The events of the 1983–1988 period shifted the aggregate supply curve rightward again and the Phillips Curve to the left, or so the Keynesian view went.

An alternative explanation of the events of the 1970s and 1980s came from the natural rate hypothesis of new classical economics. The two variants of this hypothesis were those of adaptive-expectations and rational-expectations theorists. Both adaptive- and rational-expectations theorists contend that the downsloping Phillips Curve is a figment of Keynesian imagination; that it is actually a vertical line; and that government attempts to reduce the unemployment rate below the rate at which the vertical Phillips Curve meets the horizontal axis produce a higher rate of inflation. The major difference between the adaptive expectationists and rational expectationists is that the former believe that expansionary monetary or fiscal policies can bring about a temporary decline in the unemployment rate; the latter argue that such policies do not even reduce unemployment temporarily, and any short-term instability in the macro economy is a product of price-level surprises.

New classical economists also distinguish between a short-run and a long-run aggregate supply curve. In the short run, nominal wages are fixed so an increase in the price level increases business profits and real output. In the long run, nominal wages are flexible so business profits and employment return to their original level, making the long-run aggregate supply curve vertical at the potential level of real output. Keynesians question the speed of these adjustments because of the downward inflexibility of wages and prices and hold that there are opportunities for the use of stabilization policies to reduce the high cost of unemployment or inflation.

The distinction between the short-run and long-run aggregate supply curve requires a reinterpretation of demand-pull and cost-push inflation. Although demand-pull inflation will increase the price level and real output in the short run, once nominal wages increase, the temporary increase in output will be gone, but the price level will be higher at the potential level of output for the economy. Cost-push inflation will increase the price level and decrease real output in the short run, but again, once nominal wages fall, output and the price level will return to the original level. If policy makers try to counter cost-push inflation by increasing aggregate demand, they may make matters worse by increasing the price level and causing the short-run aggregate supply curve to decrease again.

Other solutions for stagflation have been sought by the United States and other mixed market economies. Discussed in the chapter are market policies and wage-price policies that were used in the 1960s and 1970s to correct aspects of the unemployment and inflation problem. Of more recent appeal, however, was supply-side economics, which gained visibility during the Reagan administration (1981–1989). Supply-side economists pointed to the role of the Federal government in causing the slump in productivity and economic growth in the economy during the 1970s. The solutions, which became the program of Reaganomics, were to come from massive reduction in personal and corporate income taxes, reduced government regulation, cuts in social and welfare spending by government, and control over the rate of growth of the money supply. Despite its successes, this program and supply-side economics have been criticized, especially for the failure of the large cuts in the tax rates to increase significantly the aggregate supply curve beyond its historical level.

The chapter concludes with a recap of the alternative macroeconomic theories and policies presented in this and the previous chapter. You should take time to study Table 19–1 in detail so that you understand and can explain the different viewpoints.

■ CHECKLIST

When you have studied this chapter you should be able to:

☐ Explain how early Keynesian analysis was able to conclude that the economy could achieve both full employment and stable prices; and what was needed to reach these two goals simultaneously.

☐ Draw a traditional Phillips Curve (after properly labeling the two axes); and explain how to derive this curve by using the aggregate demand-aggregate supply model.

☐ State the two basic causes of the inflation shown on the Phillips Curve.

☐ Explain and use the Phillips Curve to illustrate the stabilization policy dilemma.

☐ Define stagflation; and contrast stagflation with the relationship shown by a Phillips Curve.

☐ Enumerate the supply-side shocks experienced by the American economy in the 1970s and early 1980s; and use the aggregate demand-aggregate supply model to explain why these shocks led to stagflation.

☐ List the events that contributed to stagflation's demise during the 1983–1988 period.

☐ Describe the Keynesians' view of the Phillips Curve from 1960 to 1988.

☐ Explain the natural rate hypothesis and the two variants of this hypothesis—adaptive expectations and rational expectations.

☐ Use the adaptive expectations model to explain the process of inflation and disinflation in the economy.

☐ Compare and contrast how adaptive expectations and rational expectations theorists view the Phillips Curve.

☐ Distinguish the short-run from the long-run aggregate supply curve.

☐ Compare and contrast Keynesian and new classical perspectives of stabilization policy.

☐ Apply the distinction between the short-run and long-run aggregate supply curve to explain demand-pull and cost-push inflation.

☐ State the two kinds of market policies that might be used to combat stagflation.

☐ Distinguish between wage-price guideposts and wage-price controls; and explain why they are called income policies.

☐ Explain what the advocates of supply-side economics see as the three basic causes of stagflation in the American economy; and the four policies advocated by the Reagan administration to deal with this stagflation.

☐ Criticize the program of the Reagan administration (Reaganomics) and evaluate the effectiveness of that program.

☐ Summarize the alternative macroeconomic theories and policies of various issues.

■ CHAPTER OUTLINE

1. In the simple Keynesian model of aggregate demand and aggregate supply, an assumption is made that the aggregate supply curve is shaped as a reverse "L" with a horizontal (Keynesian) range and a vertical (classical) range.

a. With this basic model, the economy may realize either unemployment or inflation, but not both problems simultaneously. The stagflation episodes of the 1970s showed this conclusion to be incorrect.

b. The model can be revised to account for the events of the 1970s by including an upsloping portion in the intermediate range of the aggregate supply curve and by allowing the aggregate supply curve to shift left.

2. If aggregate supply is constant and the economy is operating in the intermediate range on the aggregate supply curve, the greater the rate of increase in aggregate demand the greater is the rate of increase in the price level and in real output, and the lower is the rate of unemployment (and *vice versa*); and there is, therefore, an inverse relationship (or tradeoff) called the Phillips Curve between the inflation rate and the unemployment rate.

a. There are at least two reasons why inflation occurs before the economy reaches full employment.

(1) Scarcities of some kinds of labor develop before the economy's entire labor force is fully employed; and these scarcities increase wage rates, production costs, and prices.

(2) Labor unions and business firms have market power and they raise wage rates and prices as the economy approaches full employment.

b. While fiscal and monetary policy can be employed to manage aggregate demand and to affect unemployment and the rate of inflation, the nation faces a serious policy dilemma: full employment without inflation and price stability without unemployment are impossible and the nation must choose one of the combinations of inflation and unemployment that lies on the Phillips Curve.

c. Events in the 1960s seemed to confirm the inverse relationship between the unemployment and inflation rates.

3. Events of the 1970s and 1980s, however, called into question the stability of the Phillips Curve:

a. In the 1970s and early 1980s the American economy experienced both higher rates of inflation and greater unemployment rates; and this stagflation suggests either that there is no dependable relationship between the inflation and unemployment rates or that the Phillips Curve had shifted to the right.

(1) During these years six cost- or supply-side shocks decreased aggregate supply (moved the aggregate supply curve left) to increase both prices and unemployment in the United States; and the experiences of the American economy suggest that the Phillips Curve is not a stable relationship and cannot be used as the basis for economic policy.

(2) The demise of stagflation came in the 1983–1988 period because of a variety of factors; but unemployment and inflation moved in the same direction at times, not in the opposite direction implied by the Phillips Curve of the 1960s.

b. The Keynesian view is that a tradeoff between unemployment and inflation does exist; the explanation for the data problems were the supply shocks that produced a

leftward shift in the Phillips Curve during the 1971–1982 period, and changes in the economy that produced a rightward shift during the 1983–1988 period.

4. The natural rate hypothesis questions the existence of a downsloping Phillips Curve and views the economy as stable in the long run at the natural rate of unemployment. There are two variants to this hypothesis:

a. The theory of adaptive expectations suggests that an increase in aggregate demand sponsored by government may temporarily reduce unemployment as the price level increases and profits expand, but the actions also set into motion other events:

(1) The increase in the price level reduces the real wages of workers who demand and obtain higher nominal wages; these actions return unemployment to its original level.

(2) Back at the original level, there is now a higher actual and expected rate of inflation for the economy, so the short-run Phillips Curve has shifted upward.

(3) The process is repeated when government tries again to reduce unemployment and the rise in the price level accelerates as the short-run Phillips Curves shift upward.

(4) In the long run, the Phillips Curve is stable only as a vertical line at the natural rate of unemployment; there is no tradeoff between unemployment and inflation.

b. Rational expectations theory assumes that workers fully anticipate that government policies to reduce unemployment will also be inflationary, and they increase their nominal wage demands to offset the expected inflation; thus there will not even be a temporary decline in unemployment, or a short-run Phillips Curve.

5. The aggregate supply curve has short- and long-run characteristics, and implications for policy:

a. In the short run, where nominal wages are fixed, the aggregate supply curve is upward sloping: an increase in the price level will increase profits and cause a rise in real output; in contrast, when the price level decreases, profits are reduced and so is real output.

b. In the long run, where nominal wages are variable, the aggregate supply curve is vertical at the potential level of output: increases in the price level will increase in nominal wages and cause a shift to the left in the short-run aggregate supply curve; or declines in the price level reduce nominal wages and shift the short-run aggregate supply curve to the right; but in either case, although the price level changes, output returns to its potential level, so the long-run aggregate supply curve is vertical.

c. Proponents of new classical economics subscribe to the view that with flexible nominal wages the economy is basically stable at the full-employment level of output in the long run, and thus there no need for policy actions; modern Keynesians contend that nominal wages may be slow to adjust to price level changes and support the use of stabilization policies to reduce unemployment or inflation costs to the economy.

6. Knowledge of the short- and long-run features of aggregate demand and supply provide insights into these types of inflation:

a. Demand-pull inflation will shift the short-run aggregate demand curve, which increases the price level and causes a temporary increase in real output; but in the long run, nominal wages will increase and the short-run aggregate supply will shift to the left, resulting in an even higher price level with real output returning to its previous level.

b. Cost-push inflation will shift the short-run aggregate supply curve left:

(1) this action increases the price level and temporarily decreases real output;

(2) the resulting recession will reduce nominal wages, shifting the short-run aggregate supply to its original position;

(3) but if government takes actions to counter the cost-push inflation and recession by shifting aggregate demand, the price level will move to an even higher level.

c. The aggregate demand and aggregate supply curves are both vertical in the long run.

7. Because of the ineffectiveness of demand-management policies in coping with stagflation, the American economy has sought other kinds of policies to prevent decreases in or to increase aggregate supply (to shift the Phillips Curve to the left).

a. Market policies try to eliminate the causes of premature inflation and include:

(1) employment and training policies to reduce the scarcities of particular kinds of labor that occur before the labor force is fully employed;

(2) pro-competition policies to reduce the power of labor unions and business firms to raise wage rates and prices.

b. Wage-price (or incomes) policies restrict increases in wages and prices by utilizing either guideposts or controls.

(1) Wage-price guideposts are voluntary restraints. The Kennedy-Johnson guideposts restricted money-wage increases in all industries to the rate at which the productivity of labor in the economy had increased; and allowed an industry to increase the price of its product by an amount equal to the increase in its unit labor cost.

(2) Wage-price controls are mandatory (or legal) restraints; and were employed in 1971 to deal with stagflation in the American economy.

(3) Whether to employ wage-price policies has been a vigorously debated issue; and the proponents and opponents have based their arguments on the questions of workability and compliance and allocative efficiency.

(4) To improve the effectiveness of income policies it has been suggested that special tax rebates be given to (tax penalties imposed on) those who comply with (ignore) the guideposts.

c. Supply-side economists argue that the Keynesians have overemphasized the aggregate demand side and neglected the aggregate supply side in their explanation of the price level and unemployment.

(1) Taxes, they argue, are business costs and increased taxes result in an upward shift in aggregate supply.

(2) They also argue that taxes and transfer payments reduce the incentives to work, to save, and to invest and lead to a misallocation of resources which reduces aggregate supply.

(3) And the increased regulation of industry has adversely affected costs and productivity.

d. Reaganomics was based on supply-side economics and it was the policy of the Reagan administration to reduce almost all government spending (except defense expenditures), reduce government spending (except defense expenditures), reduce government regulation of private business firms, prevent the growth in the money supply from being inflationary, and reduce personal and corporate income tax rates.

(1) Sizable reductions in personal and business tax rates were contained in the Economic Recovery Tax Act of 1981 and were aimed at increasing aggregate supply to bring about a reduction in the rates of inflation and unemployment (and an expansion in real output);

(2) The Tax Reform Act of 1986 lowered marginal tax rates but broadened the tax base to keep this tax change "revenue neutral";

(3) Economist Arthur Laffer contended that lower tax rates would increase tax revenues and prevent inflationary government deficits.

(4) But critics replied that these tax-rate reductions would have little effect on incentives (and would be slow to expand national output), would so increase aggregate demand (relative to supply) that large budget deficits and more rapid inflation would result, would actually decrease tax revenues, and would increase income inequality.

e. While the programs of the Reagan administration reduced the inflation rate sharply, they appear to have brought on a sharp recession between 1980 and 1982, increased the budget deficits of the Federal government, failed to increase tax revenues, may have crowded-out private investment, and have not increased saving and investment or incentives to work; and the recovery of the economy since 1982 can be attributed to the expansionary effects of the budget deficit.

8. Table 19–1 contains a recap of the alternative macroeconomic theories and policies discussed in Chapters 18 and 19.

■ **IMPORTANT TERMS**

Phillips Curve	Demand-pull inflation
Stagflation	Cost-push inflation
Supply shocks	Market policies
Inflationary expectations	Wage-price guideposts
Natural-rate hypothesis	Wage-price controls
Adaptive expectations theory	Incomes policies
Rational-expectations theory	Supply-side economics
Disinflation	Tax "wedge"
Short-run aggregate supply curve	Reaganomics
Long-run aggregate supply curve	Economic Recovery Tax Act (ERTA) of 1981
	Tax Reform Act of 1986
New classical economics	Laffer Curve
Price-level surprises	Tax-transfer disincentives

■ **FILL-IN QUESTIONS**

1. In the simplest Keynesian view, the price level of the economy would not increase until the economy reached _____ and inflation was the result of (excess, insufficient) _____ aggregate demand; and the economy can have (either, both) _____ unemployment or/and inflation.

2. In the aggregate demand–aggregate supply model, when the economy is producing in the intermediate range along the aggregate supply curve:
 a. An increase in aggregate demand will (increase, decrease) _____ real output and employment.
 b. A decrease in aggregate supply will _____ real output and employment.

3. If aggregate supply remains constant, along the intermediate range of aggregate supply:
 a. the greater the increase in aggregate demand, the (greater, smaller) _____ will be the increase in the price level, the _____ will be the increase in real output, and the _____ will be the unemployment rate;
 b. there will be a(n) (direct, inverse) _____ relationship between the rate of inflation and the unemployment rate.

4. When prices rise before _____ _____, this is the result of the market power of _____ and _____ and of imbalances or bottlenecks in _____ markets.

5. The Phillips Curve:
 a. is the relation between the annual rate of increase in the _____ and the _____ rate;
 b. has a (positive, negative) _____ slope.

6. The stabilization policy dilemma faced by the American economy is that:
 a. to have full employment it must also have _____ and to have stable prices it must tolerate _____
 b. to reduce the unemployment rate the rate of inflation must (increase, decrease) _____ and to reduce the rate of inflation the unemployment rate must _____

7. Policies to manage aggregate demand can be used to (shift the, select a point on the) _____ Phillips Curve, but such policies do not improve the "unemployment rate-inflation rate" _____

8. List the six factors (supply-side shocks) that shifted the Phillips Curve to the right after 1972 according to Keynesians.
 a. _____
 b. _____
 c. _____
 d. _____
 e. _____
 f. _____

9. In the equation that relates unit labor costs to nominal wage rates and the productivity of labor:
 a. If the rate at which nominal wages increase is greater than the rate at which productivity increases, unit labor costs will (increase, decrease) _____
 b. If the productivity of labor decreases and nominal wage rates are constant, unit labor costs will _____

10. The expectation of inflation by workers and employers leads to (higher, lower) _____ wage rates and in turn to a (rise, fall) _____ in production costs, to a(n) (increase, decrease) _____ in aggregate supply, to a (higher, lower) _____ price level, and to a _____ rate of unemployment in the economy.

11. The rising unemployment rates and the sharp inflation following the supply-side shocks can be understood by using the aggregate demand-aggregate supply model.

a. The shocks (increased, decreased) _____ aggregate supply.

b. Which in turn increased both the _____ level and the _____ rate.

c. And these two events when they occur simultaneously are called _____

12. List four factors that contributed to stagflation's demise during the 1983–1988 period:

a. _____

b. _____

c. _____

d. _____

13. During the 1960s, the empirical data indicate that unemployment and inflation moved in the (same, opposite) _____ direction; in 1973–1974, 1979–1980, and in some years during the 1983–1988 period, unemployment and inflation moved in the _____ direction.

14. There is much debate among economists about the Phillips Curve:

a. Keynesians contend that during the stagflation of the 1970s, the Phillips Curve shifted (right, left) _____; during the demise of stagflation from 1983–1988, the Phillips Curve shifted _____

b. Other economists associated with new classical thinking conclude that the downsloping Phillips Curve does not _____ in the long run and subscribe to the _____ hypothesis, for which there are two variants—_____

and _____ expectations.

c. The theory of adaptive expectations suggests that people form their expectations of _____ based on experience and (immediately, gradually) _____ change expectations over time.

d. With this theory.

(1) the (short-run, long-run) _____ Phillips Curve may be downsloping, but the _____ Phillips Curve is vertical at the _____

(2) attempts by government to reduce the unemployment rate bring about a rate of inflation that (increases, decreases) _____

e. The rational expectations theory suggests that:

(1) attempts by government to reduce the unemployment rate lead workers to anticipate perfectly the amount of _____ this will cause and to keep their (real, nominal) _____ wages constant they obtain a(n) (increase, decrease) _____ in their _____ wages; and

(2) this brings about (a rise, a fall, no change) _____ in the price level and _____ in the unemployment rate.

15. With the aggregate supply curve:

a. In the short run, the curve is (upsloping, vertical) _____ and in the long run the curve is _____;

b. In the short run, nominal wages are (fixed, variable) _____, and in the long run, nominal wages are _____.

c. Proponents of new classical economics think that wages and prices are (flexible, inflexible) _____ and that the economy is (stable, unstable) _____ in the long run at the full employment level of real output; policy changes by government (will, will not) _____ be anticipated in advance and _____ influence the economy in the short term; only _____ surprises produce temporary changes in real output.

d. Modern Keynesians accept the distinction between short- and long-run aggregate supply, but contend that wages and prices are (flexible, inflexible) _____ downward, and therefore they advocate a(n) (active, hand-offs) _____ policy by government in the short run to reduce the (low, high) _____ cost of inflation and unemployment.

16. Demand-pull inflation will shift the (short-run, long-run) _____ aggregate demand curve (right, left) _____, which will (decrease, increase) _____ the price level and temporarily _____ real output. As a consequence, the (short-run, long-run) _____ aggregate supply curve will shift left because of a rise in (real, nominal) _____ wages, producing a (lower, higher) _____ price level at the original level of real output.

17. Cost-push Inflation will shift the short-run aggregate supply curve (right, left) _____, thus the price level will (increase, decrease) _____ and real output will temporarily _____; if government takes no actions to counter the cost-push inflation, the resulting recession will _____ nominal wages, and shift the short-run aggregate supply curve back to its original position; yet, if the government tries to counter the cost-push inflation and recession with a(n) _____ in aggregate demand, the price level will move even higher.

18. Three kinds of economic policies might be used to deal with stagflation.

a. These three policies are _____ policies, _____ – _____ policies, and the policies identified with _____ economics.

b. If effective, these policies would move the Phillips Curve to the (right, left) _____

19. Market policies to reduce unemployment include:
a. those designed to reduce bottlenecks in labor markets and are called _____ policies; and
b. those aimed at reducing the market power of business firms and labor unions and are called pro-_____ policies.

20. Wage-price policies:
a. are sometimes called _____ policies;
b. involve either:

(1) wage-price (controls, guideposts) _____ which rely upon the voluntary cooperation of labor unions and business firms

(2) or wage-price _____ which have the force of law to make them effective.

21. The wage-price guideposts for curbing inflation during the Kennedy-Johnson administrations limited **wage** increases in an industry to the overall rate of increase in the _____ of labor and limited **price** increases to an amount equal to the increase in _____ costs in that industry.

22. It is the view of supply-side economists that:
a. business costs and product prices have increased because
(1) government has raised taxes and these taxes are a business _____ and a "_____" between the price of a product and the cost of resources;
(2) high marginal tax rates reduce _____ to work, save, invest, and take risks; and
(3) increased government _____ of industry has increased its productivity;
b. the remedy for stagflation is a substantial (increase, decrease) _____ in taxes.

23. The program of the Reagan administration ("Reaganomics") to reduce inflation and unemployment in the economy had four principal elements. These were

a. _____

b. _____

c. _____

d. _____

24. The Laffer Curve depicts the relationship between tax rates and tax revenues. In theory, as the tax rates increase from 0%, tax revenues will (increase, decrease) _____ to some maximum level, after which tax revenues will _____ as the tax rates increase; or, as tax rates are reduced from 100%, tax revenues will _____ to some maximum level, after which tax revenues will _____ as tax rates decrease.

25. The main supply-side proposition was that the cut in tax rates would significantly shift the (aggregate demand, aggregate supply) _____ curve to (leftward, rightward) _____ and make the economy grow at a pace greater than historical experience. The evidence to date (does, does not) _____ appear to support that proposition.

■ PROBLEMS AND PROJECTS

1. In the next column is a traditional Phillips Curve.

a. At full employment (a 4% unemployment rate) the price level would rise by _____% each year.

b. If the price level were stable (increasing by 0% a year) the unemployment rate would be _____%.

c. Which of the combinations along the Phillips Curve would you choose for the economy? _____ Why would you select this combination? _____

_____

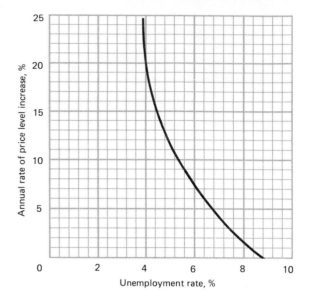

be employed to produce each of the seven real national outputs (in billions) in the aggregate supply schedule. The labor force is 80 million workers and the full-employment output of the economy is $_____

2. In columns (1) and (2) of the table below is a portion of an aggregate supply schedule. Column (3) shows the number of full-time workers (in millions) that would have to

(1) Price level	(2) Real output produced	(3) Employment	(4) Real output purchased	(5) Real output purchased	(6) Real output purchased
$3	$ 800	69	$2300	$2600	$1900
4	1300	70	2200	2500	1800
5	1700	72	2100	2400	1700
6	2000	75	2000	2300	1600
7	2200	78	1900	2200	1500
8	2300	80	1800	2100	1400
9	2300	80	1700	2000	1300

a. If the aggregate demand schedule were that shown by columns (1) and (4):

   (1) The price level would be $_____ and the real output would be $_____

   (2) the number of workers employed would be _____, the number of workers unemployed would be _____, and the unemployment *rate* would be _____ percent.

b. If aggregate demand were to increase to that shown in columns (1) and (5) and aggregate supply remained constant:

   (1) the price level would rise to $_____

and the real output would rise to $_____

   (2) employment would increase by _____

_____ workers and the unemployment rate would fall to _____%.

   (3) the price level has increased by and the rate of inflation has been _____%.

c. If aggregate demand were to decrease to that shown in columns (1) and (6) and aggregate supply remained constant:

   (1) the price level would fall to $_____

and the real output would fall to $_____

   (2) employment would decrease by _____ workers and the unemployment rate would rise to

_____%.

(3) the price level has decreased and the rate of inflation has been (positive, negative) _____

3. Below is an adaptive expectations model of the short- and long-run Phillips Curve.

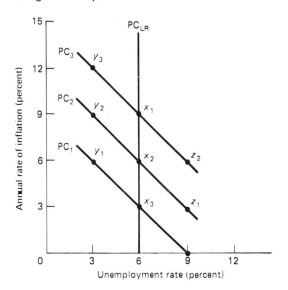

a. Suppose you begin at point **X**$_1$; then an assumption is made that nominal wages are set on the original expectation that a 3% rate of inflation will continue in the economy.

(1) If government invokes expansionary monetary and fiscal policy to reduce the unemployment rate from 6% to 3%, then the actual rate of inflation will move to

_____%. The higher product prices will lift profits of firms and they will hire more workers; thus in the short run the economy will temporarily move to point

_____

(2) If workers then demand and receive higher wages to compensate for the loss of purchasing power from higher than expected inflation, then business profits will fall from previous levels and firms will reduce employment. Therefore, employment will move from point

_____ to point _____ on the graph. The short-run Phillips Curve has shifted from _____

to _____ on the graph.

(3) If government again tries to stimulate aggregate demand with monetary and fiscal policy to reduce the unemployment rate from 6% to 3%, then prices will rise before nominal wages, and output and employment will increase, so that there will be a move from point

_____ to point _____ on the graph.

(4) But when workers get nominal wage increases,

profits fall, and employment moves from point

_____ at _____ % to point

_____ at _____%. The short-run Phillips Curve has now shifted from _____ to

_____ on the graph.

(5) The long-run Phillips Curve is the line _____

_____

b. Suppose you begin at point **X**$_3$, where the expected and actual rate of inflation is 9% and the unemployment rate is 6%.

(1) If there should be a decline in aggregate demand because of a recession and if the actual rate of inflation should fall to 6%, well below the expected rate of 9%, then business profits will fall and the unemployment rate will decrease to 9% as shown by the movement from point **X**$_3$

to point _____

(2) If firms and workers adjust their expectation to the 6% rate of inflation, then nominal wages will fall, profits will rise, and the economy will move from point

_____ to point _____. The short-run Phillips Curve has shifted from _____ to

_____

(3) If this process is repeated, the long-run Phillips Curve will be traced as line _____.

4. Below is an aggregate demand and aggregate supply model. Assume that the economy is initially in equilibrium

at AD$_1$ and AS$_1$. The price level will be _____

and the real national output will be _____

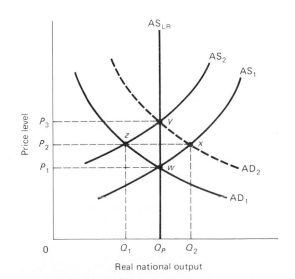

a. If there is demand-pull inflation, then:

(1) in the short run, the new equilibrium is at point _____, with the price level at _____ and real output at _____ ;

(2) in the long run, nominal wages will rise so the aggregate supply curve will shift from _____ to _____. The equilibrium will be at point _____ with the price level at _____ and real output at _____; and so the increase in aggregate demand has only moved the economy along its _____ curve.

b. Now assume that the economy is initially in equilibrium at point *W,* where AD_1 and AS_1 intersect. If there is cost-push inflation, then:

(1) in the short run, the new equilibrium is at point _____, with the price level at _____ and real output at _____

(2) If the government tries to counter the cost-push inflation with expansionary monetary and fiscal policy, then aggregate demand will shift from _____ to _____, with the price level becoming _____ and real output _____; but this policy has a trap because the price level has shifted from _____ to _____ and the new level of inflation might shift _____ leftward.

(3) If government does not counter the cost-push inflation, the price level will eventually move to _____ and real output to _____ as the recession reduces nominal wages and shifts the aggregate supply curve from _____ to _____

5. Assume that the overall rate of increase in the productivity of labor in the economy is 4% per year.

a. The general level of wages in the economy can increase by _____% a year without increasing unit labor costs and inducing cost-push inflation.

b. If the wage rate were increased by this percentage,

(1) in an industry in which the productivity of labor had increased 3%, labor costs per unit would (increase, decrease) _____ by _____%; and the application of the Kennedy-Johnson price guidepost would permit the price of the product produced by this industry to (rise, fall) _____ by _____%.

(2) In an industry in which the productivity of labor had increased by 6%, labor costs per unit would _____ by _____%; and the price guidepost would permit the price of the product to _____ by _____%.

(3) In an industry in which the productivity of labor had *decreased* by 2%, labor costs per unit would _____ by _____%; and the price guidepost would permit the price of the product to _____ by _____%.

■ **SELF-TEST**

Circle the T if the statement is true, the F if it is false.

1. In the simplest Keynesian model the aggregate-supply curve has no intermediate range.   **T   F**

2. The simple Keynesian model provides a reasonably satisfactory explanation of the macroeconomic behavior of the American economy between 1930 and 1970, but does not explain the stagflation of the 1970s and early 1980s.   **T   F**

3. When aggregate supply is constant, higher rates of inflation are accompanied by higher rates of unemployment.   **T   F**

4. According to the conventional Phillips Curve the rate of inflation increases as the level of unemployment decreases.   **T   F**

5. Labor market imbalances and market power are explanations offered by Keynesians to explain the intermediate range of the aggregate supply curve.   **T   F**

6. According to Keynesians, as the economy approaches full employment, some type of labor become fully employed before all the labor force is fully employed. **T   F**

7. Policies to manage aggregate supply can be used to choose a point on the Phillips Curve, but these policies do not improve the "unemployment rate–inflation rate" trade-off reflected in the Phillips Curve.   **T   F**

8. Stagflation refers to a situation in which both the price level and the unemployment rate are rising.   **T   F**

9. Keynesians contend that the Phillips Curve shifted left during the 1973–1982 period and shifted right during the 1983–1988 period.   **T   F**

10. Expectations of inflation induce workers to demand a higher nominal wage and their employers to pay them higher wages.   **T   F**

11. When the nominal wage rate increases at a rate greater than the rate at which the productivity of labor increases, unit labor cost will rise.   **T   F**

12. If the nominal wage rate increases by 8% and the productivity of labor remains constant, unit labor costs will rise.   **T   F**

13. The natural rate hypothesis suggests that there is a natural rate of inflation for the economy.   **T   F**

14. The theory of adaptive expectations indicates that there may be a short-run tradeoff between inflation and unemployment, but no long-run tradeoff.   **T   F**

15. From the adaptive expectations perspective, when the actual rate of inflation is higher than expected, the unemployment rate will rise.   **T   F**

16. Adaptive expectation theorists believe that they are able to explain disinflation in the economy.   **T   F**

17. The theory of rational expectations maintains that if workers believe expansionary monetary and fiscal policies will be inflationary and therefore lower their real wages, then the reaction of the workers to these expectations results in higher nominal wages, higher labor costs, and no change in employment in the economy.   **T   F**

18. Natural rate theorists conclude that demand-management policies cannot influence real output and employment in the long run, but only the price level.   **T   F**

19. The long-run aggregate supply curve is upsloping at the potential level of real national output.   **T   F**

20. New classical economists hold that price level surprises produce short-run fluctuations in the economy, but in the long run the economy is stable at the full-employment level of output.   **T   F**

21. Keynesians contend that nominal wages are inflexible upward and therefore they advocate a hands-off approach to stabilization policy.   **T   F**

22. Demand-pull inflation will increase the price level and real output in the short run, but in the long run, only the price level will increase.   **T   F**

23. An inflationary spiral is likely to result from the use of stabilization policies to maintain full-employment when the economy is experiencing cost-push inflation.   **T   F**

24. Of the policies that might be employed to deal with stagflation, the market, wage-price, and supply-side policies are designed to move the Phillips Curve to the left.   **T   F**

25. Voluntary restraint by business and labor leaders is not apt to be effective in preventing price and wage in-

creases because such restraint requires them to abandon their major goals.   **T   F**

26. The wage-price guideposts of the Kennedy-Johnson administrations for preventing cost-push inflation were to limit wage increases to the overall rate of increase in labor productivity in the economy.   **T   F**

27. Supply-side economists contend that Keynesian economics is unable to explain stagflation because costs and aggregate supply play an "active" role in the Keynesian model.   **T   F**

28. The tax "wedge" to which supply-side economists refer is the difference between the price of a product and the cost of economic resources required to produce it.   **T   F**

29. If the economy were at point **A** on the Laffer Curve shown below, a decrease in tax rates would increase tax revenues.   **T   F**

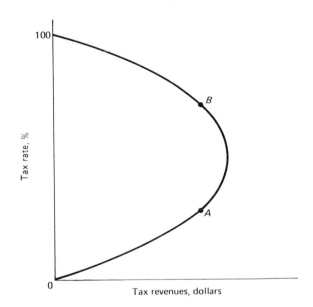

30. The supply-side economists believe that the economy is at a point such as point **B** on the Laffer Curve above, and that a substantial reduction in tax rates would both increase tax revenues and increase incentives to work, invest, innovate, and take risks.   **T   F**

Circle the letter that corresponds to the best answer.

1. In the Keynesian expenditures-output model it is impossible for the economy to experience:
(*a*) full employment
(*b*) inflation
(*c*) unemployment and inflation
(*d*) full employment and stable prices

2. As long as aggregate supply remains constant and the economy operates along the intermediate range of the aggregate-supply curve, the greater the increase in aggregate demand:

(a) the greater is the increase in the price level
(b) the greater is the increase in the unemployment rate
(c) the smaller is the increase in real output
(d) the smaller is the increase in employment

3. The conventional Phillips Curve:

(a) shows the inverse relation between the rate of increase in the price level and the unemployment rate
(b) makes it possible for the economy to achieve full employment and stable prices
(c) indicates that prices do not rise until full employment has been achieved
(d) slopes upward from left to right

4. Labor-market adjustments do not eliminate bottleneck problems when there is less than full employment in the economy. Which of the following is *not* one of the reasons for these labor-market imbalances?

(a) unemployed workers often lack the skills or training needed for a new occupation
(b) the demand for workers in the markets in which there are labor shortages is inadequate
(c) there are artificial restrictions which prevent unemployed workers from filling the job openings
(d) unemployed workers do not know of the shortages of workers in other labor markets in the economy

5. If inflation during periods of less than full employment is to be explained by market power, it must be assumed that:

(a) only unions possess considerable market power
(b) only employers possess considerable market power
(c) both unions and employers possess considerable market power
(d) neither unions nor employers possess considerable market power

6. The stabilization policy dilemma illustrated by a Phillips Curve is the mutual inconsistency of:

(a) more employment and price stability
(b) a higher unemployment rate and price stability
(c) inflation and more employment
(d) inflation and a lower unemployment rate

7. Demand-management (monetary and fiscal) policies can be employed to:

(a) shift the Phillips Curve to the right
(b) shift the Phillips Curve to the left
(c) achieve full employment without inflation
(d) reduce the unemployment rate

8. Which of the following was one of the supply-side shocks to the American economy during the 1970s and early 1980s?

(a) the imposition of wage and price controls
(b) the appreciation of the dollar
(c) the fall in the price charged by OPEC nations for oil
(d) worldwide agricultural surpluses

9. If the percentage change in the productivity of labor is 2% and the percentage change in nominal-wage rates is 5%, the percentage change in unit labor costs is:

(a) 1%
(b) 3%
(c) 7%
(d) 10%

10. Suppose the overall rate of increase in the productivity of labor in the economy is 4%. If the productivity of labor in a particular industry has increased at a rate of only 3%, the Kennedy-Johnson wage-price guideposts would have allowed this industry:

(a) to increase both the wage rate and the price of its product by 3%
(b) to increase the wage rate by 3% and would have allowed no increase in price
(c) to increase the wage rate by 4% and would have allowed no increase in price
(d) to increase the wage rate by 4% and to increase price by about 1%

11. Supply shocks which cause a leftward shift in the aggregate-supply curve, aggregate demand remaining constant, will:

(a) decrease the price level
(b) decrease the unemployment rate
(c) increase real output
(d) increase both the price level and the unemployment rate

12. Which one of the following would be a factor contributing to the demise of stagflation during the 1983–1988 period?

(a) a lessening of foreign competition
(b) a strengthening of the monopoly power of OPEC
(c) a recession brought on largely by a tight monetary policy
(d) an increase in regulation of airline and trucking industries

13. According to the Keynesian view, the collapse of the traditional unemployment rate-inflation rate tradeoff and the likely shift in the Phillips Curve during the 1980s were the consequence of a:

(a) rightward shift in aggregate demand
(b) rightward shift in aggregate supply
(c) leftward shift in aggregate demand
(d) leftward shift in aggregate supply

14. The natural rate hypothesis suggests that the economy is stable only in the:
(a) short run at the natural rate of unemployment
(b) short run at the natural rate of inflation
(c) long run at the natural rate of unemployment
(d) long run at the natural rate of inflation

15. The theory of adaptive expectations suggests that if increases in nominal wage rates lag behind increases in the price level, and government attempts to reduce unemployment by using fiscal and monetary policies, then employment:
(a) and the price level increase in the long run
(b) remains constant and the price level increases in the short run
(c) increases and the price level remains constant in the short run
(d) remains constant and the price level increases in the long run

16. The rational expectations theorists contend that when government attempts to reduce unemployment by using monetary and fiscal policies, unemployment decreases:
(a) temporarily and the price level rises
(b) permanently and the price level rises
(c) both temporarily and permanently and the price level rises
(d) neither temporarily nor permanently and the price level rises

17. In the view of natural rate theorists, the long-run Phillips Curve is:
(a) horizontal
(b) vertical
(c) upsloping
(d) downsloping

18. Disinflation, or reductions in the rate of inflation, can be explained based on the natural rate conclusion that when the:
(a) actual rate of inflation is lower than the expected rate, the unemployment rate will rise to bring the expected and actual rates into balance
(b) expected rate of inflation is lower than the actual rate, the unemployment rate will rise to bring the expected and actual rates into balance
(c) actual rate of inflation is higher than the expected rate, the unemployment rate will fall to bring the expected and actual rates into balance
(d) expected rate of inflation is higher than the actual rate, the unemployment rate will fall to bring the expected and actual rates into balance

19. The natural rate theory suggests that the aggregate supply curve:
(a) is stable in the short run so long as nominal wages

do not increase in the short run in response to the increase in the price level
(b) unstable in the long run because real wages are continually changing
(c) will shift to the right when the price of capital increases
(d) will shift to the right when nominal wages increase

20. According to new classical thinking, fully anticipated changes in the price level do **not** change the:
(a) level of real output
(b) level of prices
(c) inflexibility of wages and prices
(d) effectiveness of stabilization policy

21. In the short run, demand-pull inflation:
(a) is caused by a rightward shift in the Phillips Curve
(b) is the result of a decrease in aggregate demand
(c) produces an increase in real output
(d) creates price level surprises

22. In the long run, demand-pull inflation will:
(a) decrease the unemployment rate
(b) decrease the level of nominal wages
(c) increase the level of prices
(d) increase real national output

23. A likely result of treating cost-push inflation by stimulating aggregate demand with monetary and fiscal policies is:
(a) an inflationary spiral
(b) a price level surprise
(c) disinflation
(d) a recession

24. Which of the following is **not** one of the employment and training policies that might help relieve the problem of stagflation?
(a) application of antimonopoly laws to labor unions
(b) removal of discrimination as an obstacle to employment
(c) improvement of the flow of job information between workers without jobs and employers with unfilled positions
(d) expansion of programs that provide job training

25. From the viewpoint of supply-side economists, stagflation is the result of
(a) excessive taxation
(b) government deregulation
(c) a shifting Phillips Curve
(d) unanticipated inflation

26. Supply-side economists of the 1980s thought that the American system of taxes reduced:
(a) unemployment, but increased inflation
(b) incentives to work, save, and invest
(c) transfer payments to the poor and homeless

(d) the effectiveness of wage-price guideposts for the economy

27. Which one of the following was an element in the Reaganomics program for reducing stagflation in the American economy?
(a) a reduction in defense expenditures
(b) a reduction in personal income tax rates
(c) an increase in rate of growth of the money supply
(d) an increase in the regulation of private business firms

28. During the 1980–1982 period, the program of the Reagan administration reduced:
(a) unemployment
(b) the rate of inflation
(c) the Federal budget deficit
(d) the price of imported oil

29. One basic criticism of the central proposition of supply-side economics was that the Reaganomics program did not:
(a) slow the rate of growth in the money supply
(b) fully deregulate all sectors of the economy for optimal expansion
(c) significantly shift aggregate supply rightward more rapidly than its historical pace
(d) substantially reduce the level of unemployment in the economy and provide for retraining workers for other employment

■ **DISCUSSION QUESTIONS**

1. Why does the simplest Keynesian model imply that the economy may have either unemployment or inflation but will not experience unemployment and inflation simultaneously?

2. What is a Phillips Curve? Explain how a Phillips Curve with a negative slope may be derived by holding aggregate supply constant and mentally increasing aggregate demand.

3. What factors do Keynesians point to that underlie the Phillips Curve? How are those factors related to the intermediate range of the aggregate supply curve?

4. What is the stabilization policy dilemma illustrated by the traditional Phillips Curve? Does the manipulation of aggregate demand through monetary and fiscal policy move the Phillips Curve or cause a movement along the Phillips Curve?

5. Were the rates of inflation and of unemployment consistent with the Phillips Curve in the 1950s and 1960s?

What do these two rates suggest about the curve in the 1970s and early 1980s?

6. What were the supply-side shocks to the American economy during the 1970s and early 1980s? How did these shocks affect aggregate supply and the Phillips Curve in the United States?

7. How do expectations of inflation and declines in the productivity of labor affect aggregate supply and the Phillips Curve?

8. When do increases in nominal-wage rates increase unit labor costs, decrease aggregate supply, and increase the price level in the economy?

9. Describe the factors that contributed to stagflation's demise during the 1983–1988 period. What do Keynesians contend happened to the Phillips Curve during this period compared to the 1970s and early 1980s?

10. Explain the natural rate hypothesis and briefly describe the two variants of the interpretation of the unemployment-inflation rate data of 1960–1988.

11. What does "adaptive" refer to in the theory of adaptive expectations? Illustrate how this theory is used to explain both inflation and disinflation in the economy.

12. What are the views of the adaptive expectationists on:
(a) the effects of expansionary monetary and fiscal policy on employment in the short run and on the short-run Phillips Curve; and,
(b) the long-run Phillips Curve? How do they reach these conclusions?

13. How do rational expectationists believe expansionary monetary and fiscal policy affects the price level and employment in the short run and the long run? What assumptions do they make to reach this conclusion?

14. Compare and contrast the theories of rational expectations and adaptive expectations in terms of views on inflationary expectations, the interpretation of the Phillips Curve, and the effectiveness of demand-management policies.

15. Identify the basic difference between a short-run and a long-run aggregate supply curve. Explain what happens to aggregate supply when an increase in the price level results in an increase in nominal wages.

16. How do Keynesians and new classical economists view wage and price flexibility in the economy? What implications does each group draw about economic policy for the economy?

17. Describe the process of demand-pull inflation in the short run and in the long run. How does demand-pull inflation influence the aggregate supply curve?

18. What are two generalizations that emerge from the analysis of cost-push inflation? Describe the two scenarios that provide the basis for the generalizations.

19. What are the two kinds of market policies that might be employed to shift the Phillips Curve to the left? Within each of these two categories, what specific things might be done to reduce the causes of inflation?

20. Explain
(a) what is meant by wage-price policy;
(b) why wage-price policy is often called incomes policy; and
(c) the difference between wage-price guideposts and wage-price controls.

21. What
(a) was the wage guidepost and
(b) the price guidepost of the Kennedy-Johnson administrations? Why would adherence to these guideposts by labor and management have limited the rate of inflation?

22. What wages and prices were controlled during the Nixon administration? Why did it seem necessary to control them?

23. State the cases **for** and **against** the use of wage-price (or incomes) policy to limit inflation. Build each case upon the two points on which the wage-price policy debate has centered.

24. Why do supply-side economists believe Keynesian economics "does not come to grips with stagflation"? In the view of the supply-siders, what have been the three principal causes of stagflation in the United States?

25. What were the four major steps the Reagan administration proposed to increase employment and reduce inflation in the American economy?

26. Explain:
(a) the provisions of the Economic Recovery Tax Act of 1981;
(b) Tax Reform Act of 1986; and,
(c) the Laffer Curve. Contrast the positions of the supply-side economists and Keynesians with respect to the acts and the curve.

27. Criticize and defend the contention that Reaganomics worked well to reduce stagflation in the United States. Did supply-side economics accomplish its goals under Reaganomics?

28. Summarize the major aspects of competing macroeconomic theories and policy perspectives.

■ ANSWERS

CHAPTER 19: THE INFLATION-UNEMPLOYMENT RELATIONSHIP: KEYNESIAN, NEW CLASSICAL, AND SUPPLY-SIDE VIEWS

Fill-in questions

1. full employment, excess, either

2. a. increase; b. decrease

3. a. greater, greater, smaller; b. inverse

4. full employment is reached; business firms, labor unions, labor

5. a. price level, unemployment; b. negative

6. a. inflation, unemployment; b. increase, increase

7. select a point on the; tradeoff

8. a. the dramatic rise in the oil prices of OPEC; b. agricultural shortfalls throughout the world (higher agricultural prices); c. the devaluation of the dollar; d. the abandonment of wage-price controls; e. the fall in the rate of growth of labor productivity; f. inflationary expectations

9. a. increase; b. increase

10. higher, rise, decrease, higher, higher

11. a. decreased; b. price, unemployment; c. stagflation

12. (any order) a. recession of 1981–1982 with tight monetary policy; b. intensive foreign competition suppressed some wages and prices; c. deregulation in some industries depressed wages; d. a decline in the monopoly power of OPEC

13. opposite, same

14. a. right, left; b. exist, natural rate, adaptive, rational (either order for last two); c. inflation, gradually; d. (1) short-run, long-run, natural rate of unemployment, (2) increases; e. (1) inflation, real, increase, nominal, (2) a rise, no change

15. a. upsloping, vertical; b. fixed, variable; c. flexible, stable, will, will not, price level; d. inflexible, active, high

16. short-run, right, increase, increase, short-run, nominal, higher

17. left, increase, decrease, decrease, increase

18. a. market, wage, price, supply-side; b. left

19. a. employment and training; b. competition

20. a. incomes; b. (1) guideposts, (2) controls

21. productivity, unit labor

22. a. (1) cost, wedge, (2) incentives, (3) regulation; b. decrease

23. a. substantial reduction in Federal expenditures except those for defense; b. reduction in government regulation of private business; c. limitation of the rate of growth in the money supply; d. sharp reduction in personal and corporate income tax rates

24. increase, decrease, increase, decrease

25. aggregate supply, rightward, does not

Problems and projects

1. a. 20; b. 9; c. (it's your choice)

2. 2300; a. (1) 6, 2000, (2) 75, 5, 6.25; b. (1) 7, 2200, (2), 3, 2.5, (3) 16.67; c. (1) 5, 1700, (2) 3, 10, (3) negative

3. *a.* (1) 6, Y_1; (2) Y_1, X_2, PC_1, PC_2, (3) X_2, Y_2, (4) Y_2, 3, X_3, 6, PC_2, PC_3, (5) PC_{LR}; *b.* (1) Z_2, (2) Z_2, X_2, PC_3, PC_2, (3) PC_{LR}

4. P_1, Q_P; *a.* (1) X, P_2, Q_2, (2) AS_1, AS_2, Y, P_3, Q_P, AS_{LR}; *b.* (1) Z, P_2, Q_1, (2) AD_1, AD_2, P_3, Q_P, P_2, P_3, AS_2, (3) P_1, Q_P, AS_2, AS_1

5. *a.* 4; *b.* (1) increase, 1, rise, 1; (2) decrease, 2, fall, 2; (3) increase, 6, rise, 6

Self-test

1. T; **2.** T; **3.** F; **4.** T; **5.** T; **6.** T; **7.** F; **8.** T; **9.** F; **10.** T; **11.** T; **12.** T; **13.** F; **14.** T; **15.** F; **16.** T; **17.** T; **18.** T; **19.** F; **20.** T; **21.** F; **22.** T; **23.** T; **24.** F; **25.** T; **26.** T; **27.** F; **28.** F; **29.** F; **30.** T

1. *c;* **2.** *a;* **3.** *a;* **4.** *b;* **5.** *c;* **6.** *a;* **7.** *d;* **8.** *a;* **9.** *b;* **10.** *d;* **11.** *d;* **12.** *c;* **13.** *b;* **14.** *c;* **15.** *d;* **16.** *d;* **17.** *b;* **18.** *a;* **19.** *a;* **20.** *a;* **21.** *c;* **22.** *c;* **23.** *a;* **24.** *a;* **25.** *a;* **26.** *b;* **27.** *b;* **28.** *b;* **29.** *c*

Budget deficits and the public debt

The Federal government can operate with a budget deficit, a budget surplus, or with a balanced budget during a year. Over the past twenty-five years, the Federal government has had very few budget surpluses; in fact, it has had budget deficits in all but one year. In the past decade, these budget deficits have grown quite large and have caused problems for the American economy. Chapter 20, therefore, looks at the issues surrounding the budget deficits of the 1980s and the related public debt.

Any budget surplus or deficit affects the size of the public (sometimes called the national) debt; surpluses decrease it and deficits increase it. As a consequence of its persistent deficits during and since World War II the public debt has increased; and since 1980 the deficits have grown larger and the public debt has increased by increasing amounts from one year to the next. The Federal government finances the public debt by selling securities (bonds). To those who have purchased these securities the government pays interest each year; and as the size of the debt has increased (and interest rates in the economy have risen) the annual interest payments on the debt have also increased.

These facts are the background for this chapter. After defining a budget deficit and the public debt, the chapter examines three budget philosophies. You should be aware that the philosophies adopted by the Federal government have a significant impact on the output of and employment in the economy *and* on the public debt. A brief explanation of the reasons for the increases in the public debt (wars and recessions) and of the absolute and relative sizes of the debt and the interest payments on the debt is next. Then comes an examination of the economic implications or consequences of the debt. Here you will learn that the debt creates problems for the economy (but these problems do not include bankrupting the Federal government or shifting the cost of a war—or of other government programs—to future generations).

The problems created by the public debt and the payment of interest of the debt are four in number. They appear to make the distribution of income in the economy more unequal, to reduce the incentives which induce people and business firms to produce and expand their out-

puts, to decrease the American standard of living if a part of the debt is owed to foreigners, and to have a crowding-out effect on investment in plant and equipment in the United States.

Crowding-out is probably the most serious of these four problems; and you should be sure that you understand how crowding-out works and how it imposes a burden on future generations by reducing the growth of the nation's capital stock. To understand why it reduces the growth of the capital stock, borrowing to finance an increase in government expenditures is compared with increasing taxes to finance these expenditures.

Finally the chapter shows that government borrowing not only crowds out investment in the economy but results in a chain of events that lead to the contraction of output and employment in the United States. Be sure you follow each of the steps in this cause-and-effect chain. There is not any new theory in this chapter, only a discussion of the macroeconomic problems with budget deficits and a sizable public debt. But as you will learn at the end of the chapter, there are policy responses that are being considered or that have been undertaken to deal with the problem and its effects.

■ **CHECKLIST**

When you have studied this chapter you should be able to:

☐ Define a budget deficit (and surplus) and the public debt; and explain how the latter is related to the former.

☐ Explain each of the three budget philosophies.

☐ State the absolute and relative size of the public debt and of the annual interest charges on this debt; and the principal causes of the debt.

☐ Explain how adjusting the size of the nominal public debt for inflation affects the real size of the debt and the real size of a budget deficit; and why the accounting procedures employed by the Federal government do not accurately reflect its financial condition.

☐ Give three reasons why a large public debt will not bankrupt the government.

☐ Discuss whether the public debt imposes a burden on future generations; and why the public debt is for the most part also a public credit.

☐ Enumerate the four real issues related to the public debt.

☐ Compare the effects of an internal debt with the effects of an external debt on the economy.

☐ Describe the crowding-out effect of borrowing to finance an increase in government expenditures and the burden this method of financing expenditures places on future generations; compare the burden imposed on future generations by this method of finance with the burden placed on them if the increased expenditures are financed by increased taxation; and qualify in two ways this comparison.

☐ Trace the effects of borrowing to finance an increase in government expenditures on interest rates, the attractiveness of American securities to foreigners, the international debts of the United States, the international value of the dollar, American exports and imports, and output and employment in the United States.

☐ List four policy responses to the budget deficits of the Federal government and to the public debt of the United States; and describe the principal provisions of the Gramm-Rudman-Hollings Act of 1985.

☐ Explain why increasing debt is necessary in a growing economy if the economy is to remain at full employment and when it is necessary for the public debt to expand.

■ CHAPTER OUTLINE

1. The budget deficit of the Federal government is the amount by which its expenditures exceed its revenues in any year; and the public debt at any time is the sum of the Federal government's previous annual deficits (less any annual surpluses).

2. If the Federal government utilizes fiscal policy to combat recession and inflation its budget is not likely to be balanced in any particular year. Three budgetary philosophies may be adopted by the government; and the adoption of any of these philosophies will affect employment, real output, and the price level of the economy.

a. Proponents of an annually balanced budget would have government expenditures and tax revenues equal in every year; such a budget is pro- rather than counter-cyclical; but conservative economists favor it to prevent the expansion of the public sector (and the contraction of the private sector) of the economy without the increased payment of taxes by the public.

b. Those who advocate a cyclically balanced budget propose matching surpluses (in years of prosperity) with deficits (in depression years) to stabilize the economy; but there is no assurance that the surpluses will equal the deficits over the years.

c. Advocates of functional finance contend that deficits, surpluses, and the size of the debt are of minor importance; that the goal of full employment without inflation should be achieved regardless of the effects of the necessary fiscal policies upon the budget and the size of the public debt.

3. Any government deficit increases the size of the public debt; and the public debt has grown substantially since 1929.

a. The growth of the debt is the result of Federal borrowing during wartime and during recessions (when the built-in stability of economy generates budget deficits automatically); and in the early 1980s the debt grew as a result of reductions in tax rates without matching reductions in government expenditures.

b. The public debt in 1988 was $2.6 trillion.

(1) The size of the debt as a percentage of the economy's GNP did not grow so rapidly as the absolute size of the debt between 1940 and 1985; but relative to the GNP it has increased significantly since the 1970s.

(2) Since the 1970s the interest payments on the debt (because of increases in the size of the debt and higher interest rates in the economy) have also increased significantly; and interest payments as a percentage of the economy's GNP have grown dramatically.

(3) About one-fourth of the public debt is owed to government agencies and the Federal Reserve Banks and three-fourths to others; but, more importantly, about 13% of it is owed to foreign citizens, firms, and governments.

(4) Because the accounting system used by the Federal government records its debts but not its assets the public debt is not a true picture of its financial position; and when adjusted for inflation, the decrease in the real value of its debt can exceed its nominal deficit and result in a real budget surplus.

4. The contentions that a large debt will eventually bankrupt the government and that borrowing to finance expenditures passes the cost on to future generations are false.

a. The debt cannot bankrupt the government

(1) because the government need not retire (reduce) the debt and can refund (or refinance) it;

(2) because the government has the constitutional authority to levy and collect taxes; and

(3) because the government can always print (or create) money to pay both the principal and the interest on it.

b. The debt cannot shift the burdens of the debt to future generations because the debt is largely internally held, and repayment of any portion of the principal and the payment of interest on it does not reduce the wealth or purchasing power of Americans.

5. But the debt does create real and potential problems in the economy.

a. The payment of interest on the debt probably increases the extent of income inequality.

b. The payment of taxes to finance these interest payments may also reduce the incentives to bear risks, to innovate, to invest, and to save, and so slow economic growth in the economy.

c. The portion of the debt that is externally held requires the repayment of principal and the payment of interest to foreign citizens and institutions and transfers a part of the real output of the American economy to them.

d. An increase in government spending may or may not impose a burden on future generations.

(1) If the increase in government spending is financed by increased personal taxes, the burden of the increased spending is on the present generation whose consumption is reduced; but if it is financed by an increased public debt, the increased borrowing of the Federal government will raise interest rates, crowd-out investment spending, and future generations will inherit a smaller stock of capital goods.

(2) The burden imposed on future generations is lessened if the increase in government expenditures is for real or human capital or if the economy were initially operating at less than full employment (and it stimulates an increase in investment demand).

6. In the 1980s the Federal government has incurred deficits and the public debt has risen.

a. This has caused concern because:

(1) the deficits and the increases in the public debt have grown larger;

(2) interest costs of the debt have risen;

(3) the deficits have taken place in a peace-time economy operating close to full employment, which means there is great potential for the "crowding out" of real private investment and for demand-pull inflation; and

(4) large budget deficits make it difficult for a nation to achieve a balance in its international trade.

b. These large deficits have produced a cause-and-effect chain of events: they have increased interest rates; higher interest rates have crowded-out real private investment and made financial investment by foreigners in the United States more attractive; the latter increased the external debt of the United States and raised the international value of the dollar; and the latter reduced U.S. exports, expanded U.S. imports, and had a contractionary effect on employment and output in the American economy, which softened the overall expansionary impact of a deficit.

c. There are three loose ends to the complex chain of events as described in *b* above:

(1) The inflow of foreign funds helped keep interest rates lower than would otherwise be the case and diminished the size of the crowding-out effect;

(2) High interest rates in the United States resulting from large deficits placed an increased burden on less developed countries, thereby contributing to the world debt problem and banking problems in the United States; and

(3) The unfavorable trade balance meant that the United States had to borrow heavily from other nations and to sell assets to foreign investors, thereby affecting the course of economic growth in the future.

d. A number of policy responses have been suggested to lessen the deficits and the increases in the public debt.

(1) One suggested remedy is an amendment to the U.S. Constitution that would require Congress to balance the Federal budget each year.

(2) Congress in December of 1985 passed the Gramm-Rudman-Hollings Act which required it to reduce the deficits annually and to balance the budget by 1991 and which mandated automatic reductions in spending when Congress and the President cannot agree on how to achieve the targeted deficit reductions. This act was revised in 1987 to achieve a balanced budget by 1993.

(3) Others would have Congress impose a value-added tax or a tax on imported oil or repeal earlier reductions in the tax rates on personal incomes.

(4) And several other proposals, such as the privatization of some government assets and programs by selling them to private business firms, or giving the President the power to veto spending measures on a line-item basis.

e. Despite the problems associated with deficits and the public debt, private and public debt has an important role to play: it absorbs the saving from a growing economy at full employment and sustains the aggregate expenditures of consumers, businesses, and governments at the full-employment level; and if consumers and firms do not borrow sufficient amounts, the public debt must be increased to maintain full employment and economic growth in the economy.

■ IMPORTANT TERMS

Budget deficit	**Balanced Budget**
Public debt	**Amendment**
Annually balanced budget	**Gramm-Rudman-Hollings**
Cyclically balanced budget	**Act**
Functional finance	**Privatization**
External debt	**Line-item veto**
Crowding-out effect	

■ FILL-IN QUESTIONS

1. The budget deficit of the Federal government in any year is equal to its (expenditures, revenues) _____ less its _____ in that year; and the public debt is equal to the sum of the Federal government's past budget _____ _____ less its budget _____.

2. An annually balanced budget is (pro-, counter-) _____ cyclical because governments tend to (raise, lower) _____ taxes and to _____ their purchases of goods and services during a recession (and to do just the opposite during an inflation).

3. A cyclically balanced budget suggests that to ensure full employment without inflation, the government incur deficits during periods of _____ and surpluses during periods of _____ with the deficits and surpluses equaling each other over the business cycle.

4. Functional finance has as its main goal the achievement of _____; and would regard budget _____ and increases in the _____ as of secondary importance.

5. The principal causes of the public debt are past _____ and _____ and recent discretionary reductions in tax _____.

6. In 1988 the public debt of the United States was:
   a. equal to about $_____ billion and about _____% of the GNP, and the annual interest charges on this debt are about $_____ billion and equal about _____% of the GNP;
   b. for the most part an (internal, external) _____ debt.

7. About:
   a. one-fourth of the public debt is owed to government _____ and to American (commercial, central) _____ banks; and

b. about _____% of this debt is owed to foreigners.

8. The accounting procedures used by the Federal government reflect its (assets, debts) _____ but do not reflect its _____
   a. Eisner demonstrated that if the Federal government used a capital budget which included depreciation costs, then the 1988 Federal budget deficit would have been cut (by a third, in half) _____
   b. He also adjusted the 1988 Federal budget deficit for the effects of inflation because inflation (increases, decreases) _____ the real value of the public debt.
   c. After making inflation- and capital-adjustments to the 1988 Federal deficit and after adding the amount of state and local budget surpluses, Eisner was able to show a $42 billion government budget (deficit, surplus) _____

9. The possibility that the Federal government will go bankrupt is a false issue. It need not (reduce, refinance) _____ its debt; and it can retire maturing securities by _____ them or by creating _____. The government can also levy and collect _____ to pay its debts.

10. As long as the government expenditures which lead to the increase in the public debt are not financed by borrowing from foreigners, the public debt of the United States is also an _____ of the American people who own government securities; and the cost of a government program financed by borrowing from the American public is equal to their decreased _____ of goods and services and is a burden on (the present, a future) _____ generation.

11. The public debt is a burden on an economy if it is (internally, externally) _____ held. It and the payment of interest on it may, however (increase, decrease) _ _____ income inequality in the economy, dampen the _____ to work, take risks, save, and invest in the economy, and have a _____ effect on investment.

12. A public debt which is internally held imposes a burden on future generations if the borrowing done to finance an increase in government expenditures (increases, decreases) _____ interest rates, _____ investment spending, and leaves future generations with a smaller stock of _____ goods.

a. But if the increased government expenditures are financed by an increase in the taxes on personal income, the present generation will have fewer _____ goods and the burden of the increased government expenditures will be on _____ generation.

b. These generalizations are subject to two qualifications: The size of the burden of increased government expenditures financed by borrowing on future generations is weakened if the government expenditures finance increases in physical or human _____ or if the economy had been operating at (full, less than full) _____ employment.

13. The increased concern of the public with Federal deficits and the expanding public debt in the 1980s is the result of the large _____ of these deficits, the increased interest _____ of the debt, the fact that the economy was at (peace, war) _____ and operating close to _____, and the difficulty of achieving a _____ in international trade.

14. Large deficits during times of full employment raise two problems. First, there is great potential for the _____ of real private investment. Second, the stimulus to the economy from the deficits may create the conditions for _____

15. Large budget deficits tend to increase _____ _____ and decrease _____ to create an unfavorable trade balance. This trade imbalance has contributed to making the United States a (creditor, debtor) _____ nation and (increased, decreased) _____ the selling of domestic assets to foreign investors.

16. The deficits of the Federal government tend to (increase, decrease) _____ interest rates in the money markets.

a. This change in interest rates (expands, contracts) _____ private investment spending and makes financial investments by foreigners in the U.S.

(more, less) _____ attractive.

b. This change in the financial investments of foreigners in the U.S. (increases, decreases) _____ the external debts of the U.S. and (raises, lowers) _____ the international value of the dollar.

c. This change in the international value of the dollar (expands, contracts) _____ American exports, _____ American imports, and _____ ***net*** exports.

d. This change in American net exports has a(n) (expansionary, contractionary) _____ effect on real output and employment in the United States.

e. The overall expansionary effect of a budget deficit may be reduced somewhat by the _____ effect and the _____ effect.

17. There are other points to be considered in the chain of events from the budget deficits of the 1980s. First, the inflow of funds from abroad would (raise, lower) _____ domestic interest rates than would otherwise be the case and therefore (strengthen, weaken) _____ the crowding-out effect. Second, the high interest rates in the United States placed greater burden on (developed, underdeveloped) _____ countries and created debt problems for the _____ system. Third, the value of imports became (greater than, less than) _____, so the United States had to borrow from foreigners and sold more assets.

18. Three policy responses to the problems of large budget deficits of the Federal government are a _____ amendment requiring the Federal government to balance its budget annually, the _____ Act of 1985, and an increase in _____.

19. Other policy responses related to the deficit problem have been considered. Two topics that have received attention are the _____ of government assets and programs, and granting the President the power to use _____ on spending proposals by the Congress.

20. Public and private debts play a positive role if they absorb a sufficient amount of _____ to enable an economy that is (stationary, growing) _____ to remain at _____.

■ PROBLEMS AND PROJECTS

1. Columns (1) and (2) in the table below are the investment-demand schedule and show planned net investment (*I*) at different rates of interest (*i*). Assume the marginal propensity to consume in the economy is 0.8.

(1) *i*	(2) *I*	(3) *I'*
.08	$115	$125
.07	140	150
.06	165	175
.05	190	200
.04	215	225

a. If the Federal government were to spend an additional $20 for goods and services the equilibrium real NNP would (increase, decrease) _____ by $_____

b. If the Federal government had obtained the additional $20 by

(1) increasing taxes by $20 the equilibrium real NNP would have (increased, decreased) _____ a total of $_____;

(2) borrowing $20 in the money market and this borrowing had increased the interest rate from 5% to 6%,

(a) planned net investment spending would have (increased, decreased) _____ by $_____,

(b) the equilibrium real NNP would have _____ by $_____, and

(c) the net effect of the increased government spending of the $20 borrowed in the money market would have been to _____ the equilibrium real NNP by $_____.

c. But if the government deficit-spending had improved business profit expectations and shifted the investment-demand schedule to the one shown in columns (1) and (3) in the table above the total effect of the increased government spending of the $20 borrowed in the money market would have been to _____ the equilibrium real NNP by $_____

■ SELF-TEST

Circle the T if the statement is true, the F if it is false.

1. The budget deficit of the Federal government in any year is equal to its revenues less its expenditures. **T   F**

2. There is no assurance that a nation can both use fiscal policy to promote full employment and balance its budget cyclically. **T   F**

3. Proponents of functional finance argue that a balanced budget, whether it is balanced annually or over the business cycle, is of minor importance when compared with the objective of full employment without inflation. **T   F**

4. The primary reasons for the increase in the public debt since 1929 have been wars, recessions, and reductions in tax rates. **T   F**

5. The public debt was about $1800 billion at the end of 1988. **T   F**

6. Between 1940 and the present both the public debt and the interest charges on this debt as percentages of the GNP have decreased. **T   F**

7. About one-tenth of the public debt is currently held by foreigners and about three-fourths of it is held by agencies of the Federal government and the American central banks. **T   F**

8. Inflation increases the ***real*** value of the ***nominal*** public debt. **T   F**

9. When adjusted for inflation, Eisner and Pieper found, the Federal government had a budget surplus rather than a budget deficit in 1988. **T   F**

10. Selling government securities to foreigners to finance increased expenditures by the Federal government imposes a burden on future generations. **T   F**

11. The crowding-out effect of borrowing in the money market to finance an increase in government expenditures is the result of the rise in interest rates in these markets. **T   F**

12. Financing increased government expenditures by increasing personal taxes imposes a burden on future generations. **T   F**

13. Crowding-out shifts the investment-demand curve to the left. **T   F**

14. Higher interest rates in the United States not only crowd-out real investment but make financial investment by foreigners in the United States less attractive. **T   F**

15. Increases in the international value of the dollar tend to have an expansionary effect on output and employment in the United States. **T F**

16. New classical economists believe that large Federal deficits have significant stimulative effects on the economy. **T F**

17. The Gramm-Rudman-Hollings Act was revised in 1987 to have the Federal government achieve a balanced budget by 1993. **T F**

18. Privatization would allow the Federal government to acquire the assets of profitable privately owned business firms in order to increase the revenues and reduce the budget deficits of the Federal government. **T F**

19. The amount of saving done at full employment increases in a growing economy. **T F**

20. To maintain full employment in a growing economy it is necessary for the total of public and private debt to increase. **T F**

Circle the letter that corresponds to the correct answer.

1. The public debt is the sum of all previous:
(*a*) expenditures of the Federal government
(*b*) budget deficits of the Federal government
(*c*) budget deficits less the budget surpluses of the Federal government
(*d*) budget surpluses less the budget deficits of the Federal government

2. Which of the following would involve reducing government expenditures and increasing tax rates during a recession?
(*a*) an annually balanced budget policy
(*b*) functional finance
(*c*) a cyclically balanced budget policy
(*d*) a policy employing built-in stability

3. As a percentage of the gross national product, the public debt and interest on the debt were in 1988, respectively, about:
(*a*) 49% and 1%
(*b*) 49% and 2%
(*c*) 53% and 2%
(*d*) 53% and 3%

4. The annual interest payments on the public debt in 1988 were about:
(*a*) $154 billion
(*b*) $119 billion
(*c*) $100 billion
(*d*) $89 billion

5. Compared with the 1970s:

(*a*) both the public debt and the interest charges on the debt relative to the GNP have increased
(*b*) the public debt relative to the GNP has decreased and the interest charges on the debt relative to the GNP have increased
(*c*) the public debt relative to the GNP has increased and the interest charges on the debt relative to the GNP have decreased
(*d*) both the public debt and the interest charges on the debt relative to the GNP have decreased

6. The accounting procedures used by the Federal government record:
(*a*) only its assets
(*b*) only its debts
(*c*) both its assets and debts
(*d*) its net worth

7. Inflation is a tax on:
(*a*) the holders of the public debt and reduces the size of a budget deficit
(*b*) the holders of the public debt and expands the size of a budget deficit
(*c*) the Federal government and reduces the size of a budget deficit
(*d*) the Federal government and expands the size of a budget deficit

8. The public debt cannot bankrupt the Federal government because the Federal government:
(*a*) need not reduce the size of the debt
(*b*) is able to refinance the debt
(*c*) can create money to repay the debt and pay the interest on it
(*d*) all of the above

9. Incurring an internal debt to finance a war does not pass the cost of the war on to future generations because:
(*a*) the opportunity cost of the war is borne by the generation that fights it
(*b*) the government need not pay interest on internally held debts
(*c*) there is never a need for government to refinance the debt
(*d*) wartime inflation reduces the relative size of the debt

10. Which of the following would be a consequence of the retirement of the internally held portion of the public debt?
(*a*) a reduction in the nation's productive capacity
(*b*) a reduction in the nation's standard of living
(*c*) a redistribution of the nation's wealth among its citizens
(*d*) an increase in aggregate expenditures in the economy

11. Which of the following is an important consesquence of the public debt of the United States?

(a) it increases incentives to work and invest

(b) it transfers a portion of the American output of goods and services to foreign nations

(c) it reduces income inequality in the United States

(d) it leads to greater saving at every level of disposable income

12. The crowding-out effect of borrowing in the money market to finance an increase in government expenditures:

(a) reduces current private investment expenditures

(b) decreases the rate at which the privately owned stock of real capital increases

(c) imposes a burden on future generations

(d) does all of the above

13. The crowding-out effect of government borrowing to finance its increased expenditures is reduced:

(a) when the economy is operating at less than full employment

(b) when the expenditures expand human capital in the economy

(c) when the government's deficit financing improves the profit expectations of business firms

(d) when any one or more of the above are true

14. Which one of the following is **not** one of the sources of the recent concern with the deficits of the Federal government and the growth of the public debt?

(a) the large increases in the size of the deficits and in the public debt

(b) the operation of the economy substantially below full employment

(c) the mounting interest costs of the debt

(d) the fact that the nation was not at war

15. The increased foreign demand for American securities that results from higher interest rates in the United States:

(a) increases the external debts of the United States and the international value of the dollar

(b) increases the external debts of the United States and decreases the internationl value of the dollar

(c) decreases the external debts of the United States and increases the international value of the dollar

(d) decreases the external debts of the United States and the international value of the dollar

16. When the international value of the dollar rises:

(a) American exports tend to increase

(b) American imports tend to decrease

(c) American net exports tend to decrease

(d) all of the above tend to occur

17. The Gramm-Rudman-Hollings Act of 1985 and its revision in 1987 require that:

(a) the sizes of the Federal budget deficits be reduced annually

(b) the Federal budget be balanced by 1993

(c) the expenditures of the Federal government be automatically reduced if Congress and the President cannot agree on how to reach the targeted reductions in the budget deficits

(d) all of the above

18. Suppose the multiplier is 3. Were the amount of saving done at full employment to increase by $20 and were private borrowing to increase by $5, to maintain full employment the public debt would have to increase by:

(a) $5

(b) $15

(c) $45

(d) $60

19. New classical economists argue that recent Federal deficits have:

(a) had desirable effects on the economy because of the fiscal policy stimulus

(b) had little effect on the economy because households respond to budget deficits by increasing their present saving in anticipation of higher future taxes

(c) created a sizable trade imbalance with other nations and contributed to the selling of United States assets to foreigners

(d) caused interest rates to rise and crowded-out private investment

20. High interest rates in the United States which were related to Federal budget deficits of the 1980s tended to:

(a) contribute to the debt burden of underdeveloped nations that traded with the United States

(b) reduce the flow of funds from foreign nations to the United States

(c) increase the long-term economic growth and domestic investment of foreign nations that transferred funds to the United States

(d) enable the United States to become a major creditor nation for the first time in many decades

■ DISCUSSION QUESTIONS

1. What is the difference between the (Federal) budget deficit and the public debt?

2. Explain why an annually balanced budget is not "neutral" and how it can intensify, rather than reduce, the tendencies for NNP to rise and fall.

3. How does a cyclically balanced budget philosophy differ from the philosophy of functional finance? Why do advocates of functional finance argue that budget deficits and a mounting national debt are of secondary importance?

4. How big is the public debt of the United States absolutely and relative to the GNP? How large are the interest payments on this debt absolutely and relative to the GNP? What has happened to the size of the debt and the interest payments on it absolutely and relatively since 1930 and since 1980? Why have these changes occurred?

5. In what way do the accounting procedures of the Federal government misstate its actual financial position (its net worth)? How does inflation affect the *real* size of the public debt and the real size of the Federal government's budget deficits?

6. Why can't the public debt result in the bankruptcy of the Federal government?

7 Explain the difference between an internally held and an externally held public debt. If the debt is internally held government borrowing to finance a war does not pass the cost of the war on to future generations. Why?

8. How does the public debt and the payment of interest on this debt affect:
(*a*) the distribution of income and
(*b*) incentives? Why does the portion of the public debt externally held impose a burden on the economy?

9. How can deficit financing impose a burden on future generations? Why don't increases in government expenditures financed by increased personal taxes impose the same burden on future generations? What will lessen the burden on future generations of deficit financing?

10. What heightened the concern of the public in the early 1980s over budget deficits and the increase in the public debt? How do budget deficits (and the increase in the public debt) affect:
(*a*) interest rates;
(*b*) planned domestic investment in real capital and the financial investment of foreigners in American securities;
(*c*) the external debts of the United States and the international value of the dollar;
(*d* American exports and imports of goods and services; and
(*e*) employment and real output in the American economy?

11. Discuss other deficit-related effects on interest rates and crowding out, interest rates and the international debt crisis, and the trade imbalance and the borrowing needs of the United States.

12. What are the basic differences in Keynesian and new classical views of the effects of deficits?

13. Explain the policy responses that have been suggested for the Federal budget deficits and the increasing public debt. What were the chief provisions of the Gramm-Rudman-Hollings Act of 1985? How was the act revised in 1987?

14. How would privatization or a line-item veto help reduce budget deficits?

15. What tends to happen to the amount of saving done at full employment as the full-employment real NNP grows? Why, in a growing economy, must debt increase in order to maintain full employment and economic growth?

■ **ANSWERS**

CHAPTER 20 BUDGET DEFICITS AND THE PUBLIC DEBT

Fill-in questions
1. expenditures, revenues, deficits, surpluses
2. pro-, raise, lower
3. recession, inflation
4. full employment without inflation, deficits, public debt
5. wars, recessions, rates
6. *a.* 2600, 53, 154, 3.2; *b.* internal
7. *a.* agencies, central; *b.* 13
8. debts, assets; *a.* in half; *b.* decreases; *c.* surplus
9. reduce, refinancing, money, taxes
10. asset, consumption, the present
11. externally, increase, incentives, crowding-out
12. increases, decreases, capital; *a.* consumer, present; *b.* capital, less than full
13. size, costs, peace, full employment, balance
14. crowding-out, demand-pull inflation
15. imports, exports, debtor, increased
16. increase; *a.* contracts, more; *b.* increases, raises; *c.* contracts, expands, contracts; *d.* contractionary; *e.* crowding-out, net export (either order)
17. lower, weaken, underdeveloped, banking, greater than
18. constitutional, Gramm-Rudman-Hollings, taxes
19. privatization, line-item veto
20. saving, growing, full employment

Problems and projects
1. *a.* increase, 100; *b.* (1) increased, 20, (2) (a) decreased, 25, (b) decreased, 125, (c) decrease, 25; *c.* increase, 25

Self-test
1. F; 2. T; 3. T; 4. T; 5. F; 6. F; 7. F; 8. F; 9. T; 10. T; 11. T; 12. F; 13. F; 14. F; 15. F; 16. F; 17. T; 18. F; 19. T; 20. T
1. *c;* 2. *a;* 3. *d;* 4. *a;* 5. *a;* 6. *b;* 7. *a;* 8. *d;* 9. *a;* 10. *c;* 11. *b;* 12. *d;* 13. *d;* 14. *b;* 15. *a;* 16. *c;* 17. *d;* 18. *b;* 19. *b;* 20. *a*

Economic growth

Chapter 21 is the last of four chapters that discuss macroeconomic issues and problems. While the previous chapters focused primarily on short-term instability in output and the price level, this chapter looks at the longer-term problem of economic growth.

After briefly defining and pointing out the significance of growth, the text analyzes the six factors that make growth possible. The four *supply* factors increase the output potential of the economy. Whether the economy actually produces its full potential—that is, whether the economy has both full employment and full production—depends upon two other factors: the level of aggregate expenditures (the *demand* factor) and the efficiency with which the economy reallocates resources (the *allocative* factor).

Why has the United States grown economically? First, because the American population and the size of its labor force have grown. Second and more important, the productivity of the labor force in the United States has increased. The increase in the productivity of labor is the result of technological advances; the expansion of the stock of capital goods in the American economy; the improved education and training of its labor force; economies of scale; the reallocation of resources; the generous quantities of natural resources with which the American economy was endowed; and its social, cultural, and political environment. (Note, however, that the regulations of government tend to slow the rates at which the productivity of labor and the output of the economy grow.) But in addition to the increases in the ability of the economy to produce goods and services made possible by the supply and allocative factors, aggregate expenditures have expanded sufficiently (though unsteadily) to bring about most of the actual growth made possible by the increases in the quantity and the productivity of labor.

In the 1960s and 1970s, however, the rate at which the productivity of labor in the United States increased was dramatically less than it had been in earlier decades. This slowdown has had a number of consequences and a number of causes for the American economy. None of the consequences was, however, good; and they added to the problems that we faced in the 1980s. Productivity growth improved modestly over the 1981–1988 period, but maintaining and increasing that rate of growth is a critical long-term problem facing the United States economy.

The controversy over whether growth should be a social goal with a high priority in the United States has, of course, two sides to it. The case in defense of and the case against growth are both considered. You will have to decide for yourself which case is the stronger and whether the social benefits from growth are worth the costs.

Actually, Chapter 21 contains very little that is really new. It uses a few of the ideas, terms, and theories found in earlier chapters to explain what makes an economy capable of growing (that is, what increases the size of its full-employment or capacity output) and what is necessary if it is actually to grow (that is, if it is to produce all which its expanding capital allows). You also are presented with historical data on the United States economy to place economic growth in a long-run perspective. With careful reading you should have little or no trouble with Chapter 21, providing you have done a good job on the earlier chapters.

■ CHECKLIST

When you have studied this chapter you should be able to:

☐ Distinguish between employment theory and growth economics.

☐ Define economic growth in two different ways.

☐ Explain why economic growth is important to any economy.

☐ Identify four supply factors in economic growth.

☐ Explain demand and allocative factors in economic growth.

☐ State the two fundamental means by which an economy can increase its real GNP and the relative importance of these two means of increasing the real GNP in the United States since 1929.

☐ Describe the growth record of the American economy since 1940 and its rates of economic growth since World War II.

☐ Enumerate the several sources of the growth of the productivity of labor in the United States since 1929; and state their relative importance in the growth of its real national income.

☐ Identify the chief detriment to the increase in labor productivity; and state by how much it and other factors have slowed the growth of real national income in the United States since 1929.

☐ Explain why the actual rate of growth in the United States has been less than its potential rate of growth and why it has been unstable.

☐ Enumerate the five principal causes and the three principal consequences of the slowdown in the rate at which labor productivity has increased in the United States from 1966–1981.

☐ Discuss whether there has been a resurgence of productivity in the 1980s.

☐ Present the case against further economic growth in the United States.

☐ Defend further economic growth.

☐ Outline the three types of economic policies that might be utilized to stimulate growth in the United States.

■ **CHAPTER OUTLINE**

1. While employment theory and stabilization policy are concerned with the short run and an economy with a fixed productive capacity, growth economics deals with the long run and changes in productive capacity over time.

a. Economic growth means an increase in either the total or the per capita real output of an economy; and is measured in terms of the annual percentage rate of growth of either total or per capita real output.

b. Economic growth is important because it lessens the burden of scarcity: it provides the means of satisfying existing wants more fully and fulfilling new wants.

c. One or two percentage point differences in the rate of growth result in substantial differences in annual increases in the economy's output.

2. Whether economic growth *can* occur depends upon four supply factors (or, said another way, upon the quantity of labor employed and the productivity of labor); and whether it will occur depends upon the demand factor and the allocative factor. Most of the discussion of growth focuses on supply considerations. An economy can increase its real output by increasing the quantity of labor employed, by increasing the productivity of labor, or by doing both of these things.

3. Over the last fifty-five years or so, the growth record of the American economy has been impressive; but economic growth in America has been less impressive than the record of many advanced industrialized nations in recent decades.

a. Economic well-being may be understated by economic growth figures because the figures do not take into account improvements in product quality or increases in leisure time.

b. But growth may have adverse effects on the environment or the quality of life that are not reflected in growth figures, thus the figures may overstate the benefits of growth.

4. Denison estimates that between 1929 and 1982 the real national income in the United States grew at an average annual rate of 2.9%.

a. Two-thirds of this growth was the result of the increased productivity of labor, and one-third of it was the result of the increased quantity of labor employed in the economy.

b. During this period the American population and its labor force expanded; and despite decreases in the length of the workweek and birthrates, the increased participation of women in the labor force and the growth of its population continue to expand the size of the labor force by two million workers a year.

c. Technological advance is combining given amounts of resources in new ways that result in a larger output; and during the 1929–1982 period it accounted for 28% of the increase in real national income.

d. Saving and investment have expanded the American economy's stock of capital; increased the quantity of tools, equipment, and machinery with which each worker has to work; and accounted for 19% of the increase in real national income between 1929 and 1982.

e. Increased investment in human capital (in the training and education of workers) expands the productivity of workers; and accounted for 14% of the 1929–1982 increase in real national income.

f. Economies of scale and the improved allocation of resources also expand the productivity of workers; and in the American economy 9% and 8%, respectively, of the increase in real national income between 1929 and 1982 can be attributed to them.

g. But such detriments (or deterrents) to the growth of productivity as the government regulation of industry, of pollution, and of worker health and safety divert investment away from productivity-increasing additions to capital; and they accounted for a negative 9% of the increased real national income in the 1929–1982 period.

h. Such difficult-to-quantify factors as its general abundance of natural resources and social-cultural-political environment have also contributed to economic growth in the United States.

i. While actual growth in real national income during the 1929–1982 period averaged 2.9% a year, it would have been (an estimated) 3.2% a year if aggregate demand had not at times fallen below its full-employment levels.

j. Increases in the productivity of labor have been more important than increases in the quantity of labor employed in expanding real national income in the American economy; but these increases in productivity cannot be taken for granted, are not automatic, and are the results of the changes in the economy described above.

5. From 1973–1981 the annual rates of increase in the productivity of labor in the United States decreased substantially.

a. The significance of this slowdown was that

(1) it decreased the rates at which real wage rates and the standard of living rose;

(2) it contributed to rising unit labor costs and to inflation in the American economy; and

(3) it led to higher prices for American goods in world markets and the loss of these markets to American producers.

b. The suggested causes of this decrease in the rate at which the productivity of labor has increased included

(1) the smaller proportion of the GNP spent for investment and a change in the composition of this investment spending;

(2) a decline in the stock of capital per worker;

(3) a fall in the quality (training and experience) of the American labor force;

(4) a slowdown (as reflected in expenditures for R and D) in technological progress; and

(5) the adversarial relationship between workers and managers in the American system of industrial relations.

c. In the 1980s the decline in the rate of increase in productivity ended, in large part due to changes in the factors that depressed productivity growth in the 1973–1981 period; but the rate of productivity growth in the 1980s has still only been modest.

6. Americans today debate whether economic growth is or is not desirable.

a. Those opposed to rapid economic growth contend that

(1) it pollutes the environment;

(2) it is not needed to resolve domestic problems;

(3) it makes people more anxious and insecure; and

(4) while providing more goods and services, it does not result in a better life.

b. Those in favor of growth argue that

(1) it results in a higher standard of living and lessens the burden of scarcity;

(2) it is not the cause of pollution;

(3) it is the easiest way to bring about a more equitable distribution of income; and

(4) ending or slowing growth will not improve the quality of life.

7. To stimulate economic growth in the American economy Keynesians stress policies that would expand aggregate expenditures and constrain government spending and consumption; supply-side economists stress policies that would expand the economy's capacity output by increasing saving, investment, work effort, and risk taking; and others advocate the use of an industrial policy that would shape the structure and the composition of industry in the economy.

■ IMPORTANT TERMS

Economic growth	**Labor productivity**
Supply factor	**Productivity slowdown**
Demand factor	**Infrastructure**
Allocative factor	**Industrial policy**

■ FILL-IN QUESTIONS

1. Employment theory assumes the productive capacity of the economy is (fixed, variable) _____ while growth economics is concerned with an economy whose productive capacity (increases, remains constant) _____ over time.

2 Economic growth can mean an increase in either the _____ or the _____ of an economy.

3. A rise in output per capita (increases, decreases) _____ the standard of living and _____ the burden of scarcity in the economy.

4. Assume an economy has a GNP of $3600 billion. If the growth rate is 5%, GNP will increase by $_____ billion a year; but if the rate of growth is only 3%, the annual increase in GNP will be $_____ billion. A two percentage point difference in the growth rate results in a $_____ billion difference in the annual increase in GNP.

5. The four supply factors in economic growth are

_____ ,

_____ ,

_____, and

_____ .

The other two growth factors are the _____

_____ factor and the _____
factor.

6. The real GNP of any economy in any year is equal to

the _____ of labor employed **multiplied** by

the _____ of labor.
  a. The former is measured by the number of (workers,

hours of labor) _____ employed.
  b. The latter is equal to the real GNP per

_____ per _____

7. The quantity of labor employed in the economy in any
year depends on the size of the employed

_____ force and the

_____

_____ of the average workweek. The size
element depends upon the size of the working-age

_____ and the labor-force

_____ rate.

8. In the United States since 1940 the real GNP has

increased almost _____-fold and the real per

capita GNP has increased almost _____
times.

9. Since 1948 the rates of growth in real GNP and per

capita GNP have, on the average, been _____%

and _____%, respectively.

10. Between 1929 and 1982 the real national income of
the United States grew at an average annual rate of

_____%. Of this growth, _____/3 was the re-

sult of increases in the quantity of _____ em-

ployed and _____/3 was the result of increases in

the _____ of _____

11. In addition to (increases, decreases) _____
in the quantity of labor employed, the growth of the
American economy between 1929 and 1982 can be at-

tributed to _____ in the productivity of labor
which resulted from:

  a. technological _____ ;

  b. increases in the quantity of _____ em-

ployed and in the quantity employed per _____;

  c. the improved _____ and _____
of workers;

  d. economies of _____; and

  e. the improved _____ of resources.

12. An increase in the stock of capital of a nation is the

result of saving and _____. In the United States the
stock of capital has historically grown (more, less)

_____ rapidly than the quantity of labor employed.

13. Technological progress means that we learn how to
employ given quantities of resources to obtain greater

_____; and, more often than not, this

progress requires _____ in new machinery and
equipment.

14. The principal detriment to growth of real national
income in the 1929–1982 period seems to have been

government _____ which diverted

(consumption, investment) _____ spending away from uses that would have increased the

_____ of labor.

15. Two other factors that have led to economic growth in

the United States are its abundant _____ re-

sources and its social-cultural-political _____

16. Denison's analysis is designed to explain (actual, po-

tential) _____ real national income. When there

is a deficiency of aggregate demand the _____

rate of economic growth falls short of the _____.
Denison estimates that the rate would have been higher at

_____% per year, if the economy's (actual, potential)

_____ had been achieved year after year.

17. The annual rates of increase in the productivity of
labor, between the middle 1960s and 1981, (rose, fell,

remained constant) _____

_____

  a. This resulted in a (rise, fall) _____ in

the rates at which the standard of _____ and the (nominal, real) _____ wages of labor increased, in a (rise, fall) _____ in unit labor costs and (inflation, deflation) _____ in the United States, and the loss of international markets to (American, foreign) _____ producers of goods and services.

b. Its causes were the (rise, fall) _____ in investment spending as a percentage of GNP and changes in the composition of (consumption, investment) _____ spending, the (rise, fall) _____ in the amount of _____ available per worker, the (improvement, deterioration) _____ of the quality of the labor force, a slower rate of _____ progress, and the adversarial relationship between _____ and _____ in the United States.

c. Since about 1981 the rate of increase in the productivity of labor in the United States has (increased, decreased) _____ at a (fast, modest) _____ pace.

18. Influential economists arguing against the need for growth in the United States believe that growth _____ the environment, does not lead to the solution of _____, breeds _____ and _____, and does not result in the _____

19. Those who favor growth for the American economy argue that it is the basic way to raise the standard of _____ and lessen the _____ dilemma, that economic growth does not necessarily result in _____, that growth is the only practical way of obtaining a more _____ distribution of _____, and that limiting growth will not bring about _____

20. To stimulate economic growth in the United States:
a. Keynesians stress the (supply, demand) _____ side of growth, favor (high, low) _____ interest rates to expand _____ spending, and would use fiscal policies to (expand, contract) _____ government spending and consumption.
b. Supply-side economists stress policies that would stimulate _____, _____, _____, and entrepreneurial _____ to expand (aggregate demand, capacity output) _____
c. Others stress policies that would shape the _____ and _____ of American industry and are called _____ policy.

■ **PROBLEMS AND PROJECTS**

1. Suppose the real GNP and the population of an economy in seven different years were those shown in the next table.
a. How large would the real per capita GNP of the economy be in each of the other six years? Put your figures in the table.
b. What would have been the size of the optimum population of this economy? _____
c. What was the *amount* of growth in real GNP between year 1 and year 2? $_____
d. What was the *rate* of growth in real GNP between year 3 and year 4? _____%

Year	Population, millions	Real GNP, billions of dollars	Per capita real GNP
1	30	$ 9	$ 300
2	60	24	_____
3	90	45	_____
4	120	66	_____
5	150	90	_____
6	180	99	_____
7	210	105	_____

2. Given the data in the table below, calculate the average annual rates of growth in real GNP and real per capita GNP over the period given. (Note: Remember to adjust rate of growth for the number of years in the period so you get average annual rates.)

Year	Real GNP	Annual growth in %	Real GNP per capita	Annual growth in %
1970	$2,416		$11,785	
1975	2,695	_____	12,593	_____
1980	3,187	_____	13,978	_____
1985	3,618	_____	15,139	_____
1987	3,847	_____	15,766	_____

Source: Table 21-1 of textbook (p. 417).

3. The table below shows the quantity of labor (measured in hours) and the productivity of labor (measured in real GNP per hour) in a hypothetical economy in three different years.

Year	Quantity of labor	Productivity of labor	Real GNP
1	1000	$100	$_____
2	1000	105	_____
3	1100	105	_____

a. Compute the economy's real GNP in each of the three years and enter them in the table.

b. Between years 1 and 2, the quantity of labor remained constant; but

(1) the productivity of labor increased by _____ percent; and

(2) as a consequence, real GNP increased by _____ percent.

c. Between years 2 and 3, the productivity of labor remained constant; but

(1) the quantity of labor increased by _____ percent; and

(2) as a consequence, real GNP increased by _____ percent.

d. Between years 1 and 3

(1) real GNP increased by _____%; and

(2) this rate of increase is approximately equal to the sum of the rates of increase in the _____ and the _____ of labor.

■ **SELF-TEST**

Circle the T if the statement is true, the F if it is false.

1. Growth economics concern an economy in which productive capacity is not fixed.   **T   F**

2. The better of the two definitions of economic growth is an increase in the per capita real output of the economy.   **T   F**

3. Suppose two economies both have GNPs of $500 billion. If the GNPs grow at annual rates of 3% in the first and 5% in the second economy, the difference in their amounts of growth in one year is $10 billion.   **T   F**

4. The demand factor in economic growth refers to the ability of the economy to expand its production as the demand for products grows.   **T   F**

5. The allocative factor in economic growth refers to the ability of the economy to move resources from one use to another as the productive capacity of the economy grows.   **T   F**

6. The real GNP of an economy in any year is equal to its input of labor divided by the productivity of labor.   **T   F**

7. Real GNP has tended to increase more rapidly than real per capita GNP in the United States.   **T   F**

8. Growth and rates-of-growth estimates generally attempt to take account of changes in the quality of goods produced and in the amount of leisure members of the economy enjoy.   **T   F**

9. Increased labor productivity has been more important than increased labor inputs in the growth of the American economy since 1929.   **T   F**

10. Since 1929 improved technology has accounted for about 28% of the increase in labor productivity in the United States.   **T   F**

11. More often than not technological progress requires the economy to invest in new machinery and equipment.   **T   F**

12. The single most important source of the growth of labor productivity in the United States since 1929 has been the increase in the size of the American labor force.   **T   F**

13. During the 1960s and 1970s the United States invested a larger percentage of its GNP in capital than most of the other industrially advanced nations.   **T   F**

14. The regulation of industry, the pollution of the environment, and the health and safety of workers by government tends to reduce the rate at which labor productivity grows.   **T   F**

15. The availability of natural resources in the United States has been a significant factor in the growth of the American economy.   **T   F**

16. The American social, cultural, and political environment has, in general, worked to slow the economic growth of the United States.   **T   F**

17. Increases in labor productivity can, at least in the American economy, be taken pretty much for granted because the rate of increase has been nearly constant for well over half a century.   **T   F**

18. Between the mid-1960s and 1982 the productivity of labor in the United States fell.   **T   F**

19. The adversarial nature of industrial relations between managers and their employees in the United States tends to slow the rate at which the productivity of labor increases.   **T   F**

20. Supply-side economists favor increasing taxes to stimulate saving, investment, and economic growth in the economy.   **T   F**

Circle the letter that corresponds to the best answer.

1. Which of the following is *not* one of the benefits of economic growth to a society?
(a) everyone enjoys a greater real income
(b) the standard of living in that society increases
(c) the burden of scarcity decreases
(d) the society is better able to satisfy new wants

2. If the real output of an economy were to increase from $2000 billion to $2100 billion in one year the rate of growth of real output during that year would be:
(a) 0.5%
(b) 5%
(c) 10%
(d) 50%

3. Suppose an economy has a real GNP of $700 billion and an annual growth rate of 5%. Over a *two*-year period real GNP will increase by:
(a) $14 billion
(b) $35 billion
(c) $70 billion
(d) $71¾ billion

4. If the production possibilities curve of an economy moves from **AB** to **CD** on the following graph, and the economy changes the combination of goods it produces from **X** to **Y,** there has been:
(a) improvement in both the supply and the other growth factors
(b) an improvement in only the supply factor
(c) an improvement in only the demand and allocative growth factors
(d) an improvement in the level of total employment in the economy

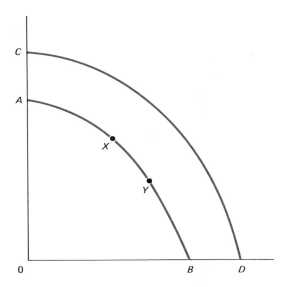

5. Which of the following is *not* a supply factor in economic growth?
(a) an expansion in purchasing power
(b) an increase in the economy's stock of capital goods
(c) more natural resources
(d) technological progress

6. Since 1940 real GNP in the United States has increased about:
(a) twofold
(b) threefold
(c) fourfold
(d) fivefold

7. Between 1870 and 1969 the total output of the American economy increased at an average **annual** rate of about:
(a) ½ of 1%
(b) 2%
(c) 3½%
(d) 5%

8. Total output per capita in the United States between 1870 and 1969 increased at an average annual rate of about:
(a) 1%
(b) 2%
(c) 3%
(d) 4%

9. Denison estimates that between 1929 and 1982 the real national income of the United States grew at an annual rate of:
(a) 2.1%
(b) 2.9%
(c) 3.3%
(d) 3.9%

10. About what fraction of the growth in the real national income of the United States since 1929 has been due to increases in the quantity of labor employed?
(a) ¼
(b) ⅓
(c) ½
(d) ⅔

11. The factor accounting for the greatest increase in the productivity of labor in the United States between 1929 and 1982 was:
(a) economies of scale
(b) technological advance
(c) the improved education and training of the labor force
(d) the expanded quantity of capital

12. The population and labor force of the United States were in 1982, respectively, about:
(a) 122 and 49 million
(b) 110 and 49 million
(c) 232 and 122 million
(d) 232 and 110 million

13. Approximately what percentages of the labor force have completed high school and four years of college?
(a) 45% and 8%
(b) 44% and 13%
(c) 60% and 8%
(d) 80% and 20%

14. During the 1948–1966 period the productivity of labor in the United States increased at an average annual rate of:
(a) 2.1%
(b) 2.9%
(c) 3.2%
(d) 3.9%

15. The decline in the rate at which the productivity of labor increased from 1966–1981 can be attributed to a number of causes. Which of the following is *not* one of these causes?
(a) the decrease in the relative prices of American goods in world markets
(b) the decrease in the quality of the American labor force
(c) the decrease in the capital-labor ratio
(d) the decrease in the rate of technological progress

16. The decline in the rate at which the productivity of labor increased from 1966–1981 in the United States has brought about:
(a) a fall in the relative prices of American goods in world markets
(b) a fall in the standard of living in the United States
(c) rising unit labor costs and inflation in the United States
(d) all of the above

17. Which of the following is *not* a part of the case against economic growth?
(a) growth produces pollution
(b) growth impedes the increased production of consumer goods
(c) growth prevents the attainment of a better life
(d) growth is not needed to provide us with the means of solving domestic social problems

18. Which of the following is *not* a part of the case in defense of economic growth?
(a) growth lessens the unlimited wants–scarce resources problem
(b) growth lessens the extent of anxiety and insecurity
(c) growth need not be accompanied by the pollution of the environment
(d) growth is the only practical way to reduce poverty

19. If a nation's real GNP is growing by 2% per year, then approximately how many years will it take for real GNP to double?
(a) 25 years
(b) 30 years
(c) 35 years
(d) 40 years

20. To promote economic growth, Keynesians would tend to give the most support to:
(a) an industrial policy
(b) an easy money policy
(c) constraints on government spending
(d) constraints on consumption spending

■ **DISCUSSION QUESTIONS**

1. How does growth economics differ from the theory of employment and stabilization policy?

2. What is meant by economic growth? Why should the citizens of the United States be concerned with economic growth?

3. What are the six basic ingredients of economic growth? What is the essential difference between the supply factors and the other two factors? Is there any relationship between the strength of the supply factors and the strength of the demand factor?

4. What is the relationship between the real GNP produced in any year and the quantity of labor employed and labor productivity?

5. In what units are the quantity of labor and the productivity of labor measured? What:
(a) are the two principal determinants of the quantity of the labor input;
(b) determines the size of the labor force?

6. What has been the growth record of the American economy since 1940 and since 1870? Compare recent American growth rates with those in other nations.

7. What have been the sources of the growth of the real national income in the United States since 1929? What has tended to slow the increase in labor productivity and in real national income?

8. What changes have occurred in the size of the American population and labor force since 1929? What factor has slowed the rate of growth of the former and what factor has speeded the growth of the latter?

9. What is the relationship between investment and the stock of capital? By how much has capital per worker expanded since 1869? What is the connection between increases in the capital stock and the rate of economic growth?

10. What is technological advance and why are technological advance and capital formation closely related processes?

11. What is meant by and, therefore, tends to increase the "quality" of labor? How is this quality usually measured?

12. What are the economic consequences if aggregate demand increases less than productive capacity increases? What are the long-term consequences of this macroeconomic instability?

13. By how much did the annual increases in the productivity of labor decline in the United States between mid-1960s and 1982? What have been:
(a) the causes; and
(b) the consequences of this decline?

14. Has economic growth resurged since 1981? What

long-term problems does productivity growth pose for the economy of the United States?

15. What arguments can be presented on both sides of the question of whether growth in the United States is desirable?

16. What:
(a) policies do Keynesians advocate to stimulate economic growth;
(b) policies do supply-side economists favor to stimulate economic growth;
(c) is meant by "industrial policy"?

■ **ANSWERS**

CHAPTER 21   ECONOMIC GROWTH

Fill-in questions

1. fixed, increases

2. total real output (NNP or GNP), real output (NNP or GNP) per capita

3. increases, decreases

4. 180, 108, 72

5. quantity and quality of natural resources, quantity and quality of human resources, the supply or stock of capital goods, technology, demand, allocative

6. quantity, productivity; a. hours of labor; b. worker, hour (either order)

7. labor, length, population, participation

8. five, three

9. 3.3, 1.9

10. 2.9, 1, labor, 2, productivity, labor

11. increases, increases; a. progress (advance); b. capital, worker; c. education, training; d. scale; e. allocation

12. investment, more

13. output (production), investment

14. regulations, investment, productivity

15. natural, environment

16. actual, actual, potential, 3.2, potential

17. fell; a. fall, living, real, rise, inflation, foreign; b. fall, investment, fall, capital, deterioration, technological, managers, employees; c. increased, modest

18. pollutes, domestic problems, anxiety, insecurity, good life

19. living, unlimited wants–scarce resources, pollution, equitable, income, a better life

20. a. demand, low, investment, contract; b. saving, investment, work effort, risk-taking, capacity output; c. structure, composition, industrial

CHAPTER 22

International trade: comparative advantage and protectionism

This is the first of two chapters dealing with international trade and finance. International trade is a subject with which most people have little firsthand experience. For this reason many of the terms, concepts, and ideas encountered in these chapters will be unfamiliar and may not be readily grasped. However, most of this material is fairly simple if you will take some pains to examine it. The ideas and concepts employed are new, but they are not especially complex or difficult.

At the beginning it is essential to recognize that international trade is important to the United States. Exports from and imports into the American economy are $519 and $612 billion a year. The United States **absolutely** is the greatest exporting and importing nation in the world. In **relative** terms, other nations have exports and imports which are larger percentages of their GNPs. They may export and import more than 35 percent of GNP, while the United States exports and imports only about 11% to 13% of GNP. It is equally important for you to understand from the beginning that international trade differs from the trade that goes on within nations. Different nations use different monies, not just one money; resources are less mobile internationally than they are **intra**nationally; and nations place more political restrictions on international trade than they do on intranational trade.

But while foreign trade differs from domestic trade, nations trade for the same basic reason that people within a nation trade: to take advantage of the benefits of specialization. Nations specialize in and export those goods and services in the production of which they have a comparative advantage. A comparative advantage means that the opportunity cost of producing a particular good or service is lower in that nation than in another nation. These nations will avoid the production of and import the goods and services in the production of which other nations have a comparative advantage. In this way all nations are able to obtain products which are produced as inexpensively as possible. Put another way, when nations specialize in those products in which they have a comparative advantage, the world as a whole can obtain more goods and services from its resources; and each of the nations of the world can enjoy a standard of living higher than it would have if it did not specialize and export and import.

But regardless of the advantages of specialization and trade among nations, people in the United States and throughout the world have for well over 200 years debated whether free trade or protection was the better policy for their nation. Economists took part in this debate and, with few exceptions, argued for free trade and against protection. Those who favor free trade contend that free trade benefits both the nation and the world as a whole. "Free traders" argue that tariffs, import quotas, and other barriers to international trade prevent or reduce specialization and decrease both a nation's and the world's production and standard of living.

But nations have and continue to erect barriers to trade with other nations. The questions upon which the latter part of this chapter focuses attention are (1) what motivates nations to impose tariffs and to limit the quantities of goods imported from abroad; (2) what effects do protection have upon a nation's own prosperity and upon the prosperity of the world; and (3) what kinds of arguments do those who favor protection employ to support their position—on what grounds do they base their contention that their nation will benefit from the erection of barriers which reduce imports from foreign nations.

The chapter's final major section is a brief review of American policy toward trade barriers since 1934. That year began a series of gradual but substantial tariff-rate reductions which have continued almost up to the present year under the General Agreement on Tariffs and Trade (GATT). There has also been economic integration among nations in an area that reduces trade restrictions. The European Economic Community, or Common Market, and the United States–Canadian Free-Trade Agreement are examples of this economic integration. Despite this progress in decreasing the barriers to trade with other nations, protectionism is not dead. Advocates of protection are alive—though not quite well—and the causes and costs of this rebirth of protectionism in the United States conclude the chapter.

Whether free trade or protection will be the policy of the United States in the years to come may well depend upon whether you understand that free trade helps everyone and that protection helps no one but the selfish.

■ **CHECKLIST**

When you have studied this chapter you should be able to:

☐ Explain the importance of international trade to the American economy in terms of the volume of this trade and American dependence on it and list the major exports and imports of the United States.

☐ Identify three features of international trade which distinguish it from the trade that takes place within a nation.

☐ State the two economic circumstances which make it desirable for nations to specialize and trade.

☐ Compute, when you are given the necessary figures, the costs of producing two commodities in two countries; determine which nation has the comparative advantage in the production of each commodity; calculate the range in which the terms of trade will be found; and explain the gains to each nation and to the world from specialization and trade.

☐ Restate the case for free trade.

☐ Identify the four principal types of artificial barriers to international trade and the motive for erecting these barriers.

☐ Explain the economic effects of a protective tariff on resource allocation, the price of the commodity, the total production of the commodity, and the outputs of foreign and domestic producers of the commodity.

☐ Enumerate the arguments used to support the case for protection and find the weakness in each of these arguments.

☐ List the major provisions of the Reciprocal Trade Agreements Act of 1934 and of the General Agreement on Tariffs and Trade (GATT) of 1947; and explain why the former was a sharp change in the trade policy of the United States.

☐ Describe the recent focus of GATT negotiations.

☐ Identify the four major goals of the European Economic Community (the Common Market).

☐ Explain the features and the economic significance of the United States–Canadian Free-Trade Agreement of 1988.

☐ Identify the interrelated factors that explain the rebirth of protectionism in the United States; present examples of this rebirth; and state the costs of increased protection to the consumers of the United States relative to its benefits.

■ **CHAPTER OUTLINE**

1. Trade among nations is large enough and unique enough to warrant special attention.

  a. While the relative importance of international trade to the United States is less than it is to other nations,

   (1) this country's imports and exports are about 11 and 13% of its GNP, about $519 and $612 billion a year, respectively, and the United States is the largest trading nation in the world;

   (2) the American economy depends on this trade for important raw materials and markets for its finished goods;

   (3) the United States imports more from the rest of the world as a whole, Japan, and the OPEC nations than it exports to them, most American trade is with other developed nations, and Canada is the largest trading partner; and

   (4) changes in the net exports (exports minus imports) have a multiplier effect on American output, employment, and prices.

  b. International trade has three characteristics that distinguish it from domestic trade: resources are less mobile, the nations use different currencies (or money), and the trade is subjected to more political restrictions.

2. Specialization and trade among nations is advantageous because the world's resources are not evenly distributed and the efficient production of different commodities necessitates different methods and combinations of resources.

3. A simple hypothetical example explains comparative advantage and the gains from trade.

  a. Suppose the world is composed of only two nations, each of which is capable of producing two different commodities and in which the production possibilities curves are different straight lines (whose cost ratios are constant but different).

  b. With different cost ratios, each nation will have a comparative (cost) advantage in the production of one of the two commodities; and if the world is to use its resources economically each nation must specialize in the commodity in the production of which it has a comparative advantage.

  c. The ratio at which one product is traded for another— the terms of trade—lies between the cost ratios of the two nations.

  d. Each nation gains from this trade because specialization permits a greater total output from the same resources and a better allocation of the world's resources.

  e. If cost ratios in the two nations are not constant, specialization may not be complete.

  f. The basic argument for free trade among nations is that it leads to a better allocation of resources and a higher standard of living in the world; but it also increases competition and deters monopoly in these nations.

4. Nations, however, retard international trade by erecting artificial barriers; and tariffs, import quotas, a variety of nontariff barriers, and voluntary export restrictions are the principal barriers to trade.

a. Special interest groups within nations benefit from protection and persuade their nations to erect trade barriers; but the costs to consumers of this protection exceed the benefits to the economy.

b. The imposition of a tariff on a good imported from abroad has both direct and indirect effects on an economy.

(1) The tariff increases the domestic price of the good, reduces its domestic consumption, expands its domestic production, decreases foreign production, and transfers income from domestic consumers to government.

(2) It also reduces the income of foreign producers and the ability of foreign nations to purchase goods and services in the nation imposing the tariff, causes the contraction of relatively efficient industries in that nation, decreases world trade, and lowers the real output of goods and services.

5. The arguments for protectionism are many but they often are of questionable validity.

a. The military self-sufficiency argument can be challenged because it is difficult to determine which industry is "vital" to national defense and must be protected; it would be more efficient economically to provide a direct subsidy to military producers rather than impose a tariff.

b. Trade barriers do not necessarily increase domestic employment because:

(1) imports may eliminate some jobs, but create others; therefore, imports may only change the composition of employment, not the overall level of employment;

(2) the exports of one nation become the imports of another; tariffs barriers can be viewed as "beggar thy neighbor" policies;

(3) there is likely to be retaliation from other nations from the imposition of trade barriers that will reduce national output and employment; and,

(4) they create a less efficient allocation of resources by shielding protected domestic industries from the rigors of competition.

c. Using tariff barriers to permit diversification for stability in economy is not necessary for advanced economies such as the United States and there may be economic costs to diversification in less developed nations.

d. It is alleged that infant-industries need protection until they are sufficiently large to compete. But the argument may not apply to developed economies; it is difficult to select which industries will prosper; protectionism tends to persist long after it is needed; and direct subsidies may be more economically efficient. The need for "breathing spell" is also questionable for some industries because it may not improve efficiency and may make the industry more dependent on protection.

e. Sometimes protection is sought against the "dumping" of excess foreign goods on American markets. Dumping is a legitimate concern and is restricted under United States trade law, but to use dumping as an excuse for widespread tariff protection is unjustified and the number of documented cases is few. If foreign companies are more efficient (low cost) producers, what may appear to be dumping may actually be comparative advantage at work.

f. Protection is sometimes sought because of the cheap foreign labor argument; it should be realized that nations gain from trade based on comparative advantage and without trade living standards will be lower.

g. In summary, most of the protectionist arguments are fallacious or based on half-truths. The only points that have some validity, under certain conditions, are the infant-industry and military-sufficiency arguments, but both are subject to abuse. The historical evidence suggests that free trade promotes and protectionism deters prosperity and economic growth in the world.

6. International trade policies have changed over the years.

a. Until 1934, the United States steadily increased tariff rates to protect private-interest groups. Since the passage of the Reciprocal Trade Agreement Act of 1934, tariff rates have been substantially reduced.

b. Many nations, including the United States, signed the General Agreement on Tariffs and Trade (GATT) in an attempt to eliminate trade barriers. The Uruguay "round" of negotiations, begun in 1986, is the current forum for multination trade negotiations and they involve reducing agricultural subsidies worldwide, removal of trade barriers in services, ending restrictions on foreign investments, and establishing worldwide recognition for patents, copyrights, and trademarks.

c. Economic integration, or the combining of markets of two or more nations into free trade zones, is another method for trade liberalization. There are two examples of economic integration:

(1) The European Common Market sought the economic integration of thirteen Western European nations to create mass markets and increase economic growth; a number of specific goals are set for 1992; but the success of the integration creates problems for nonmember nations such as the United States because of potential tariff barriers.

(2) The United States–Canadian Free-Trade Agreement of 1988 eliminated many trade restrictions between

the two nations and should be a benefit to both countries given the volume of trade between them.

d. In recent years pressures for protection from goods produced abroad have reemerged in the United States.

(1) There are several interrelated causes of these pressures including a backlash from past tariff reductions, more firms are affected by foreign competition, other nations are now more competitive with the United States, and American imports have exceeded exports in recent years.

(2) In the 1980s there were examples of restrictions placed on imports into the United States, and although tariffs overall are low, there are some very high tariffs and restrictions placed on a select list of goods.

(3) The costs to consumers in the United States of protection are high; protection is similar to a regressive tax because it redistributes income from the lowest to the highest income groups; the gains that trade barriers create for protected industries produce a much greater loss for the overall economy.

■ **IMPORTANT TERMS**

Closed economy

Open economy

Labor- (land-, capital-) intensive commodity

Cost ratio

Comparative advantage

Specialization

Terms of trade

Trading possibilities line

Tariff

Revenue tariff

Protective tariff

Import quota

Nontariff barriers (NTBs)

Voluntary export restrictions (VERs)

Smoot-Hawley Tariff Act of 1930

Dumping

Reciprocal Trade Agreements Act of 1934

Most-favored-nation clause

General Agreement on Tariffs and Trade (GATT)

Economic integration

European Common Market (European Economic Community)

United States–Canadian Free-Trade Agreement

■ **FILL-IN QUESTIONS**

1. Trade is important to the United States in màny ways.
a. The imports of the United States amount to about

_____% of the economy's GNP and exports amount

to about _____%. In absolute volume of imports and exports the United States is the world's _____ trading nation

b. The United States is _____ on world trade and the bulk of its trade is with (less developed, developed) _____ nations. The largest trading partner of the United States is (Japan, Canada)

_____.

c. Changes in net exports have _____ effects on the level of national income, employment, and prices.

2. Special attention is devoted to international trade because resources are (more, less) _____ mobile between nations than within a nation; because each nation employs a different _____; and because international trade is subject to a (greater, smaller) _____ number of political interferences and controls than domestic trade.

3. Nations tend to trade among themselves because the distribution of economic resources among them is (even, uneven) _____ and because the efficient production of various goods and services necessitates (the same, different) _____ technologies or combinations of resources.

4. The nations of the world tend to specialize in those goods in the production of which they have a

_____, to export those goods, and to import those goods in the production of which they do not

have a _____

5. If the cost ratio in country X is 4 Panama hats equal 1 pound of bananas, while in country Y, 3 Panama hats equal 1 pound of bananas:
a. In country X hats are relatively (expensive, inexpensive) _____ and bananas relatively

_____

b. In country Y hats are relatively _____ and bananas relatively _____
c. X has a comparative advantage and should specialize in the production of _____ and Y has a comparative advantage and should specialize in the production of _____
d. When X and Y specialize and trade, the terms of trade

will be somewhere between _____ and _____ hats for each pound of bananas; and will depend upon

_____

e. When the actual terms of trade turn out to be 3½ hats for 1 pound of bananas, the cost of obtaining:

(1) 1 Panama hat has been decreased from _____

to _____ pounds of bananas in Y.

(2) 1 pound of bananas has been decreased from

_____ to _____ Panama hats in X.

f. This international specialization will not be complete if the cost of producing either good (increases, decreases,

remains constant) _____ as a nation produces more of it.

6. The basic argument for free trade is that it results in a

better _____ of resources and a higher _____ of living.

7. The barriers to international trade include _____,

_____ quotas, the non_____ barriers, and _____ restrictions.

8. Nations erect barriers to international trade to benefit

the economic positions of _____ groups even though these barriers (increase, decrease)

_____ economic efficiency and trade among nations, and the benefits to a nation are (greater,

less) _____ than the costs to it.

9. When the United States imposes a tariff on a good which is imported from abroad:

a. the price of that good in the United States will (increase, decrease) _____

b. the total purchases of the good in the United States will _____

c. the output of:

(1) American producers of the good will _____

_____

(2) foreign producers will _____

d. the ability of foreigners to buy goods and services in

the United States will _____ and, as a result, output and employment in American industries that

sell goods and services abroad will _____

10. List the six arguments which protectionists employ to justify trade barriers.

a. _____

b. _____

c. _____

d. _____

e. _____

f. _____

The only two arguments containing any reasonable justifi-

cation for protection are the _____ argu-

ment and the _____ argument.

11. Until 1930 the trend of tariff rates in the United States

was (upward, downward) _____; but

since the passage of the _____ Act in 1934

the trend has been _____. This act em-

powered the President to lower _____

rates by up to _____% in return for a re-duction in foreign restrictions on American goods and

incorporated _____ clauses in American trade agreements.

12. The three main principles set down in the General Agreement on Tariffs and Trade are:

a. _____

b. _____

c. _____

13. The Uruguay _____ negotiations is focused on proposals to eliminate trade barriers and

domestic subsidies in _____; to remove

barriers to trade in _____; to end re-

strictions on foreign economic _____;

and to establish and enforce _____,

_____, and _____ rights on an international basis.

14. The specific aims of the European Common Market

were the abolition of _____

_____

among member nations, the establishment of common

tariffs on goods imported from _____

nations, the free movement of _____

and _____ among member nations, and common policies with respect to other matters.

15. A recent example of economic integration in the

Western hemisphere was the _____ of 1988. Under terms of the agreement all trade restric-

tions will be eliminated over a _____-year period. It has been estimated that the agreement will produce annual

gains to each nation of $_____ to _____ billion when fully implemented.

16. What are four interrelated factors which have resulted in the recent resurgence of pressures for the protection of American industries?

a. _____

b. _____

c. _____

d. _____

17. The costs of protecting American producers from for-

eign competition are equal to the rise in the _____ American consumers have to pay for the protected goods.

a. These costs are (greater, less) _____ than the benefits to American producers.

b. The costs of protection were borne mostly by those

consumers in the (highest, lowest) _____ income group.

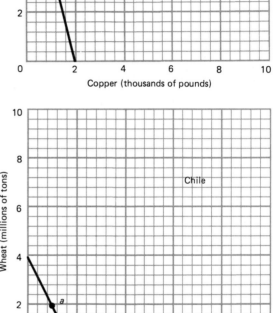

■ **PROBLEMS AND PROJECTS**

1. Shown in the next column are the production possibilities curves for two nations: the United States and Chile. Suppose these two nations do not currently engage in international trade or specialization, and suppose that points **A** and **a** show the combinations of wheat and copper they now produce and consume.

a. The straightness of the two curves indicates that the cost ratios in the two nations are (changing, constant)

_____

b. Examination of the two curves reveals that the cost ratio in:

(1) The United States is _____ million tons

of wheat for _____ thousand pounds of copper.

(2) Chile is _____ million tons of wheat

for _____ thousand pounds of copper.

c. If these two nations were to specialize and trade wheat for copper,

(1) The United States would specialize in the production of wheat because _____

_____

(2) Chile would specialize in the production of copper because _____

d. The terms of trade, if specialization and trade occur, will be greater than 2 and less than 4 million tons of wheat for 1 thousand pounds of copper because _____

_____

e. Assume the terms of trade turn out to be 3 million tons of wheat for 1 thousand pounds of copper. Draw in the trading possibilities curve for the United States and Chile.

f. With these trading possibilities curves, suppose the United States decides to consume 5 million tons of wheat and 1 thousand pounds of copper while Chile decides to consume 3 million tons of wheat and 1 thousand pounds of copper. The gains from trade to:

(1) The United States are _____ million tons of wheat and _____ thousand pounds of copper.

(2) Chile are _____ million tons of wheat and _____ thousand pounds of copper.

2. The following table shows the quantities of woolen gloves demanded (**D**) in the United States at several different prices (**P**). Also shown in the table are the quantities of woolen gloves that would be supplied by American producers (**S_a**) and the quantities that would be supplied by foreign producers (**S_f**) at the nine different prices.

a. Compute and enter in the table the total quantities that would be supplied (**S_t**) by American and foreign producers at each of the prices.

b. If the market for woolen gloves in the United States is a competitive one the equilibrium price for woolen gloves is $_____ and the equilibrium quantity is _____

c. Suppose now that the United States government imposes an 80 cent ($0.80) per pair of gloves tariff on all gloves imported into the United States from abroad. Compute and enter into the table the quantities that would be supplied (**S'_f**) by foreign producers at the nine different prices. (**Hint:** If foreign producers were willing to supply 300 pairs at a price of $1.20 when there was no tariff they are now willing to supply 300 pairs at $2.00, the $0.80 per pair tariff plus the $1.20 they will receive for themselves. The quantities supplied at each of the other prices may be found in a similar fashion.)

d. Compute and enter into the table the total quantities that would be supplied (**S'_t**) by American and foreign producers at each of the nine prices.

e. As a result of the imposition of the tariff the equilibrium price has risen to $_____ and the equilibrium quantity has fallen to _____

f. The number of pairs sold by:
(1) American producers has (increased, decreased) _____ by _____
(2) foreign producers has (increased, decreased) _____ by _____

g. The total revenues (after the payment of the tariff) of:
(1) American producers—who **do not** pay the tariff— have (increased, decreased) _____ by $_____
(2) foreign producers—who **do** pay the tariff—have (increased, decreased) _____ by $_____

h. The total amount spent by American buyers of woolen gloves has _____ by $_____

i. The tariff revenue of the United States government has _____ by $_____

j. The total number of dollars earned by foreigners has _____ by $_____; and, as a result, the total foreign demand for goods and services produced in the United States will _____ by $_____

■ **SELF-TEST**

Circle the T if the statement is true, the F if it is false.

1. Since 1970 the dollar volume of U.S. imports has increased and the dollar volume of its exports has decreased. **T F**

P	D	S_a	S_f	S_t	S'_f	S'_t
$2.60	450	275	475	____	____	____
2.40	500	250	450	____	____	____
2.20	550	225	425	____	____	____
2.00	600	200	400	____	____	____
1.80	650	175	375	____	____	____
1.60	700	150	350	____	____	____
1.40	750	125	325	____	____	____
1.20	800	0	300	____	____	____
1.00	850	0	0	____	____	____

2. The American economy's share of world trade has decreased since 1947. **T   F**

3. The United States exports and imports goods and services with a dollar value greater than any other nation in the world. **T   F**

4. The United States is completely dependent on trade for certain commodities which cannot be obtained in domestic markets. **T   F**

5. Canada is the most important trading partner for the United States in terms of the volume of exports and imports. **T   F**

Use the following production possibilities to answer questions 6, 7, and 8 below and to answer multiple-choice questions 7 and 8.

NEPAL PRODUCTION POSSIBILITIES TABLE

Product	Production alternatives					
	A	B	C	D	E	F
Yak fat	0	4	8	12	16	20
Camel hides	40	32	24	16	8	0

KASHMIR PRODUCTION POSSIBILITIES TABLE

Product	Production alternatives					
	A	B	C	D	E	F
Yak fat	0	3	6	9	12	15
Camel hides	60	48	36	24	12	0

6. In Kashmir the cost of 1 camel hide is 3 units of yak fat. **T   F**

7. Nepal has a comparative advantage in producing camel hides. **T   F**

8. With specialization and trade, the trading possibilities curves of both nations would move to the right of their production possibilities curves. **T   F**

9. Increasing production costs tend to prevent specialization among trading nations from being complete. **T   F**

10. Trade among nations tends to bring about a more efficient use of the world's resources and a greater world output of goods and services. **T   F**

11. Free trade among nations tends to increase monopoly and lessen competition in these nations. **T   F**

12. A tariff on coffee in the United States is an example of a protective tariff. **T   F**

13. The imposition of a tariff on a good imported from abroad will raise the price of the good and lower the quantity of it bought and sold. **T   F**

14. To advocate tariffs which would protect domestic producers of goods and materials essential to national defense is to substitute a political-military objective for the economic objectives of efficiently allocating resources. **T   F**

15. An increase in a nation's imports will, other things remaining constant, expand aggregate demand, real output, and employment in that nation. **T   F**

16. The Smoot-Hawley Tariff Act of 1930 reduced tariffs in the United States to the lowest level ever in an attempt to pull the nation out of the Great Depression. **T   F**

17. One crop economies may be able to make themselves more stable and diversified by imposing tariffs on goods imported from abroad; but these tariffs are apt also to lower the standard of living in these economies. **T   F**

18. Protection against the "dumping" of foreign goods at low prices on the American market is one good reason for widespread, permanent tariffs. **T   F**

19. The only argument for tariffs that has, in the appropriate circumstances, any economic justification is the increase-domestic-employment argument. **T   F**

20. If the United States concludes a tariff agreement with and lowers the tariff rates on goods imported from another nation and that trade agreement contains a most-favored-nation clause, the lower tariff rates are then charged on those goods when they are imported from (most) other nations in the world. **T   F**

21. The members of the European Economic Community have had rapid economic growth since they formed the Common Market in 1958. **T   F**

22. The economic integration of nations creates larger markets for firms within the nations that integrate and makes it possible for these firms and their customers to benefit from the economies of large-scale (mass) production. **T   F**

23. The formation of the European Economic Community (Common Market) has made it more difficult for American firms to compete with firms located within the Community for customer's there. **T F**

24. The U.S.–Canadian Free-Trade Agreement of 1988 is an example of the gains to be obtained from voluntary export restrictions. **T F**

25. The cost of protecting American firms and employees from foreign competition is the rise in the prices of products produced in the United States, and this cost almost always exceeds its benefits. **T F**

Circle the letter that corresponds to the best answer.

1. In 1988 the imports of the United States amounted to approximately what percentage of the United States' GNP?
  (*a*) 5%
  (*b*) 7%
  (*c*) 11%
  (*d*) 13%

2. Which nation is our most important trading partner in terms of the quantity of trade volume?
  (*a*) Japan
  (*b*) Canada
  (*c*) West Germany
  (*d*) United Kingdom

3. Which of the following is *not* true?
  (*a*) the greater part of the export-import trade in merchandise is with the less developed nations
  (*b*) the U.S. imports more merchandise from the OPEC nations than it exports to them
  (*c*) the U.S. imports more merchandise from Japan than it exports to it
  (*d*) the merchandise imports of the U.S. exceed its exports of merchandise

4. In recent years the total exports and imports of goods and services of the U.S. have been between:
  (*a*) $200 and $300 billion
  (*b*) $300 and $400 billion
  (*c*) $400 and $500 billion
  (*d*) $500 and $600 billion

5. International trade is a special and separate area of economic study because:
  (*a*) international trade involves the movement of goods over greater distances than trade within a nation
  (*b*) resources are more mobile internationally than domestically
  (*c*) countries engaged in international trade use different monies

  (*d*) international trade is based on comparative advantage

6. Nations would not need to engage in trade if:
  (*a*) all products were produced from the same combinations of resources
  (*b*) world resources were evenly distributed among nations
  (*c*) world resources were perfectly mobile
  (*d*) all of the above

Use the tables preceding true-false question 6 to answer the following two questions:

7. If Nepal and Kashmir engage in trade, the terms of trade will be:
  (*a*) between 2 and 4 camel hides for 1 unit of yak fat
  (*b*) between ⅓ and ½ units of yak fat for 1 camel hide
  (*c*) between 3 and 4 units of yak fat for 1 camel hide
  (*d*) between 2 and 4 units of yak fat for 1 camel hide

8. If Nepal and Kashmir, in the absence of trade between them, both produced combination C, the gains from trade would be:
  (*a*) 6 units of yak fat
  (*b*) 8 units of yak fat
  (*c*) 6 units of yak fat and 8 camel hides
  (*d*) 8 units of yak fat and 6 camel hides

9. Which one of the following is characteristic of tariffs?
  (*a*) they prevent the importation of goods from abroad
  (*b*) they specify the maximum amounts of specific commodities which may be imported during a given period of time
  (*c*) they often protect domestic producers from foreign competition
  (*d*) they enable nations to reduce their exports and increase their imports during periods of depression

10. The motive for the erection by a nation of barriers to the importation of goods and services from abroad is to:
  (*a*) improve economic efficiency in that nation
  (*b*) protect and benefit special interest groups in that nation
  (*c*) reduce the prices of the goods and services produced in that nation
  (*d*) expand the export of goods and services to foreign nations

11. When a tariff is imposed on a good imported from abroad:
  (*a*) the demand for the good increases
  (*b*) the demand for the good decreases
  (*c*) the supply of the good increases
  (*d*) the supply of the good decreases

Answer the next four questions (12, 13, 14, and 15) on the basis of the following diagram, where S_d and D_d are the domestic supply and demand for a product and P_w is the world price of that product.

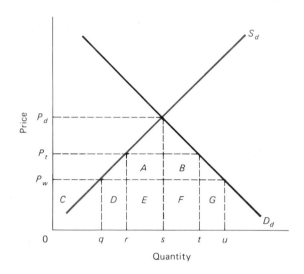

12. In a closed economy (without international trade), the equilibrium price would be:
(a) $0P_d$ but in an open economy, the equilibrium price will be $0P_t$
(b) $0P_d$ but in an open economy, the equilibrium price will be $0P_w$
(c) $0P_w$ but in an open economy, the equilibrium price will be $0P_d$
(d) $0P_w$ but in an open economy, the equilibrium price will be $0P_t$

13. If there is free trade in this economy and no tariffs, the total revenue going to the foreign producers is represented by:
(a) area **C**
(b) areas **A** and **B** combined
(c) areas **A, B, E,** and **F** combined
(d) areas **D, E, F,** and **G** combined

14. If a per unit tariff was imposed in the amount of $P_w P_t$, then domestic producers would supply:
(a) $0q$ units and foreign producers would supply qu units
(b) $0s$ units and foreign producers would supply su units
(c) $0r$ units and foreign producers would supply rt units
(d) $0t$ units and foreign producers would supply tu units

15. Given a per unit tariff in the amount of $P_w P_t$, the amount of the tariff revenue paid by consumers of this product is represented by:
(a) area **A**
(b) area **B**
(c) areas **A** and **B** combined
(d) areas **D, E, F,** and **G** combined

16. "The nation needs to protect itself from foreign countries that sell their products in our domestic markets at less than the cost of production." This quotation would be most closely associated with which protectionist argument?
(a) diversification for stability
(b) increase domestic employment
(c) protection against dumping
(d) cheap foreign labor

17. Tariffs lead to:
(a) the contraction of relatively efficient industries
(b) an overallocation of resources to relatively efficient industries
(c) an increase in the foreign demand for domestically produced goods
(d) an underallocation of resources to relatively inefficient industries

18. Which one of the following arguments for protection is the least fallacious and most pertinent in the United States today?
(a) the military self-sufficiency argument
(b) the increase-domestic-employment argument
(c) the cheap foreign labor argument
(d) the infant-industry argument

19. Which of the following is the likely result of the United States employing tariffs to protect its high wages and standard of living from cheap foreign labor?
(a) an increase in U.S. exports
(b) a rise in the American real NNP
(c) a decrease in the average productivity of American workers
(d) a decrease in the quantity of labor employed by industries producing the goods on which tariffs have been levied

20. Which of the following is a likely result of imposing tariffs to increase domestic employment?
(a) a short-run increase in domestic employment
(b) retaliatory increases in the tariff rates of foreign nations
(c) a long-run decline in exports
(d) all of the above

21. The infant-industry argument for tariffs:
(a) is especially pertinent to the advanced industrial nations
(b) generally results in tariffs that are removed after the infant industry has matured
(c) makes it rather easy to determine which infant industries will become mature industries with comparative advantages in producing their goods
(d) might better be replaced by an argument for outright subsidies for infant industries

22. Which one of the following specifically empowered

the President of the United States to reduce its tariff rates up to 50% if other nations would reduce their tariffs on American goods?

(a) the Underwood Act of 1913
(b) the Hawley-Smoot Act of 1930
(c) the Trade Agreements Act of 1934
(d) the General Agreement on Tariffs and Trade of 1947

23. Which of the following is **not** characteristic of the General Agreement on Tariffs and Trade? Nations signing the agreement were committed to:

(a) the elimination of import quotas
(b) the reciprocal reduction of tariffs by negotiation
(c) the nondiscriminatory treatment of all trading nations
(d) the establishment of a world customs union

24. One important topic for discussion during the Urguay round of GATT was:

(a) removing voluntary export restraints in manufacturing
(b) eliminating trade barriers and subsidies in agriculture
(c) abolishing the need for patent, copyright, and trademark protection
(d) increasing tariff barriers on services but reducing tariff barriers on foreign economic investments

25. The European Common Market:

(a) is designed to eliminate tariffs and import quotas among its members
(b) aims to allow the eventual free movement of capital and labor within the member nations
(c) imposes common tariffs on goods imported into the member nations from outside the Common Market area
(d) does all of the above

26. An example of economic integration would be the:

(a) Smoot-Hawley Tariff Act
(b) United States–Canadian Free-Trade Agreement
(c) Reciprocal Trade Agreements Act
(d) General Agreements on Tariffs and Trade

27. Pressures for the protection of American industries have increased in recent years because of:

(a) previous decreases in the barriers to trade
(b) persistent trade deficits in the United States
(c) increased competition from imported products
(d) all of the above

■ **DISCUSSION QUESTIONS**

1. In relative and absolute terms, how large is the volume of the international trade of the United States? What has happened to these figures over the past twenty or so years?

2. What are the principal exports and imports of the American economy? What commodities used in the economy come almost entirely from abroad and what American industries sell large percentages of their outputs abroad?

3. Which nations are the principal "trading partners" of the United States? How much of this trade is with the developed and how much of it is with the less developed nations of the world?

4. Are the American economy's exports of merchandise to greater or less than its imports of merchandise from:

(a) Japan,
(b) the OPEC nations, and
(c) the rest of the world?

5. In what ways is international trade different from the trade which takes place within a nation?

6. Why do nations specialize in certain products and export their surplus production of these goods at the same time that they are importing other goods? Why do they not use the resources employed to produce the surpluses which they export to produce the goods which they import?

7. What two facts—one dealing with the distribution of the world's resources and the other related to the technology of producing different products—are the basis for trade among nations?

8. Explain:

(a) the theory or principle of comparative advantage;
(b) what is meant by and what determines the terms of trade; and
(c) the gains from trade.

9. What is the "case for free trade"?

10. What motivates nations to erect barriers to the importation of goods from abroad and what types of barriers do they erect?

11. Suppose the United States were to increase the tariff on automobiles imported from West Germany (and other foreign countries). What would be the effect of this tariff-rate increase on:

(a) the price of automobiles in the United States;
(b) the total number of cars sold in the United States during a year;
(c) the number of cars produced by and employment in the West German automobile industry;
(d) production by and employment in the American automobile industry;
(e) West German income obtained by selling cars in the United States;

(f) the West German demand for goods produced in the U.S.;

(g) the production of and employment in those American industries which now export goods to West Germany;

(h) the standards of living in the U.S. and in West Germany;

(i) the allocation of resources in the American economy; and

(j) the allocation of the world's resources?

12. What is the "case for protection"? How valid and pertinent to the United States is each of the basic arguments for protection?

13. What was the tariff policy of the United States:

(a) between 1790 and 1930; and

(b) since 1934?

Explain the basic provisions of the Reciprocal Trade Agreements Act. How has the United States cooperated with other nations since 1945 to reduce trade barriers?

14. What were the three cardinal principles contained in the General Agreement on Tariffs and Trade?

15. What were the four main goals of the European Economic Community? How does the achievement of these goals bring about an increased standard of living within the Community? What problems and what benefits does the success of the EEC create for the United States?

16. What is the United States–Canadian Free-Trade Agreement and what is its economic significance?

17. Why have the pressures for the protection of American firms and workers increased in the last few years? What:

(a) are several examples of this increased protection; and

(b) are the costs to the American economy of protection?

■ **ANSWERS**

Fill-in questions

1. a. 13, 11, largest; b. dependent, developed, Canada; c. multiple

2. less, money (currency), greater

3. uneven, different

4. comparative advantage, comparative advantage

5. a. inexpensive, expensive; b. expensive, inexpensive; c. hats, bananas; d. 3, 4, world demand and supply for hats and bananas; e. (1) ⅓, ²⁄₇, (2) 4, 3½; f. increases

6. allocation, standard

7. tariffs, import, tariff, voluntary export

8. special interest, decrease, less

9. a. increase; b. decrease; c. (1) increase, (2) decrease; d. decrease, decrease

10. a. military self-sufficiency; b. infant industry; c. increase domestic employment; d. diversification for stability; e. protection against dumping; f. cheap foreign labor; military self-sufficiency, infant-industry

11. upward, Reciprocal Trade Agreements, downward, tariff, 50, most-favored-nation

12. a. equal, nondiscriminatory treatment of all trading nations; b. reduction of tariffs by negotiation; c. elimination of import quotas

13. Round, agriculture, services, investments, patents, copyrights, and trademarks

14. tariffs and import quotas, nonmember, capital, labor

15. U.S.–Canadian Free-Trade Agreement, 10, 1, 3

16. a. the freer trade that resulted from past reductions in trade barriers; b. the increased competition from abroad that resulted from a more open economy; c. the increased competitiveness of foreign products that resulted from lower labor costs and prices abroad; d. persistent trade deficits

17. prices; a. greater; b. lowest

Problems and projects

1. a. constant; b. (1) 8, 2, (2) 4, 2; c. (1) it has a comparative advantage in producing wheat (its cost of producing wheat is less than Chile's), (2) it has a comparative advantage in producing copper (its cost of producing copper is less than the United States'), d. one of the two nations would be unwilling to trade if the terms of trade are outside this range; f. (1) 1, 0, (2) 1, 0

2. a. 750, 700, 650, 600, 550, 500, 450, 300, 0; b. $2.00, 600; c. 375, 350, 325, 300, 0, 0, 0, 0, 0; d. 650, 600, 550, 500, 175, 150, 125, 0, 0; e. $2.20, 550; f. (1) increased, 25, (2) decreased, 75; g. (1) increased, $95, (2) decreased, $345; h. increased, $10; i. increased, $260; j. decreased, $345, decrease, $345

Self-test

1. F; **2.** T; **3.** T; **4.** T; **5.** T; **6.** F; **7.** F; **8.** T; **9.** T; **10.** T; **11.** F; **12.** F; **13.** T; **14.** T; **15.** F; **16.** F; **17.** T; **18.** F; **19.** F; **20.** T; **21.** T; **22.** T; **23.** T; **24.** F; **25.** T

1. d; **2.** b; **3.** a; **4.** d; **5.** c; **6.** d; **7.** a; **8.** a; **9.** c; **10.** b; **11.** d; **12.** b; **13.** d; **14.** c; **15.** c; **16.** c; **17.** a; **18.** a; **19.** c; **20.** d; **21.** d; **22.** c; **23.** d; **24.** b; **25.** d; **26.** b; **27.** d

Exchange rates, the balance of payments, and the trade "crisis"

In the last chapter you learned **why** nations engage in international trade and **why** they erect barriers to trade with other nations. In Chapter 23 you will learn **how** nations using different monies (or currencies) are able to trade with each other. The means they employ to overcome the difficulties that result from the use of different monies is fairly simple. When the residents of a nation (its consumers, business firms, or governments) wish to buy goods or services or real or financial assets from, make loans or gifts to, or pay interest and dividends to the residents of other nations they **buy** some of the money used in that nation. They pay for the foreign money with some of their own money. In other words, they **exchange** their own money for foreign money. And when the residents of a nation sell goods or services or real or financial assets to, receive loans or gifts from, or are paid dividends or interest by the residents of foreign nations and obtain foreign money they **sell** this foreign money—often called foreign exchange—in return for some of their own money. That is, they **exchange** foreign money for their own money. The markets in which one money is sold and is paid for with another money are called foreign exchange markets. The price that is paid (in one money) for a unit of another money is called the foreign exchange rate (or the rate of exchange). And like most prices, the foreign exchange rate for any foreign currency is determined by the demand for and the supply of that foreign currency.

As you know from Chapter 22, nations buy and sell large quantities of goods and services across national boundaries. But the residents of these nations also buy and sell such financial assets as stocks and bonds and such real assets as land and capital goods in other nations; and the governments and individuals in one nation make gifts (remittances) in other nations. At the end of a year, nations summarize their foreign transactions with the rest of the world. This summary is called the nation's international balance of payments: a record of how it obtained foreign money during the year and what it did with this foreign money. Of course, all foreign money obtained was used for some purpose—it did not evaporate—and consequently the balance of payments **always** balances. The

international balance of payments is an extremely important and useful device for understanding the amounts and kinds of international transactions in which the residents of a nation engage. But it also enables us to understand the meaning of a balance of payments imbalance (a deficit or a surplus), the causes of these imbalances, and how to deal with them.

Probably the most difficult section of this chapter is concerned with balance of payments deficits and surpluses. A balance of payments deficit (surplus) is found when the receipts of foreign money are less (greater) than the payments of foreign money and the nation must reduce (expand) its official reserves to make the balance of payments balance. You should pay particular attention to the way in which a system of **flexible** exchange rates and the way in which a system of **fixed** exchange rates will correct balance of payments deficits and surpluses; and the advantages and disadvantages of these two alternative methods of eliminating imbalances.

As examples of these two types of exchange rate systems you will find in the third section of the chapter an examination of the gold standard, of the Bretton Woods system, and of the managed floating exchange rate system. In the first two systems exchange rates are fixed; and in the third system exchange rates are fixed in the short run (to obtain the advantages of fixed exchange rates) and flexible in the long run (to enable nations to correct balance of payments deficits and surpluses).

The final section of the chapter examines what has been called the foreign-trade "crisis" of the United States. The problem is that during the early 1980s the United States imported goods and services with a dollar-and-cents value greater than the value of the goods and services it exported; and it incurred very large current-account deficits in those years. It was able to do this only by increasing its debts to (by borrowing from) the rest of the world; and by 1985 it owed more to foreigners than they owed to people in the United States. The primary (though not the only) cause of this crisis was the high international value of (exchange rate for) the American dollar during the mid 1980s. The high exchange rate for the dollar meant that the exchange rates for foreign currencies were low. The low exchange rates for other currencies and the high exchange rate for the dollar expanded American imports, contracted American exports, and produced the foreign-trade crisis in the United States.

The relatively high exchange rate for the dollar in the mid 1980s was the result of real interest rates which were higher in the United States than in the rest of the world. Real interest rates were higher in the American economy than in the rest of the world because the large budget deficits of the Federal government forced it to borrow in the American money market; and these high real interest rates in the United States increased the attractiveness to foreigners of financial investment (buying bonds or lending) in the U.S., increased the foreign demand for dollars in the foreign exchange markets, and drove the price of the dollar upward in these markets. Although the value of the dollar fell over the 1985–1987 period, the trade deficit persisted for several reasons, and only in mid-1988 did the deficit begin to fall.

The undesirable effects of the trade deficit have led to a search for policy options. Two are worthy of note while others are more limited solutions. It is thought by many economists that a reduction in the budget deficit of the Federal government would help reduce real interest rates in the United States relative to other nations, increase foreign investment in the United States and the demand for dollars, and cause the value of the dollar to fall. Putting the nation's "fiscal house" in order would help reduce the value of the dollar to fall and move exports and imports to balance in a way that would be more acceptable to the major trading partners of the United States. It is also thought that if nations with large trade surpluses with the United States, such as Japan and Germany, would take actions to increase their rate of economic growth, this condition would help increase exports from the United States to those nations.

One last word for you. This chapter is filled with new terms. Some of these are just special words used in international economies to mean things with which you are already familiar. Be very sure you learn what all of the new terms mean. It will simplify your comprehension of this chapter and enable you to understand more readily the foreign trade "crisis" of the United States examined at the end of the chapter.

■ **CHECKLIST**

When you have studied this chapter you should be able to:

☐ Explain how American exports create a demand for dollars and generate a supply of foreign exchange; and how American imports create a demand for foreign exchange and generate a supply of dollars.

☐ Define each of the five balances found in a nation's international balance of payments; and distinguish between a deficit and a surplus in each of these five balances.

☐ Explain the relationship between the current and capital account balances; and between the balance of payments and changes in the official reserves of a nation.

☐ Provide an explanation of how flexible (floating) exchange rates function to eliminate payments deficits and surpluses; and enumerate the three disadvantages of this method of correcting imbalances.

☐ Identify the five principal determinants of the demand for and supply of a particular foreign money; and explain how a change in each of these determinants would affect the rate of exchange for that foreign money.

☐ Enumerate the four means by which a nation may fix (or "peg") foreign exchange rates.

☐ Explain how a nation with a payments deficit might employ its international reserves to prevent a rise in foreign exchange rates.

☐ Describe how a nation with a payments deficit might use fiscal and monetary policies, trade policies, and exchange controls to eliminate the deficit.

☐ List the three conditions which a nation had to fulfill if it was to be on the gold standard; explain how gold flows operated to reduce payments deficits and surpluses; and identify its two advantages and its two basic drawbacks.

☐ Explain how the Bretton Woods system stabilized exchange rates and attempted to provide for orderly changes in exchange rates to eliminate payments imbalances.

☐ Define the international monetary reserves of nations in the Bretton Woods system; explain why the United States had to incur balance of payments deficits to expand these reserves; and describe the dilemma this created for the United States.

☐ Describe how the United States severed the link between gold and the international value of the dollar in 1971 that led to the floating of the dollar and brought to an end the old Bretton Woods system.

☐ Explain what is meant by a system of managed floating exchange rates; and enumerate its two alleged virtues and its three alleged shortcomings.

☐ Contrast the adjustments necessary to correct payments deficits and surpluses when exchange rates are flexible and when they are fixed.

☐ Define the American international-trade crisis.

☐ Enumerate and explain the causes of this crisis; and describe the effects of the crisis on output and employment and prices in the United States and on the indebtedness of Americans to foreigners.

☐ State what policies are needed to eliminate the foreign-trade crisis of the United States.

■ **CHAPTER OUTLINE**

1. Trade between two nations differs from domestic trade because the nations use different monies; but this problem is resolved by the existence of foreign-exchange markets in which the money used by one nation can be purchased and paid for with the money of the other nation.

  a. American exports create a demand for dollars and generate a supply of foreign money in the foreign-exchange markets; increase the money supply in the United States and decrease foreign money supplies; and earn monies that can be used to pay for American imports.

  b. American imports create a supply of dollars and generate a demand for foreign money in foreign-exchange markets; decrease the money supply in the United States and increase foreign money supplies; and use monies obtained by exporting.

2. The international balance of payments for a nation is an annual record of all its transactions with the other nations in the world; and it records all the payments received from and made to the rest of the world.

  a. The current-account section of a nation's international balance of payments records its trade in currently produced goods and services; and within this section:

  (1) the trade balance of the nation is equal to its exports of goods (merchandise) less its imports of goods (merchandise), and the nation has a trade surplus (deficit) if the exports are greater (less) than the imports;

  (2) the balance on goods and services is equal to its exports of goods and services less its imports of goods and services; and

  (3) the balance on the current account is equal to its balance on goods and services plus its net investment income (dividends and interest) from other nations and its net private and public transfers to other nations, and this balance may be either a surplus or a deficit.

  b. The capital-account section of a nation's international balance of payments records its sales of real and financial assets (which earn it foreign money) and its purchases of real and financial assets (which use up foreign money), and the nation has a capital-account surplus (deficit) if its sales are greater (less) than its purchases of real and financial assets.

  c. The current and capital accounts in a nation's international balance of payments are interrelated: a nation with a current-account deficit can finance the deficit by borrowing or selling assets abroad (with a capital-account surplus) and a nation with a current-account surplus can lend or buy assets abroad (incur a capital-account deficit).

  d. The official reserves of a nation are the foreign currencies (monies) owned by its central bank: these reserves a nation uses to finance a net deficit on its current and capital accounts, and these reserves increase when a nation has a net surplus on its current and capital ac-

counts; and in this way the nation's total outpayments and inpayments are made to equal each other (to balance).

  e. A nation is said to have a balance-of-payments surplus (deficit) when the current and capital account balance is positive (negative) and its official reserves increase (decrease).

  f. The merchandise or trade deficit of a nation implies its producers are losing their competitiveness in foreign markets, but is beneficial to consumers in that nation who receive more goods (imports) from abroad than they must pay for (export); and a balance-of-payments deficit is undesirable to the extent that the nation's official reserves are limited and require the nation to take painful macroeconomic adjustments to correct it.

3. The kinds of adjustments a nation with a balance-of-payments deficit or surplus must make to correct the imbalance depends upon whether exchange rates are flexible (floating) or fixed.

  a. If foreign exchange rates float freely the demand for and the supply of foreign exchange determine foreign exchange rates; and the exchange rate for any foreign money is the rate at which the quantity of that money demanded is equal to the quantity of it supplied.

  (1) A change in the demand for or supply of a foreign money will cause the exchange rate for that money to rise or fall; and when there is a rise (fall) in the price paid in dollars for a foreign money it is said that the dollar has depreciated (appreciated) and that the foreign money has appreciated (depreciated).

A HELPFUL HINT

The application of the terms *depreciate* and *appreciate* to foreign exchange confuses many students. Here are some hints that will help reduce the confusion.

First:
● depreciate means decrease; and appreciate means increase.

Second: what decreases when Country A's currency depreciates and increases when its currency appreciates is
● the quantity of Country B's currency that can be purchased for *one unit* of Country A's currency.

Third: when the exchange rate for B's currency:
● *rises* the quantity of B's currency that can be purchased for one unit of A's currency *decreases* (just as a rise in the price of cigars decreases the number of cigars that can be bought for a dollar) and A's currency has *depreciated*;
● *falls* the quantity of B's currency that can be purchased for one unit of A's currency *increases* (just as a fall in the price of cigars increases the number of cigars that can be bought for a dollar) and A's currency has *appreciated*.

(2) Changes in the demand for or supply of a foreign currency are largely the result of changes in tastes, relative income changes, relative price changes, changes in relative real interest rates, and speculation.

(3) When a nation has a payments deficit (surplus), foreign exchange rates will rise (fall); this will make foreign goods and services more (less) expensive, decrease (increase) imports, make a nation's goods and services less (more) expensive for foreigners to buy, increase (decrease) its exports; and these adjustments in foreign exchange rates and in imports and exports correct the nation's payments deficit (surplus).

(4) But flexible exchange rates increase the uncertainties faced by exporters, importers, and investors (and reduce international trade); change the terms of trade; and destabilize economies (by creating inflation or unemployment).

b. When nations fix (or "peg") foreign exchange rates, the governments of these nations must intervene in the foreign exchange markets to prevent shortages and surpluses of foreign monies.

(1) One way for a nation to stabilize foreign exchange rates is for its government to sell (buy) a foreign money in exchange for its own money (or gold) when there is a shortage (surplus) of the foreign money.

(2) A nation with a payments deficit might also discourage imports by imposing tariffs, import quotas, and special taxes; and encourage exports by subsidizing them.

(3) To eliminate a payments deficit a nation might require exporters who earn foreign exchange to sell it to the government; and the government would then ration the available foreign exchange among importers and make the value of imports equal to the value of exports.

(4) Another way for a nation to stabilize foreign exchange rates is to employ fiscal and monetary policies to reduce its national income and price level and to raise interest rates relative to those in other nations; and, thereby, reduce the demand for and increase the supply of the different foreign monies.

4. The nations of the world in their recent history have employed three different exchange rate systems.

a. Between 1879 and 1934 (with the exception of the World War I years) the operation of the gold standard kept foreign exchange rates relatively stable.

(1) A nation was on the gold standard when it:

(a) defined its monetary unit in terms of a certain quantity of gold;

(b) maintained a fixed relationship between its stock of gold and its money supply; and

(c) allowed gold to be exported and imported without restrictions.

(2) Foreign exchange rates between nations on the gold standard would fluctuate only within a narrow range (determined by the cost of packing, insuring, and shipping gold from country to country); and if a foreign exchange rate rose (fell) to the upper (lower) limit of the range gold would flow out of (into) a nation.

(3) But if a nation has a balance-of-payments deficit (surplus) and gold flowed out of (into) the country, its money supply would decrease (increase); this would raise (lower) interest rates and reduce (expand) aggregate demand, national output, employment, and prices in that country; and the balance-of-payments deficit (surplus) would be eliminated.

(4) The gold standard resulted in nearly stable foreign-exchange rates (which by reducing uncertainty stimulated international trade), and automatically corrected balance-of-payments deficits and surpluses; but it required that nations accept such unpleasant adjustments as recession and inflation to eliminate their balance-of-payments deficits and surpluses, and it could operate only so long as nations with deficits did not run out of gold.

(5) During the worldwide Great Depression of the 1930s nations felt that remaining on the gold standard threatened their recoveries from the Depression, and the devaluations of their currencies (to expand exports and reduce imports) led to the breakdown and abandonment of the gold standard.

b. From the end of World War II until 1971 the Bretton Woods system, committed to the adjustable-peg system of exchange rates and managed by the International Monetary Fund (IMF), kept foreign-exchange rates relatively stable.

(1) The adjustable-peg system required the United States to sell gold to other member nations at a fixed price and the other members of the IMF to define their monetary units in terms of either gold or dollars (which established fixed exchange rates among the currencies of all member nations); and for the other member nations to keep the exchange rates for their currencies from rising by selling foreign currencies, selling gold, or borrowing on a short-term basis from the IMF.

(2) The system also provided for orderly changes in exchange rates to correct a fundamental imbalance (persistent and sizable balance-of-payments deficits) by allowing a nation to devalue its currency (increase its defined gold or dollar equivalent).

(3) The other nations of the world used gold and dollars as their international monetary reserves in the Bretton Woods system: for these reserves to grow the United States had to continue to have balance-of-payments deficits, but to continue the convertibility of dollars into gold it had to reduce the deficits; and, faced with this dilemma, the United States in 1971 suspended the convertibility of the dollar, brought an end to the Bretton Woods system of fixed exchange rates, and allowed the exchange rates for the dollar and the other currencies to float.

c. Exchange rates today are managed by individual nations to avoid short-term fluctuations and allowed to float in the long term to correct balance-of-payments deficits and surpluses; and this new system of managed floating exchange rates is favored by some and criticized by others.

(1) Its proponents contend that this system has not led to any decrease in world trade and it has enabled the world to adjust to severe economic shocks.

(2) Its critics argue that it has resulted in volatile exchange rates and has not reduced balance-of-payments deficits and surpluses; and that it is a "nonsystem" that a nation may employ to achieve its own domestic economic goals.

5. The United States faces an international-trade crisis in the 1980s: its exports have grown slowly but its imports have grown rapidly; and its merchandise and current-account deficits expanded since 1980.

a. These deficits have had three major causes.

(1) The international value of the dollar rose from 1980–1985 because of large Federal-budget deficits, a tighter monetary policy during the early 1980s, and lower rates of inflation in the United States and higher real interest rates than in the rest of the world. The value of the dollar declined from 1985–1987 because of intervention by five industrial nations to supply dollars to the foreign exchange market and the increasing demand for foreign currency to purchase imports. The dollar's fall helped increase American exports, but imports continued to rise until mid-1988 in part because foreign producers kept price increases low by accepting low per unit profits.

(2) The more rapid recovery of the American economy from the 1980–1982 recession increased its imports by large amounts; and the less rapid recovery of the rest of the world increased American exports by only small amounts.

(3) American exports to the less developed nations fell and its imports from them rose because they used restrictive monetary and fiscal policies and devalued their currencies to cope with their international debts to the developed nations.

b. The trade deficits of the United States lowered real output and employment, restrained inflation, lessened the prices of imported goods in the United States, and increased the indebtedness of Americans to foreigners; had the opposite effects on its industrialized trading partners; and created additional problems for less developed nations with dollar-denominated debts.

c. To deal with the trade deficit several policies have been considered:

(1) It is argued that a decline in the Federal-budget deficits will lower the real rate of interest in the United States compared to other nations; G-7 nations would like the United States to "put its fiscal house in order" rather

than just relying on "managed" depreciation of the dollar to ease the trade imbalance.

(2) Expansionary monetary and fiscal policies by the major trading partners of the United States will tend to increase economic growth in those nations and thereby increase exports from the United States to those nations.

(3) Other policies—easy money, protective tariffs, forced recession, increasing competitiveness, and direct foreign investment—have been considered but some have limitations and drawbacks.

■ IMPORTANT TERMS

Financing exports and imports

Foreign exchange market

Export transaction

Import transaction

Rate of exchange (foreign exchange rate)

International balance of payments

Current account

Trade balance

Trade surplus

Trade deficit

Balance on goods and services

Balance on current account

Net investment income

Net transfers

Capital account

Capital inflow

Capital outflow

Balance on the capital account

Current account deficit

Current account surplus

Capital account deficit

Capital account surplus

Official reserves

Balance of payments deficit

Balance of payments surplus

Flexible (floating) exchange rate

Fixed exchange rate

Exchange rate (currency) depreciation

Exchange rate (currency) appreciation

Exchange control

Gold standard

Gold flow

Gold export point

Gold import point

Devaluation

Bretton Woods system

Adjustable pegs

International Monetary Fund

International monetary reserves

Managed floating exchange rate

G-7 nations

Foreign trade crisis

■ FILL-IN QUESTIONS

1. The rate of exchange for the French franc is the number of (francs, dollars) _____ which an American must pay to obtain one (franc, dollar) _____

2. When the rate of exchange for the Saudi Arabian riyal is 30 American cents, the rate of exchange for the American dollar is _____ riyals.

3. American:

a. exports create a (demand for, supply of) _____ foreign money, generate a _____ dollars, (increase, decrease) _____ the money supply in the United States, and _____ money supplies abroad;

b. imports create a _____ foreign money, generate a _____ dollars, and _____ the money supply in the United States, and _____ money supplies abroad.

4. In addition to the demand for foreign currency by American firms that wish to import goods from foreign countries, Americans also demand foreign money to purchase _____ and _____ services abroad and to pay _____ and _____ on foreign investments in the United States.

5. The balance of payments of a nation records all payments its residents make to and receive from residents in _____

a. Any transaction that *earns* foreign exchange for that nation is a (debit, credit) _____ and is shown with a (+, −) _____ sign.

b. A transaction that *uses up* foreign exchange is a _____ and is shown with a _____ sign.

6. When a nation has a:

a. balance of trade deficit its exports are (greater, less) _____ than its imports of _____;

b. balance-on-goods-and-services surplus its exports are _____ than its imports of goods and services;

c. current-account deficit its balance on goods and services plus its net _____ income and net _____ is (positive, negative) _____.

7. The capital account records the capital inflows and capital outflows of a nation.

a. The capital inflows are the expenditures made (in that nation, abroad) _____ by residents of (that nation, other nations) _____;

and the capital outflows are the expenditures made _____ by residents of _____ for _____ and _____ assets.

b. A nation has a capital-account surplus when its capital-account inflows are (greater, less) _____ than its outflows.

8. A nation:

a. may finance a current-account deficit by (buying, selling) _____ assets or by (borrowing, lending) _____ abroad; and

b. may use a capital-account surplus to (buy, sell) _____ assets or to (borrow, lend) _____ abroad.

9. The official reserves of a nation are the quantities of (foreign monies, its own money) _____ owned by its _____ bank. If that nation has

a. a deficit on the current and capital accounts its official reserves (increase, decrease) _____;

b. a surplus on the current and capital accounts its official reserves _____;

c. either a current and capital account deficit or surplus, the sum of the current and capital balances and the increases or decreases in its official reserves total _____

10. A country has a balance-of-payments deficit if the sum of its current and capital accounts balance is (positive, negative) _____ and its official reserves (increase, decrease) _____; and a payments surplus when the sum of its current and capital accounts balance is _____ and its official reserves _____

11. If foreign exchange rates float freely and a nation has a balance of payments *deficit:*

a. that nation's money in the foreign exchange markets will (appreciate, depreciate) _____ and foreign monies will _____

b. as a result of these changes in foreign exchange rates, the nation's imports will (increase, decrease) _____, its exports will _____, and the size of its deficit will _____

12. What effect (depreciation or appreciation) would each of the following have upon the French franc in the foreign exchange market (**ceteris paribus**)?

a. The increased preference in the United States for domestic wines over wines produced in France: _____

b. A rise in the national income of the United States:

_____

c. An increase in the price level in France: _____

_____

d. A rise in real interest rates in the United States:

_____

e. The belief of speculators in France that the dollar will appreciate in the foreign exchange market: _____

13. There are three disadvantages of freely floating foreign exchange rates: The risks and uncertainties associated with flexible rates tend to (expand, diminish)

_____ trade between nations; when a nation's currency depreciates, its terms of trade with other nations are (worsened, bettered) _____; and fluctuating exports and imports can destabilize an economy and result in _____ or in

_____ in that economy.

14. To fix or "peg" the rate of exchange for the West German mark when:

a. the exchange rate for the mark is rising, the United States would (buy, sell) _____ marks in exchange for dollars;

b. the exchange rate for the mark is falling, the United States would _____ marks in exchange for dollars.

15. A nation with a balance of payments deficit:

a. might attempt to eliminate the deficit by (taxing, subsidizing) _____ imports or by _____ exports;

b. might employ exchange controls and ration foreign exchange among those who wish to (export, import)

_____ goods and services and require all those who _____ goods and services to sell the foreign exchange they earn to the

_____

16. If the United States has a payments deficit with Japan and the exchange rate for the Japanese yen is rising, the United States might employ (expansionary, contraction-

ary) _____ fiscal and monetary policies to reduce the demand for the yen; but this would bring about (inflation, recession) _____ in the United States.

17. A nation is on the gold standard when it defines its money in terms of _____, maintains a fixed relationship between its _____ supply and gold _____, and allows gold to be freely _____ from and _____ into the nation.

18. When the nations of the world were on the gold standard

a. exchange rates were relatively (stable, unstable)

_____,

b. but when a nation had a payments deficit:

(1) gold flowed (into, out of) _____ the nation;

(2) its money supply and price level (increased, decreased) _____ and its interest rates

_____;

(3) its payments deficit (rose, fell) _____ and it experienced (inflation, recession) _____

_____

19. The Bretton Woods system was established to bring about (flexible, fixed) _____ exchange rates; and, to accomplish this, it employed the _____ system of exchange rates. Under the Bretton Woods system;

a. a member nation defined its monetary unit in terms of

_____ or _____;

b. each member nation stabilized the exchange rate for its currency and prevented it from rising by (buying, selling) _____ foreign currency which it obtained from its _____ fund, by (buying, selling) _____ gold, or by (borrowing from, lending to) _____ the International Monetary Fund;

c. a nation with a deeply rooted payments deficit could (devalue, revalue) _____ its currency;

d. international monetary reserves included both

_____ and _____;
e. it was hoped that exchange rates in the short run

would be (stable, flexible) _____ enough to promote international trade and in the long run would be

_____ enough to correct balance of payments imbalances.

20. The role of the dollar as a component of international monetary reserves produced a dilemma:
a. For these reserves to grow the United States had to incur balance of payments (surpluses, deficits)

_____

b. This resulted in an increase in the foreign holding of American dollars and in a decrease in the American re-

serves (stock) of _____.

c. The ability of the United States to convert dollars into gold and the willingness of foreigners to hold dollars (because they were "as good as gold") therefore (increased,

decreased) _____

d. For the dollar to remain an acceptable international monetary reserve the U.S. payments deficits had to be

(eliminated, continued) _____ ; but for international monetary reserves to grow the U.S. pay-

ments deficits had to be _____

21. The United States completed the destruction of the Bretton Woods system in 1971 when it suspended the

convertibility of dollars into _____ and allowed the value of the dollar to be determined by

_____

Since then the international monetary system has moved from exchange rates which (for all practical purposes)

were (fixed, floating) _____ to ex-

change rates which are _____

22. The system of exchange rates which has developed

since 1971 has been labeled a system of _____ exchange rates. This means that individual nations will:
a. in the short term buy and sell foreign exchange to

keep exchange rates _____

b. in the long term allow exchange rates to rise or fall to

correct payments _____

23. The crisis in the foreign trade of the United States

concerns the (increases, decreases) _____ in the size of the American merchandise and current-ac-

count (surpluses, deficits) _____ during the 1980s which were brought about by the sharp in-

creases in its (exports, imports) _____ and

the small increases in its _____

24. The three causes of this trade crisis were
a. the (strong, weak) _____ dollar,

b. the (slow, rapid) _____ growth of the American economy, and

c. the (expanded, reduced) _____ exports of the United States to less developed nations.

25. The rise in the international value of the dollar from 1980–1985
a. made American goods (more, less) _____ expensive and foreign goods _____ expensive, (increased, decreased) _____ American exports,

and _____ American imports;

b. was the result of relatively (high, low) _____ real interest rates in the United States caused by large

Federal-budget (surpluses, deficits) _____, a

(tight, easy) _____ monetary policy, and relatively (high, low) _____ rates of inflation in the United States.
c. From 1985–1987, the value of the dollar (rose, fell)

_____ but imports continued to rise because foreign producers accepted lower per unit

_____ and in 1987 _____ nations agreed to halt the decline of the dollar.
d. Finally, in mid-1988, the deficit began to (increase,

decrease) _____

26. American:
a. imports increased sharply in the mid-1980s because

its national income (rose, fell) _____ rapidly after the 1980–1982 recession.
b. exports to many less developed nations declined because their foreign debt problem forced them to apply

(expansionary, restrictive) _____ monetary and fiscal policies to their economies and to (revalue,

devalue) _____ their currencies in order to

expand their (exports, imports) _____ and

reduce their _____

27. The effects of the American foreign-trade crisis have

been to (expand, contract) _____ real national output and employment in the United States, to (speed, slow) _____ its rate of inflation, to

(raise, lower) _____ the prices of goods it

imported, and to (increase, decrease) _____
American indebtedness to foreigners. It has also changed
the United States from a net (creditor, debtor)

_____ to a net _____ na-
tion.

28. Two policies to correct the trade deficit include a(n)

(expansion, contraction) _____ in the bud-
get deficit of the Federal government to help lower real
interest rates in the United States relative to other nations,

and a(n) _____ in the economies of major
trading partners, such as Japan and West Germany, to
help increase demand for exports for the United States.

■ **PROBLEMS AND PROJECTS**

1. Assume an American exporter sells $3 million worth of
wheat to an importer in Colombia. If the rate of exchange
for the Colombian peso is $0.02 (two cents), the wheat
has a total value of 150 million pesos.
  a. There are two ways the importer in Colombia may pay
for the wheat. It might write a check for 150 million pesos
drawn on its bank in Bogota and send it to the American
exporter.
  (1) The American exporter would then sell the check to
its bank in New Orleans and its demand deposit there

would increase by $_____ million.
  (2) This New Orleans bank now sells the check for 150
million pesos to a correspondent bank (an American commercial bank that keeps an account in the Bogota bank).
  (*a*) The New Orleans bank's account in the corre-

spondent bank increases by _____ million

(dollars, pesos) _____; and
  (*b*) the correspondent bank's account in the Bogota

bank increases by _____ million (pesos, dol-

lars) _____
  b. The second way for the importer to pay for the wheat
is to buy from its bank in Bogota a draft on an American
bank for $3 million, pay for this draft by writing a check for
150 million pesos drawn on the Bogota bank, and send
the draft to the American exporter.

  (1) The American exporter would then deposit the draft
in its account in the New Orleans bank and its demand

deposit account there would increase by $_____
million.
  (2) The New Orleans bank collects the amount of the
draft from the American bank on which it is drawn through
the Federal Reserve Banks.

  (*a*) Its account at the Fed increases by $_____
million; and
  (*b*) the account of the bank on which the draft was

drawn decreases by $_____ million.
  c. Regardless of the way employed by the Colombian
importer to pay for the wheat:
  (1) The export of the wheat created a (demand for,

supply of) _____ dollars and a

_____ pesos
  (2) The number of dollars owned by the American ex-

porter has (increased, decreased) _____
and the number of pesos owned by the Colombian im-

porter has _____

2. The table below contains hypothetical international balance of payments data for the United States. All figures
are in billions.
  a. Compute with the appropriate sign (+ or −) and
enter in the table the six missing items.
  b. The United States had a payments (deficit, surplus)

_____ of $_____

Current account	
(1) U.S. merchandise exports	$ +150
(2) U.S. merchandise imports	−200
(3) Balance of trade	_____
(4) U.S. exports of services	+75
(5) U.S. imports of services	−60
(6) Balance on goods and services	_____
(7) Net investment income	+12
(8) Net transfers	−7
(9) Balance on current account	_____
Capital account	
(10) Capital inflows to the U.S.	+80
(11) Capital outflows from the U.S.	−55
(12) Balance on capital account	_____
(13) Current and capital account balance	_____
(14) Official reserves	_____
	$ _____ 0

3. Following are the supply and demand schedules for the British pound.

Quantity of pounds supplied	Price $	Quantity of pounds demanded
400	5.00	100
360	4.50	200
300	4.00	300
286	3.50	400
267	3.00	500
240	2.50	620
200	2.00	788

a. If the exchange rates are flexible:
(1) What will be the rate of exchange for the pound?

$_____

(2) What will be the rate of exchange for the dollar?

£ _____

(3) How many pounds will be purchased in the market?

_____

(4) How many dollars will be purchased in the market?

_____

b. If the government of the United States wished to fix or "peg" the price of the pound at $5.00 it would have to (buy, sell) _____ (how many) _____ pounds for $_____

c. And if the British government wishes to fix the price of the dollar at £⅖ it would have to (buy, sell) _____ (how many) _____ pounds for $_____

■ **SELF-TEST**

Circle the T if the statement is true, the F if it is false.

1. The importation of goods and services by Americans from abroad creates a supply of dollars in the foreign exchange market. **T F**

2. American exports expand foreign money supplies and reduce the supply of money in the United States. **T F**

3. The international balance of payments of the United States records all the payments its residents receive from and make to the residents of foreign nations. **T F**

4. Exports are a debit item and are shown with a plus sign (+) and imports are a credit item and are shown with a minus sign (−) in the international balance of payments of a nation. **T F**

5. The United States had a balance of trade deficit in 1987. **T F**

6. The balance on goods and services of the United States in 1987 was positive (a surplus). **T F**

7. In 1987 the United States had positive net investment income and negative net transfers from the rest of the world. **T F**

8. In 1987 there was a net capital outflow from the United States and the United States had a capital-account deficit. **T F**

9. The United States would have a balance of payments surplus if the balance on its current and capital accounts were positive. **T F**

10. Any nation with a balance of payments deficit must reduce its official reserves. **T F**

11. The sum of a nation's current-account balance, its capital-account balance, and the change in its official reserves in any year is always equal to zero. **T F**

12. A large trade deficit in Brazil is harmful to consumers in Brazil. **T F**

13. If a nation has a balance of payments deficit and exchange rates are flexible, the price of that nation's money in the foreign exchange markets will fall and this will reduce its imports and increase its exports. **T F**

14. The expectations of speculators in the United States that the exchange rate for the Japanese yen will fall in the future will increase the supply of yen in the foreign exchange market and decrease the exchange rate for the yen. **T F**

15. Were the United States' terms of trade with Nigeria to worsen, Nigeria would obtain a greater quantity of American goods and services for every barrel of oil it exported to the United States. **T F**

16. If a nation wishes to fix (or "peg") the foreign exchange rate for the Swiss franc, it must buy Swiss francs with its own currency when the rate of exchange for the Swiss franc rises. **T F**

17. If exchange rates are stable and a nation has a payments surplus, prices and money incomes in that nation will tend to rise. **T F**

18. A nation using exchange controls to eliminate a payments surplus might depreciate its currency. **T F**

19. If country A defined its money as worth 100 grains of gold and country B defined its money as worth 20 grains of gold, then, ignoring packing, insuring, and shipping charges, 5 units of country A's money would be worth 1 unit of country B's money. **T F**

20. When nations were on the gold standard, foreign exchange rates fluctuated only within limits determined by the cost of moving gold from one nation to another. **T F**

21. If a nation maintains an exchange stabilization fund it would purchase its own money with gold or foreign monies when the value of its money falls in foreign exchange markets. **T F**

22. In the Bretton Woods system a nation could not devalue its currency by more than 10% without the permission of the International Fund. **T F**

23. In the Bretton Woods system a nation with persistent balance of payments surpluses had an undervalued currency and should have increased the pegged value of its currency. **T F**

24. Because the world's stock of gold did not grow very rapidly it became necessary for the United States to have payments deficits if international monetary reserves were to increase. **T F**

25. One of the basic shortcomings of the Bretton Woods system was its inability to bring about the changes in exchange rates needed to correct persistent payments deficits and surpluses. **T F**

26. Another basic shortcoming of the Bretton Woods system was its failure to maintain stable foreign exchange rates. **T F**

27. The United States shattered the Bretton Woods system in August 1971 by raising tariff rates on nearly all the goods it imported by an average of 40%. **T F**

28. Using the managed floating system of exchange rates, a nation with a persistent balance of payments surplus should allow the value of its currency in foreign exchange markets to decrease. **T F**

29. The foreign-trade crisis experienced by the American economy in the 1980s was characterized by sharp increases in American exports and slight increases in American imports. **T F**

30. The principal reason for the strong dollar in the early 1980s was the high real interest rates in the United States. **T F**

31. High real interest rates in the United States increased the attractiveness of financial investment in the United States to foreigners and the foreign demand for American dollars. **T F**

32. The rapid growth of the American economy after 1982 lessened its foreign-trade crisis because its exports are directly related to its national income. **T F**

33. The strong international value of the dollar in the

mid-1980s imposed special hardships on American firms dependent on export markets and those that competed with imported goods. **T F**

34. The negative net exports of the United States have increased the indebtedness of Americans to foreigners. **T F**

35. In 1985 the status of the United States was changed from net-debtor to net-creditor nation. **T F**

36. The major trading partners of the United States contend that it must work to reduce the Federal budget deficit if it is to achieve a better balance of international trade. **T F**

37. Improved economic growth in the major economies of the major trading partners of the United States would tend to worsen the trade deficit. **T F**

Circle the letter that corresponds to the best answer.

1. If an American could buy £25,000 for $100,000, the rate of exchange for the pound would be:
 (*a*) $40
 (*b*) $25
 (*c*) $4
 (*d*) $.25

2. American residents demand foreign currencies in order:
 (*a*) to pay for goods and services imported from foreign countries
 (*b*) to receive interest payments and dividends on their investments outside the United States
 (*c*) to make real and financial investments in foreign nations
 (*d*) to do all of the above

3. A nation's balance of trade is equal to its:
 (*a*) exports less its imports of merchandise (goods)
 (*b*) exports less its imports of goods and services
 (*c*) exports less its imports of goods and services plus its net investment income and net transfers
 (*d*) exports less its imports of goods, services, and capital

4. A nation's balance on the current account is equal to its:
 (*a*) exports less its imports of merchandise (goods)
 (*b*) exports less its imports of goods and services
 (*c*) exports less its imports of goods and services plus its net investment income and net transfers
 (*d*) exports less its imports of goods, services, and capital

5. The net investment income of the United States in its international balance of payments is:

(a) the interest income it receives from foreign residents

(b) the dividends it receives from foreign residents

(c) the interest payments and dividends it receives from foreign residents

(d) the interest payments, dividends, and transfers it receives from foreign residents

6. Capital flows into the United States include the purchase by foreign residents of:

(a) a factory building owned by Americans

(b) shares of stock owned by Americans

(c) bonds owned by Americans

(d) all of the above

7. An American current account deficit may be financed by:

(a) borrowing abroad

(b) selling real assets to foreigners

(c) selling financial assets to foreigners

(d) doing any of the above

8. The official reserves of the United States are:

(a) the stock of gold owned by the Federal government

(b) the foreign currencies owned by the Federal Reserve Banks

(c) the money supply of the United States

(d) all of the above

9. A nation may be able to correct or eliminate a persistent (long-term) balance of payments deficit by:

(a) lowering the barriers on imported goods

(b) reducing the international value of its currency

(c) expanding its national income

(d) reducing its official reserves

10. If exchange rates float freely the exchange rate for any currency is determined by:

(a) the demand for it

(b) the supply of it

(c) the demand for and the supply of it

(d) the official reserves that "back" it

11. If a nation had a balance of payments surplus and exchange rates floated freely:

(a) the foreign exchange rate for its currency would rise, its exports would increase, and its imports would decrease

(b) the foreign exchange rate for its currency would rise, its exports would decrease, and its imports would increase

(c) the foreign exchange rate for its currency would fall, its exports would increase, and its imports would decrease

(d) the foreign exchange rate for its currency would fall, its exports would decrease, and its imports would increase

12. Assuming exchange rates are flexible, which of the following should increase the dollar price of the Swedish krona?

(a) a rate of inflation greater in Sweden than in the United States

(b) real interest-rate increases greater in Sweden than in the United States

(c) national-income increases greater in Sweden than in the United States

(d) the increased preference of Swedes for American over Swedish automobiles

13. Which of the following would be one of the results associated with the use of freely floating foreign exchange rates to correct a nation's balance of payments surplus?

(a) the nation's terms of trade with other nations would be worsened

(b) importers in the nation who had made contracts for the future delivery of goods would find that they had to pay a higher price than expected for the goods

(c) if the nation were at full employment the decrease in exports and the increase in imports would be inflationary

(d) exporters in the nation would find their sales abroad had decreased

14. When exchange rates are fixed and a nation at full employment has a payments surplus, the result in that nation will be:

(a) a declining price level

(b) falling money income

(c) inflation

(d) rising real income

15. The use of exchange controls to eliminate a nation's balance of payments deficit results in:

(a) decreasing the nation's imports

(b) decreasing the nation's exports

(c) decreasing the nation's price level

(d) decreasing the nation's income

16. A nation with a balance of payments surplus might attempt to eliminate this surplus by employing:

(a) import quotas

(b) higher tariffs

(c) subsidies on items which the nation exports

(d) none of the above

17. Which one of the following conditions did a nation **not** have to fulfill if it was to be one under the gold standard?

(a) use only gold as a medium of exchange

(b) maintain a fixed relationship between its gold stock and its money supply

(c) allow gold to be freely exported from and imported into the nation

(d) define its monetary unit in terms of a fixed quantity of gold

18. If the nations of the world were on the gold standard and one nation has a balance of payments surplus:
(a) foreign exchange rates in that nation would rise toward the gold import point
(b) gold would tend to be imported into that country
(c) the level of prices in that country would tend to fall
(d) employment and output in that country would tend to fall

19. Under the gold standard a nation with a balance of payments deficit would experience all but one of the following. Which one?
(a) gold would flow out of the nation
(b) the nation's money supply would contract
(c) interest rates in the nation would fall
(d) real national output, employment, and prices in the nation would decline

20. Which of the following was the principal disadvantage of the gold standard?
(a) unstable foreign exchange rates
(b) persistent payments imbalances
(c) the uncertainties and decreased trade that resulted from the depreciation of gold
(d) the domestic macroeconomic adjustments experienced by a nation with a payments deficit or surplus

21. All but one of the following were elements in the adjustable-peg system of foreign exchange rates. Which one?
(a) each nation defined its monetary unit in terms of gold or dollars
(b) nations bought and sold their own currencies to stabilize exchange rates
(c) nations were allowed to devalue their currencies when faced with persistent payments deficits
(d) the deposit by all nations of their international reserves with the IMF

22. Which one of the following was *not* characteristic of the International Monetary Fund in the Bretton Woods system?
(a) made short-term loans to member nations with balance of payments deficits
(b) tried to maintain relatively stable exchange rates
(c) required member nations to maintain exchange stabilization funds
(d) extended long-term loans to less developed nations for the purpose of increasing their productive capacities

23. The objective of the adjustable-peg system was exchange rates which were:
(a) adjustable in the short run and fixed in the long run
(b) adjustable in both the short and long run

(c) fixed in both the short and long run
(d) fixed in the short run; adjustable in the long run

24. Which of the following is the best definition of international monetary reserves in the Bretton Woods system?
(a) gold
(b) dollars
(c) gold and dollars
(d) gold, dollars, and British pounds

25. The dilemma created by the U.S. payments deficits was that:
(a) to maintain the status of the dollar as an acceptable international monetary reserve the deficit had to be reduced and to increase these reserves the deficits had to be continued
(b) to maintain the status of the dollar the deficit had to be continued and to increase reserves the deficit had to be eliminated
(c) to maintain the status of the dollar the deficit had to be increased and to expand reserves the deficit had to be reduced
(d) to maintain the status of the dollar the deficit had to be reduced and to expand reserves the deficit had to be reduced

26. "Floating" the dollar means:
(a) the value of the dollar is determined by the demand for and the supply of the dollar
(b) the dollar price of gold has been increased
(c) the price of the dollar has been allowed to crawl upward at the rate of one-fourth of 1% a month
(d) the IMF decreased the value of the dollar by 10%

27. A system of managed floating exchange rates:
(a) allows nations to stabilize exchange rates in the short term
(b) requires nations to stabilize exchange rates in the long term
(c) entails stable exchange rates in both the short and long term
(d) none of the above

28. Floating exchange rates:
(a) tend to correct payments imbalances
(b) reduce the uncertainties and risks associated with international trade
(c) increase the world's need for international monetary reserves
(d) tend to expand the volume of world trade

29. The foreign-trade crisis of the United States is the:
(a) increases in its merchandise and current-account surpluses
(b) decreases in its merchandise and current-account surpluses

(c) increases in its merchandise and current-account deficits

(d) decreases in its merchandise and current-account deficits

30. Which of the following is *not* one of the causes of the growth of American trade deficits during the 1980s?

(a) the strong dollar

(b) the rapid growth of the American economy

(c) the reduced imports of heavily indebted less developed nations from the United States

(d) the high rate of inflation experienced by the American economy relative to rates in other nations

31. High real interest rates in the United States during the mid-1980s were the result of all but one of the following. Which one?

(a) the budget deficits of the Federal government

(b) the low demand of foreign investors for the dollar

(c) the tight money policy of the Federal Reserve Banks

(d) the relatively low rate of inflation in the United States

32. The external debt problems of less developed nations forced many of them to apply:

(a) restrictive monetary and fiscal policies and to devalue their currencies

(b) restrictive monetary and fiscal policies and to revalue their currencies

(c) expansionary monetary and fiscal policies and to devalue their currencies

(d) expansionary monetary and fiscal policies and to revalue their currencies

33. The effect of the trade deficit in the United States during the early and mid-1980s was to:

(a) increase the rate of inflation

(b) increase output and employment

(c) decrease aggregate demand

(d) decrease the international value of the dollar

34. One policy solution for the trade crisis is to reduce the Federal-budget deficit because it will tend to:

(a) increase the demand for dollars and real interest rates in the United States

(b) increase the demand for dollars and decrease real interest rates in the United States

(c) decrease the demand for dollars and real interest rates in the United States

(d) decrease the demand for dollars and increase real interest rates in the United States

35. It is suggested that the large trade deficits of the United States can best be reduced with:

(a) an easy money policy in the United States

(b) an expansionary fiscal policy in the United States

(c) economic policies that increase the rate of growth in the G-7 nations

(d) an appreciation in the value of the currencies of less developed nations

■ DISCUSSION QUESTIONS

1. What is foreign exchange and the foreign exchange rate? Who are the demanders and suppliers of a particular foreign exchange, say, the French franc? Why is a buyer (demander) in the foreign exchange markets always a seller (supplier) also?

2. What is meant when it is said that "a nation's exports pay for its imports"? Do nations pay for all their imports with exports?

3. What is an international balance of payments? What are the principal sections in a nation's international balance of payments and what are the principal "balances" to be found in it?

4. How can a nation finance a current account deficit and what can it do with a current account surplus? How does a nation finance a balance of payments deficit and what does it do with a balance of payments surplus?

5. Is it good or bad for a nation to have a balance of payments deficit or surplus?

6. What types of events cause the exchange rate for a foreign currency to appreciate or to depreciate? How will each of these events affect the exchange rate for a foreign money and for a nation's own money?

7. How can freely floating foreign exchange rates eliminate balance of payments deficits and surpluses? What are the problems associated with this method of correcting payments imbalances?

8. How may a nation employ its international monetary reserves to fix or "peg" foreign exchange rates? Be precise. How does a nation obtain or acquire these monetary reserves?

9. What kinds of trade controls may nations with payments deficits employ to eliminate their deficits?

10. How can foreign exchange controls be used to restore international equilibrium? Why do such exchange controls necessarily involve the rationing of foreign exchange? What effect do these controls have upon prices, output, and employment in nations that use them?

11. If foreign exchange rates are fixed, what kind of domestic macroeconomic adjustments are required to eliminate a payments deficit? To eliminate a payments surplus?

12. When was a nation on the gold standard? How did the international gold standard correct payments imbalances? What were the disadvantages of this method of eliminating payments deficits and surpluses?

13. Why does the operation of the international gold standard ensure relatively stable foreign exchange rates, that is, rates which fluctuate only within very narrow limits? What are limits and what are the advantages of stable exchange rates?

14. What is the "critical difference" between the adjustments necessary to correct payments deficits and surpluses under the gold standard and those necessary when exchange rates are flexible? How did this difference lead to the demise of the gold standard during the 1930s?

15. Explain:
(a) why the International Monetary Fund was established and what the objectives of the adjustable-peg (or Bretton Woods) system were
(b) what the adjustable-peg system was and the basic means it employed to stabilize exchange rates in the short run; and
(c) when and how the system was to adjust exchange rates in the long run.

16. What did nations use as international monetary reserves under the Bretton Woods system? Why was the dollar used by nations as an international money and how could they acquire additional dollars?

17. Explain the dilemma created by the need for expanding international monetary reserves and for maintaining the status of the dollar.

18. Why and how did the United States shatter the Bretton Woods system in 1971? If the international value of the dollar is no longer determined by the amount of gold for which it can be exchanged, what does determine its value?

19. Explain what is meant by a managed floating system of foreign exchange rates. When are exchange rates managed and when are they allowed to float?

20. Explain the arguments of the proponents and the critics of the managed floating system.

21. What was the foreign-trade crisis of the United States during the 1980s? What were
(a) its causes; and
(b) its effects on the American economy?

22. What policies are needed to ease the trade crisis of the United States and how would such policies affect output and employment in the United States?

■ **ANSWERS**

CHAPTER 23 EXCHANGE RATES, THE BALANCE OF PAYMENTS, AND THE TRADE "CRISIS"

Fill-in questions

1. francs, dollar

2. 3⅓

3. a. supply of, demand for, increase, decrease; b. demand for, supply of, decrease, increase

4. transportation, insurance (either order), interest, dividends (either order)

5. the other nations of the world: a. credit, + ; b. debit, −

6. a. less, merchandise; b. greater; c. investment, transfers, negative

7. a. in that nation, other nations, in other nations, that nation, real, financial (either order); b. greater

8. a. selling, borrowing; b. buy, lend

9. foreign monies, central; a. decrease; b. increase; c. zero

10. negative, decrease, positive, increase

11. a. depreciate, appreciate; b. decrease, increase, decrease

12. a. depreciate; b. appreciate; c. depreciate; d. depreciate; e. depreciate

13. diminish, worsened, recession, inflation (either order)

14. a. sell; b. buy

15. a. taxing, subsidizing; b. import, export, government

16. contractionary, recession

17. gold, money, stock, exported, imported

18. a. stable; b. (1) out of, (2) decreased, rose, (3) fell, recession

19. fixed, adjustable-peg; a. gold, dollars (either order); b. buying, exchange-stabilization, selling, borrowing from; c. devalue; d. gold, dollars (either order); e. stable, flexible

20. a. deficits; b. gold; c. decreased; d. eliminated, continued

21. gold, market forces (demand and supply), fixed, floating

22. managed floating; a. stable; b. imbalances

23. increases, deficits, imports, exports

24. a. strong; b. rapid; c. reduced

25. a. more, less, decreased, increased; b. high, deficits, tight, low; c. fell, profits, G-7; d. decrease

26. a. rose; b. restrictive, devalue, exports, imports

27. contract, slow, lower, increase, creditor, debtor

28. contraction, expansion

Problems and projects

1. *a.* (1) 3, (2) (*a*) 3, dollars, (*b*) 150, pesos; *b.* (1) 3, (2) (*a*) 3, (*b*) 3; *c.* (1) demand for, supply of, (2) increased, decreased

2. *a.* −50, −35, −30, +25, −5, +5; *b.* deficit, 5

3. *a.* (1) 4.00, (2) ¼, (3) 300, (4) 1200; *b.* buy, 300, 1500; *c.* sell, 380, 950

Self-test

1. T; **2.** F; **3.** T; **4.** F; **5.** T; **6.** F; **7.** T; **8.** F; **9.** T; **10.** T; **11.** T; **12.** F; **13.** T; **14.** T; **15.** T; **16.** F; **17.** T; **18.** F; **19.** F; **20.** T; **21.** T; **22.** T; **23.** T; **24.** T; **25.** T; **26.** F; **27.** F; **28.** F; **29.** F; **30.** T; **31.** T; **32.** F; **33.** T; **34.** T; **35.** F; **36.** T; **37.** F

1. *c;* **2.** *d;* **3.** *a;* **4.** *c;* **5.** *c;* **6.** *d;* **7.** *d;* **8.** *b;* **9.** *b;* **10.** *c;* **11.** *b;* **12.** *b;* **13.** *d;* **14.** *c:* **15.** *a;* **16.** *d;* **17.** *a;* **18.** *b;* **19.** *c;* **20.** *d;* **21.** *d;* **22.** *d;* **23.** *d;* **24.** *c;* **25.** *a;* **26.** *a;* **27.** *a;* **28.** *a;* **29.** *c;* **30.** *d;* **31.** *b;* **32.** *a;* **33.** *c;* **34.** *c;* **35.** *c*

Growth and the less developed countries

This chapter looks at the problem of raising the standard of living faced by the less developed nations of the world. Economic growth both in these less developed nations and in the developed or the industrially advanced nations requires that the nation's resources and technological knowledge be expanded. Application of this principle in the less developed nations, however, faces a set of obstacles quite different from those that limit economic growth in the United States. The emphasis in this chapter is on the obstacles to economic growth in the poor and less developed nations of the world. You should concentrate your attention on these obstacles. You will then understand why increasing the quantity and quality of resources and improving technology is especially difficult in the world's less developed nations.

The existence of these special obstacles does not mean that increases in the living standards of the less developed nations are impossible. What it does mean is that the less developed nations are going to have to do things that did not need to be done in the United States (or in the other industrial nations) in order to grow. Governments of the poor countries will have to take an active role in promoting growth and limit public sector problems for economic development. Population increases are going to have to be limited. And dramatic changes in social practices and institutions will be required. If these things are not done it will not be possible to eliminate or reduce the obstacles to growth.

No matter how successful the less developed nations are in eliminating these obstacles they probably will still not be able to grow very rapidly without the help of the developed nations. There seem to be at least two reasons why the developed nations will offer the less developed ones some amount of assistance. The citizens of the more advanced nations feel some moral obligation to aid the less fortunate peoples of the world; and they may feel it is in their own self-interest to aid the poor of the world.

The debts of less developed countries have risen significantly in the past two decades. In fact, in 1987 the external debt of less developed nations that was owed to foreign governments and financial institutions was equal to about 39% of the combined gross national products of the less developed nations. The causes of this debt crisis are due in part to the events of the 1970s and early 1980s. During this period, less developed nations had to pay more for imported oil, incurred high borrowing costs because of higher interest rates, and faced reduced net export earnings because of the appreciation of the dollar. In recent years, to reduce the debt burdens these nations have been forced to enact restrictive domestic programs that often have adverse effects on net export earnings and economic growth. There are two proposed solutions to the debt crisis, but as you will learn, each proposal has some adverse secondary effects.

Less developed nations have (on the whole) grown during the past twenty-five years; but the rate at which they have grown has been about the same as that at which the developed nations have grown. This has meant (because the GNPs per capita in the former nations were initially so much smaller) that the gap between the two groups has widened over this period of time. For this and other reasons less developed countries have become increasingly dissatisfied with their relationships with the advanced industrial nations; and they have argued for the establishment of a New International Economic Order. Here you should look at these relationships from the viewpoint of the less developed nations that are not oil exporters. To understand the proposals they have made you must understand why they feel their relationships with the developed nations benefit mostly the developed and largely hurt the less developed nations.

■ CHECKLIST

When you have studied this chapter you should be able to:

☐ Distinguish between industrially advanced, oil-exporting, and less developed countries and describe the economic characteristics of the three groups.

☐ Explain why the gap between the standards of living in less developed countries and the industrially advanced countries has widened and calculate differences when given a simple example.

☐ Enumerate the human implications of the poverty in the less developed nations.

☐ Identify the four factors which make growth in real GNP possible.

☐ Identify the three specific problems related to human resources that plague the less developed nations; and the problems population growth creates in these nations.

☐ Describe the conditions of unemployment and underemployment in less developed countries.

☐ State reasons for low labor productivity in less developed countries.

☐ Present three reasons for the emphasis on capital formation in the less developed nations; and explain the obstacles to saving and the obstacles to investment in these nations.

☐ Explain why transferring the technologies used in the industrially advanced nations to the less developed ones may not be a realistic method of improving the technology of the latter nations.

☐ Enumerate several of the sociocultural and institutional factors which inhibit growth in the less developed nations.

☐ Explain why poverty in the poor nations is a vicious circle.

☐ List five reasons why governments in the less developed nations will have to play a crucial role if the vicious circle is to be broken.

☐ Describe the problems with the public sector in fostering economic development.

☐ Identify the three ways in which the industrially advanced nations may help the less developed nations to grow economically.

☐ Explain the causes and consequences of the debt crisis in less developed countries; evaluate the proposed solutions.

☐ State the six proposals made by less developed nations that would, if implemented, result in a New International Economic Order; and the arguments made by them in support of these proposals.

■ **CHAPTER OUTLINE**

1. There is considerable inequality in income among nations.

a. Nations can be classified into three major groups.

(1) Industrially advanced countries (IACs) are characterized by high per capita incomes, large stocks of capital goods, advanced technology for production, and a highly educated work force. These nations include the United States, Canada, Japan, Australia, New Zealand and nations in Western Europe.

(2) Oil exporting countries such Saudia Arabia and Kuwait have high per capita incomes, but are not highly industrialized.

(3) Most of the remaining 97 nations are considered less developed countries (LDCs). LDCs are poor, not industrialized, are heavily dependent on agriculture, have high population growth, and have low rates of literacy. These nations comprise about three-fourths of the world's population. Of this group, there are 58 middle-income LDCs with average annual per capita income of $1,270 and 39 low-income LDCs with per capita income averaging $270.

b. The newly industrialized nations such as Hong Kong, South Korea, Taiwan, and Singapore have experienced high rates of economic growth in the 1980s while many other LDCs have experienced a decrease in GNP per capita; if the growth rates were the same for high and low income nations, the gap in per capita income would widen because the income base is higher.

c. Compared with the developed nations, LDCs have not only lower per capita incomes but also lower life expectancies, higher infant mortality, lower literacy rates, less food per person, and fewer nonhuman sources of energy.

2. Economic growth requires that the quantity and quality of economic resources be increased and that technological knowledge be expanded; but there are many obstacles to such a program in LDCs.

a. Many (but not all) LDCs possess inadequate natural resources and the farm products which LDCs typically export are subject to significant price variation.

b. Many LDCs are overpopulated, there is substantial unemployment and underemployment of labor, and labor productivity is low.

c. LDCs are short of capital goods and these nations find it difficult to accumulate capital because of low savings potential, the flight of capital to IACs, and the absence of investors and incentives to invest.

d. Technological knowledge is primitive in LDCs; although they might adopt the technologies of the advanced nations, those technologies are not always appropriate to the resource endowments of the LDCs and they must therefore develop their own technologies.

e. In addition, it is difficult for LDCs to alter the social, cultural, and institutional environment in the process of promoting economic growth.

3. In summary, LDCs save little and, therefore, invest little in real and human capital because they are poor; and because they do not invest, their outputs per capita remain low and they remain poor. Even if the vicious circle were to be broken, a rapid increase in population would leave the standard of living unchanged.

4. There are differing views about the role that government plays in fostering economic growth in LDCs.

a. The positive view holds that in the initial stages of economic development government action is needed to help overcome such obstacles as the lack of law and order, entrepreneurship, and infrastructure. Government policies may also assist capital formation, and in resolving social and institutional problems.

b. There are also problems and disadvantages with government involvement in promoting growth from such factors as bureaucratic impediments, corruption, maladministration, and the importance of political objectives over economic goals. The use of central planning restricts competition and individual incentives, which are important ingredients in the growth process.

5. Industrially advanced nations of the world can help the poor nations develop in a number of ways.

a. They can lower the barriers which prevent the LDCs from selling their products in the developed nations.

b. Loans and grants from governments and international organizations also enable the LDCs to accumulate capital.

c. The flow of private capital from industrially advanced nations helps the LDCs increase their productive capacities and per capita outputs.

6. There is a crisis because of the large external debts of LDCs.

a. The debt that LDCs owe to foreign governments and foreign financial institutions has increased significantly over the last two decades, and is roughly equal to 39% of the total amount of the gross national products of LDCs, but for some countries it is much larger.

b. The causes of the debt crisis rest with world events during the 1970s and early 1980s.

(1) Higher prices for imported oil during the 1970s and early 1980s forced LDCs to borrow to cover current account deficits.

(2) The United States and other industrially advanced nations imposed tight monetary policies in the early 1980s to restrain inflation but this policy raised interest rates and costs for LDC borrowing and brought on recession to industrially advanced nations, which reduced imports from LDCs.

(3) The appreciation in the international value of the dollar during the 1981–1985 period forced LDCs to pay more for imported manufactured goods from the United States and to receive less in return for exports to the United States.

(4) And, severe debt problems in Mexico in 1982 signaled problems with LDC loans in the financial community and resulted in reduced loans from private sources; increasing Federal budget deficits in the United States during most of the 1980s absorbed more private capital that might otherwise be lent to LDCs.

c. In recent years, the International Monetary Fund worked with nations on an individual basis to resolve debt problems; in return for debt rescheduling, LDCs often must impose austerity measures and use net export earning to pay for debt retirement, but these conditions have reduced economic development funds, retarded economic growth, and lowered capital income.

d. The conditions of the 1970s and 1980s that contributed to the LDC debt crisis have reversed and the problem has eased somewhat. For the future, the two basic solutions focus on continuation of country-by-country negotiations, which may require too many years to solve the problem, and debt forgiveness by industrially advanced countries, which might have an adverse effect on private lending.

7. Because they have not grown so rapidly as they had hoped and are dissatisfied with their relationship with industrially advanced nations, the LDCs have urged the creation of a New International Economic Order which would involve six controversial features: changing the rules of the game in world economic institutions, preferential tariff treatment, less exploitation by and dependence on foreign corporations, improved terms of trade for LDC products, debt relief, and increased foreign aid from governments in industrially advanced nations.

■ **IMPORTANT TERMS**

Less developed countries (LDCs)

Industrially advanced countries (IACs)

Unemployment

Underemployment

Investment in human capital

Brain drain

Domestic capital formation

Capital flight

Infrastructure

Nonfinancial (in-kind) investment

Capital-saving technological advance

Capital-using technological advance

The will to develop

World Bank

Neocolonialism

New International Economic Order (NIEO)

Preferential tariff treatment

Stabilization fund

Terms of trade

■ **FILL-IN QUESTIONS**

1. There is income inequality among nations.

a. Industrially advanced countries (IACs) have (high, low) _____ per capita incomes while there are less developed nations (LDCs) that have _____ per capita incomes. Oil exporting nations have _____ per capita income but are not highly industrialized.

b. Among the _____ LDCs, there is a group of 58 nations which are classified as (middle, low) _____

-income LDCs with per capita GNP of $_____ and 39 nations which are classified as _____-income LDCs with per capita GNP of $_____ . In 1986, GNP of the United States was $_____ trillion but the combined GNP of the _____ LDCs that year was $_____ trillion.

c. Singapore, Hong Kong, South Korea, and Taiwan are considered _____ nations and had rates of economic growth in real GNP from 1960–1987 of _____ to _____%; many LDCs have experienced _____ real per capita GNP in the 1980s.

d. IACs have a (higher, lower) _____ starting base for per capita income than LDCs, so the same percentage growth rate for both IACs and LDCs means an increase in the _____ income gap.

e. Also, low per capita income in LDCs means that life _____, adult _____, daily _____ supply, and _____ consumption are (higher, lower) _____ and infant mortality is _____

2. The process for economic growth is the same for IACs and LDCs. It involves more _____ use of existing resources and also increasing supplies of _____ _____, _____, _____, and improving its _____

3. The distribution of natural resources among LDCs is (even, uneven) _____; many LDCs lack vital natural resources. Although _____ nations have been able to use oil resources for economic growth, much of the natural resources in LDCs are owned or controlled by companies in _____; exports of products from LDCs are subject to _____ fluctuations.

4. In terms of human resources:

a. Many LDCs are _____ and have population growth rates of about _____% compared to _____% for IACs; given the growth rate for LDCs, "rule of 70" would suggest that the population of LDCs will double in about _____ years. Rapid population growth can cause per capita GNP to (increase, decrease) _____

b. There is both _____ and _____ among workers in LDCs.

c. Labor _____ is also very low in most LDCs in part because these nations have not been able to invest in _____; and the so-called _____ contributes to the decline in skill level and productivity as the best-trained workers leave LDCs to work in IACs.

5. Capital accumulation is critical to the development of LDCs.

a. If there were more capital goods, this would improve _____ and help boost per capita GNP; an increase in capital goods is necessary because the _____ of arable land is limited; the process of capital formation is "cumulative," investment increases the (population, output, natural resources) _____ _____ of the economy and this in turn makes it possible for the economy to save more and invest more in capital goods.

b. The formation of domestic capital requires that a nation save and invest. The former is difficult in LDCs because of a low _____ and the latter is difficult because of a lack of _____ and of _____ to invest; there is also the problem of _____ where savings are transferred to IACs.

c. Many LDCs do not have much public capital goods, or _____, that are necessary for productive _____ investment.

d. Nonfinancial (or in-kind) investment involves the transfer of surplus labor from (agriculture, industry) _____ to the improvement of agricultural facilities or the _____

6. The technologies used in the advanced industrial nations might be borrowed by and used in the less developed nations; but

a. the technologies used in the advanced nations are based upon a labor force that is (skilled, unskilled) _____, labor that is relatively (abundant, scarce) _____, and capital that is relatively _____, and their technologies tend to be (labor, capital)-_____ using; while

b. the technologies required in the underdeveloped

countries must be based on a labor force that is
_____, labor that is relatively
_____, and capital that is relatively
_____, and their technologies need to be
_____-using.

   c. If technological advances make it possible to replace a worn-out plow, costing $10 when new, with a new $5 plow, the technological advance is capital (saving, using) _____

7. The "will to develop" in less developed nations involves a willingness to change the _____
and _____ arrangements of the nation.

8. In most less developed nations saving is small because the _____ per capita is small. Because saving is small, _____ in real and human capital is also small. And for this reason the _____ of labor and _____ per capita remain small.

9. List five reasons why the role of government in fostering economic development will need to be large in the less developed nations, especially during the early stages of development:

   a. _____

   b. _____

   c. _____

   d. _____

   e. _____

10. There can also be _____ with government's role in the economy of LDCs because government _____ can impede social and economic change, central planners give too much emphasis to _____ objectives rather than economic objectives, and there can be _____-administration and _____ in government. Central planning models also restrict _____ and individual _____ which are factors in economic development.

11. The three major ways in which the United States can assist economic development in the LDCs are _____
_____

_____,
and _____

12. The LDC debt crisis arises from the large (internal, external) _____ debts that have accumulated over the past two decades. In 1987, these debts were about $_____ billion and equal to about _____% of the total of the gross national products of LDCs.

13. The causes of the LDC debt crisis are due to world events during the 1970s and early 1980s.

   a. Oil prices (increased, decreased) _____
during the 1970s and this event _____ the borrowing needs of LDCs to pay for imported oil.

   b. In the early 1980s, the United States had a (tight, easy) _____ monetary policy that (increased, decreased) _____ real interest rates and _____ the cost to LDCs of servicing debts; the recession of the early 1980s in the United States also _____ the exports of farm products from LDCs to the United States.

   c. Over the 1981–1984 period, the international value of the dollar (appreciated, depreciated) _____ which meant that LDCs had to pay (more, less) _____ for imports and receive _____ in return for exports.

   d. The debt crisis in _____ in 1982 shook confidence in LDCs and reduced private _____ by banks and financial institutions; the increasing Federal budget _____ during the early 1980s also absorbed more private capital.

14. The economic consequence of the LDC debt crisis has been that creditor nations and the International Monetary Fund have _____ debts to reduce the annual burden of interest and principal repayments; in return, LDCs have had to implement domestic _____ programs that tend to reduce the _____ of living and transfer _____ earnings to debt repayment and away from investment; some experts have also worried that the LDCs' debts are a threat to the _____ systems of the _____

15. One solution to the LDC debt crisis is to negotiate (separately with, with the group of) _____ indebted nations, but the problem is that it will take too many _____ and thwart _____ in those LDCs; another solution is to _____ the debts but this action might have an adverse effect on private lending and encourage further _____.

16. In pressing for the establishment of a New International Economic Order the LDCs have argued (among other things) that:

a. because LDCs had no part in their formation and because they are "stacked" against them, there should be a change in the _____ by which international trade, finance, and investment are conducted;

b. the IACs, to deprive LDCs of their export markets, have erected barriers to _____ and the LDCs should be accorded preferential _____

c. the dealings of the LDCs with corporations in the advanced nations have led to the greater part of the benefits from the _____ of their natural resources going to others and to the increased _____ of LDCs on world markets;

d. there has been, as a result of the higher prices charged for manufactured goods by corporations in the IACs, a shift against them in the _____ of _____ and that these might be improved by the establishment of _____ funds and by _____

e. except for the oil-exporting countries, the size of their _____ abroad has increased and these should either be _____ or _____

f. the foreign aid which they have received has been _____ and should be increased to _____% of the GNP of the IACs, have no _____ attached to it, and should be provided on a long-term and _____ basis.

■ **PROBLEMS AND PROJECTS**

1. Suppose that the real GNP per capita in the average industrially advanced nation is $8000 per year and in the average less developed nation is $500 per year.

a. The gap between their standards of living is $_____ per year.

b. If GNP per capita were to grow at a rate of 5% during a year in both the industrially advanced and the less developed nations:

(1) the standard of living in the industrially advanced nations would rise to $_____ a year;

(2) the standard of living in the less developed nations would rise to $_____ a year; and

(3) the gap between their standards of living would (narrow, widen) _____ to $_____ a year.

2. While economic conditions are not identical in all less developed nations, there are certain conditions common to or typical of most of them. In the spaces after each of the following characteristics, indicate briefly the nature of this characteristic in most less developed nations.

a. Standard of living (per capita income). _____

b. Average life expectancy. _____

c. Extent of unemployment. _____

d. Literacy. _____

e. Technology. _____

f. Percentage of the population engaged in agriculture. _____

g. Size of the population relative to the land and capital available. _____

h. The birth and death rates. _____

i. Quality of the labor force. _____

j. Amount of capital equipment relative to the labor force. _____

k. Level of saving. _____

l. Incentive to invest. _____

m. Amount of basic social capital. _____

n. Extent of industrialization. _____

o. Size and quality of the entrepreneurial class and the supervisory class. _____

p. Per capita public expenditures for education and per capita energy consumpion. _____

q. Per capita consumption of food. _____

r. Disease and malnutrition. _____

3. Suppose that it takes a minimum of 5 units of food to keep a person alive for a year, that the population can double itself every 10 years, and that the food supply can increase every 10 years by an amount equal to what it was in the beginning (year 0).

a. Assume that both the population and the food supply grow at these rates. Complete the following table by computing the size of the population and the food supply in years 10 through 60.

Year	Food supply	Population
0	200	20
10	_____	_____
20	_____	_____
30	_____	_____
40	_____	_____
50	_____	_____
60	_____	_____

b. What happens to the relationship between the food supply and the population in the 30th year?

_____

c. What would actually prevent the population from growing at this rate following the 30th year?

_____

d. Assuming that the actual population growth in the years following the 30th does not outrun the food supply, what would be the size of the population in:

(1) Year 40: _____

(2) Year 50: _____

(3) Year 60: _____

e. Explain why the standard of living failed to increase in the years following the 30th even though the food supply increased by 75% between years 30 and 60. _____

_____

■ SELF-TEST

Circle the T if the statement is true, the F if it is false.

1. About three-fourths of the world's population lives in 97 less developed countries. **T F**

2. The United States has about 5% of the world's population and produces approximately one-fourth of the world's output. **T F**

3. Per capita GNP in 1986 was about $6000 in India and about $17,500 in the United States. **T F**

4. The difference between the per capita incomes in the less developed nations and the per capita incomes in the developed nations has decreased over the past years. **T F**

5. Economic growth in both industrially advanced and less developed nations requires using resources more efficiently or increasing the supplies of these resources. **T F**

6. It is impossible to achieve a high standard of living with a small supply of natural resources. **T F**

7. Nations with large populations are less developed. **T F**

8. The chief factor preventing the elimination of unemployment in the less developed nations is the small number of job openings available in the cities. **T F**

9. Saving in LDCs is a smaller percentage of national output than in IACs, and this is the chief reason total saving in LDCs is small. **T F**

10. Before private investment can be increased in less developed nations it is necessary to reduce the amount of investment in infrastructure. **T F**

11. Technological advances in LDCs will be made rapidly because they do not require pushing forward the frontiers of technological knowledge and the technologies used in IACs can be easily transferred to the less developed ones. **T F**

12. When technological advances are capital-saving it is possible for an economy to increase its productivity without any *net* investment in capital goods. **T F**

13. Emancipation from custom and tradition is often the fundamental prerequisite of economic development. **T F**

14. The policies of the governments of less developed nations have often tended to reduce the incentives of foreigners to invest in the less developed nations. **T F**

15. Governments always play a positive role in the economic development of LDCs. **T F**

16. LDCs will not need foreign aid if the developed nations will reduce tariffs and import quotas on the goods which the less developed nations export. **T F**

17. An increase in the output and employment of the United States works to the advantage of the less developed nations because it provides the less developed nations with larger markets for their exports. **T F**

18. Foreign aid from the United States to the less developed nations has consistently exceeded 1% of its GNP.
T   F

19. Many in LDCs believe that the public and private aid extended by the IACs to the LDCs is designed to increase profits in the former and to exploit the latter countries.
T   F

20. In 1987 the total external debts of LDCs was equal to about 39% of the total of the gross national products of LDCs.
T   F

21. During the 1970s and early 1980s, higher prices on imported oil, a fall in the export earnings of LDCs, an appreciation of the dollar, and a decrease in private lending all contributed to create the LDC debt crisis.
T   F

22. The simplest solution to the LDC debt crisis and the one with fewest repercussions would be to have the creditors in IACs forgive the debts of LDCs.
T   F

23. Were a fund to be established to stabilize the price of a commodity such as copper, the fund would be used to purchase the commodity when its price fell.
T   F

24. Preferential tariff treatment for LDCs means that the IACs would set their tariffs on commodities imported from LDCs below those established for the same commodities imported from IACs.
T   F

25. One of the proposals associated with the establishment of a New International Economic Order is that the aid from IACs to LDCs be automatic, have no "strings" attached to it, and equal at least .7% of the GNPs of the IACs.
T   F

Circle the letter that corresponds to the best answer.

1. Which of the following would be considered a LDC?
(*a*) China
(*b*) Kuwait
(*c*) Taiwan
(*d*) New Zealand

2. If per capita income is $600 a year in a LDC and per capita income is $12,000 in an IAC, then a 2% growth rate increases the absolute income gap by:
(*a*) $120
(*b*) $228
(*c*) $240
(*d*) $252

3. When the average annual rate of growth in per capita GNP in a LDC is 1%, approximately how many years will it take for the standard of living to double?

(*a*) 27 years
(*b*) 35 years
(*c*) 57 years
(*d*) 70 years

4. Which of the following is high in the less developed nations?
(*a*) life expectancy
(*b*) infant mortality
(*c*) literacy
(*d*) per capita energy consumption

5. Which of the following is the most serious obstacle to economic growth in less developed nations?
(*a*) the supply of natural resources
(*b*) the size and quality of the labor force
(*c*) the supply of capital equipment
(*d*) technological knowledge

6. An increase in the total output of consumer goods in a less developed nation may not increase the average standard of living because:
(*a*) of diminishing returns
(*b*) it may provoke an increase in the population
(*c*) of disguised unemployment
(*d*) the quality of the labor force is so poor

7. Which of the following best describes the unemployment found in the less developed nations?
(*a*) the result of cyclical fluctuations in aggregate demand
(*b*) the agricultural workers who have migrated from rural to urban areas and failed to find employment in the cities
(*c*) the workers in excess of the optimum population
(*d*) workers whose productivity is subject to diminishing returns

8. Which of the following is *not* a reason for placing special emphasis on capital accumulation in less developed nations?
(*a*) the inflexible supply of arable land
(*b*) the low productivity of workers
(*c*) the low marginal contribution of capital equipment
(*d*) the possibility that capital accumulation will be "cumulative"

9. Which of the following is *not* a factor limiting saving in less developed nations?
(*a*) the output of the economy is too low to permit a large volume of saving
(*b*) those who do save do not make their saving available to their own economies
(*c*) the highly unequal distribution of income
(*d*) the low marginal contribution of capital equipment to production

10. When citizens of LDCs transfer savings or invest

savings in IACs, it is referred to as:
(a) brain drain
(b) capital flight
(c) savings potential
(d) in-kind investment

11. Which of the following is **not** an obstacle to capital formation (investment) in less developed nations?
(a) the absence of strong incentives to invest
(b) the lack of basic social capital
(c) the absence of a large entrepreneurial class
(d) the lack of capital-saving changes in technology

12. Which of the following is an example of infrastructure?
(a) a steel plant
(b) an electric power plant
(c) a farm
(d) a deposit in a financial institution

13. Which of the following seems to be the **most** needed and widespread institutional change required of less developed nations?
(a) adoption of birth control
(b) development of strong labor unions
(c) increase in the nation's public capital
(d) land reform

14. Assume the total real output of a LDC increases from $100 billion to $115.5 billion while its population expands from 200 million to 210 million people. Real income per capita has, as a result, increased by:
(a) $50
(b) $100
(c) $150
(d) $200

15. The role of government in the early stages of economic development will probably be a major one for several reasons. Which one of the following is **not** one of these reasons?
(a) only government can provide a larger amount of the needed infrastructure
(b) the absence of private entrepreneurs to accumulate capital and take risks
(c) the necessity of creating **new** money to finance capital accumulation
(d) the slowness and uncertainty of the market system in fostering development

16. In recent years, many LDCs have come to recognize that:
(a) competition and economic incentives for individuals are necessary for economic development
(b) there are few disadvantages from government involvement in the development process

(c) private capital is not required for economic development
(d) the World Bank serves as an institutional barrier to economic growth

17. An event that occurred during the 1970s or early 1980s that contributed to the LDC debt crisis was:
(a) a sharp decline in price of oil charged by OPEC nations
(b) a depreciation in the international value of the dollar
(c) a tight monetary policy and recession in the United States
(d) a rise in net export earnings of the LDCs

18. To raise funds to pay interest and principal on external debt, LDCs have had to put into place domestic economic policies that tend to:
(a) decrease imports, increase exports, and lower the standard of living
(b) increase imports, decrease exports, and lower the standard of living
(c) decrease imports, decrease exports, and lower the standard of living
(d) increase imports, decrease exports, and raise the standard of living

19. The terms of trade for a nation exporting tin worsen whenever:
(a) the price of tin rises
(b) the price of tin falls
(c) the price of tin rises and the prices of imported goods decline
(d) the price of tin falls and the prices of imported goods rise

20. Which one of the following is **not** one of the proposals included in the New International Economic Order for which LDCs have argued?
(a) a change in the rules by which international financial institutions are governed
(b) the elimination of OPEC
(c) the renegotiation and cancellation of the debts of LDCs to the IACs
(d) abandonment of the neo-colonial policies of the IACs

■ **DISCUSSION QUESTIONS**

1. What is the degree of income inequality among nations of the world? Classify nations into three groups and describe this inequality. What further division can be made among poor nations? How do the overall level of GNP per capita and the rates of GNP growth compare among rich nations and poor nations?

2. What are the "human implications" of poverty found in LDCs? (Use the socioeconomic indicators found in Table 41–2 of the text to contrast the quality of life in IACs and LDCs).

3. Describe the basic avenues of economic growth. Do these avenues differ for IACs and LDCs?

4. How would you describe the natural resource situation for LDCs? In what ways do price fluctuations affect LDC exports? Is a weak natural resource base an obstacle to economic growth?

5. Describe the implications of the high rate of growth in population and its effects on the standard of living. Can the standard of living be raised by merely increasing the output of consumer goods in LDCs? What is the meaning of the cliche, "the rich get richer and the poor get children," and how does it apply to LDCs?

6. What obstacles do the human resources of LDCs place in the path of economic development? What is the distinction between unemployment and underemployment and how do the concepts apply to LDCs? What are the reasons for the low level of labor productivity in LDCs? How does "brain drain" affect LDCs?

7. What reasons exist for placing special emphasis on capital accumulation as a means of promoting economic growth in LDCs?

8. Why is domestic capital accumulation difficult in LDCs? Answer both in terms of the saving side and the investment side of capital accumulation. Is there "capital flight" from LDCs?

9. In addition to the obstacles which limit domestic investment, what other obstacles tend to limit the flow of foreign capital into LDCs? What role does infrastructure play in capital formation?

10. How might the LDCs improve their technology without engaging in slow and expensive research? Why might this be an inappropriate method of improving the technology used in the LDCs?

11. What is meant by the "will to develop"? How is it related to social and institutional change in LDCs?

12. Explain the "vicious circle" of poverty found in the LDCs. How does population growth make an escape from this vicious circle difficult?

13. Why is the role of government expected to be a positive one in the early phases of development in LDCs? What have been the problems with the involvement of government in economic development?

14. How can the United States help LDCs? What types of aid can be offered? How is it possible for the United States

to assist LDCs without spending a penny on "foreign aid"? Is this type of aid sufficient to ensure rapid and substantial development in LDCs?

15. Discuss the World Bank in terms of its purposes, characteristics, sources of funds, promotion of private capital flows, and success. What are its affiliates and their purposes?

16. Describe the dimensions of the LDC debt crisis. What were the causes of the crisis? Explain the economic consequences for LDCs and IACs of the debt crisis. Are there any solutions?

17. Explain the principal proposals which constitute the program of the LDCs for the establishment of a New International Economic Order. Explain the arguments made by the LDCs to support each of these proposals.

■ **ANSWERS**

CHAPTER 24 GROWTH AND THE LESS DEVELOPED COUNTRIES

Fill-in questions

1. *a.* high, low, high; *b.* 97, middle, 1270, low, 270, 4.2, 97, 2.4; *c.* new industrialized, 8, 9, declining; *d.* higher, absolute; *e.* expectancies, literacy, calorie, energy, lower, higher

2. efficient, natural resources, human resources, capital goods, technology

3. uneven, OPEC, IACs, price

4. *a.* overpopulated, 2, .6, 35, decrease; *b.* unemployment, underemployment; *c.* productivity, human capital, brain drain

5. *a.* labor productivity, supply, output; *b.* saving potential, investors, incentives, capital flight; *c.* infrastructure, private; *d.* agriculture, infrastructure

6. *a.* skilled, scarce, abundant, capital; *b.* unskilled, abundant, scarce, labor; *c.* saving

7. institutions, social

8. income, investment, productivity, output (income)

9. *a.* the existence of widespread banditry and intertribal warfare in many less developed nations; *b.* the absence of a sizable and vigorous entrepreneurial class; *c.* the great need for public goods and services; *d.* government action may be the only means of promoting saving and investment; *e.* government can more effectively deal with the social-institutional obstacles to growth

10. public sector problems, bureaucracy, political, mal, corruption, competition, incentives

11. by expanding trade with the underdeveloped nations (lowering the barriers to trade), private flows of capital, foreign aid (public loans and grants)

12. external, 1217, 39

13. *a.* increased, increased; *b.* tight, increased, increased, decreased; *c.* appreciated, more, less; *d.* Mexico, lending, deficits

14. rescheduled, austerity, standard, net export, banking and financial, IACs

15. separately with, decades (years), economic growth, forgive, defaults

16. *a.* rules; *b.* trade, tariff treatments; *c.* exploitation, dependence; *d.* terms, trade, stabilization, indexing; *e.* debts, canceled, rescheduled; *f.* insufficient, 0.7, strings, automatic

Problems and projects

1. *a.* 7500; *b.* (1) 8400, (2) 525, (3) widen, 7875

2. *a.* low; *b.* short; *c.* widespread; *d.* low; *e.* primitive; *f.* large; *g.* large; *h.* high; *i.* poor; *j.* small; *k.* low; *l.* absent; *m.* small; *n.* small; *o.* small and poor; *p.* small; *q.* low; *r.* common

3. *a.* food supply: 400, 600, 800, 1000, 1200, 1400; population: 40, 80, 160, 320, 640, 1280; *b.* the food supply is just able to support the population; *c.* the inability of the food supply to support a population growing at this rate; *d.* (1) 200, (2) 240, (3) 280; *e.* the population increased as rapidly as the food supply

Self-test

1. T; **2.** T; **3** F; **4.** F; **5.** T; **6.** F: **7.** F; **8.** T; **9.** F; **10.** F; **11.** F; **12.** T; **13.** T; **14.** T; **15.** F; **16.** F; **17.** T; **18.** F; **19.** T; **20.** T; **21.** T; **22.** F; **23.** T; **24.** T; **25.** T

1. *a;* **2.** *b;* **3.** *d;* **4.** *b;* **5.** *a;* **6.** *b;* **7.** *b;* **8.** *c;* **9.** *d;* **10.** *b;* **11.** *d;* **12.** *b;* **13.** *d;* **14.** *a;* **15.** *c;* **16.** *a;* **17.** *c;* **18.** *a;* **19.** *d;* **20.** *b*

The economy of the Soviet Union

During the first few years following the Russian Revolution in 1917 many people in the United States were convinced that the economic system of the Soviet Union was unworkable and that it would sooner or later break down—proof that Marx, Lenin, and Stalin were unrealistic dreamers—and that the reconversion of their economy to a free enterprise, market system would follow. Slowly it dawned upon these people that the breakdown would not occur and, on the contrary, the Soviet economy was becoming more workable and more productive, and that Soviet Russia was becoming a very strong nation. In part this early belief that Soviet Russia would collapse was based on prejudice—they wanted it to collapse in order to prove to themselves that the system called capitalism was both the only feasible system of economic organization and an almost perfectly operated system—and in part it was based on ignorance of the institutions and methods employed by Russian communism.

The aim of Chapter 25 is to dispel some of the ignorance surrounding Soviet institutions and methods and by doing so eliminate the basis for much of the unwarranted prejudice against the Soviet *economic system*. (Chapter 25, of course, does not try to convince you that the United States should adopt the Soviet economic system, or to persuade you that the Russian way of life is morally, politically, or socially preferable.)

To accomplish its aim the chapter first examines the ideology and the two institutions of the Soviet economy which are remarkably different from anything found in American capitalism and which are the framework of the Russian economy. Within this framework the Fundamental Economic Problems are solved through central economic planning. Central economic planning has no counterpart in the United States, and it is to further central economic planning that the Soviet institutional framework is maintained. The better part of the chapter is devoted to explaining what central planning is and how it is employed in the U.S.S.R. to obtain answers to the Fundamental Economic Problems.

If you learn anything from this chapter you ought to learn that the Soviet *economy* is the source of its political and military strength and that the performance and growth of the Soviet and American economic systems (and the social and political institutions that accompany them) are watched throughout the world by people who will be inclined to adopt the economic and political and social system which promises them the best prospect of improving their own material well-being. In addition, you should be aware that it is not a question of "Will the Soviet system work?" but of how well it works.

There is strength in the Soviet Union because the government is able to control the economy. The large and almost continuous increases in Soviet output are mostly the result of central economic planning and the direction of the economy toward the achievement of these plans by central authority. But there seems to have been trouble in the Soviet Union in recent decades. While it grew at a dramatic rate and become a major industrial power over the last seventy or so years, its growth rate and the increases in the productivity of its labor force have slowed since the late 1960s. The reasons for the slowdowns are explained in the text along with a brief discussion of the problems with consumer goods and living standards.

In an attempt to overcome problems with production and consumption that have plagued the Soviet economy since the 1960s, the Soviet General Secretary, Mikhail Gorbachev, embarked in 1985 on an ambitious program (called **perestroika**) to reform and restructure the economy. These changes include modernizing industry, decentralizing decision making, expanding the private sector, improving incentives for workers, relying more on the price system, and increasing the role of the Soviet Union in the international economy. Combined with the economic reforms would be more openness (called **glasnost**) to give participants in the economy and in government more freedom to discuss problems and to seek solutions. The features of Gorbachev's economic program are outlined for you in the final section of the chapter so you can discover what measures are being taken to revitalize this centrally planned economy. Whether the reforms will work and what the outcomes will be are still unknown, but the examination of another economic system in the process of change should deepen your understanding of the dynamics of economics as you conclude your study of the text.

■ CHECKLIST

When you have studied this chapter you should be able to:

☐ Outline the ideology underlying the command economy of the U.S.S.R.

☐ Identify the two outstanding institutions of the Soviet economy; and the ways in which the freedoms of consumers and workers are limited.

☐ Define central economic planning; and explain the difference between the Five-year Plan and the One-year Plans of the Soviet economy.

☐ List and explain the five techniques used in the Soviet planning system to achieve coordination.

☐ Explain how *Gosbank* helps *Gosplan* to achieve the objectives of the economic plan.

☐ Describe the incentive system employed in the U.S.S.R.

☐ Explain what determines the prices producers pay for inputs and receive for final products in the Soviet Union; and contrast the role of profits and losses and the significance of input prices in the U.S.S.R. and a market economy.

☐ Explain how the prices of consumer goods are determined in the Soviet economy and the function these prices perform.

☐ Compare the GNPs and the growth rates of the Soviet and American economies.

☐ Enumerate the five factors which have produced rapid growth in the past and four factors which have slowed recent growth in the U.S.S.R.

☐ Present four reasons why the rate at which the productivity of labor increases has fallen in the Soviet economy in recent years.

☐ Describe the problems with consumer goods and living standards in the Soviet Union.

☐ Explain the six elements of Gorbachev's economic program and discuss the obstacles and resistance it faces.

■ CHAPTER OUTLINE

1. The U.S.S.R. is a command economy which is better understood by examining its ideology and institutions.

a. Seen by its government as a dictatorship of the proletariat (or working class), the Soviet economy is based on an ideology of a classless society in which there is no private property and workers are not, therefore, exploited by capitalists who pay workers a subsistence wage that is less than the value of their production (in which there is no surplus value).

b. There are two major economic institutions in the Soviet Union.

(1) The state owns most of the property resources and little property is privately owned.

(2) Government uses central economic planning (rather than a market system) to allocate resources.

(3) In addition to these two institutions, consumers and workers have limited freedom of choice.

(a) Government, instead of consumer demand, determines the volume and composition of the production of consumer goods.

(b) Government control over education and wage rates determines the composition of the labor force and allocates it among alternative uses.

2. Central planning is used in the Soviet Union to answer the Five Fundamental Economic Questions.

a. Government in the U.S.S.R. sets forth the goals of the economy in its Five-year and its One-year Plans.

b. The basic problem encountered in planning for an entire economy is the difficulty of coordinating the many interdependent segments of the economy and the avoidance of the chain reaction that would result from a bottleneck in any one of these segments.

c. To coordinate its different sectors the Soviet economy establishes material balances, plans by negotiation, employs the priority principle, draws upon inventories to offset bottlenecks, and utilizes the "second economy."

d. To achieve the objectives of central planning the Soviet government relies upon such control agencies as *Gosplan,* other planning groups, and especially upon *Gosbank.*

e. To motivate economic units to fulfill the plan the U.S.S.R. employs monetary incentives, nonmonetary incentives, and admonitions to work.

f. Prices in the Soviet economy are established by the state and are used to promote the achievement of the plans.

(1) Producer prices are used to measure the efficiency of production.

(2) Consumer goods prices are employed to ration goods and services.

3. By engaging in central planning the government of the Soviet Union has sought to industrialize its economy and to achieve rapid economic growth.

a. It is today one of the world's leading industrial nations; historically its growth rate was greater than that of the United States; but its GNP is still only about 50% of that of the United States.

b. The sources of past growth in the Soviet Union were

its large endowment of natural resources, its totalitarian government, its surplus farm labor, its adoption of the superior technologies developed in Western nations, and its virtual elimination of cyclical unemployment.

c. But at least four factors have slowed the Soviet growth rate in the past twenty or so years.

(1) Their military expenditures divert resources from uses that would lead to greater growth.

(2) Their labor force has failed to expand as rapidly as it had during the 1970s and a shortage of labor has developed.

(3) Their inefficient agricultural sector has not expanded its output at a rate that would make greater overall growth possible.

(4) And the productivity of Soviet labor (which is only about 40% as productive as American workers) has grown at a low and declining rate because of the depletion of its natural resources, the lack of incentives for innovation and technological advance, poor worker discipline, and a planning system that may now be obsolete.

d. Much of the cost of rapid industrialization and economic growth in the past has been borne by consumers; in the Soviet Union real per capita consumption is about one-third of that in the United States.

(1) The consumer goods that are provided are of poor quality and limited in selection; there are shortages, corruption, and "secondary markets" for consumer goods.

(2) The lack of a market system to provide signals to producers and consumers causes problems in the Soviet economy; product quality and variety are less important when there are quantitative targets for production.

4. In response to the need to improve economic performance, General Secretary Gorbachev offered a series of proposals for economic reform (*perestroika*) and also called for more openness (*glasnost*) in discussions among workers, consumers, government officials, and others to encourage efforts to find solutions to the economy's problems.

a. There are six interrelated features to Gorbachev's economic program.

(1) Industry needs to be modernized which means there will be increased investment, relative to consumption, and more use of advanced technology.

(2) The decision making in the nation will be decentralized to give more authority to state enterprises and to encourage self-financing of production costs and investment.

(3) Private production of goods and services will be encouraged to a limited degree in the hope that it will help reduce shortages of consumer goods and services; the reform will also legitimize the existing "second economy."

(4) Efficiency in the work force will be improved by eliminating incompetent managers, reducing corruption, and disciplining workers for absenteeism and alcoholism;

in addition, wages and bonuses will be more closely related to productivity and the "profitability" of an enterprise.

(5) Prices for many goods and services will be free to vary to reflect relative scarcities; fewer prices will be set by central planners.

(6) The Soviet Union will be more involved in the international economy through closer economic relationships with the European Common Market and other western nations, possible participating in international economic organizations, and through joint ventures.

b. Gorbachev's economic program is not completely implemented and is still being shaped for the 1991–1995 Five-year Plan. The reforms face significant obstacles and resistance because they may:

(1) threaten the job status of some workers and party bureaucrats;

(2) give too low a priority to consumer goods production;

(3) arouse suspicion about a return to capitalist ways and be unsettling to workers and managers accustomed to the previous procedures and methods; and

(4) lead to calls for change in the political system and more autonomy in regions of the nation.

■ **IMPORTANT TERMS**

Labor theory of value	**Priority principle**
Surplus value	**"Second economy"**
State ownership	**Gosbank**
Central economic planning	**"Control by the ruble"**
Five-year Plan	**Turnover tax**
Gosplan	**Gorbachev's economic program**
One-year Plan	
Material balances	

■ **FILL-IN QUESTIONS**

1. The ideology of the Soviet economy is that:

a. the value of any commodity is determined by the amount of _____ required to produce it;

b. in capitalistic economies where capital is (privately, publicly) _____ owned capitalists exploit workers by paying them a wage that is equal to the _____ wage and obtain _____ value at their expense; and *c.* in a communist economy capital and other property will be _____ owned, society will be _____ -less, and it will be governed by the Communist Party as a dictatorship of the _____.

2. The two institutions of the U.S.S.R. which are in sharp contrast with private property and the price-market system in the American economy are the ownership by the _____ of property resources and _____ planning.

3. In the Soviet Union,
a. the volume and the composition of the production of consumer goods is determined by (consumer demand, government) _____;
b. the composition and allocation of the labor force is determined by government which controls the _____ system and _____ rates.

4. The goals or objectives of the Soviet economy are set by the _____ (which means they are set by the _____ Party).

5. The two most important plans made in the Soviet economy are the _____-year and the _____-year Plans.

6. The basic planning problem in the Soviet Union is the _____ of the various sectors of the economy. The failure of any one of these sectors to produce its planned output results in a _____ which has a _____ reaction throughout the remainder of the economy.

7. To coordinate the various segments of the economy the Soviet government _____ or matches the quantities of _____ demanded and supplied; plans by _____; and when bottlenecks appear it applies the _____ principle and draws upon its _____. The achievement of the plans for the economy are also aided by the illegal activities in the "_____ _____."

8. The agency primarily responsible for the construction of the economic plan in the Soviet Union is (**Gosplan,**

Gosbank) _____ and the agency primarily responsible for ensuring that the provisions of the plan are enforced is _____.

9. Production in the Soviet Union is motivated by _____ incentives, by _____ incentives, and by admonitions to _____.

10. In the U.S.S.R. prices are used as an accounting device for assessing the productive _____ of plants and industries and as a means of _____ products among consumers.

11. If a plant or industry in the United States were profitable its output and employment of resources would tend to (expand, contract) _____ but in the Soviet Union this would not occur; these unplanned profits would, however, indicate that the Soviet plant or industry was (more, less) _____ efficient than average.

12. The gross national product of the U.S.S.R. is about (what percentage) _____ of the GNP of the U.S. From 1966–1970, real GNP increased by _____% in the Soviet Union and _____% in the United States; but from 1983–1988 real GNP increased by _____% in the Soviet Union and _____% in the United States.

13. List five specific reasons for the past economic growth of the Soviet economy.

a. _____

b. _____

c. _____

d. _____

e. _____

14. What four factors have retarded economic growth in the Soviet Union since the late 1960s?

a. _____

b. _____

c. _____

d. _____

15. The recent decline in the rate at which worker productivity in the Soviet Union has increased is the result of the depletion of _____, the lack of incentives for _____ and _____ advances, poor worker _____, and the possible obsolescence of the _____ mechanism.

16. Overall, real per capita consumption in the Soviet Union is only about _____ of that in the United States. Soviet consumer goods are of _____ quality and the _____ is limited; the distribution of consumer goods is characterized by _____, _____, _____, and _____; and because of the lack of market incentives and the use of central planning, many consumer goods are produced for which there is little or no consumer _____

17. Reform of the Soviet economy has been proposed by _____. This economic program for reform and restructuring the Soviet economy is referred to as _____; it is to be accompanied by _____ which means that there is to be more openness in the discussion of economic issues among participants in the economy.

18. List the six elements of the economic reform program.

a. _____.

b. _____.

c. _____.

d. _____.

e. _____.

f. _____.

19. The economic changes are only goals or options and the reform faces obstacles from party members and bureaucrats who are _____ by the possible loss of job or status; the economic _____ for workers and managers may be insufficient to increase productivity; there will be _____ raised about the capitalist nature of some of the reforms; and the encouragement of _____ in the debate over economic issues may affect the _____ system.

■ **PROBLEMS AND PROJECTS**

1. On the left of the table on the top of page 266 are several of the major institutions or characteristics of American capitalism. In the spaces to the right, name the institution or characteristic of the Soviet economy which compares with the American institution or characteristic.

American institution or characteristic	Russian institution or characteristic
Private ownership of economic resources	_____
Consumer freedom to spend income as he or she sees fit	_____
Consumer sovereignty	_____
Worker freedom to select occupation and place of work	_____
Profit motive	_____
Entrepreneurial freedom to select product, output, price, etc.	_____
System of prices and markets	_____
Self-interest	_____
Privately owned farms	_____
Privately owned industrial firms and retail stores	_____

2. Below is a market demand schedule for product X.

Price, rubles	Quantity demanded (million)
90	25
80	30
70	35
60	40
50	45
40	50
30	55

a. If Soviet planners decide to produce 50 million units of product X, the price of the product *plus* the turnover tax

will be set at _____ rubles.

b. If the accounting cost of producing product X is 25

rubles, the turnover tax *rate* will be set at
_____%.

■ **SELF-TEST**

Circle the T if the statement is true, the F if it is false.

1. The Soviet government sets the economic objectives of the economy, directs the resources of the economy toward the achievement of these objectives, and uses the market system as one of the means of achieving these objectives.　　　　　　**T　F**

2. Consumers in the U.S.S.R. are free to spend their incomes on any of the consumer goods provided by the economy's central plan.　　　　　　**T　F**

3. The government of the U.S.S.R. determines the composition and the allocation of the labor force by setting the wage rates paid for different types of workers and by controlling the educational system.　　　　　**T　F**

4. A One-year Plan is less general and more detailed and specific than a Five-year Plan.　　　　　　**T　F**

5. *Gosplan* is the agency in the Soviet Union primarily responsible for preparing the economic plan.　　**T　F**

6. The basic planning problem in the Soviet Union is the determination of the overall goals of the economy. **T　F**

7. The equating of the planned requirements with the available supplies of different inputs and commodities in the One- and Five-year Plans of the Soviet Union is called "material balance."　　　　　　**T　F**

8. In the U.S.S.R. individual plants and industries play no part in the formulation of the final economic plan. **T　F**

9. Application of the priority principle means that when production bottlenecks develop in the economy, inventories are used to prevent a chain reaction.　　**T　F**

10. The communist nations of Eastern Europe to whom the U.S.S.R. exports and from whom it imports goods and services are the "second economy."　　　**T　F**

11. "Control by the ruble" is a device utilized by *Gosbank* to supervise the activities of the plants that produce goods in the Soviet economy.　　　　　**T　F**

12. Most workers in the Soviet Union are paid on a piece-rate basis.　　　　　　**T　F**

13. The labor-force participation rates of both men and women are greater in the Soviet Union than in other industrialized nations.　　　　　**T　F**

14. The turnover tax does not affect the price of consumer goods, but it does affect the consumer income available for the purchase of consumer goods.　**T　F**

15. The GNP of the U.S.S.R. is about 50% as large as the GNP in the United States.　　　　　**T　F**

16. The productivity of labor is 40% greater in the Soviet economy than in the American economy.　　**T　F**

17. Real per capita consumption in the Soviet Union is about 70% of that in the United States.　　**T　F**

18. The "radical reform" of the Soviet economy proposed by Mikhail Gorbachev is referred to as *glasnost*. **T　F**

19. Gorbachev's economic program calls for the elimination of wages and bonuses for workers as a means of reducing corruption.　　　　　**T　F**

20. The fact that many Soviet workers, managers, and planners have little experience with features of a market system may be an obstacle to the success of Gorbachev's economic reforms.　　　　　**T　F**

Circle the letter that corresponds to the best answer.

1. Which of the following is *not* an element in the ideology of the Soviet Union?
(*a*) a dictatorship of the working class
(*b*) the creation of surplus value by government
(*c*) the labor theory of value
(*d*) the public ownership of property

2. Marxian (or communist) ideology is highly critical of capitalist societies because in them:
(*a*) property is privately owned by the capitalists
(*b*) capitalists pay workers a wage that is less than the value of their production
(*c*) capitalists obtain surplus value
(*d*) all of the above are true

3. In the U.S.S.R.:

(*a*) all property is owned by the state or by collective farms and cooperatives

(*b*) all property except urban housing and farms is owned either by the state or by cooperatives

(*c*) all property except retail and wholesale enterprises is owned either by the state or by collective farms and cooperatives

(*d*) all property except small tools, clothing, household furnishings, and some housing is owned by the state or by collective farms and cooperatives

4. Which of the following helps to make central economic planning work in the Soviet Union?

(*a*) the existence of the "second economy"

(*b*) application of the priority principle

(*c*) planning by negotiation

(*d*) all of the above

5. Which of the following is the most important agency in enforcing and carrying out the central economic plan in the Soviet Union?

(*a*) *Gosplan*

(*b*) *Gosbank*

(*c*) the Communist Party

(*d*) the secret police

6. Labor unions in the Soviet Union do ***not***:

(*a*) exist

(*b*) engage in strikes or slowdowns

(*c*) bargain collectively with their employers to determine wage rates

(*d*) encourage workers to be more productive

7. Prices in the Soviet Union:

(*a*) are used as a device for rationing consumer goods

(*b*) are determined by the demands for and the supplies of products and resources

(*c*) are used to allocate resources among different firms and industries

(*d*) perform a guiding function, but not a rationing function

8. Profits and losses in the U.S.S.R. are used to determine whether:

(*a*) the production of various consumer goods should be expanded or contracted

(*b*) various goods are being produced efficiently or inefficiently

(*c*) more or fewer resources should be devoted to the production of various goods

(*d*) a product should be exported or imported

9. Suppose the Soviet government determined that the annual output of a certain quality of wristwatch would be 100,000 and that the accounting cost of producing a watch is 300 rubles. If the demand schedule for these watches were as given in the table below, what turnover rate would be placed on watches?

(*a*) 33⅓%

(*b*) 66⅔%

(*c*) 100%

(*d*) 133⅓%

Price, rubles	Quantity demanded
700	85,000
600	90,000
500	100,000
400	120,000
300	150,000
200	190,000
100	240,000

10. The annual rates of growth in real GNP in the Soviet Union and in the United States during the 1983–1988 period were, respectively:

(*a*) 2.0% and 4.0%

(*b*) 1.0% and 3.0%

(*c*) 5.0% and 3.0%

(*d*) 4.0% and 3.0%

11. In comparing the composition of GNP in the U.S.S.R. and the United States it can be said that:

(*a*) over 25% of the GNP in the United States is devoted to capital goods while less than 20% is so devoted in the U.S.S.R.

(*b*) government in the U.S.S.R. absorbs over 20% and in the United States absorbs less than 10% of the GNP

(*c*) over 75% of the GNP in both nations is represented by consumer goods

(*d*) gross investment in the U.S.S.R. is about twice again as large a percentage of the GNP as it is in the United States

12. Which of the following is ***not*** true?

(*a*) the standard of living in the U.S.S.R. is below the standard of living of the U.S.

(*b*) the output of the Russian economy exceeds the output of the American economy

(*c*) the output of the Russian economy is growing at a less rapid rate than the output of the American economy

(*d*) the Soviet economy devotes a larger percentage of its output to capital accumulation than does the American economy

13. Which of the following is ***not*** a significant factor in explaining the past economic growth in the Soviet Union?

(*a*) Extensive investments by foreigners in the Soviet economy

(*b*) high levels of domestic investment in basic industries (*c*) adoption of the advanced technological methods employed in Western nations

(*d*) the reallocation of labor from the agricultural to the industrial sector of the economy

14. All but one of the following contributed to the slower rate of growth of the Soviet Union after the late 1960s. Which one?

(*a*) the burden of military expenditures

(*b*) agricultural drag

(*c*) an overall shortage of labor

(*d*) a rise in the productivity of labor

15. The comparison of consumption in the Soviet Union and in the United States shows that in the Soviet Union there are more:

(*a*) public transportation services and less housing services than in the United States

(*b*) health services and less household services than in the United States

(*c*) education services and less consumer durables than in the United States

(*d*) food products and less alcoholic beverages than in the United States

16. The restructuring of the Soviet economy under Gorbachev is referred to as:

(*a*) **Gosplan**

(*b*) **glasnost**

(*c*) **perestroika**

(*d*) the "second" economy

17. The modernization proposals of Gorbachev's economic program basically involve:

(*a*) providing more consumption for consumers and the production of more modern consumer products to distribution

(*b*) increasing investment relative to consumption and reallocating investment toward research and development in high technology

(*c*) the building of new housing facilities to address the pressing problems of overcrowding and deterioration in dwellings

(*d*) increasing the productivity of agriculture by improving the quality of the equipment available to agricultural workers

18. Self-financing as part of the economic reforms for the Soviet Union refers to plans to:

(*a*) give private entrepreneurs the "seed" money to start a business that will eventually generate profits

(*b*) hire workers at state wages and then pay for wage increases based on productivity and performance

(*c*) legalize the "market economy" to help provide more consumer goods without requiring state investment

(*d*) let state enterprises use the proceeds from some portion of sales to pay for their production costs and their investments

19. If you are a director of a state enterprise in the Soviet Union and a policy tells you that you are permitted to spend 40 rubles on wages for every 100 rubles of output, then this situation would be an example of a:

(*a*) directive

(*b*) norm

(*c*) turnover tax

(*d*) surplus value

20. What is meant by the phrase "more rational pricing" in terms of Gorbachev's economic program?

(*a*) letting prices more accurately reflect supply and demand conditions

(*b*) providing a stronger rationale for the setting of prices by central planners

(*c*) increasing state subsides for production to lower prices for consumer goods that are in short supply

(*d*) conducting more market surveys to find out what products consumers are able and willing to buy based on projected incomes

■ **DISCUSSION QUESTIONS**

1. What are the essential features of the Marxian ideology on which the command economy of the U.S.S.R. is based?

2. What are the two principal economic institutions of the U.S.S.R.? How do these institutions compare with the economic institutions of the United States?

3. In what ways are the freedoms of consumers and workers circumscribed in the Soviet Union?

4. What is the basic planning problem in the U.S.S.R.? What techniques are used to overcome this problem and make central planning workable?

5. How is an economic plan drawn up in the Soviet Union? How is such a plan made "realistic and workable"? Why is the process of obtaining the final plan referred to as a "down-and-up evolution"?

6. What is meant by the priority principle of resource allocation? What sectors of the Soviet economy have received high priorities in the past?

7. What means and agencies are used in the Soviet Union to facilitate the achievement of the objectives of the economic plan? What types of incentives and inducements are offered to encourage the achievement of these objectives?

8. Explain the role **Gosbank** plays in the enforcement of the central economic plan in the U.S.S.R.

9. What functions do prices perform in the U.S.S.R.? How does the Russian government use the turnover tax to set the prices of consumer goods?

10. Plants and firms in the U.S.S.R. can earn profits or suffer losses just as plants and firms can in the United States. What role do profits and losses play in the U.S.S.R and what role do they play in the United States?

11. How is the turnover tax used in the Soviet Union to match the quantities demanded of various consumer goods with the quantities of these goods which **Gosplan** has decided to produce?

12. Compare the GNPs of the Soviet Union and the United States with respect to size, composition, and rate of growth.

13. Why was it possible for the U.S.S.R. to achieve economic growth in the past?

14. Why has the growth of the Soviet economy slowed since the late 1960s? Why in particular has the rate at which labor productivity rises slowed?

15. What are consumer goods and living standards like in the Soviet Union? What are the problems with central planning in providing consumer goods and producer goods?

16. Explain the six elements of Gorbachev's economic program. What features of a market economy are being used for the program? What will be the effect on consumers?

17. Why might there be obstacles or resistance to Gorbachev's economic reforms?

■ **ANSWERS**

CHAPTER 25 THE ECONOMY OF THE SOVIET UNION

Fill-in questions

1. *a.* labor; *b.* privately, subsistence, surplus; *c.* publicly, class, proletariat

2. state, central economic

3. *a.* government; *b.* educational, wage

4. government (state), Communist

5. Five, One (either order)

6. coordination, bottleneck, chain

7. balances, materials (inputs), negotiation, priority, reserve stocks (inventories), second economy

8. **Gosplan, Gosbank**

9. monetary, nonmonetary (either order), work

10. efficiency, rationing

11. expand, more

12. 50, 5.0, 3.0, 20, 4.0

13. *a.* the large natural resource base; *b.* the totalitarian government has allocated resources to promote growth; *c.* the surplus of farm labor; *d.* the employment of the superior technologies developed in Western nations; *e.* the absence of cyclical unemployment

14. *a.* the diversion of resources to military uses; *b.* a labor shortage; *c.* the backwardness of Soviet agriculture; *d.* a lower rate of increase in labor productivity

15. natural resources, innovation, technological, discipline, planning

16. one-third, poor, selection (choice); shortages, queues, black markets, corruption (any order); demand

17. Mikhail Gorbachev, **perestroika, glasnost**

18. *a.* modernization of industry and increased investment in high technology; *b.* decentralization of decision making and more self-financing of production costs and investment by state enterprises; *c.* limited expansion by the private sector to provide more consumer goods and services; *d.* improved discipline of workers and more wage and bonus incentives for workers; *e.* let prices reflect more accurately supply and demand conditions; *f.* increased role in the international economy through trade and joint ventures

19. threatened, incentives, suspicion, **glasnost** (openness), political

Problems and projects

1. state ownership of property resources; relative consumer freedom to spend income as he or she sees fit; central economic planning; workers are generally free to choose occupation and place of work; central economic planning and various forms of incentives; central economic planning; central economic planning with prices playing an implemental role; central economic planning and various forms of incentives which appeal to self-interest; state and collective farms; state-owned and cooperative firms and retail stores

2. *a.* 40; *b.* 60

Self-test

1. T; **2.** T; **3.** T; **4.** T; **5.** T; **6.** F; **7.** T; **8.** F; **9.** F; **10.** F; **11.** T; **12.** T; **13.** T; **14.** F; **15.** T; **16.** F; **17.** F; **18.** F; **19.** F; **20.** T

1. *b;* **2.** *d;* **3.** *d;* **4.** *d;* **5.** *b;* **6.** *c;* **7.** *a;* **8.** *b;* **9.** *b;* **10.** *a;* **11.** *d;* **12.** *b;* **13.** *a;* **14.** *d;* **15.** *a;* **16.** *c;* **17.** *b;* **18.** *d;* **19.** *b;* **20.** *a*

Glossary

Ability-to-pay principle The belief that those who have the greater income (or wealth) should be taxed absolutely and relatively more than those who have less.

Abstraction Elimination of irrelevant and non-economic facts to obtain an economic principle.

Actual budget The amount spent by the Federal government (to purchase goods and services and for transfer payments) less the amount of tax revenue collected by it in any (fiscal) year; and which can **not** reliably be used to determine whether it is pursuing an expansionary or contractionary fiscal policy. Compare (**see**) the Full-employment budget.

Actual deficit The size of the Federal government's Budget deficit (**see**) or surplus actually measured or recorded in any given year.

Actual investment The amount which business Firms do invest; equal to Planned investment plus Unplanned investment.

Actual reserves The amount of funds which a Member bank has on deposit at the Federal Reserve bank of its district (plus its Vault cash).

Adaptive expectations theory The idea that people determine their expectations about future events (for example, inflation) on the basis of past and present events (rates of inflation) and only change their expectations as events unfold.

Adjustable pegs The device utilized in the Bretton Woods system (**see**) to change Exchange rates in an orderly way to eliminate persistent Payments deficits and surpluses: each nation defined its monetary unit in terms of (pegged it to) gold or the dollar, kept the Rate of exchange for its money stable in the short run, and changed (adjusted) it in the long run when faced with international disequilibrium.

Aggregate demand A schedule or curve which shows the total quantity of goods and services that will be demanded (purchased) at different price levels.

Aggregate demand–aggregate supply model The macroeconomic model which uses Aggregate demand and Aggregate supply (**see** both) to determine and explain the Price level and the real National output.

Aggregate expenditures The total amount spent for final goods and services in the economy.

Aggregate expenditures–national output approach Determination of the Equilibrium net national product (**see**) by finding the real NNP at which Aggregate expenditures are equal to the National output.

Aggregate expenditures schedule A schedule or curve which shows the total amount spent for final goods and services at different levels of real NNP.

Aggregate supply A schedule or curve which shows the total quantity of goods and services that will be supplied (produced) at different price levels.

Aggregation Combining individual units or data into one unit or number. For example, all prices of individual goods and services are combined into a Price level, or all units of output are aggregated into Real net national product.

Allocative factor The ability of an economy to reallocate resources to achieve the Economic growth which the Supply factors (**see**) make possible.

Annually balanced budget The equality of government expenditures and tax collections during a year.

Anticipated inflation Inflation (**see**) at a rate which was equal to the rate expected in that period of time.

Applied economics (**See** Policy economics.)

Appreciation of the dollar An increase in the value of the dollar relative to the currency of another nation; a dollar now buys a larger amount of the foreign currency. For example, if the dollar price of a British pound changes from $3 to $2, the dollar has appreciated.

Asset Anything with a monetary value owned by a firm or individual.

Asset demand for money The amount of money people want to hold as a Store of value (the amount of their financial assets they wish to have in the form of Money); and which varies inversely with the Rate of interest.

ATS account Automatic transfer services account (**see**).

Authoritarian capitalism An economic system (method of organization) in which property resources are privately owned and government extensively directs and controls the economy.

Authoritarian socialism (*See* Command economy.)

Automatic transfer services account The combination of a Checking account and an interest-bearing Savings account at a Commercial bank that automatically transfers funds from the latter to the former account when checks are written against it.

Average product The total output produced per unit of a resource employed (total product divided by the quantity of a resource employed).

Average propensity to consume Fraction of Disposable income which households spend for consumer goods and services; consumption divided by Disposable income.

Average propensity to save Fraction of Disposable income which households save; Saving divided by Disposable income.

Average tax rate Total tax paid divided by total (taxable) income; the tax rate on total (taxable) income.

Balanced budget multiplier The effect of equal increases (decreases) in government spending for goods and services and in taxes is to increase (decrease) the Equilibrium net national product by the amount of the equal increases (decreases).

Balance of payments deficit The sum of the Balance on current account (*see*) and the Balance on the capital account (*see*) is negative.

Balance of payments surplus The sum of the Balance on current account (*see*) and the Balance on the capital account (*see*) is positive.

Balance on current account The exports of goods (merchandise) and services of a nation less its imports of goods (merchandise) and services plus its Net investment income and Net transfers.

Balance on goods and services The exports of goods (merchandise) and services of a nation less its imports of goods (merchandise) and services.

Balance on the capital account The Capital inflows (*see*) of a nation less its Capital outflows (*see*).

Balance sheet A statement of the Assets (*see*), Liabilities (*see*), and Net worth (*see*) of a firm or individual at some given time.

Balanced-budget amendment Proposed constitutional amendment which would require Congress to balance the Federal budget annually.

Bankers' bank A bank which accepts the deposits of and makes loans to Depository institutions; a Federal Reserve Bank.

Barrier to entry Anything that artificially prevents the entry of Firms into an industry.

Barter The exchange of one good or service for another good or service.

Base year The year with which prices in other years are compared when a Price index (*see*) is constructed.

Benefit-cost analysis Deciding whether to employ resources and the quantity of resources to employ for a project or program (for the production of a good or service) by comparing the benefit with the cost.

Benefits-received principle The belief that those who receive the benefits of goods and services provided by government should pay the taxes required to finance them.

Big business A business Firm which either produces a large percentage of the total output of an industry, is large (in terms of number of employees or stockholders, sales, assets, or profits) compared with other Firms in the economy, or both.

Board of Governors The seven-member group that supervises and controls the money and banking system of the United States; formally, the Board of Governors of the Federal Reserve System; the Federal Reserve Board.

Brain drain The emigration of highly educated, highly skilled workers from a country.

Break-even income The level of Disposable income at which Households plan to consume (spend) all of their income (for consumer goods and services) and to save none of it; also denotes that level of earned income at which subsidy payments become zero in an income maintenance program.

Bretton Woods system The international monetary system developed after World War II in which Adjustable pegs (*see*) were employed, the International Monetary Fund (*see*) helped to stabilize Foreign exchange rates, and gold and the dollar (*see*) were used as International monetary reserves (*see*).

Budget deficit The amount by which the expenditures of the Federal government exceed its revenues in any year.

Built-in stability The effect of Nondiscretionary fiscal policy (*see*) upon the economy; when Net taxes vary directly with the Net national product, the fall (rise) in Net taxes during a recession (inflation) helps to eliminate unemployment (inflationary pressures).

Business cycle Recurrent ups and downs over a period of years in the level of economic activity.

Capital Human-made resources used to produce goods and services; goods which do not directly satisfy human wants; capital goods.

Capital account The section in a nation's International balance of payments (*see*) in which are recorded the Capital inflows (*see*) and the Capital outflows (*see*) of that nation.

Capital account deficit A negative Balance on the capital account (*see*).

Capital account surplus A positive Balance on the capital account (*see*).

Capital consumption allowances Estimate of the amount of Capital worn out or used up (consumed) in producing the Gross national product; depreciation.

Capital flight The transfer of savings from less developed to industrially advanced countries to avoid government expropriation, taxation, and high rates of inflation or to realize better investment opportunities.

Capital gain The gain realized when securities or properties are sold for a price greater than the price paid for them.

Capital goods (*See* Capital.)

Capital inflow The expenditures made by the residents of foreign nations to purchase real and financial capital from the residents of a nation.

Capital-intensive commodity A product which requires a relatively large amount of Capital to produce.

Capital outflow The expenditures made by the residents of a nation to purchase real and financial capital from the residents of foreign nations.

Capital-saving technological advance An improvement in technology that permits a greater quantity of a product to be produced with a given amount of Capital (or the same amount of the product to be produced with a smaller amount of Capital).

Capital-using technological advance An improvement in technology that requires the use of a greater amount of Capital to produce a given quantity of a product.

Causation A cause-and-effect relationship; one or several events bring about or result in another event.

CEA (*See* Council of Economic Advisers.)

Central bank A bank whose chief function is the control of the nation's money supply.

Central economic planning Government determination of the objectives of the economy and the direction of its resources to the attainment of these objectives.

Ceteris paribus assumption (*See* "other things being equal" assumption.)

Change in amount consumed Increase or decrease in consumption spending that results from an increase or decrease in Disposable income, the Consumption schedule (curve) remaining unchanged; movement from one row (point) to another on the same Consumption schedule (curve).

Change in amount saved Increase or decrease in Saving that results from an increase or decrease in Disposable income, the Saving schedule (curve) remaining unchanged; movement from one row (point) to another on the same Saving schedule (curve).

Change in the consumption schedule An increase or decrease in consumption at each level of Disposable income caused by changes in the Nonincome determinants of consumption and saving (*see*); an upward or downward movement of the Consumption schedule.

Change in the saving schedule An increase or decrease in Saving at each level of Disposable income caused by changes in the Nonincome determinants of

consumption and saving (*see*); an upward or downward movement of the Saving schedule.

Checkable deposit Any deposit in a commercial bank or Thrift institution against which a check may be written; includes Demand deposits and NOW, ATS, and Share draft accounts.

Checking account A Checkable deposit (*see*) in a Commercial bank or Thrift institution.

Circuit velocity of money (*See* Velocity of money.)

Circular flow of income The flow of resources from Households to Firms and of products from Firms to Households accompanied in an economy using money by flows of money from Households to Firms and from Firms to Households.

Classical range The vertical segment of the Aggregate supply curve along which the economy is at Full employment.

Classical theory The Classical theory of employment (*see*).

Classical theory of employment The Macroeconomic generalizations which were accepted by most economists prior to the 1930s and which led to the conclusion that a capitalistic economy would tend to employ its resources fully.

Closed economy An economy which neither exports nor imports goods and services.

Coincidence of wants The item (good or service) which one trader wishes to obtain is the same item which another trader desires to give up and the item which the second trader wishes to acquire is the same item the first trader desires to surrender.

COLA (*See* Cost-of-living adjustment.)

Collection of checks The process by which funds are transferred from the checking accounts of the writers of checks to the checking accounts of the recipients of the checks; also called the "clearing" of checks.

Command economy An economic system (method of organization) in which property resources are publicly owned and Central economic planning (*see*) is used to direct and coordinate economic activities.

Commercial bank Firm which has a charter from either a state government or the Federal government to engage in the business of banking.

Commercial banking system All Commercial banks and Thrift institutions as a group.

Communism (*See* Command economy.)

Comparative advantage A lower relative or Comparative cost (*see*) than another producer.

Comparative cost The amount the production of one product must be reduced to increase the production of another product; Opportunity cost (*see*).

Compensation to employees Wages and salaries paid by employers to workers plus Wage and salary supplements (*see*).

Competing goods (*See* Substitute goods.)

Competition The presence in a market of a large number of independent buyers and sellers and the freedom of buyers and sellers to enter and to leave the market.

Complementary goods Goods or services for which there is an inverse relationship between the price of one and the demand for the other; when the price of one falls (rises) the demand for the other increases (decreases).

Complex multiplier The Multiplier (**see**) when changes in the Net national product change Net taxes and Imports, as well as Saving.

Conglomerate combination A group of Plants (**see**) owned by a single Firm and engaged at one or more stages in the production of different products (of products which do not compete with each other).

Consumer goods Goods and services which satisfy human wants directly.

Consumer sovereignty Determination by consumers of the types and quantities of goods and services that are produced from the scarce resources of the economy.

Consumption schedule Schedule which shows the amounts Households plan to spend for Consumer goods at different levels of Disposable income.

Contractionary fiscal policy A decrease in Aggregate demand brought about by a decrease in Government expenditures for goods and services, an increase in Net taxes, or some combination of the two.

"Control by the ruble" The requirement in the U.S.S.R. that each plant's receipts and expenditures be completed through the use of checks drawn on **Gosbank** (**see**) which enables **Gosbank** to record the performance and progress of each plant toward the fulfillment of the production targets assigned it by **Gosplan**.

Corporate income tax A tax levied on the net income (profit) of Corporations.

Corporation A legal entity ("person") chartered by a state or the Federal government, and distinct and separate from the individuals who own it.

Correlation Systematic and dependable association between two sets of data (two kinds of events).

Cost-of-living adjustment An increase in the incomes (wages) of workers which is automatically received by them when there is inflation in the economy and guaranteed by a clause in their labor contracts with their employer.

Cost-push inflation Inflation that results from a decrease in Aggregate supply (from higher wage rates and raw material prices) and which is accompanied by decreases in real output and employment (by increases in the Unemployment rate).

Cost ratio The ratio of the decrease in the production of one product to the increase in the production of another product when resources are shifted from the production of the first to the production of the second product; the amount the production of one product decreases when the production of a second product increases by one unit.

Council of Economic Advisers A group of three persons which advises and assists the President of the United States on economic matters (including the preparation of the economic report of the President to Congress).

Credit An accounting notation that the value of an asset (such as the foreign money owned by the residents of a nation) has increased.

Credit union An association of persons who have a common tie (such as being employees of the same Firm or members of the same Labor union) which sells shares to (accepts deposits from) its members and makes loans to them.

Crowding-out effect The rise in interest rates and the resulting decrease in planned net investment spending in the economy caused by increased borrowing in the money market by the Federal government.

Currency Coins and Paper money.

Currency appreciation (**See** Exchange rate appreciation.)

Currency depreciation (**See** Exchange rate depreciation.)

Current account The section in a nation's International balance of payments (**see**) in which are recorded its exports and imports of goods (merchandise) and services, its net investment income, and its net transfers.

Current account deficit A negative Balance on current account (**see**).

Current account surplus A positive Balance on current account (**see**).

Customary economy (**See** Traditional economy.)

Cyclical deficit A Federal Budget deficit which is caused by a recession and the consequent decline in tax revenues.

Cyclical unemployment Unemployment caused by insufficient Aggregate expenditures.

Cyclically balanced budget The equality of Government expenditures for goods and services and Net tax collections over the course of a Business cycle; deficits incurred during periods of recession are offset by surpluses obtained during periods of prosperity (inflation).

Debit An accounting notation that the value of an asset (such as the foreign money owned by the residents of a nation) has decreased.

Declining economy An economy in which Net private domestic investment (**see**) is less than zero (Gross private domestic investment is less than Depreciation).

Decrease in demand A decrease in the Quantity demanded of a good or service at every price; a shift of the Demand curve to the left.

Decrease in supply A decrease in the Quantity supplied of a good or service at every price; a shift of the Supply curve to the left.

Deduction Reasoning from assumptions to conclusions; a method of reasoning that tests a hypothesis (an assumption) by comparing the conclusions to which it leads with economic facts.

Deflating Finding the Real gross national product (*see*) by decreasing the dollar value of the Gross national product produced in a year in which prices were higher than in the Base year (*see*).

Deflation A fall in the general (average) level of prices in the economy.

Demand A Demand schedule or a Demand curve (*see both*).

Demand curve A curve which shows the amounts of a good or service buyers wish to purchase at various prices during some period of time.

Demand deposit A deposit in a Commercial bank against which checks may be written; a Checking account or checking-account money.

Demand-deposit multiplier (*See* Monetary multiplier.)

Demand factor The increase in the level of Aggregate demand which brings about the Economic growth made possible by an increase in the productive potential of the economy.

Demand management The use of Fiscal policy (*see*) and Monetary policy (*see*) to increase or decrease Aggregate demand.

Demand-pull inflation Inflation which is the result of an increase in Aggregate demand.

Demand schedule A schedule which shows the amounts of a good or service buyers wish to purchase at various prices during some period of time.

Dependent variable A variable which changes as a consequence of a change in some other (independent) variable; the "effect" or outcome.

Depository institution A Firm that accepts the deposits of Money of the public (businesses and persons); Commercial banks, Savings and loan associations, Mutual savings banks, and Credit unions.

Depository Institutions Deregulation and Monetary Control Act Federal legislation of 1980 which, among other things, allowed Thrift institutions to accept Checkable deposits and to use the check-clearing facilities of the Federal Reserve and to borrow from the Federal Reserve Banks; subjected the Thrifts to the reserve requirements of the Fed; and provided for the gradual elimination of the maximum interest rates that could be paid by Depository institutions on Savings and Time deposits.

Depreciation (*See* Capital consumption allowances.)

Depreciation of the dollar A decrease in the value of the dollar relative to another currency; a dollar now buys a smaller amount of the foreign currency. For example, if

the dollar price of a British pound changes from $2 to $3, the dollar has depreciated.

Derived demand The demand for a good or service which is dependent upon or related to the demand for some other good or service; the demand for a resource which depends upon the demand for the products it can be used to produce.

Descriptive economics The gathering or collection of relevant economic facts (data).

Devaluation A decrease in the defined value of a currency.

DI (*See* Disposable income.)

DIDMCA (*See* Depository Institutions Deregulation and Monetary Control Act.)

Directing function of prices (*See* Guiding function of prices.)

Directly related Two sets of economic data that change in the same direction; when one variable increases (decreases) the other increases (decreases).

Direct relationship The relationship between two variables which change in the same direction, for example, product price and quantity supplied.

Discount rate The interest rate which the Federal Reserve Banks charge on the loans they make to Depository institutions.

Discouraged workers Workers who have left the Labor force (*see*) because they have not been able to find employment.

Discretionary fiscal policy Deliberate changes in taxes (tax rates) and government spending (spending for goods and services and transfer payment programs) by Congress for the purpose of achieving a full-employment noninflationary Net national product and economic growth.

Disinflation A reduction in the rate of Inflation (*see*).

Disposable income Personal income (*see*) less Personal taxes (*see*); income available for Personal consumption expenditures (*see*) and Personal saving (*see*).

Dissaving Spending for consumer goods and services in excess of Disposable income; the amont by which Personal consumption expenditures (*see*) exceed Disposable income.

Division of labor Dividing the work required to produce a product into a number of different tasks which are performed by different workers; Specialization (*see*) of workers.

Dollar votes The "votes" which consumers and entrepreneurs in effect cast for the production of the different kinds of consumer and capital goods, respectively, when they purchase them in the markets of the economy.

Domestic capital formation Adding to a nation's stock of Capital by saving a part of its own national output.

Domestic economic goal Assumed to be full employment with little or no inflation.

Double counting Including the value of intermediate goods (**see**) in the Gross national product; counting the same good or service more than once.

Double taxation Taxation of both corporate net income (profits) and the dividends paid from this net income when they become the Personal income of households.

Dumping The sale of products below cost in a foreign country.

Durable good A consumer good with an expected life (use) of one year or more.

Dynamic progress The development over time of more efficient (less costly) techniques of producing existing products and of improved products; technological progress.

Earnings The money income received by a worker; equal to the Wage (rate) multiplied by the quantity of labor supplied (the amount of time worked) by the worker.

Easy money policy Expanding the Money supply.

Economic analysis Deriving Economic principles (**see**) from relevant economic facts.

Economic cost A payment that must be made to obtain and retain the services of a resource; the income a Firm must provide to a resource supplier to attract the resource away from an alternative use; equal to the quantity of other products that cannot be produced when resources are employed to produce a particular product.

Economic efficiency The relationship between the input of scarce resources and the resulting output of a good or service; production of an output with a given dollar-and-cents value with the smallest total expenditure for resources; obtaining the largest total production of a good or service with resources of a given dollar-and-cents value.

Economic growth (1) An increase in the Production possibilities schedule or curve that results from an increase in resource supplies or an improvement in Technology; (2) an increase either in real output (Gross national product) or in real output per capita.

Economic integration Cooperation among and the complete or partial unification of the economies of different nations; the elimination of the barriers to trade among these nations; the bringing together of the markets in each of the separate economies to form one large (a common) market.

Economic law (**See** Economic principle.)

Economic model A simplified picture of reality; an abstract generalization.

Economic perspective A viewpoint which envisions individuals and institutions making rational or purposeful decisions based upon a consideration of the benefits and costs associated with their actions.

Economic policy Course of action that will correct or avoid a problem.

Economic principle Generalization of the economic behavior of individuals and institutions.

Economic profit The Total revenue of a firm less all its Economic costs; also called "pure profit" and "above normal profit."

Economic Recovery Tax Act The Federal act of 1981 which reduced personal income tax rates, lowered Capital gains tax rates, allowed a more rapid writeoff against taxes of business expenditures for new plants and equipment, lowered the rates at which corporate incomes are taxed, and provided for the adjustment of tax brackets for inflation.

Economic rent The price paid for the use of land and other natural resources, the supply of which is fixed (perfectly inelastic).

Economics Social science concerned with using scarce resources to obtain the maximum satisfaction of the unlimited material wants of society.

Economic theory Deriving Economic principles (**see**) from relevant economic facts; an Economic principle (**see**).

Economizing problem Society's material wants are unlimited but the resources available to produce the goods and services that satisfy wants are limited (scarce); the inability of any economy to produce unlimited quantities of goods and services.

Efficient allocation of resources That allocation of the resources of an economy among the production of different products which leads to the maximum satisfaction of the wants of consumers.

Employment Act of 1946 Federal legislation which committed the Federal government to the maintenance of economic stability (Full employment, stable prices, and Economic growth); established the Council of Economic Advisers (**see**); and the Joint Economic Committee (**see**); and provided for the annual economic report of the President to Congress.

Employment rate The percentage of the Labor force (**see**) employed at any time.

Entrepreneurial ability The human resource which combines the other resources to produce a product, makes nonroutine decisions, innovates, and bears risks.

Equation of exchange $MV = PQ$; in which M is the Money supply (**see**), V is the Income velocity of money (**see**), P is the Price level, and Q is the physical volume of final goods and services produced.

Equilibrium national output The real National output at which the Aggregate demand curve intersects the Aggregate supply curve.

Equilibrium NNP The Net national product at which the total quantity of final goods and services produced (the National output) is equal to the total quantity of final goods and services purchased (Aggregate expenditures).

Equilibrium price The price in a competitive market at which the Quantity demanded (**see**) and the Quantity supplied (**see**) are equal; at which there is neither a shortage nor a surplus; and at which there is no tendency for price to rise or fall.

Equilibrium price level   The price level at which the Aggregate demand curve intersects the Aggregate supply curve.

Equilibrium quantity   The Quantity demanded (**see**) and Quantity supplied (**see**) at the Equilibrium price (**see**) in a competitive market.

Equilibrium real national output   The real national output which is determined by the equality (intersection) of Aggregate demand and Aggregate supply.

ERTA   (**See** Economic Recovery Tax Act.)

European Common Market   The association of thirteen European nations initiated in 1958 to abolish gradually the tariffs and Import quotas that exist among them, to establish common Tariffs for goods imported from outside the member nations, to allow the eventual free movement of labor and capital among them, and to create other common economic policies.

European Economic Community   (**See** European Common Market.)

Excess reserves   The amount by which a Member bank's Actual reserves (**see**) exceed its required reserves (**see**); Actual reserves minus required reserves.

Exchange control   (**See** Foreign exchange control.)

Exchange rate   The Rate of exchange (**see**).

Exchange rate appreciation   An increase in the value of a nation's money in foreign exchange markets; an increase in the Rates of exchange for foreign monies.

Exchange rate depreciation   A decrease in the value of a nation's money in foreign exchange markets; a decrease in the Rates of exchange for foreign monies.

Exchange rate determinant   Any factor other than the Rate of exchange (**see**) that determines the demand for and the supply of a currency in the Foreign exchange market (**see**).

Excise tax   A tax levied on the expenditure for a specific product or on the quantity of the product purchased.

Exclusion principle   The exclusion of those who do not pay for a product from the benefits of the product.

Exhaustive expenditure   An expenditure by government that results directly in the employment of economic resources and in the absorption by government of the goods and services these resources produce; Government purchase (**see**).

Expanding economy   An economy in which Net private domestic investment (**see**) is greater than zero (Gross private domestic investment is greater than Depreciation).

Expanding industry   An industry in which Economic profits are obtained by the firms in the industry and which will, therefore, increase its output as new firms enter the industry.

Expansionary fiscal policy   An increase in Aggregate demand brought about by an increase in Government expenditures for goods and services, a decrease in Net taxes, or some combination of the two.

Expectations   What consumers, business Firms, and others believe will happen or what conditions will be in the future.

Expected rate of net profits   Annual profits which a firm anticipates it will obtain by purchasing Capital (by investing) expressed as a percentage of the price (cost) of the Capital.

Expenditures approach   The method which adds all the expenditures made for Final goods and services to measure the Gross national product.

Expenditures-output approach   (**See** Aggregate expenditures–national output approach.)

Exports   Goods and services produced in a given nation and sold to customers in other nations.

Export transactions   A sale of a good or service which increases the amount of foreign money held by the citizens, firms, and governments of a nation.

External benefit   (**See** Spillover benefit.)

External cost   (**See** Spillover cost.)

External debt   Public debt (**see**) owed to foreign citizens, firms, and institutions.

External economic goal   (**See** International economic goal.)

Externality   (**See** Spillover.)

Face value   The dollar or cents value stamped on a coin.

Factors of production   Economic resources: Land, Capital, Labor, and Entrepreneurial ability.

Fallacy of composition   Incorrectly reasoning that what is true for the individual (or part) is therefore necessarily true for the group (or whole).

FDIC   (**See** Federal Deposit Insurance Corporation.)

Federal Advisory Committee   The group of twelve commercial bankers which advises the Board of Governors (**see**) on banking policy.

Federal Deposit Insurance Corporation   The Federally chartered corporation which insures the deposit liabilities of Commercial banks (Member and qualified nonmember banks).

Federal Open Market Committee   (**See** Open Market Committee.)

Federal Reserve Bank   Any one of the twelve banks chartered by the United States government to control the Money supply and perform other functions; (**See** Central bank, Quasi-public bank, **and** Banker's bank.)

Federal Reserve Note   Paper money issued by the Federal Reserve Banks.

Federal Savings and Loan Insurance Corporation   The federally chartered corporation which insures the deposit liabilities of Savings and loan associations.

Feedback effects   The effects which a change in the money supply will have (because it affects the interest rate, planned investment, and the equilibrium NNP) on the demand for money which is itself directly related to the NNP.

Fiat money Anything that is Money because government has decreed it to be Money.

Final goods Goods which have been purchased for final use and not for resale or further processing or manufacturing (during the year).

Financial capital (*See* Money capital.)

Financing exports and imports The use of Foreign exchange markets by exporters and importers to receive and make payments for goods and services they sell and buy in foreign nations.

Firm An organization that employs resources to produce a good or service for profit and owns and operates one or more Plants (*see*).

Fiscal federalism The system of transfers (grants) by which the Federal government shares its revenues with state and local governments.

Fiscal policy Changes in government spending and tax collections for the purpose of achieving a full-employment and noninflationary national output.

Five fundamental economic questions The five questions which every economy must answer: what to produce, how to produce, how to divide the total output, how to maintain Full employment, and how to assure economic flexibility.

Five-year Plan A statement of the basic strategy for economic development and resource allocation which is prepared by *Gosplan* (*see*) and which includes target rates of growth for the Soviet economy and its major sectors and the general composition of the national output for a five-year period.

Fixed exchange rate A rate of exchange that is prevented from rising or falling.

Flexible exchange rate A rate of exchange that is determined by the demand for and supply of the foreign money and is free to rise or fall.

Floating exchange rate (*See* Flexible exchange rate.)

Foreign exchange control The control a government may exercise over the quantity of foreign money demanded by its citizens and business firms and over the Rates of exchange in order to limit its outpayments to its inpayments (to eliminate a Payments deficit, *see*).

Foreign exchange market A market in which the money (currency) used by one nation is used to purchase (is exchanged for) the money used by another nation.

Foreign exchange rate (*see* Rate of exchange.)

Foreign purchases effect The inverse relationship between the Net exports (*see*) of an economy and its Price level (*see*) relative to foreign Price levels.

Foreign-trade crisis The large and expanding trade (merchandise and current-account) deficits of the United States during the 1980s.

45-degree line A line along which the value of the NNP (measured horizontally) is equal to the value of Aggregate expenditures (measured vertically).

Fractional reserve A Reserve ratio (*see*) that is less than 100 percent of the deposit liabilities of a Commercial bank.

Freedom of choice Freedom of owners of property resources and money to employ or dispose of these resources as they see fit, of workers to enter any line of work for which they are qualified, and of consumers to spend their incomes in a manner which they deem to be appropriate (best for them).

Freedom of enterprise Freedom of business Firms to employ economic resources, to use these resources to produce products of the firm's own choosing, and to sell these products in markets of their choice.

Freely floating exchange rates Rates of exchange (*see*) which are not controlled and which may, therefore, rise and fall; and which are determined by the demand for and the supply of foreign monies.

Free-rider problem The inability of those who might provide the economy with an economically desirable and indivisible good or service to obtain payment from those who benefit from the good or service because the Exclusion principle (*see*) cannot be applied to it.

Free trade The absence of artificial (government imposed) barriers to trade among individuals and firms in different nations.

Frictional unemployment Unemployment caused by workers voluntarily changing jobs and by temporary layoffs; unemployed workers between jobs.

FSLIC (*see* Federal Savings and Loan Insurance Corporation.)

Full employment (1) Using all available resources to produce goods and services; (2) when the Unemployment rate is equal to the Full-employment unemployment rate and there is Frictional and Structural but no Cyclical unemployment (and the Real output of the economy is equal to its Potential real output).

Full Employment and Balanced Growth Act of 1978 The Federal act which supplements the Employment Act of 1946 (*see*), and requires the Federal government to establish five-year goals for the economy and to make plans to achieve these goals.

Full-employment budget What the government expenditures and revenues and its surplus or deficit would be if the economy were to operate at Full employment throughout the year.

Full-employment unemployment rate The Unemployment rate (*see*) at which there is no Cyclical unemployment (*see*) of the Labor force (*see*); and because some Frictional and Structural unemployment is unavoidable, equal to about 5 or 6 percent.

Full production The maximum amount of goods and services that can be produced from the employed resources of an economy; the absence of Underemployment (*see*).

Functional distribution of income The manner in which the economy's (the national) income is divided among those who perform different functions (provide the economy with different kinds of resources); the division of National income (*see*) into wages and salaries, proprietors' income, corporate profits, interest, and rent.

Functional finance Use of Fiscal policy to achieve a full-employment noninflationary Net national product without regard to the effect on the Public debt (*see*).

GATT (*See* General Agreement on Tariffs and Trade.)

General Agreement on Tariffs and Trade The international agreement reached in 1947 by twenty-three nations (including the United States) in which each nation agreed to give equal and nondiscriminatory treatment to the other nations, to reduce tariff rates by multinational negotiations, and to eliminate Import quotas.

Generalization Statistical or probability statement; statement of the nature of the relation between two or more sets of facts.

Gentleman's agreement An informal understanding on the price to be charged among the firms in an Oligopoly.

GNP (*See* Gross national product.)

GNP deflator The Price index (*see*) for all final goods and services used to adjust the money (or nominal) GNP to measure the real GNP.

GNP gap Potential Real gross national product less actual Real gross national product.

Gold export point The rate of exchange for a foreign money above which—when nations participate in the International gold standard (*see*)—the foreign money will not be purchased and gold will be sent (exported) to the foreign country to make payments there.

Gold flow The movement of gold into or out of a nation.

Gold import point The Rate of exchange for a foreign money below which—when nations participate in the International gold standard (*see*)—a nation's own money will not be purchased and gold will be sent (imported) into that country by foreigners to make payments there.

Gorbachev's economic program A recent series of reforms designed to revitalize the Soviet economy. The reforms stress the modernization of productive facilities, less centralized control, improved worker discipline and productivity, more emphasis upon market prices, and an expansion of private economic activity.

Gosbank The state owned and operated (and the only) bank in the U.S.S.R.

Gosplan The State Planning Commission in the U.S.S.R.

Government purchase Disbursement of money by government for which government receives a currently produced good or service in return.

Government purchases of goods and services The expenditures of all governments in the economy for Final goods (*see*) and services.

Government transfer payment The disbursement of money (or goods and services) by government for which government receives no currently produced good or service in return.

Grain reserve program A program in which grain is put into a reserve to reduce market supply when prices are low and sold from the reserve when prices are unusually high in order to increase the market supply.

Gramm-Rudman-Hollings Act Legislation enacted in 1985 by the Federal government requiring annual reductions in Federal budget deficits and, as amended, a balanced budget by 1993; and mandating an automatic decrease in expenditures when Congress and the President cannot agree on how to meet the targeted reductions in the budget deficit.

Gross national product The total market value of all Final goods (*see*) and services produced in the economy during a year.

Gross private domestic investment Expenditures for newly produced Capital goods (*see*)—machinery, equipment, tools, and buildings—and for additions to inventories.

Guiding function of prices The ability of price changes to bring about changes in the quantities of products and resources demanded and supplied (*see* Incentive function).

Horizontal axis The "left-right" or "west-east" axis on a graph or grid.

Horizontal combination A group of Plants (*see*) in the same stage of production and owned by a single Firm (*see*).

Household An economic unit (of one or more persons) which provides the economy with resources and uses the money paid to it for these resources to purchase goods and services that satisfy material wants.

Humphrey-Hawkins Act (*See* Full Employment and Balanced Growth Act of 1978.)

Hyperinflation A very rapid rise in the price level.

IMF (*See* International Monetary Fund.)

Import quota A limit imposed by a nation on the quantity of a good that may be imported from abroad during some period of time.

Imports Spending by individuals, Firms, and governments of an economy for goods and services produced in foreign nations.

Import transaction The purchase of a good or service which decreases the amount of foreign money held by citizens, firms, and governments of a nation.

Income approach The method which adds all the incomes generated by the production of Final goods and services to measure the Gross national product.

Income effect The effect which a change in the price of a product has upon the Real income (purchasing power) of a consumer and the resulting effect upon the quantity of that product the consumer would purchase after the consequences of the Substitution effect (**see**) have been taken into account (eliminated).

Income inequality The unequal distribution of an economy's total income among persons or families in the economy.

Incomes policy Government policy that affects the Money incomes of individuals (the wages workers receive) and the prices they pay for goods and services and thereby affects their Real incomes (**see** Wage-price policy).

Income velocity of money (**See** Velocity of money.)

Increase in demand An increase in the Quantity demanded of a good or service at every price; a shift in the Demand curve to the right.

Increase in supply An increase in the Quantity supplied of a good or service at every price; a shift in the Supply curve to the right.

Independent goods Goods or services such that there is no relationship between the price of one and the demand for the other; when the price of one rises or falls the demand for the other remains constant.

Independent variable The variable which causes a change in some other (dependent) variable.

Indirect business taxes Such taxes as Sales, Excise, and business Property taxes (**see all**), license fees, and Tariffs (**see**) which Firms treat as costs of producing a product and pass on (in whole or in part) to buyers of the product by charging them higher prices.

Individual demand The Demand schedule (**see**) or Demand curve (**see**) of a single buyer of a good or service.

Individual supply The Supply schedule (**see**) or Supply curve (**see**) of a single seller of a good or service.

Induction A method of reasoning that proceeds from facts to Generalization (**see**).

Industrially advanced countries (IACs) Countries such as the United States, Canada, Japan, and the nations of western Europe which have developed Market economies based upon large stocks of technologically advanced capital goods and skilled labor forces.

Industry The group of (one or more) Firms that produce identical or similar products.

Inferior good A good or service of which consumers purchase less (more) at every price when their incomes increase (decrease).

Inflating Finding the Real gross national product (**see**) by increasing the dollar value of the Gross national product produced in a year in which prices are lower than they were in the Base year (**see**).

Inflation A rise in the general (average) level of prices in the economy.

Inflationary expectations The belief of workers, business Firms, and consumers that there will be substantial inflation in the future.

Inflationary gap The amount by which the Aggregate-expenditures schedule (curve) must decrease (shift downward) to decrease the nominal NNP to the full-employment noninflationary level.

Inflationary recession (**See** Stagflation.)

Infrastructure For the economy, the capital goods usually provided by the Public sector for the use of its citizens and Firms (e.g., highways, bridges, transit systems, waste-water treatment facilities, municipal water systems, and airports). For the Firm, the services and facilities which it must have to produce its products, which would be too costly for it to provide for itself, and which are provided by governments or other Firms (e.g., water, electricity, waste treatment, transportation, research, engineering, finance, and banking).

Injection An addition of spending to the income-expenditure stream: Investment, Government purchases of goods and services, and Exports.

Injunction An order from a court of law that directs a person or organization not to perform a certain act because the act would do irreparable damage to some other person or persons; a restraining order.

In-kind investment Nonfinancial investment (**see**).

Innovation The introduction of a new product, the use of a new method of production, or the employment of a new form of business organization.

Inpayments The receipts of (its own or foreign) money which the individuals, Firms, and governments of one nation obtain from the sale of goods and services, investment income, Remittances, and Capital inflows from abroad.

Interest The payment made for the use of money (of borrowed funds).

Interest income Income of those who supply the economy with Capital (**see**).

Interest rate The Rate of interest (**see**).

Interest-rate effect The tendency for increases (decreases) in the Price level to increase (decrease) the demand for money; raise (lower) interest rates; and, as a result, to reduce (expand) total spending in the economy.

Intermediate goods Goods which are purchased for resale or further processing or manufacturing during the year.

Intermediate range The upsloping segment of the Aggregate supply curve that lies between the Keynesian range and the Classical range (**see both**).

Internal economic goal (**See** Domestic economic goal.)

Internally held public debt Public debt (**see**) owed to

(United States government securities owned by) American citizens, Firms, and institutions.

International balance of payments Summary statement of the transactions which took place between the individuals, Firms, and governments of one nation and those in all other nations during the year.

International balance of payments deficit (*See* Balance of payments deficit.)

International balance of payments surplus (*See* Balance of payments surplus.)

International Bank for Reconstruction and Development (*See* World Bank.)

International economic goal Assumed to be a current-account balance of zero.

International gold standard An international monetary system employed in the nineteenth and early twentieth centuries in which each nation defined its money in terms of a quantity of gold, maintained a fixed relationship between its gold stock and money supply, and allowed the free importation and exportation of gold.

International Monetary Fund The international association of nations which was formed after World War II to make loans of foreign monies to nations with temporary Payments deficits (*see*) and to administer the Adjustable pegs (*see*).

International monetary reserves The foreign monies and such assets as gold a nation may use to settle a Payments deficit. (*see*)

International value of the dollar The price that must be paid in foreign currency (money) to obtain one American dollar.

Interstate Commerce Commission Act The Federal legislation of 1887 which established the Interstate Commerce Commission (*see*).

Intrinsic value The value in the market of the metal in a coin.

Inverse relationship The relationship between two variables which change in opposite directions, for example, product price and quantity demanded.

Investment Spending for (the production and accumulation of) Capital goods (*see*) and additions to inventories.

Investment curve A curve which shows the amounts firms plan to invest (along the vertical axis) at different income (Net national product) levels (along the horizontal axis).

Investment-demand curve A curve which shows Rates of interest (along the vertical axis) and the amount of Investment (along the horizontal axis) at each Rate of interest.

Investment schedule A schedule which shows the amounts Firms plan to invest at different income (Net national product) levels.

Invisible hand The tendency of Firms and resource suppliers seeking to further their self-interests in competitive markets to further the best interest of society as a whole (the maximum satisfaction of wants).

JEC (*See* Joint Economic Committee.)

Joint Economic Committee Committee of Senators and Congressmen which investigates economic problems of national interest.

Keynesian economics The macroeconomic generalizations which are today accepted by most (but not all) economists and which lead to the conclusion that a capitalistic economy does not always employ its resources fully and that Fiscal policy (*see*) and Monetary policy (*see*) can be used to promote Full employment (*see*).

Keynesianism The philosophical, ideological, and analytical views of the prevailing majority of American economists; and their employment theory and stabilization policies.

Keynesian range The horizontal segment of the Aggregate-supply curve along which the price level is constant as real national output changes.

Labor The physical and mental talents (efforts) of people which can be used to produce goods and services.

Labor force Persons sixteen years of age and older who are not in institutions and who are employed or are unemployed and seeking work.

Labor-intensive commodity A product which requires a relatively large amount of Labor to produce.

Labor productivity Total output divided by the quantity of labor employed to produce the output; the Average product (*see*) of labor or output per worker per hour.

Labor theory of value The Marxian notion that the economic value of any commodity is determined solely by the amount of labor required to produce it.

Labor union A group of workers organized to advance the interests of the group (to increase wages, shorten the hours worked, improve working conditions, etc.).

Laffer Curve A curve which shows the relationship between tax rates and the tax revenues of government and on which there is a tax rate (between zero and 100 percent) at which tax revenues are a maximum.

Laissez faire capitalism (*See* Pure capitalism.)

Land Natural resources ("free gifts of nature") which can be used to produce goods and services.

Land-intensive commodity A product which requires a relatively large amount of Land to produce.

Law of demand The inverse relationship between the price and the Quantity demanded (*see*) of a good or service during some period of time.

Law of diminishing returns When successive equal increments of a Variable resource (*see*) are added to the

Fixed resources (**see**), beyond some level of employment, the Marginal product (**see**) of the Variable resource will decrease.

Law of increasing opportunity cost As the amount of a product produced is increased, the Opportunity cost (**see**)—Marginal cost (**see**)—of producing an additional unit of the product increases.

Law of supply The direct relationship between the price and the Quantity supplied (**see**) of a good or service during some period of time.

Leakage (1) a withdrawal of potential spending from the income-expenditures stream: Saving (**see**), tax payments, and Imports (**see**); (2) a withdrawal which reduces the lending potential of the Commercial banking system.

Leakages-injections approach Determination of the Equilibrium net national product (**see**) by finding the Net national product at which Leakages (**see**) are equal to Injections (**see**).

Least-cost combination rule (of resources) The quantity of each resource a Firm must employ if it is to produce any output at the lowest total cost; the combination on which the ratio of the Marginal product (**see**) of a resource to its Marginal resource cost (**see**) (to its price if the resource is employed in a competitive market) is the same for all resources employed.

Legal reserves (deposit) The minimum amount which a Depository institution (**see**) must keep on deposit with the Federal Reserve Bank in its district, or in Vault cash (**see**).

Legal tender Anything that government has decreed must be accepted in payment of a debt.

Lending potential of an individual commercial bank The amount by which a single Commercial bank can safely increase the Money supply by making new loans to (or buying securities from) the public; equal to the Commercial bank's Excess reserves (**see**).

Lending potential of the banking system The amount by which the Commercial banking system (**see**) can increase the Money supply by making new loans to (or buying securities from) the public; equal to the Excess reserves (**see**) of the Commercial banking system multiplied by the Monetary multiplier (**see**).

Less developed countries (LDCs) Many countries of Africa, Asia, and Latin America which are characterized by a lack of capital goods, primitive production technologies, low literacy rates, high unemployment, rapid population growth, and labor forces heavily committed to agriculture.

Liability A debt with a monetary value; an amount owed by a Firm or an individual.

Limited Liability Restriction of the maximum that may be lost to a predetermined amount; the maximum amount that may be lost by the owners (stockholders) of a Corporation is the amount they paid for their shares of stock.

Line-item veto A proposal to give the President the power to delete specific expenditure items from spending legislation passed by Congress.

Liquidity Money or things which can be quickly and easily converted into Money with little or no loss of purchasing power.

Liquidity preference theory of interest The theory in which the demand for Liquidity (the quantity of Money firms and households wish to possess) and the supply of Liquidity (the quantity of Money available) determine the equilibrium Rate of interest in the economy.

Loaded terminology Terms which arouse emotions and elicit approval or disapproval.

Long-run aggregate supply curve The aggregate supply curve associated with a time period in which input prices (especially nominal wages) are fully responsive to changes in the price level.

M1 The narrowly defined Money supply; the Currency and Checkable deposits (**see**) not owned by the Federal government, Federal Reserve Banks, or Depository institutions.

M2 A more broadly defined Money supply; equal to *M1* (**see**) plus Noncheckable savings deposits and small Time deposits (deposits of less than $100,000).

M3 A still more broadly defined Money supply; equal to *M2* (**see**) plus large Time deposits (deposits of $100,000 or more).

Macroeconomics The part of economics concerned with the economy as a whole; with such major aggregates as the household, business, and governmental sectors and with totals for the economy.

Managed floating exchange rate An Exchange rate that is allowed to change (float) to eliminate persistent Payments deficit and surpluses and is controlled (managed) to reduce day-to-day fluctuations.

Marginal propensity to consume Fraction of any change in Disposable income which is spent for Consumer goods; equal to the change in consumption divided by the change in Disposable income.

Marginal propensity to save Fraction of any change in Disposable income which households save; equal to change in Saving (**see**) divided by the change in Disposable income.

Marginal tax rate The fraction of additional (taxable) income that must be paid in taxes.

Margin requirement The minimum percentage down payment which purchasers of shares of stock must make.

Market Any institution or mechanism that brings together the buyers (demanders) and sellers (suppliers) of a particular good or service.

Market demand (*See* Total demand.)

Market economy An economy in which only the private decisions of consumers, resource suppliers, and business Firms determine how resources are allocated;

the Market system.

Market failure The failure of a market to bring about the allocation of resources that best satisfies the wants of society (that maximizes the satisfaction of wants). In particular, the over- or underallocation of resources to the production of a particular good or service (because of Spillovers) and no allocation of resources to the production of Public goods (**see**).

Market policies Government policies designed to reduce the market power of labor unions and large business firms and to reduce or eliminate imbalances and bottlenecks in labor markets.

Market socialism An economic system (method of organization) in which property resources are publicly owned and markets and prices are used to direct and coordinate economic activities.

Market system All the product and resource markets of the economy and the relationships among them; a method which allows the prices determined in these markets to allocate the economy's scarce resources and to communicate and coordinate the decisions made by consumers, business firms, and resource suppliers.

"Material balance" Preparation of the Five- and One-year Plans (**see each**) by **Gosplan** (**see**) so that the planned requirements and the available supplies of each input and commodity are equal.

Medium of exchange Money (**see**); a convenient means of exchanging goods and services without engaging in Barter (**see**) what sellers generally accept and buyers generally use to pay for a good or service.

Member bank A Commercial bank (**see**) which is a member of the Federal Reserve system; all National banks (**see**) and the State banks (**see**) which have chosen to join the system.

Member bank deposits The deposits which Member banks (**see**) have at the Federal Reserve Banks (**see**).

Member bank reserves Member bank deposits (**see**) plus their Vault cash (**see**).

Microeconomics The part of economics concerned with such individual units within the economy as Industries, firms, and Households; and with individual markets, particular prices, and specific goods and services.

Mixed capitalism An economy in which both government and private decisions determine how resources are allocated.

Monetarism An alternative to Keynesianism (**see**); the philosophical, ideological, and analytical view of a minority of American economists; and their employment theory and stabilization policy which stress the role of money.

Monetary multiplier The multiple of its Excess reserves (**see**) by which the Commercial banking system (**see**) can expand the Money supply and Demand deposits by making new loans (or buying securities); and equal to one divided by the Required reserve ratio (**see**).

Monetary policy Changing the Money supply (**see**) in order to assist the economy to achieve a full-employment, noninflationary level of total output.

Monetary rule The rule suggested by Monetarism (**see**); the Money supply should be expanded each year at the same annual rate as the potential rate of growth of the Real gross national product; the supply of money should be increased steadily at from 3 to 5 percent.

Money Any item which is generally acceptable to sellers in exchange for goods and services.

Money capital Money available to purchase Capital goods (**see**).

Money income (*See* Nominal income.)

Money interest rate The Nominal interest rate (**see**).

Money market The market in which the demand for and the supply of money determine the Interest rate (or the level of interest rates) in the economy.

Money supply Narrowly defined (**see**) *M*1, more broadly defined (**see**) *M*2 and *M*3.

Money wage The amount of money received by a worker per unit of time (hour, day, etc.); nominal wage.

Money wage rate (*See* Money wage.)

Monopoly (1) A market in which the number of sellers is so small that each seller is able to influence the total supply and the price of the good or service; (2) a major industry in which a small number of Firms control all or a large portion of its output (Business monopoly).

Moral suasion The statements, pronouncements, and appeals made by the Federal Reserve Banks which are intended to influence the leaning policies of Commercial banks.

Most-favored-nation clause A clause in a trade agreement between the United States and another nation which provides that the other nation's Imports into the United States will be subjected to the lowest tariff levied then or later on any other nation's Imports into the United States.

Multiplier The ratio of the change in the Equilibrium NNP to the change in Investment (**see**), or to the change in any other component of the Aggregate expenditures schedule or to the change in Net taxes; the number by which a change in any component in the Aggregate expenditures schedule or in Net taxes must be multiplied to find the resulting change in the Equilibrium NNP.

Multiplier effect The effect upon the Equilibrium net national product of a change in the Aggregate expenditures schedule (caused by a change in the Consumption schedule, Investment, Net taxes, Government expenditures for goods and services, or Exports).

Mutually exclusive goals Goals which conflict and cannot be achieved simultaneously.

Mutual savings bank A Firm without stockholders which accepts deposits primarily from small individual savers and which lends primarily to individuals to finance the purchases of residences.

National bank   A Commercial bank (**see**) chartered by the United States government.

National income   Total income earned by resource suppliers for their contributions to the production of the Gross national product (**see**); equal to the Gross national product minus the Nonincome charges (**see**).

National income accounting   The techniques employed to measure (estimate) the overall production of the economy and other related totals for the nation as a whole.

National output   The Net (or gross) national product; the total output of final goods and services produced in the economy.

Natural monopoly   An industry in which the Economies of scale (**see**) are so great that the product can be produced by one Firm at an average cost which is lower than it would be if it were produced by more than one Firm.

Natural rate hypothesis   Contends that the economy is stable in the long run at the natural rate of unemployment; views the long-run Phillips Curve (**see**) as being vertical at the natural rate of unemployment.

Natural rate of unemployment   (**See** Full-employment unemployment rate.)

Near-money   Financial assets, the most important of which are Noncheckable savings accounts, Time deposits, and U.S. short-term securities and savings bonds, that are not a medium of exchange but can be readily converted into Money.

Negative relationship   (**See** Inverse relationship.)

Negotiable order of withdrawal account   An account (deposit) in a Savings and loan association (**see**) or Mutual savings bank (**see**) against which a check may be written and which pays interest to the depositor.

Net capital movement   The difference between the real and financial investments and loans made by individuals and Firms of one nation in the other nations of the world and the investments and loans made by individuals and Firms from other nations in a nation; Capital inflows less Capital outflows.

Net export effect   The notion that the impact of a change in Monetary policy (Fiscal policy) will be strengthened (weakened) by the consequent change in Net exports (**see**). For example, a tight (easy) money policy will increase (decrease) domestic interest rates; thereby increasing (decreasing) the foreign demand for dollars. As a result, the dollar appreciates (depreciates) and causes American net exports to decrease (increase).

Net exports   Exports (**see**) minus Imports (**see**).

Net investment income   The interest and dividend income received by the residents of a nation from residents of other nations less the interest and dividend payments made by the residents of that nation to the residents of other nations.

Net national product   Gross national product (**see**) less that part of the output needed to replace the Capital goods worn out in producing the output (Capital consumption allowances, **see**).

Net private domestic investment   Gross private domestic investment (**see**) less Capital consumption allowances (**see**); the addition to the nation's stock of Capital during a year.

Net taxes   The taxes collected by government less Government transfer payments (**see**).

Net transfers   The personal and government transfer payments made to residents of foreign nations less the personal and government transfer payments received from residents of foreign nations.

Net worth   The total Assets (**see**) less the total Liabilities (**see**) of a Firm or an individual; the claims of the owners of a firm against its total Assets.

New classical economies   The theory that, although unanticipated price level changes may create macroeconomic instability in the short run, the economy is stable at the full-employment level of national output in the long run because of price and wage flexibility.

New International Economic Order   A series of proposals made by the Less developed countries (LDCs) (**see**) for basic changes in their relationships with the advanced industrialized nations that would accelerate the growth of and redistribute world income to the LDCs.

NIEO   New International Economic Order (**see**).

NNP   (**See** Net national product.)

Nominal income   The number of dollars received by an individual or group during some period of time.

Nominal interest rate   The rate of interest expressed in dollars of current value (not adjusted for inflation).

Nominal national output (NNP)   The NNP (**see**) measured in terms of the price level at the time of measurement (unadjusted for changes in the price level).

Nominal wage rate   The Money wage (**see**).

Noncheckable savings account   A Savings account (**see**) against which a check may not be written; a Savings account which is not a NOW, ATS, or share draft account.

Nondiscretionary fiscal policy   The increases (decreases) in Net taxes (**see**) which occur without Congressional action when the Net national product rises (falls) and which tend to stabilize the economy.

Nondurable good   A Consumer good (**see**) with an expected life (use) of less than one year.

Nonexhaustive expenditure   An expenditure by government that does not result directly in the employment of economic resources or the production of goods and services; **see** Government transfer payment.

Nonfinancial investment   An investment which does not require households to save a part of their money incomes; but which uses surplus (unproductive) labor to build Capital goods.

Nonincome charges Capital consumption allowances (*see*) and Indirect business taxes (*see*).

Nonincome determinants of consumption and saving All influences on consumption spending and saving other than the level of Disposable income.

Noninterest determinants of investment All influences on the level of investment spending other than the rate of interest.

Noninvestment transaction An expenditure for stocks, bonds, or second-hand Capital goods.

Nonmarket transactions The production of goods and services not included in the measurement of the Gross national product because the goods and services are not bought and sold.

Nonprice determinant of demand Factors other than its price which determine the quantities demanded of a good or service.

Nonprice determinant of supply Factors other than its price which determine the quantities supplied of a good or service.

Nonprice-level-determinants of aggregate demand Factors such as consumption, investment, government, and net export spending which, if they change, will shift the aggregate demand curve.

Nonprice-level-determinants of aggregate supply Factors such as input prices, productivity, and the legal-institutional environment which, if they change, will shift the aggregate supply curve.

Nonproductive transaction The purchase and sale of any item that is not a currently produced good or service.

Nontariff barriers All barriers other than Tariffs (*see*) which nations erect to impede trade among nations; Import quotas (*see*), licensing requirements, unreasonable product-quality standards, unnecessary red tape in customs procedures, etc.

Normal good A good or service of which consumers will purchase more (less) at every price when their incomes increase (decrease).

Normal profit Payment that must be made by a Firm to obtain and retain Entrepreneurial ability (*see*); the minimum payment (income) Entrepreneurial ability must (expect to) receive to induce it to perform the entrepreneurial functions for a Firm; an Implicit cost (*see*).

Normative economics That part of economics which pertains to value judgments about what the economy should be like; concerned with economic goals and policies.

NOW account Negotiable order of withdrawal account (*see*).

NTBs (*See* Nontariff barriers.)

Official reserves The foreign monies (currencies) owned by the central bank of a nation.

Okun's law The generalization that any one percentage point rise in the Unemployment rate above the Full-employment unemployment rate will increase the GNP gap by 2.5 percent of the Potential output (GNP) of the economy.

One-year Plan A detailed operational plan which is prepared by *Gosplan* (*see*) and which specifies the inputs and outputs of each enterprise in the U.S.S.R. for a one-year period.

OPEC An acronym for the Organization of Petroleum Exporting Countries (*see*).

Open economy An economy which both exports and imports goods and services.

Open Market Committee The twelve-member group that determines the purchase-and-sale policies of the Federal Reserve Banks in the market for United States government securities.

Open-market operations The buying and selling of United States government securities by the Federal Reserve Banks.

Opportunity cost The amount of other products that must be forgone or sacrificed to produce a unit of a product.

Organization of Petroleum Exporting Countries The cartel formed in 1970 by thirteen oil-producing countries to control the price at which they sell crude oil to foreign importers and the quantity of oil exported by its members and which accounts for a large proportion of the world's export of oil.

"Other things being equal" assumption Assuming that factors other than those being considered are constant.

Outpayments The expenditures of (its own or foreign) money which the individuals, Firms, and governments of one nation make to purchase goods and services, for Remittances, as investment income, and Capital outflows abroad.

Paper money Pieces of paper used as a Medium of exchange (*see*); in the United States, Federal Reserve Notes (*see*).

Paradox of thrift The attempt of society to save more results in the same amount of, or less, Saving.

Partnership An unincorporated business Firm owned and operated by two or more persons.

Payments deficit (*See* Balance of payments deficit.)

Payments surplus (*See* Balance of payments surplus.)

Payroll tax A tax levied on employers of Labor equal to a percentage of all or part of the wages and salaries paid by them; and on employees equal to a percentage of all or part of the wages and salaries received by them.

Personal consumption expenditures The expenditures of Households for Durable and Nondurable consumer goods and services.

Personal distribution of income   The manner in which the economy's Personal or Disposable income is divided among different income classes or different households.

Personal income   The income, part of which is earned and the remainder of which is unearned, available to resource suppliers and others before the payment of Personal taxes (**see**).

Personal income tax   A tax levied on the taxable income of individuals (households and unincorporated firms).

Personal saving   The Personal income of households less Personal taxes (**see**) and Personal consumption expenditures (**see**); Disposable income not spent for Consumer goods (**see**).

Phillips Curve   A curve which shows the relationship between the Unemployment rate (**see**) (on the horizontal axis) and the annual rate of increase in the Price level (on the vertical axis).

Planned economy   An economy in which only government determines how resources are allocated.

Planned investment   The amount which business firms plan or intend to invest.

Plant   A physical establishment (Land and Capital) which performs one or more of the functions in the production (fabrication and distribution) of goods and services.

Policy economics   The formulation of courses of action to bring about desired results or to prevent undesired occurrences (to control economic events).

Political business cycle   The tendency of Congress to destabilize the economy by reducing taxes and increasing government expenditures before elections and to raise taxes and lower expenditures after the elections.

Positive economics   The analysis of facts or data for the purpose of establishing scientific generalizations about economic behavior; compare Normative economics.

Positive relationship   The relationship between two variables which change in the same direction, for example, product price and quantity supplied.

Post hoc, ergo propter hoc fallacy   Incorrectly reasoning that when one event precedes another the first event is the cause of the second.

Potential output   The real output (GNP) an economy is able to produce when it fully employs its available resources.

Preferential tariff treatment   Setting Tariffs lower for one nation (or group or nations) than for others.

Premature inflation   Inflation (**see**) which occurs before the economy has reached Full employment (**see**).

Price   The quantity of money (or of other goods and services) paid and received for a unit of a good or service.

Price-decreasing effect   The effect in a competitive market of a decrease in Demand or an increase in Supply upon the Equilibrium price (**see**).

Price guidepost   The price charged by an industry for its product should increase by no more than the increase in the Unit labor cost (**see**) of producing the product.

Price increasing effect   The effect in a competitive market of an increase in Demand or a decrease in Supply upon the Equilibrium price.

Price index   An index number which shows how the average price of a "market basket" of goods changes through time. A price index is used to change nominal output (income) into real output (income).

Price level surprises   Unanticipated changes in the price level.

Price-wage flexibility   Changes in the prices of products and in the Wages paid to workers; the ability of prices and Wages to rise or to fall.

Priority principle   The assignment of priorities to the planned outputs of the various sectors and industries in the economy of the U.S.S.R. and the shifting of resources, when bottlenecks develop, from low- to high-priority sectors and industries to assure the fulfillment of the production targets of the latter sectors and industries.

Private good   A good or service to which the Exclusion principle (**see**) is applicable and which is provided by privately owned firms to those who are willing to pay for it.

Private property   The right of private persons and Firms to obtain, own, control, employ, dispose of, and bequeath Land, Capital, and other Assets.

Private sector   The Households and business firms of the economy.

Production possibilities curve   A curve which shows the different combinations of two goods or services that can be produced in a Full-employment (**see**), Full-production (**see**) economy in which the available supplies of resources and technology are constant.

Production possibilities table   A table which shows the different combinations of two goods or services that can be produced in a Full-employment (**see**), Full-production (**see**) economy in which the available supplies of resources and technology are constant.

Productive efficiency   The production of a good in the least-costly way: employing the minimum quantity of resources needed to produce a given output and producing the output at which Average total cost is a minimum.

Productivity   A measure of average output or real output per unit of input. For example, the productivity of labor may be determined by dividing hours of work into real output.

Productivity slowdown   The recent decline in the rate at which Labor productivity (**see**) in the United States has increased.

Product market   A market in which Households buy and Firms sell the products they have produced.

Profit   (**See**) Economic profit and Normal profit; without an adjective preceding it, the income of those who supply the economy with Entrepreneurial ability (**see**) or Normal profit.

Progressive tax　A tax such that the Average tax rate increases as the taxpayer's income increases and decreases as income decreases.

Property tax　A tax on the value of property (Capital, Land, stocks and bonds, and other Assets) owned by Firms and Households.

Proportional tax　A tax such that the Average tax rate remains constant as the taxpayer's income increases and decreases.

Proprietors' income　The net income of the owners of unincorporated Firms (proprietorships and partnerships).

Prosperous industry　(**See** Expanding industry.)

Protective tariff　A Tariff (**see**) designed to protect domestic producers of a good from the competition of foreign producers.

Public debt　The total amount owed by the Federal government (to the owners of government securities) and equal to the sum of its past Budget deficits (less its budget surpluses).

Public finance　The branch of economics which analyzes government revenues and expenditures for "Social" goods, now called "Public" goods.

Public good　A good or service to which the Exclusion principle (**see**) is not applicable; and which is provided by government if it yields substantial benefits to society.

Public sector　The part of the economy that contains all its governments; government.

Pure capitalism　An economic system (method of organization) in which property resources are privately owned and markets and prices are used to direct and coordinate economic activities.

Pure competition　(1) A market in which a very large number of Firms sells a Standardized product (**see**), into which entry is very easy, in which the individual seller has no control over the price at which the product sells, and in which there is no Nonprice competition (**see**); (2) a market in which there is a very large number of buyers.

Pure profit　(**See** Economic profit.)

Quantity-decreasing effect　The effect in a competitive market of a decrease in Demand or a decrease in Supply upon the Equilibrium quantity (**see**).

Quantity demanded　The amount of a good or service buyers wish (or a buyer wishes) to purchase at a particular price during some period of time.

Quantity-increasing effect　The effect in a competitive market of an increase in Demand or an increase in Supply upon the Equilibrium quantity (**see**).

Quantity supplied　The amount of a good or service sellers offer (or a seller offers) to sell at a particular price during some period of time.

Quasi-public bank　A bank which is privately owned but governmentally (publicly) controlled; each of the Federal Reserve banks.

Quasi-public good　A good or service to which the Exclusion principle (**see**) could be applied, but which has such a large Spillover benefit (**see**) that government sponsors its production to prevent an underallocation of resources.

R&D　Research and development; activities undertaken to bring about Technological progress.

Ratchet effect　The tendency for the Price level to rise when Aggregate demand increases, but not fall when Aggregate demand declines.

Rate of exchange　The price paid in one's own money to acquire one unit of a foreign money; the rate at which the money of one nation is exchanged for the money of another nation.

Rate of interest　Price paid for the use of Money or for the use of Capital; interest rate.

Rational　An adjective that describes the behavior of any individual who consistently does those things that will enable him or her to achieve the declared objective of the individual; and that describes the behavior of a consumer who uses money income to buy the collection of goods and services that yields the maximum amount of Utility (**see**).

Rational expectations theory　The hypothesis that business firms and households expect monetary and fiscal policies to have certain effects on the economy and take, in pursuit of their own self-interests, actions which make these policies ineffective.

Rationing function of price　The ability of a price in a competitive market to equalize Quantity demanded and Quantity supplied and to eliminate shortages and surpluses by rising or falling.

Reagonomics　The policies of the Reagan administration based on Supply-side economics (**see**) and intended to reduce inflation and the Unemployment rate (Stagflation).

Real-balances effect　The tendency for increases (decreases) in the price level to lower (raise) the real value (or purchasing power) of financial assets with fixed money values; and, as a result, to reduce (expand) total spending in the economy.

Real capital　(**See** Capital.)

Real gross national product　Gross national product (**see**) adjusted for changes in the price level; Gross national product in a year divided by the GNP deflator (**see**) for that year.

Real income　The amount of goods and services an individual or group can purchase with his, her, or its Nominal income during some period of time; Nominal income adjusted for changes in the Price level.

Real interest rate　The rate of interest expressed in

dollars of constant value (adjusted for inflation); and equal to the Nominal interest rate (**see**) less the rate of inflation.

Real net national product (NNP) The NNP (**see**) measured in terms of a constant price level (adjusted for changes in the price level).

Real rate of interest The Real interest rate (**see**).

Real wage The amount of goods and services a worker can purchase with his or her Money wage (**see**); the purchasing power of the Money wage; the Money wage adjusted for changes in the Price level.

Real wage rate (See Real wage.)

Recessionary gap The amount by which the Aggregate expenditures schedule (curve) must increase (shift upward) to increase the real NNP to the full-employment noninflationary level.

Reciprocal Trade Agreements Act of 1934 The Federal act which gave the President the authority to negotiate agreements with foreign nations and lower American tariff rates by up to 50 percent if the foreign nations would reduce tariff rates on American goods and which incorporated Most-favored-nation clauses (**see**) in the agreements reached with these nations.

Refinancing the public debt Paying owners of maturing United States government securities with money obtained by selling new securities or with new securities.

Regressive tax A tax such that the average tax rate decreases (increases) as the taxpayer's income increases (decreases).

Remittance A gift or grant; a payment for which no good or service is received in return; the funds sent by workers who have legally or illegally entered a foreign nation to their families in the nations from which they have migrated.

Rental income Income received by those who supply the economy with Land (**see**).

Required reserve ratio (See Reserve ratio.)

Reserve ratio The specified minimum percentage of its deposit liabilities which a Member bank (**see**) must keep on deposit at the Federal Reserve Bank in its district, or in Vault cash (**see**).

Resource market A market in which Households sell and Firms buy the services of resources.

Retiring the public debt Reducing the size of the Public debt by paying money to owners of maturing United States government securities.

Revaluation An increase in the defined value of a currency.

Revenue tariff A Tariff (**see**) designed to produce income for the (Federal) government.

Roundabout production The construction and use of Capital (**see**) to aid in the production of Consumer goods (**see**).

Rule of 70 A method by which the number of years it will take for the Price level to double can be calculated; divide 70 by the annual rate of inflation.

Sales tax A tax levied on expenditures for a broad group of products.

Saving Disposable income not spent for Consumer goods (**see**); not spending for consumption; equal to Disposable income minus Personal consumption expenditures (**see**).

Savings account A deposit in a Depository institution (**see**) which is interest-earning and which can normally be withdrawn by the depositor at any time (though the institution may legally require fourteen days' notice for withdrawal).

Savings and loan association A Firm which accepts deposits primarily from small individual savers, and lends primarily to individuals to finance purchases of residences.

Saving schedule Schedule which shows the amounts Households plan to save (plan not to spend for Consumer goods, **see**) at different levels of Disposable income.

Savings institution A Thrift institution (**see**).

Say's Law The (discredited) macroeconomic generalization that the production of goods and services (supply) creates an equal Aggregate demand for these goods and services.

Scarce resources The fixed (limited) quantities of Land, Capital, Labor, and Entrepreneurial ability (**see all**) which are never sufficient to satisfy the material wants of humans because their wants are unlimited.

Seasonal variation An increase or decrease during a single year in the level of economic activity caused by a change in the season.

"Second economy" The semilegal and illegal markets and activities which exist side by side with the legal and official markets and activities in the U.S.S.R.

Secular trend The expansion or contraction in the level of economic activity over a long period of years.

Selective controls The techniques the Federal Reserve Banks employ to change the availability of certain specific types of credit.

Self-interest What each Firm, property owner, worker, and consumer believes is best for itself and seeks to obtain.

Separation of ownership and control Difference between the group that owns the Corporation (the stockholders) and the group that manages it (the directors and officers) and between the interests (goals) of the two groups.

Service That which is intangible (invisible) and for which a consumer, firm, or government is willing to exchange something of value.

Share draft account A deposit in a Credit union (**see**) against which a check may be written and which earns interest for the depositor (member).

Short-run aggregate supply curve The aggregate supply curve relevant to a time period wherein input prirce (particularly nominal wages) remain constant when the price level changes.

Simple multiplier   The Multiplier (**see**) in an economy in which government collects no Net taxes (**see**), there are no Imports (**see**), and Investment (**see**) is independent of the level of income (Net national product); equal to one divided by the Marginal propensity to save (**see**).

Slope of a line   The ratio of the vertical change (the rise or fall) to the horizontal change (the run) in moving between two points on a line. The slope of an upward sloping line is positive, reflecting a direct relationship between two variables; the slope of a downward sloping line is negative, reflecting an inverse relationship between two variables.

Smoot-Hawley Tariff Act   Passed in 1930, this legislation established some of the highest tariffs in United States history. Its objective was to reduce imports and stimulate the domestic economy.

Social accounting   (**See** National income accounting.)

Sole proprietorship   An unincorporated business firm owned and operated by a single person.

Specialization   The use of the resources of an individual, a Firm, a region, or a nation to produce one or a few goods and services.

Spillover   A benefit or cost associated with the consumption or production of a good or service which is obtained by or inflicted without compensation upon a party other than the buyer or seller of the good or service; (**see** Spillover benefit and Spillover cost).

Spillover benefit   The benefit obtained neither by producers nor by consumers of a product but without compensation by a third party (society as a whole).

Spillover cost   The cost of producing a product borne neither by producers nor by consumers of the product but without compensation by a third party (society as a whole).

Stabilization fund   A stock of money and of a commodity that is used to prevent the price of the commodity from changing by buying (selling) the commodity when its price decreases (increases).

Stabilization policy dilemma   The use of monetary and fiscal policy to decrease the Unemployment rate increases the rate of inflation, and the use of monetary and fiscal policy to decrease the rate of inflation increases the Unemployment rate.

Stagflation   Inflation accompanied by stagnation in the rate of growth of output and a high unemployment rate in the economy; simultaneous increases in both the Price level and the Unemployment rate.

State bank   A Commercial bank chartered to engage in the business of banking by a state government.

State ownership   The ownership of property (Land and Capital) by government (the state); in the U.S.S.R. by the central government (the nation).

Static economy   (1) An economy in which Net private domestic investment (**see**) is equal to zero—Gross private domestic investment (**see**) is equal to the Capital consumption allowances (**see**); (2) an economy in which the supplies of resources, technology, and the tastes of consumers do not change and in which, therefore, the economic future is perfectly predictable and there is no uncertainty.

Structural deficit   The difference between Federal tax revenues and expenditures when the economy is at full employment.

Structural unemployment   Unemployment caused by changes in the structure of demand for Consumer goods and in technology; workers who are unemployed either because their skills are not demanded by employers or because they lack sufficient skills to obtain employment.

Subsidy   A payment of funds (or goods and services) by a government, business firm, or household for which it receives no good or service in return. When made by a government, it is a Government transfer payment (**see**).

Substitute goods   Goods or services such that there is a direct relationship between the price of one and the Demand for the other; when the price of one falls (rises) the Demand for the other decreases (increases).

Substitution effect   (1) The effect which a change in the price of a Consumer good would have upon the relative expensiveness of that good and the resulting effect upon the quantity of the good a consumer would purchase if the consumer's Real income (**see**) remained constant; (2) the effect which a change in the price of a resource would have upon the quantity of the resource employed by a firm if the firm did not change its output.

Superior good   (**See** Normal good.)

Supply   A Supply schedule or a Supply curve (**see both**).

Supply curve   A curve which shows the amounts of a good or service sellers (a seller) will offer to sell at various prices during some period of time.

Supply factor   An increase in the available quantity of a resource, an improvement in its quality, or an expansion of technological knowledge which makes it possible for an economy to produce a greater output of goods and services.

Supply schedule   A schedule which shows the amounts of a good or service sellers (a seller) will offer to sell at various prices during some period of time.

Supply shock   One of several events of the 1970s and early 1980s which increased production costs, decreased Aggregate supply, and generated Stagflation in the United States.

Supply-side economics   The part of modern macroeconomics that emphasizes the role of costs and Aggregate supply in its explanation of Inflation and unemployed labor.

Supply-side view The view of fiscal policy held by the advocates of Supply-side economics which emphasizes increasing Aggregate supply (**see**) as a means of reducing the Unemployment rate and Inflation and encouraging Economic Growth.

Tangent The point at which a line touches, but does not intersect, a curve.

Target dilemma A problem which arises because monetary authorities cannot simultaneously stabilize both the money supply and the level of interest rates.

Tariff A tax imposed (only by the Federal government in the United States) on an imported good.

Tax A nonvoluntary payment of money (or goods and services) to a government by a Household or Firm for which the Household or Firm receives no good or service directly in return and which is not a fine imposed by a court for an illegal act.

Tax incidence The income or purchasing power which different persons and groups lose as a result of the imposition of a tax after Tax shifting (**see**) has occurred.

Tax Reform Act of 1986 Federal legislation which broadened the personal income tax base, but also lowered both tax rates and the number of tax brackets.

Tax shifting The transfer to others of all or part of a tax by charging them a higher price or by paying them a lower price for a good or service.

Tax "wedge" Such taxes as Indirect business taxes (**see**) and Payroll taxes (**see**) which are treated as a cost by business firms and reflected in the prices of the products produced by them; equal to the price of the product less the cost of the resources required to produce it.

Technology The body of knowledge that can be used to produce goods and services from Economic resources.

Terms of trade The rate at which units of one product can be exchanged for units of another product; the Price (**see**) of a good or service; the amount of one good or service that must be given up to obtain one unit of another good or service.

Thrift institution A Savings and loan association, Mutual savings bank, or Credit union (**see all**).

Tight money policy Contracting or restricting the growth of the nation's Money supply (**see**).

Till money (See Vault cash.)

Time deposit An interest-earning deposit in a Depository institution (**see**) which may be withdrawn by the depositor without a loss of interest on or after a specific date or at the end of a specific period of time.

Token money Coins which have a Face value (**see**) greater than their Intrinsic value (**see**).

Total demand The Demand schedule (**see**) or the Demand curve (**see**) of all buyers of a good or service.

Total demand for money The sum of the Transactions demand for money (**see**) and Asset demand for money (**see**); the relationship between the total amount of money demanded, nominal GNP, and the Rate of Interest.

Total product The total output of a particular good or service produced by a firm (a group of firms or the entire economy).

Total revenue The total number of dollars received by a Firm (or Firms) from the sale of a product; equal to the total expenditures for the product produced by the Firm (or Firms); equal to the quantity sold (demanded) multiplied by the price at which it is sold—by the Average revenue (**see**) from its sale.

Total spending The total amount buyers of goods and services spend or plan to spend.

Total supply The Supply schedule (**see**) or the Supply curve (**see**) of all sellers of a good or service.

Trade balance The export of merchandise (goods) of a nation less its imports of merchandise (goods).

Trade controls Tariffs (**see**), export subsidies, Import quotas (**see**), and other means a nation may employ to reduce Imports (**see**) and expand Exports (**see**) in order to eliminate a Balance of payments deficit (**see**).

Trade deficit The amount by which a nation's imports of merchandise (goods) exceed its exports of merchandise (goods).

Trading surplus The amount by which a nation's exports of merchandise (goods) exceed its imports of merchandise (goods).

Trade possibilities line A line which shows the different combinations of two products an economy is able to obtain (consume) when it specializes in the production of one product and trades (exports) this product to obtain the other product.

Traditional economy An economic system (method of organization) in which traditions and customs determine how the economy will use its scarce resources.

Transactions demand for money The amount of money people want to hold to use as a Medium of exchange (to make payments); and which varies directly with the nominal GNP.

Transfer payment A payment of money (or goods and services) by a government or a Firm to a Household or Firm for which the payer receives no good or service directly in return.

Turnover tax The tax added to the accounting price of a good in the U.S.S.R. to determine the price at which the quantity of the good demanded will equal the quantity of the good it has been decided to produce, the rate of taxation being higher on relatively scarce and lower on relatively abundant goods.

Unanticipated inflation Inflation (**see**) at a rate which was greater than the rate expected in that period of time.

Underemployment Failure to produce the maximum amount of goods and services that can be produced from the resources employed; failure to achieve Full production (**see**).

Undistributed corporate profits   The after-tax profits of corporations not distributed as dividends to stockholders; corporate or business saving.

Unemployment   Failure to use all available Economic resources to produce goods and services; failure of the economy to employ fully its Labor force (**see**).

Unemployment compensation   (*See* Unemployment insurance.)

Unemployment rate   The percentage of the Labor force (**see**) that is unemployed at any time.

United States–Canadian Free-Trade Agreement   An accord signed in 1988 to eliminate all trade barriers between the two nations over a 10-year period.

Unit labor cost   Labor costs per unit of output; equal to the Money wage rate (**see**) divided by the Average product (**see**) of labor.

Unlimited liability   Absence of any limit on the maximum amount that may be lost by an individual and that the individual may become legally required to pay; the amount that may be lost and that a sole proprietor or partner may be required to pay.

Unlimited wants   The insatiable desire of consumers (people) for goods and services that will give them pleasure or satisfaction.

Unplanned investment   Actual investment less Planned investment; increases or decreases in the inventories of business firms that result from production greater than sales.

Unprosperous industry   (*See* Declining industry.)

Utility   The want-satisfying power of a good or service; the satisfaction or pleasure a consumer obtains from the consumption of a good or service (or from the consumption of a collection of goods and services).

Value added   The value of the product sold by a Firm less the value of the goods (materials) purchased and used by the Firm to produce the product; and equal to the revenue which can be used for Wages, rent, interest, and profits.

Value-added tax   A tax imposed upon the difference between the value of the goods sold by a firm and the value of the goods purchased by the firm from other firms.

Value judgment   Opinion of what is desirable or undesirable; belief regarding what ought or ought not to be (regarding what is right or just and wrong or unjust).

Value of money   The quantity of goods and services for which a unit of money (a dollar) can be exchanged; the purchasing power of a unit of money; the reciprocal of the Price level.

VAT   Value-added tax (**see**).

Vault cash   The Currency (**see**) a bank has in its safe (vault) and cash drawers.

Velocity of money   The number of times per year the average dollar in the Money supply (**see**) is spent for Final goods (**see**).

VERs   (*See* Voluntary export restrictions.)

Vertical axis   The "up–down" or "north–south" axis on a graph or grid.

Vertical combinations   A group of Plants (**see**) engaged in different stages of the production of a final product and owned by a single Firm (**see**).

Vertical intercept   The point at which a line meets the vertical axis of a graph.

Vicious circle of poverty   A problem common to the less developed countries wherein their low per capita incomes are an obstacle to realizing the levels of saving and investment requisite to acceptable rates of economic growth.

Voluntary export restrictions   The limitation by firms of their exports to particular foreign nations in order to avoid the erection of other trade barriers by the foreign nations.

Wage   The price paid for Labor (for the use or services of Labor, **see**) per unit of time (per hour, per day, etc.).

Wage and salary supplements   Payments made by employers of Labor into social insurance and private pension, health, and welfare funds for workers; and a part of the employer's cost of obtaining Labor.

Wage guidepost   Wages (**see**) in all industries in the economy should increase at an annual rate equal to the rate of increase in the Average product (**see**) of Labor in the economy.

Wage-price controls   A Wage-price policy (**see**) that legally fixes the maximum amounts by which Wages (**see**) and prices may be increased in any period of time.

Wage-price guideposts   A Wage-price policy (**see**) that depends upon the voluntary cooperation of Labor unions and business firms.

Wage-price inflationary spiral   Increases in wage rates which bring about increases in prices which in turn result in further increases in wage rates and in prices.

Wage-price policy   Government policy that attempts to alter the behavior of Labor unions and business firms in order to make their Wage and price decisions more nearly compatible with the goals of Full employment and a stable price level.

Wage rate   (*See* Wage.)

Wages   The income of those who supply the economy with Labor (**see**).

Wealth effect   (*See* Real balances effect.)

(The) "will to develop"   Wanting economic growth strongly enough to change from old to new ways of doing things.

World bank   A bank supported by 151 nations which lends (and guarantees loans) to less developed nations to assist them to grow; formally, the International Bank for Reconstruction and Development.